Frontiers of Computing Systems Research

Volume 1

Essays on Emerging Technologies, Architectures, and Theories

A Continuation Order Plan is available for this series. A continuation order will bring delivery of each new volume immediately upon publication. Volumes are billed only upon actual shipment. For further information please contact the publisher.

Frontiers of Computing Systems Research

Volume 1
Essays on Emerging Technologies, Architectures, and Theories

Edited by
S. K. Tewksbury
AT&T Bell Laboratories
Holmdel, New Jersey

Plenum Press • New York and London

ISBN-13: 978-1-4612-7902-0   e-ISBN-13: 978-1-4613-0633-7
DOI: 10.1007/978-1-4613-0633-7

© 1990 Plenum Press, New York
Softcover reprint of the hardcover 1st edition 1990
A Division of Plenum Publishing Corporation
233 Spring Street, New York, N.Y. 10013

ADVISORY BOARD

Foreword

Computing systems researchers confront two serious problems. (1) The increasingly monolithic, or pseudo-monolithic, integration of complex computing functions and systems imposes an environment which integrates advanced principles and techniques from a broad variety of fields. Researchers not only must confront the increased complexity of topics in their specialty field but also must develop a deeper general understanding of a broadening number of fields. (2) There has been a proliferation of journals, books, workshops and conferences through which research results are reported. Remaining familiar with recent advances in our specific fields is a major challenge. Casually browsing through journals and conference proceedings to remain aware of developments in areas outside our specialization has become an even greater challenge.

Frontiers of Computing Systems Research has been established to address these two issues. With the assistance of an advisory board of experts from a wide variety of specialized areas, we hope to provide roughly annual volumes of invited chapters on a broad range of topics and designed for an interdisciplinary research audience. No single volume can cover all the relevant topics and no single article can convey the full set of directions being pursued within a given topic. For this reason, a chapter listing technical reports available from universities is also included. Often, such unpublished reports are designed for a general research audience and provide a good, informal look at trends in specialized research topics. Through invited contributions and such report listings, it is our objective to develop a resource which conveys to those in specialized fields a sense of the direction and excitement seen in other specialized fields impacting computer systems research.

Frontiers of Computing Systems Research evolved from an earlier book of interdisciplinary articles, *Concurrent Computations: Algorithms, Architecture, and Technology*, edited by Tewksbury, Dickinson, and Schwartz (Plenum, 1989). I extend my gratitude to the advisory board of *Frontiers of Computing Systems Research* for their early support of this series and for their suggestions regarding authors and topics. I am particularly indebted to the authors who have provided chapters for this inaugural volume. Proposals for chapters are welcomed, as are suggestions for improving the format and content of the series.

Stuart Tewksbury, Editor

Contents

Contents

CHAPTER 1

UNUSUAL GRAPHIC REPRESENTATIONS OF COMPLEX DATA

Clifford A. Pickover
IBM Thomas J. Watson Research Center
Visualization Systems Group
Yorktown Heights, NY 10598

Abstract

An informal potpourri of novel graphics techniques for signal analysis is presented. Some areas of the work are touched upon to give the reader just a flavor of an application. Additional information is in the referenced publications. In order to encourage reader involvement, computational hints and recipes for producing the figures are provided.

> *"Who knows what secrets of nature lay buried in the terabytes of data being generated each day by physicists studying the results of numerical simulations or the image of a distant galaxy. Given the volume and complexity of scientific data, visualization in the physical sciences has become a necessity in the modern scientific world."* Robert Wolff

1.1 Introduction

This informal article describes several interesting ways of displaying data which are applied to a range of fields including acoustics and genetics. Some areas of the work are touched upon to give the reader just a flavor of an application. Much of the information has been discussed in previous papers, and additional information is in the referenced publications. In order to encourage reader involvement, computational hints and recipes for producing the figures are provided. The symbols [and] are used to delimit

Frontiers in Computing Systems Research, Vol. 1
Edited by S.K. Tewksbury
Plenum Press, New York, 1990

material which the reader can skip upon a casual reading. Note that some of the display methods devised by the author are new and speculative; however, it is hoped that many of the methods presented here will stimulate other researchers to extend and test these techniques in related fields.

This paper does not attempt to give a detailed historical background to the visual display of quantitative information. The computer graphical experiments in this paper only hint at the important past graphical work of others from which the author has received considerable inspiration. For background, the reader should consult the various books in the reference section, and in particular, the famous works of Tufte (Graphics Press, 1983), Wainer and Thissen (*Ann. Rev. Psychol*, 1981), and Wolff (*Comput. in Sci.*, 1988).

As background, perhaps the most common example of a technique used to capture patterns in data is the 3-D Fourier transform – often displayed as a 3-D map indicating energy, time, and frequency. The various mountain peaks indicate the frequency composition of data ranging from speech to breathing proteins (1). Unfortunately, traditional techniques such as this do not always distinguish potentially interesting features in input data. As an example, let's first consider speech. With the traditional Fourier representation, many perceptibly different sounds may give rise to only very subtle differences in the spectra. There has been past research which points out the limitations of the Fourier method in displaying acoustic features which are of importance in auditory perception. Such limitations naturally motivate the development of novel display techniques to help capture subtleties which may be difficult to see in the traditional displays.

1.2 Acoustics

From the dull, stentorian roar of a lion to the clanging of a cathedral bell, the remarkable range of audible sounds makes analysis exceedingly difficult. It is difficult to rigorously compare and characterize sounds by ear alone since the listening process is subject to the limitations and artifacts of both memory and perception. Also, there are individual variations in listeners' ability to localize and describe acoustic features. This problem is the primary motivation for graphic displays of speech. Some novel ways of graphically representing speech waveforms in order to capture information missing in the spectrogram will be discussed in the following sections; these include *phase-vectorgrams* displaying phase, frequency and amplitude in a cylindrical plot resembling a pipe cleaner, and *autocorrelation-faces* displaying speech in visually memorable ways for children.

The speech waveform is a complex entity which is difficult to manage, manipulate and characterize. Simply recording the pressure variation over time in the acoustic signal generated by human speech produces a complicated waveform. The signal itself alternates between quasi-periodic vowel-like sounds, which often look something like smooth rippling ocean waves when plotted, and certain consonants "looking" much like plots of random noise. Scattered through the signal are rapidly occurring high-energy pops known as plosives [1] interspersed by perceptually important silences.

While traditional graphic analyses, such as the spectrogram (intensity vs. frequency vs. time), have been invaluable in showing the general frequency content of an input signal, sometimes it is difficult for users to see on the spectrogram differences which are perceptible to the ear. These difficulties motivate representations which can make subtle differences in input signals obvious to the human analyst. First, a review of data display methods in general is presented.

1.3 New Ways of Displaying Data

The use of visual displays to present quantitative material has had a long history. There are many examples in the chronicle of science where important phenomena have been detected using visual displays and have heralded the emergence of entire new fields of scientific endeavor. Examples include the cloud, bubble, and spark chambers in physics, computer graphics of Julia Sets and other fractals in mathematics, and molecular graphics in drug design and structure-function assessment in biophysics. The usefulness of a particular display is determined by the embodiment of desirable characteristics such as descriptive capacity, potential for comparison, aid in focussing attention, and versatility. In contrast to the most common graphs which are restricted to two or three dimensions, "icons" (or symbols) such as computer-generated faces are now sometimes used to represent multidimensional data. With icons, the data parameters are mapped into figures with n features, each feature varying in size or shape according to the point's coordinate in that dimension (2,3). Such figures capitalize on the feature-integration abilities of the human visual system. Icons will be described in more detail in following sections.

---

[1] A plosive is a type of consonant sound made by sudden release of air impounded behind an occlusion of the vocal tract.

1.4   Snowflakes from Sound: Art and Science

Of the many displays of acoustical data developed, one of the most strik-
ing and colorful data-display techniques produces figures with the six-fold
symmetry of a snowflake. The trick is to convert sound waves (or any data)
into a collection of dots which are then reflected through mirror planes by a
simple computer program (see Pseudocode at end of paper). The resulting
representation, a *symmetrized dot-pattern* (SDP), provides a stimulus in
which local visual correlations are integrated to form a global percept. It
can potentially be applied to the detection and characterization of significant features of any sampled data. The symmetry, color and redundancy
of the dot-pattern is useful in the visual detection and memorization of
patterns by the human analyst.[2] The *J. Acoust. Soc. Am.* paper (1986)
describes a simple recipe for taking points on a speech amplitude-time waveform and computing the pattern (4).[3]

Figure 1.1 shows a symmetrized dot-pattern (SDP) for the "EE" sound
of a human and a synthesizer producing the same vowel sound. Since SDPs
can be considered, to a first approximation, merely a replotting of the time
waveform, it could be suggested that one would do as well to "look" at
the waveform to compare and contrast signals. However, as indicated by
the superimposed input signals, waveform similarities can often obscure
differences.

Figure 1.2 shows some more SDP examples – three different occurrences
of the sound "OO" as in "boot" spoken by three people. Despite sensitivity
to speaker individualities, SDPs have a global similarity for all "OO's".
SDPs may also help differentiate nasalized and nonnasalized sounds (Figure
1.3). In general, it is hoped that SDPs can supplement traditional analysis
to make for faster detection and diagnosis of certain important features in
data. To implement a symmetrized dot-pattern on a personal computer,
start with a digitized waveform. The waveform may represent sound where
the jagged trace on a graph indicates how the sound's loudness changes

---

[2] Pilot tests indicate that people without formal training in phonetics or acoustics, and
with no preparation, can recognize certain speech sounds represented by symmetrized
dot-patterns (SDPs). In some cases people can also identify a particular speaker by
looking at the speech-SDPs (see Pickover, C. (1986) On the use of computer generated
symmetrized dot-patterns for the visual characterization of speech waveforms and other
sampled data. *Acoust. Soc. Am.* 80(3): 955-960).

[3] Since most of the author's work with SDPs are in the field of speech, and since
the plots vaguely resemble snowflakes, the representation has informally been called a
"speech flake" by Ivars Peterson of *Science News* (see color cover of *Science News*, 131,
June 1987).

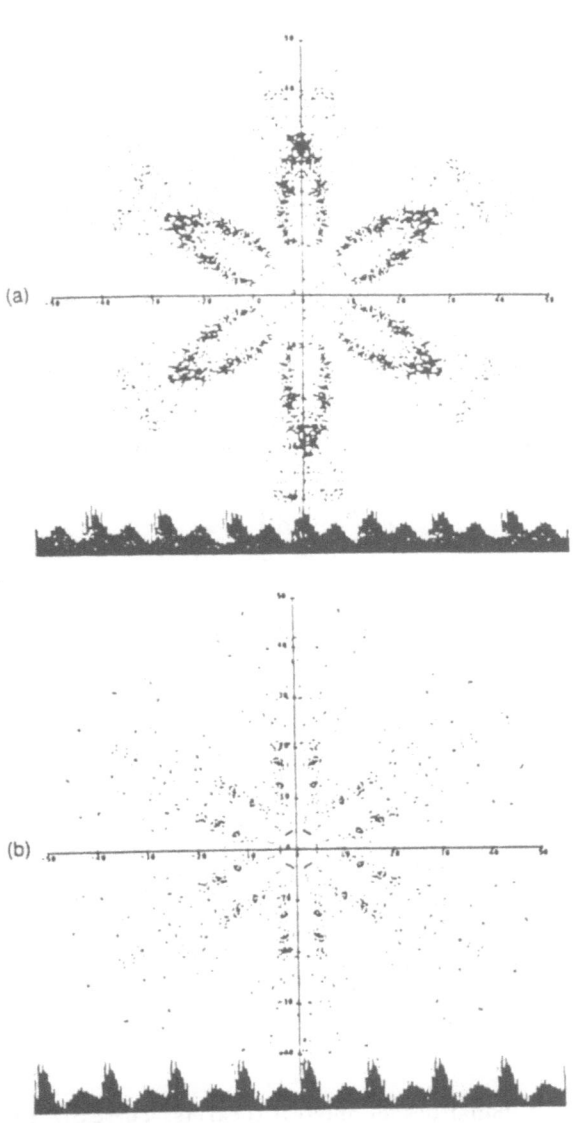

Figure 1.1: Symmetrized dot-patterns for "EE" vowel sound. Human-made "EE" sound (top) and a synthesized version of the same sound (bottom). Despite similar waveforms, symmetrized dot-patterns clearly show differences. (This figure and several others in this section first appeared in *J. Acoust. Soc. Am.* (Pickover, 1986).)

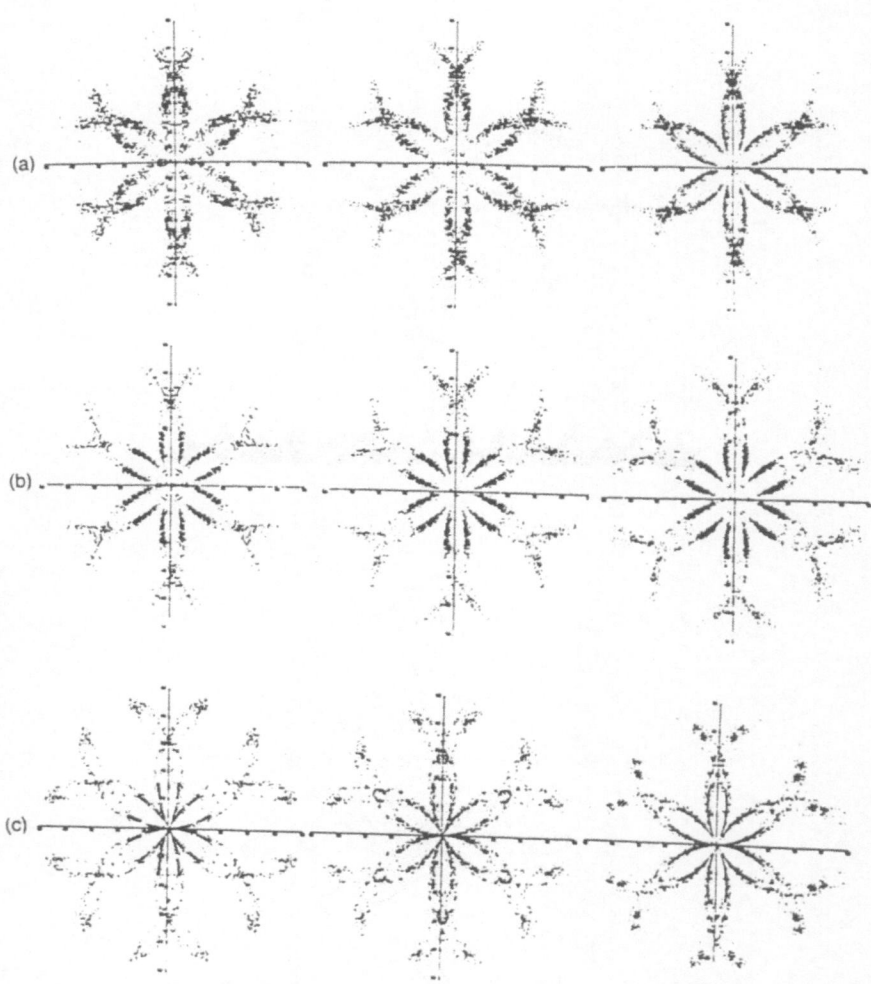

Figure 1.2: Family similarities for different speakers. These SDPs were computed from three individuals ((a), (b), and (c)) for three different occurrences of the sound "OO" as in "boot". Despite sensitivity to speaker individualities, SDPs have a global similarity for all "OO's".

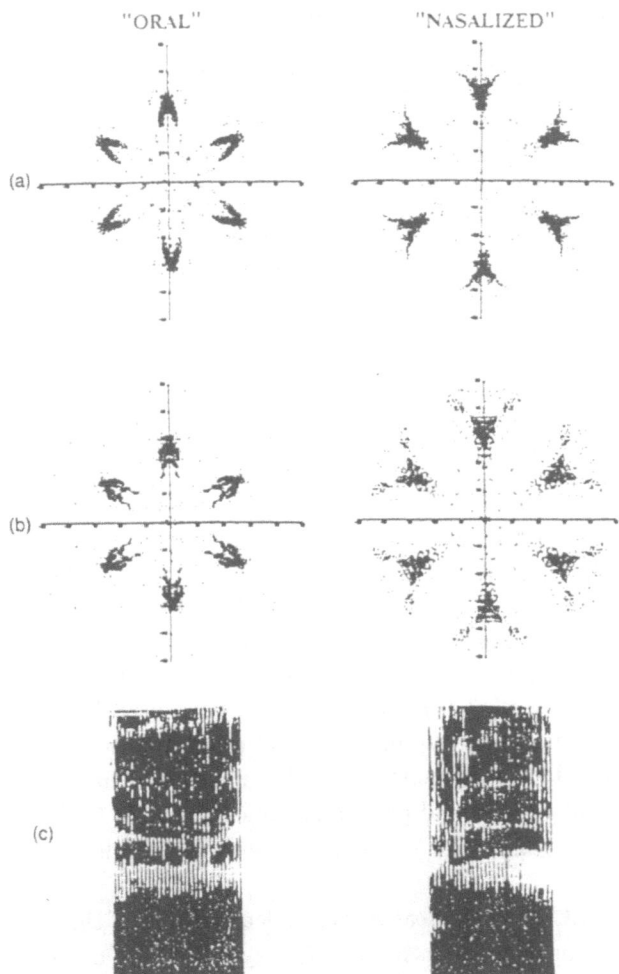

Figure 1.3: SDPs computed for oral and nasalized sounds. (a) "AH" and nasalized "AH" produced by a male speaker (as in the first vowel sound in "father" and "mom", respectively). (b) "AH" and nasalized "AH" produced by a female speaker. (c) Spectrograms for "AH" and nasalized "AH". SDPs can make the differences obvious, even for inexperienced users of SDPs. For comparisons of these patterns before and after symmetrization, see ref. (4).

through time. The data is mapped to a snowflake-like pattern by comparing the loudness of pairs of adjacent points and plotting the result on a polar coordinate graph (a graph that looks likes a polar view of the earth, with the North Pole at the graph's center). The points are then reflected, as though looking at them through a kaleidoscope (see pseudocode in the Appendix). The correlations (relationships) between adjacent pairs of points determine the structure of the SDP.

The concentration in this section is focused on human speech sounds, but the SDP can also be applied to handwriting, and musical and animal sounds. See the pseudocode in the Appendix for SDP color options, which make SDPs more useful in detecting data features (and more interesting from an artistic standpoint).

The use of this data display in representing cardiac sounds is discussed in the next section.

1.5   Medicine: Cardiology and SDPs

Symmetrized dot-patterns may have applications in representing heart sounds. Nearly a million Americans die each year of cardiovascular disease, according to the American Heart Association. The traditional diagnostic methods for cardiac disease – listening with a stethoscope (auscultation), examination of graphic records of the audible sounds (phonocardiography), or electrocardiogram (ECG) analysis – have been used for years by physicians and other medical personnel to detect abnormalities of the heart. I've used the symmetrized dot-pattern display mentioned in the previous section to represent normal and pathological heart sounds (mild mitral stenosis, and mitral regurgitation). Figure 1.4 shows example SDPs for cardiac sounds.

Unlike the ECG which measures electrical activity of the heart, the SDP described here uses acoustic input. The symmetrized dot-pattern (SDP) characterizes waveforms using patterns of dots and requires very limited computational time as prerequisite. Previous studies in texture discrimination and pattern recognition have shown that symmetry elements can make features more obvious to the human observer, and for this reason the SDPs have a high degree of induced symmetry (and redundancy) in order to aid the human analyst in recognizing and remembering patterns. In Figure 1.4 the SDP marked "normal" was computed from a normal heart beat. Another SDP represents the sounds from a patient with mild mitral stenosis. Mitral stenosis is an abnormal narrowing of the mitral valve usu-

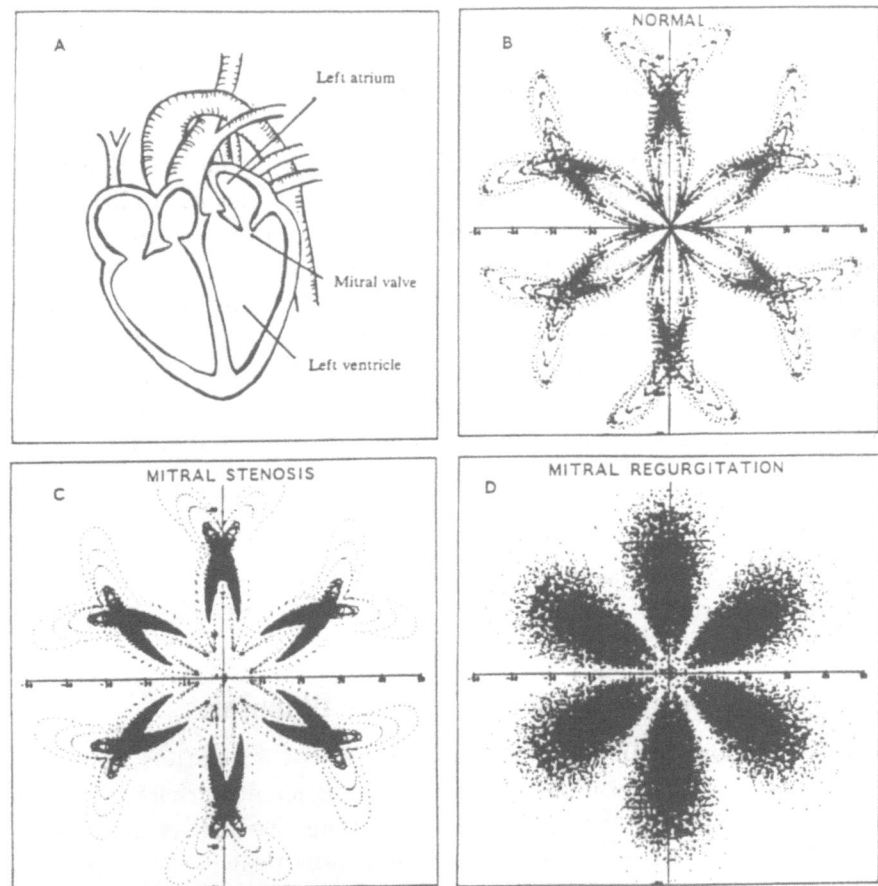

Figure 1.4: Heart sounds. A normal heart sound can be contrasted with cardiac sounds associated with various pathological conditions.

ally resulting from a disease such as rheumatic fever, and obstructing the free flow of blood from left atrium to left ventricle. Figure 1.4 also shows an SDP computed from a patient with mitral regurgitation, the abnormal back-flow of blood into the left atrium. Prior work in speech (last section) has suggested that the SDP functions somewhat like an autocorrelator and is also sensitive to general frequency content and waveform variability. The higher frequency noise characterizing the back-flow segment in mitral regurgitation gives rise to the characteristic "fuzzy" pattern in the SDP in Figure 1.4. An intermediate amplitude region in mitral stenosis gives rise to the dark "flying v" formations. These SDPs were computed for samples of about one-half second duration; however, other time-lengths were tried, including the capturing of several heart beats per frame, with essentially identical results. Also, when studying different segments in time, essentially the same SDP was generated.

The several demonstrations included in this section indicate that SDPs can make differences obvious even to inexperienced persons. Unlike SDPs, the traditional cardiac displays are not the same as pictures, since pictures have numerous visual features that can be readily identified, labeled, remembered, and integrated into a coherent whole. The ease with which patterns can be recognized may have value in instances where feedback to the patient or other medical personnel is useful, particularly when a physician is unavailable. This recognition ease and SDP-sensitivity may also be useful for researchers and physicians when comparing and studying heart sounds. Obviously, more cardiac sounds and many subjects need to be studied to fully assess the extent of SDPs'. usefulness. The specific visual correlates of acoustic-cardiac features which people use to distinguish one member of a cardiac class from another would provide an interesting avenue of future research.

1.6   A Dot-Display Used in Molecular Biophysics

The previous section showed how symmetrized dot-patters can represent data. Another example of a display used for data characterization at a more fundamental level of perception than the SDP is the random dot-display. This type of pattern was first researched in detail by Leon Glass in 1969 while studying visual perception (5). These patterns, also called random-dot moire patterns, are potentially useful in the global characterization of conformational changes occurring in biomolecules (6). As background, if a pattern of random dots is superimposed on itself and rotated by a small angle, concentric circles are perceived about the point of rotation. If the angle of rotation is increased, the perceived circles gradually disappear until a totally unstructured dot display is seen. This effect demonstrates the ability of the human visual system to detect local autocorrelations and may suggest a physiological basis of form perception in higher animals (Glass, 1969). Figure 1.5 shows an example of a dot interference pattern. The pattern is comprised of a set of ten thousand random dots which was superimposed on itself and subsequently rotated and uniformly expanded. Though the pattern was calculated by computer, similar patterns can easily be generated using sprinkled ink and transparencies.

Figure 1.5: Random dot-patterns. Random dot-display produced by superimposing a figure containing 10,000 random dots upon itself and subsequent rotation by three degrees and uniform expansion by a factor of 1.1. Note: if the rotation is much larger, the eye looses the ability to perceive the spiral patterns.

I've applied the "Glass patterns" to a problem in biophysics. By placing random dots on a graphics representation of a protein molecule before and after rotation, the center of rotation can easily be found (just as we can easily perceive the center in Figure 1.5). There are sometimes crystal structures of two forms of a biomolecule related by a conformational change. Often it is desirable to ascertain an equivalent axis of rotation relating two structures in conformational space regardless of the fact that the actual

transformation between the starting and ending form of the molecule may
have involved many small intermediate rotational and translational components. (To learn more about how to use these techniques to visually capture
motions in proteins and advantages over brute-force numerical methods, see
ref. 6)

1.7   Autocorrelation Cartoon-Faces for Speech

*"The most exotic journey would not be to see a thousand differ-
ent places, but to see a single place through a thousand person's
eyes." - Anon.*

Presented in this section is a rather unorthodox computer graphics characterization of sound and DNA sequences using computer generated cartoon faces. As background, computer graphics has become increasingly
useful in the representation and interpretation of multidimensional data
with complex relationships. Pseudo-color, animation, three-dimensional
figures, and a variety of shading schemes are among the techniques used
to reveal relationships not easily visible from simple correlations based on
two-dimensional linear theories.

Showing correlations between two or three variables is easy: simply plot
a two-dimensional or three-dimensional graph. But what if one is trying
to present four or five or even ten different variables at once? The face
method of representing multivariate data was first presented in 1973 by
Chernoff, a Harvard statistician (7). Using gradations of various facial features, such as the degree of eyebrow slant or pupil size, a single face can
convey the value of many different variables at the same time (Figure 1.6).
Such faces have been shown to be more reliable and more memorable than

5 5 5 5 5 5 5 5 5   6 5 5 5 5 5 5 5 5   7 5 5 5 5 5 5 5 5

Figure 1.6: Cartoon faces and data analysis. These cartoon faces can be used to
represent the values of as many as 10 variables, each variable corresponding to
a facial feature. Here only one facial feature, horizontal eye length, is changed.
Other facial coordinates are set to a constant middle-position.

Figure 1.7: The diversity of computer-generated faces. The settings for each of the ten facial parameters were computed using a random number generator.

other tested icons (or symbols), and allow the human analyst to grasp many of the essential regularities and irregularities in the data. In general, n data parameters are mapped into a figure with n features, each feature varying in size or shape according to the point's coordinate in that dimension. The data sample variables are mapped to facial characteristics; thus, each multivariate observation is visualized as a computer-drawn face. This aspect of the graphical point displays capitalizes on the feature integration abilities of the human visual system and is particularly useful for higher levels of cognitive processing. Figure 1.7 shows the range of faces produced when random numbers ("white noise") are mapped to facial coordinates.

puter generated cartoon faces can be used to represent speech sounds (8). The autocorrelation of a signal $x(n)$ with lag k is defined as

$$\phi(k) = \sum_{n=-\infty}^{\infty} x(n)x(n+k). \tag{1.1}$$

The autocorrelation function for data describes the general dependance of the values of the data at one time on its values at another time. On a computer an autocorrelation function for a finite window in time can be implemented as shown in the pseudocode in the Appendix. For more on autocorrelation theory, see (9,10).

To implement an "autocorrelation-face", 10 facial parameters are computed from the first 10 points of the autocorrelation function of a 50 ms sample of the speech sound. The process is described in more detail in ref. 8.

In this and the following applications, ten facial parameters, represented by $F(1, 2, 3, 4, 5, 6, 7, 8, 9, 10)$ are used, and each facial characteristic has ten settings, $S(1, 2, 3, 4, 5, 6, 7, 8, 9, 10)$, providing for 10 billion possible different faces. The controlled features are: head eccentricity, eye eccentricity, pupil size, eyebrow slant, nose size, mouth shape, eye spacing, eye size, mouth length, and degree of mouth opening. Head eccentricity, for example, controls how elongated the head is in either the horizontal or vertical direction. The mouth is constructed using parabolic interpolation routines, and the other features are derived from circles, lines, and ellipses. Figure 1.8 shows some examples computed from human speech.[4] The resultant speech-faces could provide useful biofeedback targets for helping deaf and severely hearing-impaired individuals to modify their vocalizations in selective ways – especially since they may provide simple and memorable features to which children could relate. The traditional speech spectrogram displays are not the same as pictures, since pictures have numerous visual features that can be readily identified, labeled, and integrated into a coherent whole. To compare SDPs (previous section) and faces: note that unlike faces, SDPs do not elicit an emotional reaction. Emotion does confer a mnemonic advantage for the faces, but can sometimes obscure the association, e.g. a smiling face representing cancer statistics.

---

[4] Various tests were done to assess whether people can differentiate sounds by looking at the faces. Test subjects were given sets of cards to sort into nine different categories of sound. The average percent correct for classification into 9 separate groups was 89 % ± 8%, with 3 perfect scores. (See ref. 8).

Figure 1.8: Faces from sound. Cartoon faces can be used to characterize sounds. The top row represents the fricative sound "s"; the second, "sh"; the third, "z"; and the fourth, "v". Sounds were repeated three times. For vowel and nasal sounds, see *J. Educ. Tech. Syst.*

1.8 Phase Vectorgrams

In this section, we return to a discussion of graphics for representing sounds. Presented here is the "phase vectorgram" representation, developed with colleagues in 1985 (11).

Until recently it had been believed that the perceived sound of an audio signal could be completely characterized by its power spectrum (energy vs. frequency). A sine wave is characterized by amplitude (or extreme height), its period (the time between one peak and the next) and its phase (the position of the sine wave in time). Recent psychoacoustic experiments have revealed that phase relations between the sinusoidal components in signals can be perceived – yet they are not represented on spectrograms. This suggests that there is a more appropriate domain than that of the power spectrum in which to process signals. The phase information normally discarded via transformation to the domain of the power spectrum must be reconsidered. Unfortunately, the short-term phase of a dynamic signal is difficult to quantify and plot. [These difficulties are overcome in an analysis using an autocorrelation-based pitch detector, followed by discrete Fourier transform, and normalization of the plot to the phase of the fundamental frequency (ϕ_1):

$$\phi_i = \phi_i - k\phi_1 \tag{1.2}$$

where k is the harmonic number and ϕ_1 is the phase of the fundamental. (These terms may be unfamiliar to some readers; see (12) for more information.) With knowledge of the fundamental frequency we can adjust the Fourier analysis so the reference point is synchronized to the fundamental period of the waveform, and the frequency sample points can be taken at more meaningful points corresponding to the harmonics of the fundamental.]

In the phase vectorgram (Figure 1.9) amplitude, frequency and phase are presented in a cylindrical plot resembling a pipe-cleaner or bottle-brush. Shown is a vectorgram for different regions in time for the human utterance "ee", as in "meet". Given the amplitudes for components k and the corrected phases (see Eq. 2), the "bristles" in the cylindrical plot may be drawn. The length of each bristle is determined by the gain at each frequency. Frequency extends from low frequency (0 Hz) to high frequency

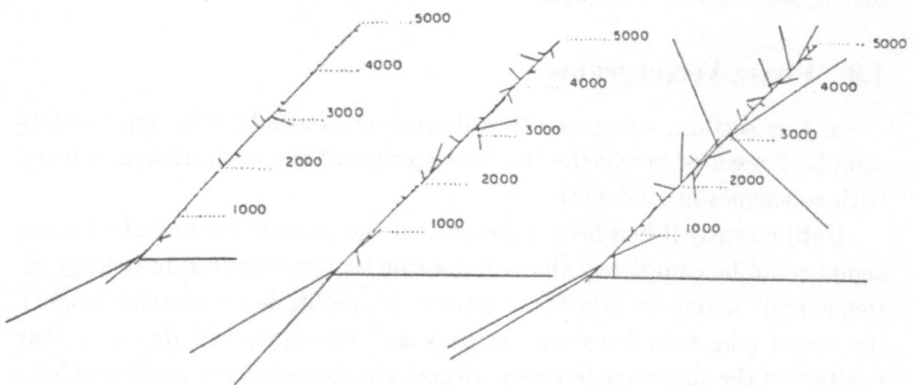

Figure 1.9: Phase vectorgram. Harmonics of a vowel sound are plotted as "bristles" emanating from a central axis, with an angle equal to the phase of each harmonic.

(5000 Hz) as the cylinder goes from front to back. Phase is represented by the angle the bristle makes with the central axis. Cylindrical plots are normalized so that all bristles may be accommodated in the same size graph. The cylindrical plot represents the phases more meaningfully than traditional two dimensional phase-vs.-frequency plots which typically have phase from -180 to +180 degrees on the ordinate and frequency on the abscissa – amplitude is not a factor in such plots. In our plots, the length of the bristle reflects the importance of that particular phase component since the bristle length is related to the amplitude. Low amplitude bristles due to noise or computational artifacts therefore do not obscure the plot. In addition, the cylindrical representation eliminates the need for "phase unwrapping" (12). Generally, the cylindrical plot gives a clear indication of both phase and amplitude as a function of frequency. It may be of use in a variety of signal processing applications. Evidence of speaker-independent phase "signatures" for phonemes (the basic building blocks of speech) suggests the use of phase vectorgrams in speech recognition.

1.9 Molecular Genetics: DNA Vectorgram

1.9.1 Background

DNA contains the basic genetic information of all living cells. The sequences of bases of DNA (adenine, cytosine, guanine, and thymine – A,C,G, and T) may hold information concerning protein synthesis as well as a variety of regulatory signals. For example, specific AT-rich regions are thought to be codes for beginning transcription. Also, certain *specific* viral sequences elicit cancerous changes in cells in artificial media and in animals. In addition to containing such regulatory codes and tumor-promoting codes, DNA sequence and composition are often correlated with physical properties of the DNA such as the DNA melting temperature.

Fairly detailed comparisons between DNA sequences are useful and can be achieved by a variety of brute-force statistical computations, but sometimes at a cost of the loss of an intuitive feeling for the structures. Differences between sequences may obscure the similarities. Even determining whether a particular sequence is *random* is curiously difficult. The approaches described in this section provide a way for simply representing and comparing random and DNA sequences in such a way that several sequence features may be detected by the analyst's eye.

1.9.2 DNA Vectorgram

The "vectorgrams" sometimes look like the steps a drunkard would take wandering in an open field. They can also be used to search for patterns in the sequence of bases in DNA. The method involves the conversion of the DNA sequence to binary data and subsequent mapping of the data to a two-dimensional pattern on a cellular lattice. For the example presented in this section, triply bonded bases (GC) are differentiated from doubly bonded bases (AT) by assigning nucleotide input values as follows: $G = 1$, $C = 1$, $A = 0$, $T = 0$. As the sequence generated by this means are strings of 0's and 1's, the human observer may find difficulty in distinguishing between different sequences (Figure 1.10).

A technique which has proved useful in overcoming this drawback involves the transformation of the digit strings into characteristic two-dimensional patterns traced out on a unit cellular lattice. This approach was applied to the shift-registers of digital computers by D.II. Green (14). The

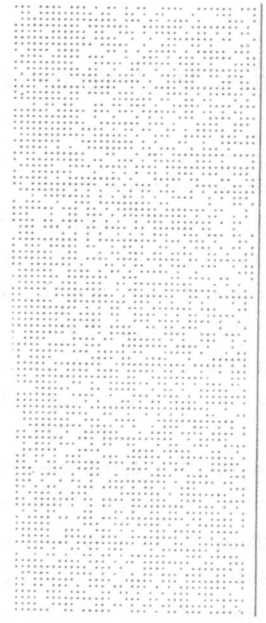

Figure 1.10: Representation of DNA by dots. G's and C's are mapped to dots in this representation of a 4000-base cancer gene. The human observer may have difficulty in distinguishing between different sequences using this representation. The DNA vectorgram makes this clear.

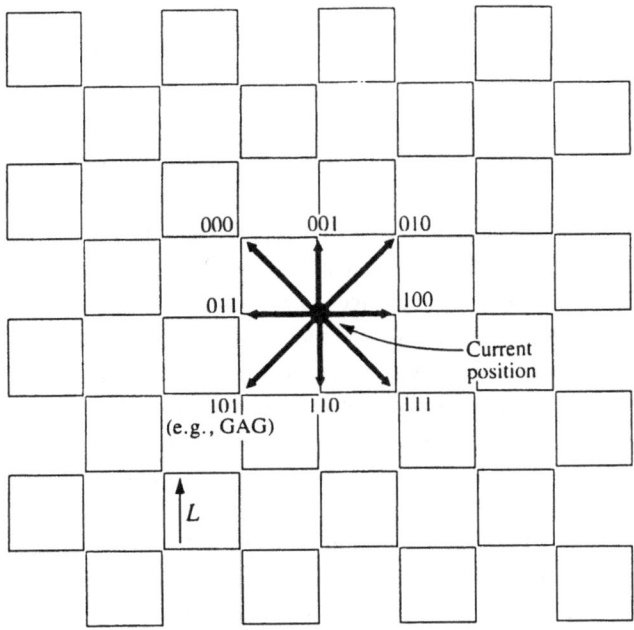

Figure 1.11: DNA transformation. The mapping of the digit strings into characteristic two-dimensional patterns traced out on a cellular lattice of cell length L. Each of the three digit combinations causes a vector to be drawn from a point on the lattice to one of the eight points immediately adjacent according to the coding system shown.

simple conversion pattern used for the DNA work follows that of Green (14). Three digits at a time are inspected and assigned a direction of movement over a cellular lattice. "010" would indicate to move up and to the right. Therefore, each of the three digit combinations causes a vector to be drawn from a point on the lattice to one of the eight points immediately adjacent according to the coding system shown. This procedure is repeated using serial overlapping windows of length three, and therefore a pattern characteristic of the DNA sequence is drawn on the lattice.

Using this approach, sequences with a predominance of repeating G's or C's, for example, will show a net movement along the right lower diagonal. In general, sequences with high G-C content will show a downward tendency. Using the transformation diagramed in Figure 1.11, you can see that if for each combination of 3 bases found in the sequence, there exists at some other region another combination which is the logical inverse (e.g.

G and A interchanged; 010 vs. 101), then the net movement will be zero. A repeating sequence such as ... GGGGAAGAATACGAGGGGAA ... generates a trace that returns to its starting point.

Figure 1.12 shows a DNA vectorgram for a random input sequence. This is useful for comparison with the DNA sequence to follow which is visually far from random. The radius of the circle centered at the origin indicates how far the sequence is expected to travel by chance.

It was quite startling to see such a large difference in the vectorgram produced by a real DNA sequence as compared with the vectorgram in Figure 1.13. An example of the output of the graphics system for a large DNA sequence represented by the dots in Figure 1.11 is presented in Figure 1.13 The calculation was performed for a human bladder oncogene consisting of about 4000 bases. The vectorgram, far from being random, travels a mostly downward course indicating strings containing a predominance of 1's (011,101,111). The most prominent feature on the map is the "kink" (global shift in direction) at about 1350, and interestingly this feature corresponds to a biologically important area of the DNA sequence. Magnifications of the fine structure of the vectorgram reveal additional interesting patterns

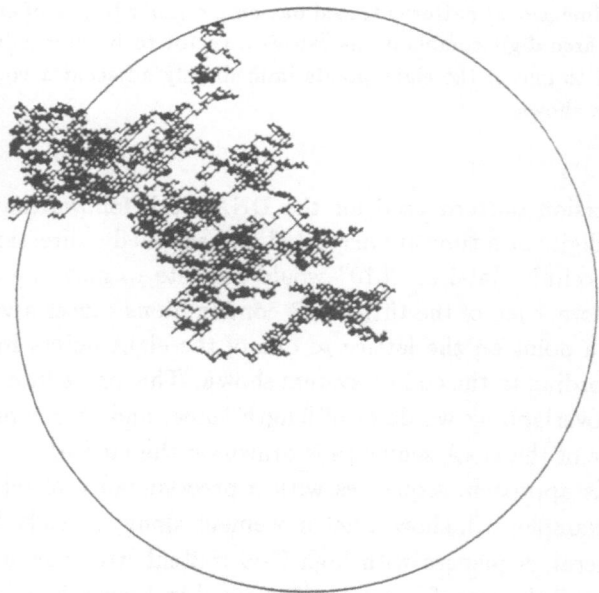

Figure 1.12: Random nucleotide-base input sequence. This is useful for visual comparison with the DNA sequence in Figure 1.11, which is far from random.

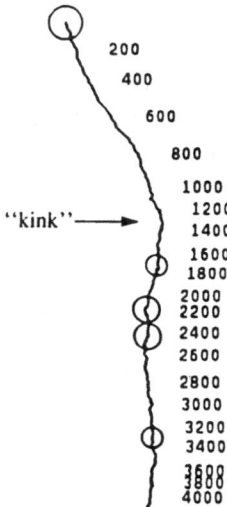

Figure 1.13: Human bladder oncogene (cancer gene). The vectorgram, computed from the same data as Figure 1.10 is far from random; it travels a mostly downward course indicating strings containing a predominance of 1's (011,101,111). The most prominent feature on the map is the "kink" at about 1350, and interestingly this feature corresponds to a biologically important area of the DNA sequence.

(loops, hairpins, etc.) (15). One can study a number of other cancer genes with this approach and examine the usefulness of the vectorgram in capturing patterns not easy to find using other traditional approaches. (See ref. (15) for magnifications of the regions in bubbles in Figure 1.13.)

1.10   Directed Reading List

Several excellent reference books describing prior work in the field of unusual graphic representations were listed in the beginning of this paper. In addition, there is a growing literature on the Chernoff face representation. For some good references, see: Chernoff, H. (1973), Chernoff and Rizvi (1975), Flury and Riedwyl (1981), and Jacob et al. (1976) (refs. 17,18,19).

Cancer genes (oncogenes) continue to be of significant interest to molecular geneticists, and the reader should consult Bishop (1982) (ref. 20) for an introductory description of these genes. For a more recent discussion of oncogenes, see Holden (1987) (ref. 21) The sequence data for the oncogene oncogenes, see Holden (1987) (ref. 21) The sequence data for the oncogene graphics experiments in this book come from Reddy (1983) (ref. 22). The search for patterns in DNA is also an active research area for molecular geneticists, and the reader should see Friedland and Kedes (1985), and Lewin (1986) for more information (refs. 23, 24).

1.11   Summary

This paper illustrates just a few of the many ways to cope with the vast quantities of data generated by modern instruments and computer techniques. Particular attention was given to identifying patterns and trends in various types of data. The displays were a mixture of old ideas used in new contexts and new ideas brought to bear on long-standing data analysis problems. Some of the displays described included: the DNA vectorgram, auto-correlation face, symmetrized dot-pattern, phase vectorgram, and random dot-display. Notice that the choice of data representation depends on the attributes of the phenomena under study, what the researcher is looking for, and the intended target audience (e.g. technical colleagues vs. children vs. general public). For a survey of work described in this paper and references to the work of others in related fields, see Peterson's article in *Science News* 131: 392-394, 1987). Much of the material in this chapter appears in [25].

Appendix

In order to encourage reader involvement, the following computer pseudocode is given. Typical parameters are given within the code. The reader should be able to program the concepts outlined here in the programming language of his or her choice.

ALGORITHM: How to create a Symmetrized Dot-Pattern

INPUT: W(t) a waveform with npts sample points
OUTPUT: snowflake-like SDP
VARIABLES: npts is the number of data points.
   angle controls the symmetry angle of the dot pattern.
   lag determines the time relationship between points.
Notes: Try changing the angle, top and lag parameters to optimize
   these values for finding features of interest in the data.

```
top = 50;        (* scaling upper bound *)
(* find low and high values in data *)
hi=1.0 e-10; lo=1.0 e10;
do i = 1 to npts;
   if W(i) > hi then hi = W(i);
   if W(i) < low then low = W(i);
end;
do i = 1 to npts;  (* rescale data to range: 0 - top *)
   W(i) = (W(i)-low)*top/(hi-low);
end;
call set('POLAR'); (* place graphics in polar mode   *)
call axis(-top,top,0,360); (* set up axes in r and theta    *)
angle=60;                (* choose a symmetry angle    *)
lag= 1;                  (* choose a lag               *)
do j = 1 to npts-lag;
   (* Color dots              *)
   if W(j+lag)-W(j) >= 0 then Color(Red) else Color(Green);
   do i = 1 to 360 by angle;
      PlotDot(W(j),i+W(j+lag));  (* place dot at (r,theta)   *)
      PlotDot(W(j),i-W(j+lag));
   end;
end;
```

ALGORITHM: How to Create a Moire Dot-Pattern

Variables:
NumDots = the number of dots (e.g. 10,000)
Angle   = the rotation angle (e.g. 1 degree)
sf   = scale factor   (e.g. 1.1)
Notes: The display area is assumed to go from 0 to 100. Random
   numbers are generated on the interval (0,1). The reader may
   experiment by gradually increasing the angle until the eye can no
   longer detect correlations.

```
DO i = 1 to NumDots;
   GenRand(randx); GenRand(randy);  (* Generate random numbers *)
   randx=randx*100; randy=randy*100;
   PrintDot(randx,randy);
   (* Rotate and Scale; Center is at (50,50) *)
   randxx =sf*((randx-50)*cosd(angle)+(randy-50)*sind(angle)) + 50;
   randy =sf*((randy-50)*cosd(angle)-(randx-50)*sind(angle)) + 50;
   randx = randxx;
   PrintDot(randx,randy);  (* Print superimposed pattern *)
END;
```

ALGORITHM: Autocorrelation Function

Variables: npts = the number of data points
    Input = array of samples from a digitized
        waveform.
    Auto = autocorrelation function
Notes: If the input data is a function of time
    then the autocorrelation function is
    also a function of time.

```
auto(*) = 0; (* initialize array *)
do p = 0 to npts;
  do q = 1 to npts - p;
    auto(p) = auto(p) + input(q)*input(q+p);
  end;
  (* correction factor *)
  auto(p) = auto(p)* (1/(npts-p));
end;
```

**ALGORITHM:
Create a DNA Vectorgram**

Variables:
  (x,y) - current position in lattice
  s   - step size for walk on lattice

```
select(argument);
   when('000') do; x=x-s;y=y+s; end;
   when('001') do; y=y+s; end;
   when('010') do; x=x+s;y=y+s; end;
   when('011') do; x=x-s; end;
   when('100') do; x=x+s; end;
   when('101') do; x=x-s;y=y-s; end;
   when('110') do; y=y-s; end;
   when('111') do; x=x+s;y=y-s; end;
end;/*select*/
call MovePen(x,y);
```

References

[1] C. Pickover, *Spectrographic representations of globular protein breathing motions*, Science, Vol. 223, p. 181 (1984); C. Pickover, *Frequency representations of DNA sequences: Application to a bladder cancer gene*, Journal of Molecular Graphics, Vol. 2, p. 50 (1984); C. Pickover, *Novel Graphics Allow Computer Synthesis of Singing "Human" Voices*, Computer Technology Review (Winter Issue), Vol. 7(16), pp. 79-89 (1988).

[2] H. Wainer and D. Thissen, *Graphical Data Analysis*, Ann. Rev. Psychol., Vol. 32, pp. 191-241 (1981).

[3] E. Tufte, *The Visual Display of Quantitative Information*, Graphics Press: Connecticut (1983).

[4] C. Pickover, *On the use of computer generated symmetrized dot-patterns for the visual characterization of speech waveforms and other sampled data*, J. Acoust. Soc. Am., Vol. 80(3), pp. 955-960 (1986).

[5] L. Glass, *Moire effect from random dots*, Nature, Vol. 223, pp. 578 (1969).

[6] C. Pickover, *The use of random-dot displays in the study of biomolecular conformation*, Journal of Molecular Graphics, Vol. 2, pp. 34 (1984).

[7] H. Chernoff, *The use of faces to represent points in k-dimensional space graphically*, J. Amer. Statist. Assoc., Vol. 68, pp. 361-367 (1973).

[8] C. Pickover, *On the educational uses of computer-generated cartoon faces*, Journal of Educational Technology Systems, Vol. 13, pp. 185-198 (1985).

[9] J. Bendat and R. Piersol, *Measurement and Analysis of Random Data*. John Wiley and Sons: New York (1966).

[10] I. Witten, *Principals of Computer Speech*. Academic Press: N.Y (1982).

[11] C. Pickover and M. Kubovy, *Speech vectorgram*, IBM Technical Disclosure Bulletin, Vol. 27, pp. 6774-6775 (1985); C. Pickover and M. Martin, *Short-term phase characterization in dynamic signal analysis*, IBM Technical Disclosure Bulletin, Vol. 27, pp. 6769-6771 (1985).

[12] R. K. Otnes and L. Enochson, *Applied Time Series Analysis, Vol I: Basic Techniques.* Wiley: N.Y (1978).

[13] L. Cohen and C. Pickover, *A comparison of joint time frequency distribution for speech signals,* invited talk, IEEE International Conference on Circuits & Systems, Vol. 1, pp. 42-45 (1986).

[14] D. H. Green, *Shift-register derived patterns,* In *Cybernetic Serendipity,* J. Reichardt (ed), Prager: New York, p. 99 (1968).

[15] C. Pickover, *DNA Vectorgrams: representation of cancer gene sequences as movements along a 2-D cellular lattice,* IBM J. Res. Dev., Vol. 31, pp. 111-119 (1987).

[16] R. Wolff, *The visualization challenge in the physical sciences,* Computers in Science, Vol. 2(1), pp. 16-31 (Jan./Feb., 1988).

[17] H. Chernoff and M. Rizvi, *Effect on classification error of random permutations of features in representing multivariate data by faces,* J. Amer. Statistical Assoc., Vol. 70, pp. 548-554 (1975).

[18] B. Flury and H. Riedwyl, *Graphical representation of multivariate data by means of asymmetrical faces,* J. Amer. Statistical Assoc., Vol. 76, pp. 757-765 (1981).

[19] R. Jacob, H. Egeth and W. Bevan, *The face as a data display,* Human Factors, Vol. 18, pp. 189-200 (1976).

[20] J. Bishop, *Oncogenes,* Scientific American, pp. 81-92 (March, 1982).

[21] C. Holden, *Oncogene linked to fruit-fly development,* Science, Vol. 238, pp. 160-161 (1987).

[22] E. Reddy, *Nucleotide sequence analysis of the T24 human bladder carcinoma oncogene,* Science, Vol. 220, pp. 1061 (1983).

[23] P. Friedland and L. Kedes, *Discovering the secrets of DNA,* Communications of the ACM, Vol. 28, pp. 1164-1186 (1985).

[24] R. Lewin, *Proposal to sequence the human genome stirs debate,* Science, Vol. 232, pp. 1598-1599 (1986).

[25] C. Pickover, *Computers, Pattern, Chaos and Beauty.* St. Martin's Press: New York (1990).

CHAPTER 2

STABILITY OF CONTINUOUS
CELLULAR AUTOMATA

Martin Grant
Dept. of Physics
McGill University
Montreal, Quebec H3A 2T8
Canada

J.D. Gunton
Dept. of Physics
Lehigh University
Bethlehem, PA 18015
USA

Abstract

We formally coarse-grain the microscopic equations of motion which determine the dynamical behavior of a class of cellular automata by projection-operator methods. Thus, we obtain a macroscopic description in terms of Langevin equations for the slow long-lifetime thermodynamic variables, such as order parameters. The dynamical rules for the automata are modeled by equations which are similar to Hamilton's equations. For reversible automata, we obtain the standard results of nonequilibrium statistical physics, namely, fluctuation-dissipation relations, Onsager's symmetry relations, and Green-Kubo relations. For dynamical rules which have both reversible and irreversible parts we find that none of these results apply. For irreversible rules, we obtain an exact result: the slow variable is linearly unstable due to a "fluctuation-enhancement" relation. This can imply that the structure in the irreversible cellular automata grows exponentially for early times. We also discuss the relationship of our results to the growth of ordered structure in physical systems.

2.1 Introduction

Cellular automata are dynamical systems consisting of many identical components [1]. Their time dependence is determined by a prescribed set of rules, to make the automata idealized models for the kinetics of pattern

Frontiers in Computing Systems Research, Vol. 1
Edited by S.K. Tewksbury
Plenum Press, New York, 1990

formation in natural systems. Examples which are often cited include the formation of dendrites, flow in turbulent fluids, and the growth of structure in biological systems. This potential richness in the field has generated a great deal of interest. Much of the current work involves the study of cellular automata by direct numerical simulation.

In this paper we analytically classify cellular automata on the basis of their signature under time reversal. Purely reversible rules, which we will also call reactive, are those whose equations of motion are invariant as time $t \to -t$. Purely irreversible rules, called dissipative, are those whose equations of motion have a minus-sign signature under time reversal. In general, rules can have both reactive and dissipative parts. It is often found numerically that cellar automata with irreversible rules rapidly form complicated structure, as time goes on, regardless of initial conditions [2,3,4]. It is this novel feature of self-organization into self-similar structures which is of most interest in cellular automata. This is reminiscent of complex dynamical systems which form structures spontaneously.

We shall discuss one aspect of self-organization in cellular automata: the instability leading to the growth of structure. Usually there are strong reasons for systems to become less ordered as time goes on. Thermodynamics requires isolated systems to evolve to a state of greater disorder. In nonequilibrium theory the analog of this consists of three results which constrain the dynamic Langevin equations for macroscopic variables: fluctuation-dissipation relations [5], Onsager's relations [6], and Green-Kubo relations [7,8]. These affect the dissipative parts of Langevin equations of motion, requiring disorder to increase. Microscopic equations for physical systems are reactive and, in some sense, these constraints are the price one pays for breaking time-reversal symmetry in the derivation of irreversible kinetic equations. Regardless, some physical systems do form structures spontaneously. These systems are typically not isolated, however. As examples, we will review spinodal decomposition and dendritic growth below.

Cellular automata are isolated systems, but their "microscopic" equations of motion need not be reactive. Thus the results from nonequilibrium theory mentioned above need not apply. This has been anticipated by Grinstein, Jayaprakesh and IIe [4]. They argued that Onsager's symmetry relations for transport coefficients need not apply to cellular automata.

Hence, we felt it worthwhile to find the analog of these standard results for irreversible automata. The derivation of macroscopic Langevin equations from first principles involves the coarse-graining of a large number of microscopic equations of motion [9,10,11,12,13]. Below, we use these standard methods to coarse-grain a class of dynamical systems [14] which we argue are the continuum analogs of discrete cellular automata. The novelty is that we can consider microscopic equations of motion which can be reversible, irreversible, or a combination of those behaviors. The irreversible parts we consider have been shown in other contexts [15] to be equivalent to the effect of walls. Thus some connection between self-organization in irreversible automata and open physical systems can be made.

We derive Langevin equations for the macroscopic behavior of the slowly varying thermodynamic quantities in the system. As one might expect, the results mentioned above, fluctuation-dissipation relations, Onsager's relations, and Green-Kubo relations only apply to the reversible automata we consider. Cellular automata with other signatures under time reversal do not obey these relations. A noteworthy consequence of the analysis is the following exact result: for irreversible rules, the evolution of the slow variable, if it exists, must be linearly unstable. This implies that the slow variable grows exponentially for early times. Exponential growth for early times is often a signature of pattern formation in nonequilibrium systems. It occurs, for example, in the Cahn [16] theory of spinodal decomposition [17], and the Mullins-Sekerka [18] theory of interfacial instability in dendritic growth [19]. The result here, however, has a dramatically different origin: it is a consequence of a "transport coefficient" becoming negative due to fluctuation-enhancement relation which forces order to grow in irreversible automata, rather than being a thermodynamic instability. Our treatment is analogous to the usual derivation of the fluctuation-dissipation theorem, and applies to a large class of automata.

An outline for the remainder of this paper follows. In section 2.2, we review the nature of self-organization in physical systems. We discuss spinodal decomposition in section 2.2.1, and dendritic growth in section 2.2.2. These are two of the most studied problems in the kinetics of pattern formation. In section 2.3, we coarse-grain microscopic equations of motion. We review the standard derivation of macroscopic Langevin equations by the projection-operator method in section 2.3.1. In section 2.3.2, we study a class of irreversible cellular automata. They are coarse-grained by the methods reviewed in section 2.3.1. Finally, in section 2.4, we summarize and discuss our results.

2.2   Instabilities and Self-Organization in Physical Systems

2.2.1   Spinodal Decomposition

Before giving the analysis presented in the next section, we briefly review two examples of pattern formation in physical systems. If a system is prepared at a high temperature in a disordered state, then rapidly cooled to a low temperature T where it is ordered in equilibrium, it orders kinetically [17]. Small domains of ordered phase form and then grow to macroscopic size as time increases. For example, in an AlZn binary alloy, the disordered state corresponds to a random mixture of Al and Zn atoms. Following the quench, small domains of Al and Zn form, which grow as the two phases separate. This time dependent process, by which the system evolves to its final equilibrium state, where the Al and Zn phases are completely separated, is a first-order phase transition.

During spinodal decomposition, a long-wavelength instability (briefly identified below) creates an interconnected structure. In Fig. 2.1, we show some typical Monte Carlo configurations for very early times [20]. There, one can see the disordered phase becoming unstable and leading to the formation of domains of ordered phase. For later times, the interconnected structure of domains coarsens. A macroscopic description of the instability requires a field $\psi(\vec{x}, t)$ corresponding to the local order at site $\vec{x}$ and time t. For a binary alloy, like AlZn, which undergoes spinodal decomposition by phase separation as the two phases unmix, the order parameter ψ is the excess concentration of either phase, normalized to be $+1$ or -1, when only one phase is present. In that case, ψ is conserved, since the fractional amount of either species can never increase or decrease. A binary alloy like Cu_3Au undergoing an order-disorder transition has a nonconserved order parameter (we shall call this "spinodal decomposition" also, even though this term is, strictly speaking, only used for the case in which the order parameter is conserved). There, the two species Cu and Au preferentially order at low temperatures on different sublattices, like an antiferromagnet. The relative concentration on a sublattice then determines ψ, which is not conserved. In Fig. 2.1, the order parameter is not conserved; snapshots for a system with a conserved ψ are similar. Below we shall only consider a nonconserved ψ.

To explain the physics of spinodal decomposition, one must first identify the origin of the long-wavelength instability which causes the interconnected inter-twining of domains. This was done by Cahn [16]. A dynamical equation can be prescribed by assuming that all time variation is due to the slowly varying order parameter ψ. Furthermore, all time dependence is due to the minimization of the local free energy, with all other degrees of freedom modeled by a random noise whose intensity is determined in part by the temperature. That equation is

$$\frac{\partial \psi(\vec{x}, t)}{\partial t} = -D \frac{\delta F[\psi]}{\delta \psi} + \eta, \qquad (2.1)$$

where $F[\psi]$ is the free energy functional, the transport coefficient D is a constant if ψ is nonconserved, and D is related to the intensity of the "noise" η by a fluctuation-dissipation relation:

$$\langle \eta(\vec{x}, t) \eta(\vec{x}', t') \rangle = 2D k_B T \delta(\vec{x} - \vec{x}') \delta(t - t'), \qquad (2.2)$$

where k_B is Boltzmann's constant. The free energy functional F is the sum of the local free energies f at all sites $\vec{x}$, which typically has the form $f = -r\psi^2 + u\psi^4$ where r and u are positive constants, plus the sum of all the exchange interactions, each one of which is proportional to $(\nabla \psi)^2$. In Cahn's theory, one simply linearizes around the initial value $\psi = 0$. Then, $f \approx -r\psi^2$, and ψ grows exponentially, since the Langevin equation becomes

$$\frac{\partial \psi}{\partial t} \approx Dr\psi, \qquad (2.3)$$

for long wavelengths where we can neglect the exchange interaction. The origin of the instability is the mechanical instability in the middle of the van-der-Waals loop, given by the chemical potential $\partial f / \partial \psi = -2r\psi + 4u\psi^3$.

Such a theory only addresses the early stages of spinodal decomposition. Roughly speaking, neglecting the quartic term implies $\psi(t) \sim e^t [1 + \mathcal{O}(\psi^2)]$. But the higher-order term itself behaves like e^t, so the expansion breaks down quickly. Nonlinearities, and coupled Fourier modes make the full problem exceedingly complicated.

2.2.2 Dendritic Growth

Another area involving instabilities leading to pattern formation is crystal growth [19]. There, a single crystal in an undercooled melt grows by the diffusion of latent heat from the crystal to the melt into a complex dendritic structure. The problem is usually formulated in terms of, say, the diffusion equation for temperature in the supercooled melt with moving boundary conditions at the crystal-melt interface. Perturbations of the flat crystal-melt interface into the supercooled melt are linearly unstable and eventually grow into complex dendritic patterns. The linear stability

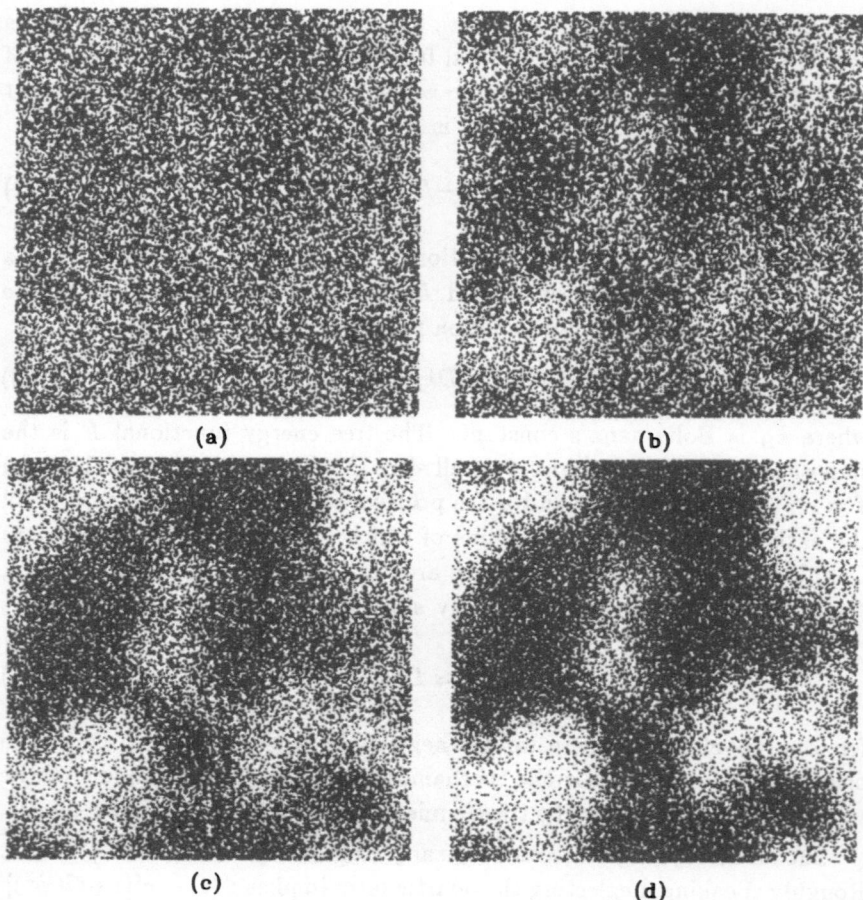

Figure 2.1: Monte Carlo simulation of spinodal decomposition in a system with a nonconserved order parameter [20]. White is order parameter +1, black is order parameter −1. Shown are very early times, as the linearly unstable initial state decays, leading to the formation of domains.

analysis of the equations of motion, which we will not reproduce here, was done by Mullins and Sekerka [18]. Again, a thermodynamic instability due to a phase transition gives rise to the eventual structure, and the linear analysis is valid for only the very early stages of growth. The slow thermodynamic variables do not only consist of the order parameter field; the phenomenological dynamic description is made up of a nonconserved order parameter which is coupled to a conserved field controlling thermal diffusion. This implies the instability of the surface separating two phases of the order parameter mentioned above.

Both systems we have discussed in this section have instabilities leading to the growth of patterns. The derivation of the macroscopic equations of motion is phenomenological, and the instabilities are of thermodynamic origin: note that transport coefficients are well defined for both problems. Finally, coupling to thermal effects in externally-controlled walls is essential. In spinodal decomposition, one prepares the system at high T and then rapidly quenches temperature, while in dendritic growth, one supercools the melt through externally-controlled walls.

2.3 Langevin Equations for Slow Variables

2.3.1 Reversible Microscopic Dynamics

In this section we review the derivation of macroscopic kinetic equations by coarse-graining microscopic equations. The subtlety is that although the microscopic equations of motion for a many-body system are invariant under time reversal, coarse-graining gives macroscopic Langevin equations which have dissipative parts. One begins with Hamilton's equations of motion for all the canonical momenta and positions of the many-body system. A useful way to write these coupled equations of motion is

$$\frac{\partial a_j}{\partial t} = i\mathcal{L}(a_k)a_j, \tag{2.4}$$

where a_j are the dynamical variables, and the index j runs over positions and momenta of all the particles in the system. The operator $\mathcal{L}$ is called the Liouvillian which is defined by $\mathcal{L} \equiv -i[\mathcal{H}, \ ]$, where $\mathcal{H}$ is the Hamiltonian, and the square brackets denote a Poisson bracket. For the analysis below, note that the linear operator $\mathcal{L}$ may be any function of a_j, with one constraint: time-reversal invariance of Hamilton's equations implies $\mathcal{L}$ is Hermitean, if one associates a vector space with the variables a_j.

Eq. (2.4) provides a complete description of classical many-body mechanics. This description can be intractable, however, since, for example, many initial conditions $a_j(t = 0)$ are required. Note that Eq. (2.4) need not be a linear equation since $\mathcal{L}(a_j)$ has not been specified. Instead, Eq. (2.4) states that there is a universal function, $\mathcal{L}$ or $\mathcal{H}$, which is coupled in an identical fashion to all the variables a_j in the system, and which determines the dynamics. Furthermore, the coupling of the dynamics of different a_j's, which makes this a many-body problem, enters through $\mathcal{L}(a_j)$ alone.

To derive kinetic equations for the macroscopic modes of the system, we must make a statistical assumption. We assume that, out of the large set of variables a_j, there are a handful, renamed ψ_j, which are more slowly varying than the remainder, called a'_j. Thus, as ψ_j changes from $\psi_j(t)$ to $\psi_j(t + dt)$, the rapidly varying quantities $a'_j(t + dt)$ are uncorrelated with $a'_j(t)$. Then we will find that the macroscopic Langevin equations we shall derive for ψ_j will be dissipative, with the strength of that dissipation controlled by the fast variables which were neglected.

The slow variables ψ_j are identified by physical arguments. Since they must determine the long-time, long-wavelength behavior of a system, the set includes broken-symmetry variables such as order parameters (which describe structures, and so are persistent in space), and conserved variables (which are persistent in time) [12]. Other choices of the long-lifetime relevant variables can be made, and some are controversial [13], although it is well established that a useful expanded set also includes polynomial combinations of broken symmetry and conserved variables. We shall explicitly consider the case where ψ is a scalar variable, and there are not conservation laws. By assumption, it must determine all structure on long length and time scales. This is analogous to the order parameter for spinodal decomposition mentioned above. Nevertheless ψ need not be an "order parameter" in the strict sense which is used in the field of critical phenomena. (A counter-example would be the interface variable for the instability leading to dendritic growth.)

It now remains to separate the dynamics of ψ_j from a'_j, in the Liouvillian $\mathcal{L}(a_j) = \mathcal{L}(\psi_j, a'_j)$, where this coupling occurs. This has been done by Zwanzig [9] and Mori [10] with an exact version of linear-response theory called the projection-operator method. The method exploits the fact that $\mathcal{L}$ is a linear operator, and one projects the dynamics onto the linear subspace of slow variables ψ_j. A vector space is given by associating a bra $\langle \; |$ or ket $| \; \rangle$ with each a_j. Inner products satisfy the following properties:

$$\frac{\partial}{\partial t} \langle \cdots | \cdots \rangle_{(t=0)} = 0, \tag{2.5}$$

$$\langle \psi_j(t = 0) \rangle = 0, \tag{2.6}$$

and

$$\mathcal{L}\langle \cdots \rangle = \langle \cdots \rangle \mathcal{L}. \tag{2.7}$$

This corresponds to, for example, a system which is prepared in an equilibrium state at $t = 0$, where the inner product gives an ensemble average and $\psi_j(t)$ corresponds to a small deviation from equilibrium. Eqs. (2.5)-(2.7) asserts that the initial state of the system is a quiescent equilibrium one.

Note that this is a property of an inner product which is a macroscopic observable, rather than a property of the vectors, which are microscopic variables.

The projection operator onto the space of slow modes is

$$\mathcal{P} \equiv |\psi_j(0)\rangle\langle\psi_j(0)|\psi_k(0)\rangle^{-1}\langle\psi_k(0)| \qquad (2.8)$$

$$\mathcal{P} \equiv 1 - \mathcal{Q},$$

where a summation convention over the indices j and k is implicit. One begins with

$$\frac{\partial\psi_j}{\partial t} = i\mathcal{L}(a_k)\psi_j = i\mathcal{L}(\psi_k, a'_k)\psi_j,$$

and expresses $\mathcal{L}$ as $(\mathcal{PL} + \mathcal{QL})$. The subsequent algebra is well known [12], and is most easily accomplished with the help of Laplace transforms. The generalized Langevin equation one obtains is

$$\frac{\partial\psi_j(t)}{\partial t} = i\Omega_{jk}(0)\psi_j(t) - \int_0^t dt' M_{jk}(t - t')\psi_k(t') + f_j(t), \qquad (2.9)$$

where a summation over k is implicit. This expression is formally equivalent to Eq. (2.4). The terms in Eq. (2.9) have the following forms. The streaming term is

$$i\Omega_{jk}(0) \equiv \langle i\mathcal{L}\psi_j(0)|\psi_l(0)\rangle\langle\psi_l(0)|\psi_k(0)\rangle^{-1}, \qquad (2.10)$$

and the memory kernel is

$$M_{jk}(t) = \langle f_j(t)|f_l(0)\rangle\langle\psi_l(0)|\psi_k(0)\rangle^{-1}, \qquad (2.11)$$

where sums over l are implicit and $t > 0$. The "noise" is

$$f_j(t) \equiv e^{t\mathcal{Q}i\mathcal{L}\mathcal{Q}}\mathcal{Q}i\mathcal{L}\psi_j(0), \qquad (2.12)$$

so that $\langle\psi_j(0)|f_k(t)\rangle = 0$. The fast variables a'_j enter the equation for ψ_j through f_j, (note that f_j is a microscopic quantity, defined in terms of $\mathcal{Q}$).

No coarse-graining has been done to Eq. (2.4) yet, since Eq. (2.9) is only a rearrangement of that equation. We have yet to make use of our statistical assumption that ψ_j is slow, since any of the a_j's satisfy Eq. (2.9). We shall do this and consider the important case of a single slow nonconserved variable $\psi_j = \psi$, then ψ is a variable associated with global structure, as we have discussed. The generalized Langevin equation now has a simpler form,

$$\frac{\partial\psi(t)}{\partial t} = -\int_0^t dt' M(t - t')\psi(t') + f(t), \qquad (2.13)$$

where $\langle f(t)|f(0)\rangle = M(t)\langle\psi^2(0)\rangle$, for $t > 0$. The streaming term vanishes by virtue of Eq. (2.5). Now, if the characteristic time τ over which $f(t)$ is correlated is much smaller than a typical observation time dt over which $\psi(t)$ varies, then

$$\langle f(t)|f(t')\rangle \sim \delta(t - t'), \tag{2.14}$$

which is called a Markov approximation.

Eq. (2.14) gives the complete coarse-graining, and is where the assumption that ψ and a'_j have vastly different characteristic time scales enters. Note that it is an assumption about correlations in time. Clearly, we may now write

$$M(t) = D\delta(t - t'), \tag{2.15}$$

where D is a constant. Furthermore,

$$\langle f(t)|f(t')\rangle = 2D\langle\psi^2(0)\rangle\delta(t - t'), \tag{2.16}$$

where the factor of 2 arises because either t or t' can be the greater now. Since everything in Eq. (2.16) is positive, except possibly D,

$$D > 0. \tag{2.17}$$

Thus the macroscopic Langevin equation for the slow variable is

$$\frac{\partial\psi}{\partial t} = -D\psi + f, \tag{2.18}$$

which has been obtained from first principles. The equation is no longer time-reversal invariant, because of the coarse-graining due to the Markov approximation. It is dissipative, roughly speaking, $\psi \sim e^{-Dt}$, so structure decreases with time, as thermodynamics requires.

The three results mentioned above appear here in simplified form. Eq. (2.16) gives the fluctuation-dissipation relation, which expresses the transport coefficient for dissipation, D, in terms of the microscopic fluctuations f. Onsager's relations require the matrix of the transport coefficients to be symmetric, though for a scalar ψ we obtain the much simpler restriction Eq. (2.17). Finally, one can readily see that Eqs. (2.18) and (2.16) give a correlation-function expression for D, namely

$$D^{-1} = \int_0^\infty dt\langle\psi(t)\psi(0)\rangle\langle\psi^2(0)\rangle^{-1}, \tag{2.19}$$

which is a Green-Kubo relation.

Note that the equation of motion for ψ must be dissipative and not reactive, despite the fact that ψ satisfied Eq. (2.4) which is time-reversal invariant. This is because ψ has been assumed to be much more slowly varying than the other a_j's. It is worth mentioning that "slow" and "fast" imply relations involving correlations. As a counter-example, consider N uncoupled oscillators of frequencies ω_1, ω_2, ..., where $\omega_7 \ll \omega_j$, $j \neq 7$. Even though the seventh oscillator is slower than the others it is still oscillating and not relaxing. It is the coupling between slow and fast variables which gives dissipation. In Eq. (2.18), the dissipative macroscopic motion of ψ is due to fluctuations alone, from Eq. (2.16). That is, the dynamics of $\psi(t)$ are only due to its coupling to the fast microscopic variables a'_j, which are represented by f. The fast variables obey reversible microscopic equations with frequencies ω'_j, say. At a microscopic level, each of these fast oscillators pushes ψ in a different direction, due to the coupling between fast and slow variables. This quickly oscillating background, however, does not appear in the macroscopic description provided by the Markov approximation. Instead, the macroscopic Langevin equation implies that ψ decays with time. This decay is, however, with respect to the rapidly varying microscopic background which has been coarse-grained away.

The projection-operator method, provides one way to approach nonequilibrium statistical physics. The advantage of this approach is that we begin from first principles, and the assumptions which one must make to obtain Langevin equations are particularly well defined. An alternative strategy is to introduce a master equation for the probability distribution function. However, master equations are postulated with broken time-reversal symmetry. For example, in kinetic Ising models, spins flip or exchange positions due to a macroscopic heat bath. The microscopic variables which are the origin of this heat bath have been coarse-grained away to obtain the master equation. It is worth noting that, if moments in the initial state are determined by a Gaussian distribution, Eq. (2.18) is equivalent to a Fokker-Planck equation for the probability distribution function ρ, namely

$$\frac{\partial \rho}{\partial t} = D \frac{\partial}{\partial \psi}(\psi + \langle \psi^2 \rangle \frac{\partial}{\partial \psi})\rho. \tag{2.20}$$

Alternatively, this is what one obtains from the continuum limit of a master equation by the Kramers-Moyal expansion.

2.3.2   Irreversible Cellular Automata

We now apply the techniques reviewed above to a class of dynamical systems. Langevin equations for the slow thermodynamic variables will be obtained for irreversible microscopic equations.

First, we require a set of coupled dynamical equations to coarse-grain. Cellular automata are defined as discrete dynamical systems where identical local kinetic rules are applied to each variable. The prescribed rules are often chosen to be irreversible, although reversible rules are also considered. This is analogous to Hamilton's equations, where a universal function $\mathcal{L}$ acts identically on each dynamical variable. The two main differences are that cellular automata involve discrete time (which we shall not consider), and the rules are often irreversible. It may also be that some cellular automata involve rules which cannot be expressed as a linear operator. Such an operator, however, provides the most simple nontrivial way for rules to enter first-order dynamical equations. Motivated by these remarks, we introduce the following coupled set of dynamical equations which determine the behavior of a class of continuous cellular automata,

$$\frac{\partial a_j}{\partial t} = i(\mathcal{L}_R(a_k) + i\mathcal{L}_I(a_k))a_j. \tag{2.21}$$

In this equation, a_j are the dynamical variables, and $\mathcal{L}_R$ and $\mathcal{L}_I$ are both Hermitean linear operators. The first term, $\mathcal{L}_R$, gives reversible dynamics while the second, $\mathcal{L}_I$, gives irreversible behavior. All the novel results we obtain below are due to this second term. We expect that Eq. (2.21) has universal features which address the following question: how does the microscopic signature under time reversal affect the macroscopic equations of motion for the thermodynamic variables?

It should be noted that operators like $\mathcal{L} = \mathcal{L}_R + i\mathcal{L}_I$ have been introduced in other related contexts. Prigogine [21] attributed $\mathcal{L}_I$ to the breaking of time-reversal symmetry in macroscopic systems. Another motivation for studying a "microscopic" many-body equation which includes irreversible, as well as reversible parts is as follows. Although dynamics is time-reversal invariant at a microscopic level, at the macroscopic level there is a direction in time. Some macroscopic systems, in say biology, have many degrees of freedom, and therefore are sufficiently complicated so as to be intractable. Eq. (2.21) provides a simple example of such a complicated system. It is of interest to coarse-grain some of that complicated behavior, and thus simplify the description of such systems.

For our purposes, it is important to note that McLennan [15] has attributed $\mathcal{L}_I$ to coupling of the canonical variables to external sources and sinks. This provides an explicit connection of the irreversible cellular automata to the systems we discussed in the previous section, where pattern formation was due to externally imposed constraints. In some sense, we are presenting a derivation of, for example, the unstable van-der-Waals-loop contribution to the coarse-grained free energy in Eq. (2.1).

The class of reversible automata given by Eq. (2.21), with $\mathcal{L}_I \equiv 0$, correspond to Hamilton's equations. Thus, all the results of the previous section apply: fluctuation-dissipation relations, Onsager's relations, and Green-Kubo relations.

Automata containing reversible and irreversible parts correspond to both $\mathcal{L}_R$ and $\mathcal{L}_I$ being nonzero. The projection-operator formalism can be applied to such systems, since only linear operators are involved, provided the constraints given by Eqs. (2.5)-(2.7) for the inner product are satisfied. Before presenting the results, note that Eq. (2.5) requires detailed balancing of the initial ensemble. One can think of the following as a linear stability analysis; given an initial equilibrium state for the dynamical system, is it stable. Alternatively, it is instructive to give one example of such an initial state. In dissipative systems, one can enforce the time-translation invariance of an ensemble average with a forcing function, $\mu(t)$, such that

$$\frac{\partial a_j}{\partial t} = i(\mathcal{L}_R + i\mathcal{L}_I)a_j + \epsilon_j \mu(t) \qquad (2.22)$$

We have introduced a parameter ϵ_j, and a Gaussian noise (e.g., $\langle \mu(t) \rangle = 0$, and $\langle \mu(t)\mu(t') \rangle \sim \delta(t - t')$). The deterministic cellular automata in which we are interested correspond to $\epsilon_j = 0$. Time-translation invariance of the initial state is satisfied by the following prescription: for $t < 0$, $\epsilon_j \gg 1$, while for $t > 0$, $\epsilon_j \ll 1$. This corresponds to a "quench" from random initial conditions.

One can now introduce projection operators onto the space of slow modes ψ_j, as we did above. The generalized Langevin equation which corresponds to Eq. (2.21) is

$$\frac{\partial \psi_j(t)}{\partial t} = i\Omega_{jk}(0)\psi_k(t) - \int_0^t dt' M_{jk}(t - t')\psi_k(t') + f_j(t), \qquad (2.23)$$

where a summation convention is implicit over k. The streaming term and the noise have the same algebraic form as given in Eqs. (2.10) and (2.12) above. The noise f is, however, not related to the memory kernel $M_{jk}(t)$

through Eq. (2.11). Instead we obtain

$$\langle f_j(t)|f_k(0)\rangle = M_{jl}(t)\langle\psi_l(0)|\psi_k(0)\rangle^{-1} - 2\langle f_j(t)|Q\mathcal{L}_I\psi_k(0)\rangle, \qquad (2.24)$$

or

$$\langle f_j(t)|f_k(0)\rangle = -M_{jl}(t)\langle\psi_l(0)|\psi_k(0)\rangle^{-1} + 2\langle f_j(t)|Q\mathcal{L}_R\psi_k(0)\rangle, \qquad (2.25)$$

where there is an implicit sum over l, and $t > 0$. Again, as above, no coarse-graining has been done to these equations, until we make assumptions about the time correlations of $f_j(t)$. Nevertheless, one can already see that the standard results of nonequilibrium theory will not apply. For example, the fluctuation-dissipation relation no longer holds because of the extra piece involving $\mathcal{L}_I$ in Eq. (2.24). Similarly, Onsager's relations and Green-Kubo relations no longer apply. This explicitly verifies the argument of Grinstein, Jayaprakesh and He [4] that symmetry relations should not exist in such a case.

The more interesting and important result concerning Eq. (2.23) can be seen by considering the class of purely irreversible cellular automata which are given by $\mathcal{L}_R \equiv 0$ in Eq. (2.21). We shall, as we did above, consider a scalar slow variable $\psi_j = \psi$. In that case it is again natural to interpret ψ as the variable determining global structure. Usually physical intuition is used to choose the set of slow variables, e.g., one identifies an order parameter empirically. Here, however, we shall assume first that a slow variable does exist. Making the same Markov approximation to Eq. (2.25) as above, we obtain $M(t) = D\delta(t - t')$, and

$$\langle f(t)|f(t')\rangle = -2D\langle\psi^2(0)\rangle\delta(t - t'). \qquad (2.26)$$

Thus,

$$D < 0,$$

and the transport coefficient is negative. The Langevin equation for the slow variable becomes

$$\frac{\partial\psi(t)}{\partial t} = |D|\psi(t) + f(t), \qquad (2.27)$$

with

$$\langle f(t)|f(t')\rangle = 2|D|\langle\psi^2(0)\rangle\delta(t - t'), \qquad (2.28)$$

which we shall call a "fluctuation-enhancement" relation. It may be worth noting that if one replaces t by it in Eq. (2.21) (with $\mathcal{L}_R = 0$) we have an equation of the form of Hamilton's equations, i.e., $\partial|a_j\rangle/\partial(it) = i\mathcal{L}_I|a_j\rangle$. From section 2.2.1, we know this leads to Eqs. (2.16) and (2.18) with $t \to it$. Since $\delta(it - it') = \delta(t - t')/i$, one straightforwardly obtains Eqs. (2.27) and (2.28).

Note that we have not specified the dissipative operator $\mathcal{L}_I(a_j)$. This linear operator can be any function of the set of "microscopic" variables a_j. An example of a one-dimensional irreversible automata is [2], $a_j(t + 1) = a_{j-1}(t) \cdot a_{j+1}(t)$, where the N variables $a_j = \pm 1$ at every lattice site $j = 1$, $\ldots$, N. Then, one has $\partial a_j/\partial t = -\mathcal{L}_I a_j$ with $\partial a_j/\partial t \equiv a_j(t + 1) - a_j(t)$, and $\mathcal{L}_I \equiv \sum_k [a_k(t) - a_{k+1}(t) \cdot a_{k-1}(t)]\partial/\partial a_k$. This is similar to what we have considered, although the lattice structure in both space and time could cause subtle differences from the continuous cellular automata above.

The result above implies the following: if a slow variable exists for irreversible rules, such as we have given, it is linearly unstable. The slow variable grows exponentially for early times since, roughly speaking, Eq. (2.27) gives $\psi \sim e^{|D|t}$. For later times as ψ becomes large it is clear that the set of relevant variables must be enlarged to include polynomials such as ψ^2 and ψ^3. These are only negligible for sufficiently early times, since $\langle \psi(0) \rangle \equiv 0$. A straightforward way to do this is to consider the set of slow variables [11] $\psi_j = [\psi, \psi^2, \psi^3, \ldots]$. These nonlinear effects will modify the late-time behavior of the irreversible cellular automata. It is also straightforward to consider a continuous set where the slow variable is a field, $\psi(\vec{x}, t)$. Finally, although the result requires $\mathcal{L}_R = 0$, if an automata has nonzero reversible and irreversible parts, where a Markov approximation can separately be made for both pieces, one obtains a Langevin equation as above with the sign of D determined by the relative strength of $\mathcal{L}_R$ to $\mathcal{L}_I$. It is difficult, however, to determine how to compare these two contributions in general.

It is worth mentioning at this point, as we did above, a counter-example which clarifies the origin of the unstable behavior. Note that, by choosing a single slow variable, its macroscopic dynamics were unstable. Consider many uncoupled dissipative modes, where $\mathcal{L}_I$ is replaced by a constant λ_j. Even if, say, $\lambda_7 \ll \lambda_j$ and $j \neq 7$, so that the seventh mode was much "slower" than the others, there is no instability. Again, it is the coupling of the variables which is ultimately responsible for the instability. The fluctuation-enhancement relation implies that all unstable motion of ψ is due to fluctuations at the microscopic level. The fast variables, a'_j, dissipate with damping constants λ'_j, say. Their effect due to coupling on the slow variable ψ becomes less intense as time goes on. This background is not present in the macroscopic description provided by the Langevin equation.

Instead, ψ is unstable and grows. This growth, however, is with respect to the microscopic background which has been coarse-grained away by a Markov approximation.

A virtue of this approach is that the instability leading to structure growth can readily be identified. This is more difficult to accomplish by simulations of discrete cellular automata. Instabilities in spinodal decomposition and dendritic growth are also easier to establish from such formulations. Our explicit prediction, that $\psi(t)$ grows exponentially for early times, could be seen in simulations of automata by monitoring, for example, the decrease in entropy. For later times, it is natural to expect crossovers to power-law growth due to nonlinear effects of the kind discussed above, which we have not considered. Indeed, it is often found numerically that structure grows in many complex ways for irreversible automata. The present theory only predicts an instability, and the early-time growth behavior due to that instability. Thus the self-similar, but far-from-equilibrium, shapes which form during the growth of cellular automata are not described by the present theory. It seems possible, however, that non-linear effects could result in self-similar behavior. This is certainly the case for both spinodal decomposition and dendritic growth, where early-time growth is exponential and late-time growth is self-similar and follows a power law.

2.4   Discussion

We have analyzed the dynamical behavior of a class of cellular automata by the methods of first-principles nonequilibrium statistical physics. Both reversible and irreversible automata were considered. The class of dynamical systems were modeled after Hamilton's equations of motion for a many-body system. Thus, we studied the consequences of breaking time-reversal symmetry, at the microscopic level, in a many-component system.

The equations of motion for the automata were coarse-grained by Zwanzig-Mori projection-operator methods. Thus we obtained a macroscopic description of the system in terms of generalized Langevin equations. Our most interesting result applies to irreversible automata, which are often considered in numerical simulations. If there is a slow variable, it must be linearly unstable, and thus grow, due to a fluctuation-enhancement relation.

Such equations, where a slow variable is linearly unstable, are common in theories of pattern formation in far-from-equilibrium systems. They are often applied to the theory of biological systems to model the growth of structure [22]. Thus our analysis relates these complementary approaches, and may provide a partial justification for the use of such equations to model biological systems. The origin of the instability here, however, from microscopic irreversible equations resulting in a fluctuation-enhancement relation for the transport coefficient, is quite different from what is usually considered.

Our results (in particular, the spontaneous growth of structure due to irreversible rules) are consistent with the possibility, which is mentioned in the literature, that self-organization in nature is related to irreversible rules in many-component systems. The main qualifications concerning our results are that they apply to the class of cellular automata defined by Eq. (2.21) above, and that we have assumed the existence of a slow variable. Nevertheless, it seems possible that the qualitative result, irreversibility leading to instability, might have more general validity.

There are several important problems our analysis does not address. The central one to our minds is a method by which one could systematically obtain Langevin equations for particular discrete cellular automata. While, our treatment suggests the possibility of a general result, it is an inconvenient formalism for the study of a given system. There are other formalisms for nonequilibrium theory which might be more appropriate [23], e.g., Boltzmann's kinetic theory of gases. Finally, we have not studied *nonlinear* Langevin equations for automata, which could involve connections to the complex structures and morphologies that are studied in nonequilibrium physical systems.

Acknowledgements

This work was supported by the Natural Sciences and Engineering Research Council of Canada, and les Fonds pour la Formation de Chercheurs et l'Aide à la Recherche de la Province du Québec, and National Science Foundation grant # DMR-86-12609.

References

[1] J. von Neumann, in *Theory of Self-Reproducing Automata*, edited by A. W. Birks (Univ. of Illinois Press, Urbana, IL, 1966).

[2] *Theory and Applications of Cellular Automata* edited by S. Wolfram (World Science, Singapore, 1986). T. Toffolli and N. Margolus, *Cellular Automata Machines* (MIT press, Cambridge MA, 1987). S. Wolfram,

Rev. Mod. Phys. **55**, 601 (1983). Physica (Amsterdam) **10D**, 1–247 (1984).

[3] E. Domany and W. Kinzel, Phys. Rev. Lett. **53**, 311 (1984). C. H. Bennett and G. Grinstein, Phys. Rev. Lett. **55**, 657 (1985).

[4] G. Grinstein, C. Jayaprakesh, and Y. He, Phys. Rev. Lett. **55**, 2527 (1985).

[5] S. Chandrasekhar, Rev. Mod. Phys. **15**, 1 (1943). S. Chandrasekhar, Rev. Mod. Phys. **21**, 383 (1949). A. Einstein, Ann. Phys. (Leipzig) **17**, 549 (1905). P. Langevin, C. R. Acad. Sci. (Paris) **146**, 530 (1908).

[6] L. Onsager, Phys. Rev. **37**, 405 (1931). L. Onsager, Phys. Rev. **38**, 2265 (1931).

[7] M. S. Green, J. Chem. Phys. **20**, 1281 (1952).

[8] R. Kubo, J. Phys. Soc. Jpn. **12**, 570 (1957). R. Kubo, M. Yokota, and S. Nakajima, J. Phys. Soc. Jpn. **12**, 1203 (1957). R. Kubo, Rep. Prog. Phys. **29**, 255 (1966).

[9] R. Zwanzig, J. Chem. Phys. **33**, 1338 (1960). R. Zwanzig, on *Lectures in Theoretical Physics*, edited by W. E. Brittin, B. W. Downs, and J. Downs (Interscience, New York, 1961), Vol. 3.

[10] H. Mori, Prog. Theor. Phys. **33**, 423 (1965). H. Mori, Prog. Theor. Phys. **34**, 399 (1965).

[11] R. Zwanzig, Phys. Rev. **124**, 983 (1961). H. Mori, Prog. Theor. Phys. **49**, 764 (1973). H. Mori, Prog. Theor. Phys. **49**, 1516 (1973). K. Kawasaki, Ann. Phys. (N. Y.) **61**, 1 (1970).

[12] D. Forster, *Hydrodynamic Fluctuations, Broken Symmetry, and Correlation Functions* (Benjamin, Reading, MA, 1975). J. P. Boon and S. Yip, *Molecular Hydrodynamics* (McGraw-Hill, New York, 1980).

[13] N. G. van Kampen, *Stochastic Methods in Physics and Chemistry* (North-Holland, Amsterdam, 1981). P. Resibois, in *Proceedings of the Sixth IUPAP Conference on Statistical Mechanics*, edited by S. Rice (Univ. of Chicago Press, Chicago, IL, 1972).

[14] M. Grant and J. D. Gunton, Phys. Rev. Lett. **57**, 1970 (1986).

[15] J. A. McLennan, Adv. Chem. Phys. **5**, 260 (1963). K. Kawasaki, J. Phys. A **6**, 1289 (1973), has used projection-operator techniques to study nonequilibrium steady states..

[16] J. W. Cahn, Trans. Mettal. Soc. AIME **242**, 166 (1968). J. E. Hilliard, in *Phase Transformations*, edited by H. I. Aronson (American Society of Metals, Ohio, 1970). H. E. Cook, Acta Metall. **18**, 297 (1970)

[17] J. D. Gunton, M. San Miguel, and P. S. Sahni, in *Phase Transitions and Critical Phenomena*, edited by C. Domb and J. L. Lebowitz (Academic, London, 1983), Vol. 8.

[18] W. W. Mullins and R. F. Sekerka, J. Appl. Phys. **34**, 323 (1963). W. W. Mullins and R. F. Sekerka, J. Appl. Phys. **35**, 444 (1964).

[19] J. S. Langer, Rev. Mod. Phys. **52**, 1 (1980).

[20] M. Laradji, M. Sc. thesis (McGill University, 1989). M. Laradji, M. Grant, M. J. Zuckermann, and W. Klein, McGill University preprint.

[21] I. Prigogine, in *Order and Fluctuations in Equilibrium and Nonequilibrium Statistical Physics*, edited by G. Nicolis, G. Dewer, and J. W. Turner (Wiley, New York, 1981), p. 35.

[22] H. Haken, *Synergetics* (Springer-Verlag, New York, 1983). P. Glansdorff and I. Prigogine, *Thermodynamic Theory of Structure, Stability and Fluctuations* (Wiley, New York, 1971). G. Nicolis and I. Prigogine, *Self-Organization in Nonequilibrium Systems* (Wiley, New York, 1977).

[23] J. L. Lebowitz, Physica **140A**, 232 (1986).

CHAPTER 3

ARCHITECTURES AND DEVICES FOR ULSI

D. K. Ferry
R. O. Grondin
L. A. Akers and
L. C. Shiue
Center for Solid State Electronic Research
Arizona State University
Tempe, AZ 85287

3.1 Introduction

Since the introduction of integrated circuits in the late 1950's, the number of individual transistors that can be placed upon a single circuit has approximately doubled every three years. Today, even university design laboratories for teaching of students can access chip foundries which produce 1.2 μm (and smaller) design rule circuits. Compared with this, many commercial companies are experimenting with the production of chips with critical dimensions of 0.1 μm, and university laboratories have produced individual devices with gate lengths much smaller than this [1,2]. The creation of devices whose spatially important scales may be only a few tens of nanometers opens the door to the study of many new and important physical effects, some of which have been described earlier [3]. Indeed, it can rightfully be said that it will be impossible to understand fully the operation of these devices without a full understanding of these newly appearing physical effects.

We can understand the driving forces (and the need for further understanding of the physics) quite easily. In the early 1980's, Hewlett-Packard produced a single-chip microprocessor containing approximately 0.5M devices in its 1 cm^2 area [4]. This chip was fabricated with essentially 1.25

μm gate length transistors. Today, we are talking about megabit memories and dense signal processing chips with devices of these same dimensions. Yet, *we are also talking about reaching chip densities of* 10^9 *devices within a short period of time.* While the first question is what would we use so many devices to accomplish, even if we could reliably fabricate the chips with a meaningful yield, we must also ask just what this does to the required device technology. In general, progress in the integrated circuit field has followed a complicated scaling relationship [5]. This scaling reduces feature sizes by an amount α. To reach a billion transistors, as envisaged, requires a scale-up of a factor of 2000 over the HP chip, which means $\alpha = 45$. Thus, if we follow the scaling relationships, we expect to see transistors with gate lengths of only 30 nm! Very few laboratories have produced research devices with gate lengths on this scale and little is understood about the limitations (from the physics) that will determine whether or not these devices are practical.

What is happening in the reduction of individual feature sizes of a transistor, used as the basic building block for ULSI, is that the critical length (e.g. the gate length or a depletion length) will become so small that it approaches the *coherence length* of the electrons that provide the operation. Over the past several years, it has become evident that this latter length is not the wavelength of the electron itself, but the *inelastic mean free path*, or the length over which the energy coherence is maintained by the electron. With modern modulation doping techniques in heterojunction device structures, this latter length can be more than 1 μm at low temperatures, but there is also evidence that it can be as much as 0.1 μm at room temperature. The consequence is that such small devices must now be treated as quantum mechanical objects, and many phenomena become important that have never been treated in the normal classical and semi-classical treatments of semiconductor devices. While this has served to invigorate studies of quantum behavior in device structures, we are limited in that many of these quantum phenomena are only poorly understood at best.

In the following section, a number of small device effects that are important are reviewed. No comprehensive treatment of each, nor a comprehensive treatment of all effects, is intended. Rather, the selection is governed by those effects which have been shown to already occur in devices. Here we try to establish the connection between a few such effects. Nearly all semiconductor devices operate on the principle of hindering the transport of carriers from the source (or emitter) to the drain (or collector) by the presence of a potential barrier, which is modulated by the gate (or base potential). As the size of devices has been reduced, so-called second-order effects have introduced unintended modifications to this barrier through parasitic effects such as drain-induced barrier lowering [6]. In the ultra-submicron regime, we must begin to consider that many carriers will actually tunnel through the barrier, and encounter strong potential variations, further changing the basic operation of the device. In addition, the active channel length can be much less than 0.1 μm after the barriers have been surpassed. Carriers then have the possibility of transiting this region *ballistically;* e.g. without scattering, or perhaps suffering just a few elastic collisions [7]. Then we can expect to see quantum effects and quantum resonances in this ballistic transport, such as that seen in transport through thin oxides in MOS devices [8,9].

Even if the fabrication of these small devices can be obtained, what computational scheme is best suited for architectures with large numbers of coupled devices. In conventional descriptions of VLSI circuits, each switching device is assumed to behave in the same manner within the total system as it does when it is isolated. The full function of the system or integrated circuit (IC) is determined solely by the interconnections used to join the individual devices together. A different function can only be assigned to the system by redesigning the interconnections – a practical impossibility for most systems, but in practice accomplished in some programmable systolic arrays. The conventional clear separation of device design from system design thus depends upon being able to isolate each individual device from the environment of the other devices except for the planned effects occurring through the interconnection network. This simplification is likely to be seriously in error for submicron configured systems, where the devices are packed much closer together. As a result of the much closer packing, the isolation of one device from another will be difficult to achieve. Instead, one is driven to begin to think about methods of actually using the interactions between devices as a tool to accomplish distributed information processing within the VLSI chip. This approach is exactly the approach used by architectures modeled after biological systems, called neural architectures.

In Section 3.3 concurrent processing in highly parallel systems will be discussed. This topic naturally leads to Section 3.4, neural architectures. Lastly, Section 3.5 will describe our views of future integrated systems.

3.2 Small Device Physics

Most simple models of semiconductor devices are built upon the gradual channel approximation, in which a one-dimensional problem is solved for the potential along the channel length. In the simplest of these models, the mobility is assumed to be constant, and the velocity rises along the channel as the electric field rises (the density drops in going from the source to the drain, which leads to the rise in field). This leads to the general behavior that the drain current is proportional to $(V_{GS} - V_{DS})^2$. The important first modification to this behavior, and one seen in most submicron devices, is that the velocity cannot continue to increase, but is limited to the saturation value, typically 10^7 cm/sec. The current density through the device is then limited to a value given by the product of the saturation velocity and the carrier density at the position in the device where velocity saturation sets in. Beyond this point, both the velocity and total current through the device remains constant, and this point acts as the injection point for the saturated region. Thus, typically, we find that

$$J = nev = C_o v_{sat} \left(V_{GS} - V_{sat} \right), \qquad (3.1)$$

where v_{sat} is the saturation velocity and V_{sat} is the voltage in the channel at the saturation point – the position at which the velocity rises to v_{sat}. Equation (3.1) is written for a MOSFET, but the equivalent behavior is found in MESFETs [10]. We also note from (3.1) that the transconductance no longer increases for further decreases in the gate length, since the gate length dependence has disappeared from the current equation. If we are to obtain any further increase in performance by down-scaling the device size, we must go sufficiently far to see increases in the saturation velocity due to *non-stationary transport*. In this latter case, the gate length is sufficiently short that electrons transit the entire gate region without ever stabilizing to the saturation velocity. Due to *velocity overshoot*, the effective velocity can be greater than the saturation value [11].

3.2.1 Velocity Saturation and Velocity Overshoot

In low fields, and in equilibrium, the rates of emission and absorption of phonons by the electrons balance each other. In high electric fields, however, the carriers gain energy from the field, and this energy must be eventually dissipated to the lattice through an increase in phonon emission. We can make an estimate of the actual velocity that can be sustained stably in the high field by equating the drift energy to the phonon energy and some adjusting factors. First, we expect from simple energy balance that

$$\frac{1}{2}m^* v_{sat}^2 \approx \hbar\omega_0.$$

Now, we must modify the right-hand side to account for the net emission rate. The total scattering rate is proportional to the sum of the emission and absorption processes, while the net emission rate is proportional to the difference. In general, the ratio of the difference to the sum is just

$$\frac{(N_q + 1) - N_q}{(N_q + 1) + N_q} = \tanh\left(\frac{\hbar\omega_0}{2k_B T}\right),$$

where N_q is the phonon distribution function (the Bose-Einstein distribution). Finally, there is a correction factor for the electron distribution function (the Maxwellian distribution), which is $4/3\hbar$, which finally gives us the saturated velocity

$$v_{sat} = \left[\frac{8\hbar\omega_0}{3\pi m^*} \tanh\left(\frac{\hbar\omega_0}{2k_B T}\right)\right]^{1/2}. \tag{3.2}$$

Equation (3.2) is found to give very good fits to the actual values obtained for a great many semiconductors [12].

In order for the electrons to have a net emission of phonons, the distribution function must change from the equilibrium one [13]. Increases of momentum are accompanied by a shift of the distribution in the applied field, which is just the momentum relaxation process. In high fields, however, the change in the distribution function is generally a heating of the distribution, which means a spread in energy space. This is the energy relaxation process. If a system of electrons is subjected to the combined influence of an electric field and the scattering centers, the drift velocity of the particles will asymptotically approach a velocity given by

$$v = \frac{e\tau_m}{m^*} E. \tag{3.3}$$

However, this does not agree with the saturation value discussed above. For saturation to occur, we require that the momentum relaxation time τ_m decrease (asymptotically at very high fields) as $1/E$. However, at $t = 0$ in a time dependent process, τ_m has its equilibrium or low-field value. The time it takes for τ_m to relax to the high-field value is the energy relaxation time τ_e. If the energy relaxation time is longer than the momentum relaxation time, the velocity will initially rise to a level given approximately by (3.3), and then decay slowly (with the energy relaxation time) to the saturated value. This process is that of *velocity overshoot*. Velocity overshoot is greatly enhanced in materials such as GaAs, where there is an additional decrease of the velocity due to an increase of the effective mass, and a large increase in the scattering rates, as the carriers scatter from the central Γ valley to the satellite L valleys.

3.2.2 Energy and Momentum Relaxation

Most field-dependent velocities, necessary to give the saturation effect at high electric fields, assume that steady-state conditions are reached. Clearly this is not the case, particularly in small devices. Electrons entering the high field region are accelerated, and may leave the region before settling into the steady-state saturation velocity. Thus, the velocity overshoot discussed above may induce effective velocities higher than the saturation velocity. The key factor that governs these effects is the transient velocity and its related velocity autocorrelation function. The physics is somewhat more complicated than that treated in most texts on statistical physics, in that the hot carrier conditions arising in high electric fields are really characteristic of a system which is far from equilibrium. The dominant factor that arises from this is the concept of retardation (and memory) effects. Thus, our dominant equation is a *retarded* Langevin equation [14,15].

We consider an ensemble of carriers initially at equilibrium with the lattice, and characterized by a Maxwellian distribution function with $< v^2 >= 3k_B T/m^*$, and T is the lattice temperature. At a certain time, $t = 0$, we apply a macroscopic and homogeneous electric field whose amplitude is sufficiently large to generate a hot carrier distribution. These conditions give rise to a transient dynamic response (TDR) of the carriers, velocity overshoot, and retarded relaxation, all of which arise from the retarded Langevin equation [16]

$$m^* \frac{dv}{dt} = -m^* \int_0^t \gamma(t-u)v(u)\, du + R(t) + eE\, h(t), \qquad (3.4)$$

where $R(t)$ is a random force, $h(t)$ is the Heavyside step function, and γ is a relaxation function. The random force is the non-regular (non-averaging) part of the interaction of the carriers with the lattice. Equation (3.4) is a non-Markovian form of the Langevin equation, since the rate of change of the average velocity depends upon past values of the velocity. Further, it is non-stationary in that the value of the velocity depends upon all past time since application of the field. Only such an equation as this can describe the essentially non-Boltzmann behavior at the short time scales included in the TDR.

We may easily solve (3.4) using Laplace transforms. We introduce a function $\mathcal{X}(t)$ defined by its transform as

$$\mathcal{X}(s) = \frac{1}{s + \gamma(s)},$$

and this leads to the time response (after inverse transforming)

$$v(t) = v(0)\mathcal{X}(t) + \frac{eE}{m^*}\int_0^t \mathcal{X}(u)du + \frac{1}{m^*}\int_0^t R(t-u)\mathcal{X}(u)du, \qquad (3.5)$$

which is a general expression of the evolution of the velocity of each carrier. We get $\mathcal{X}(t)$ by averaging (3.5) over the ensemble (assuming that R is uncorrelated to the velocity, which in essence means noninteracting carriers). This yields

$$\mathcal{X}(t) = \frac{m^*}{eE}\frac{dv_d}{dt},$$

where v_d is the drift velocity and approaches the saturation velocity. Thus, $\mathcal{X}(t)$ represents the macroscopic acceleration of the ensemble, but also has another meaning. If we introduce the non-stationary correlation function

$$\phi_{\Delta v}(t,t') = <v(t)v(t')> - v_d(t)v_d(t'),$$

we can relate $\mathcal{X}(t)$ to this by multiplying both sides of (3.5) with $v(0)$ and averaging over the ensemble, so that

$$\phi_{\Delta v}(0,t) = <v^2(0)>\mathcal{X}(t)$$

Thus, we recognize $\mathcal{X}(t)$ as the non-stationary correlation function for the velocity which is initially at rest at $t = 0$. Then,

$$v_d(t) = \frac{eE}{m^* <v^2(0)>}\int_0^t \phi_{\Delta v}(0,t')dt'. \qquad (3.6)$$

This result is a particular form of the general relationship known as the Kubo formula for velocity response [17]. This relationship between the first and second moments of the velocities of the carrier ensemble is an intrinsic property of the retarded Langevin equation used to describe the TDR.

We can work backwords through the equations to identify the critical points. In equilibrium situations, we know that the correlation functions have simple exponential decays; e.g. $\mathcal{X}(t) = exp(-t/\tau)$. In this case, we note that (3.6) admits only a simple monotonic increase of the drift velocity, and no overshoot can occur. Moreover, we note that the relaxation function $\gamma = (1/\tau)\delta(t)$, so that (3.4) reduces to the normal Langevin equation. Thus, overshoot can be inferred to be related to the expansion of the time dependence of the relaxation function from this simple delta function form. Indeed, this is just where the energy relaxation process occurs in the equations (we could of course do what is normally done and write another retarded Langevin equation for the energy, but that is not really necessary). If we include another time constant in the process, we achieve the necessary retardation. Thus, let us write

$$\gamma(t) = \frac{1}{\tau_m \tau_e} \exp\left(-\frac{t}{\tau_e}\right),$$

where we have now introduced an energy relaxation time. We note that the choice of coefficients still provides the proper normalization. This now leads to

$$\mathcal{X}(s) = \frac{\tau_m(s\tau_e + 1)}{s\tau_m(s\tau_e + 1) + 1},$$

and

$$\mathcal{X}(t) = \exp\left(-\frac{t}{2\tau_e}\right)\left[\cos(\beta t) + \frac{1}{2\beta\tau_e}\sin(\beta t)\right], \qquad (3.7)$$

where

$$\beta^2 = \frac{1}{\tau_e}\left[\frac{1}{\tau_m} - \frac{1}{4\tau_e}\right].$$

As long as β is real, there is a region near $\beta t \leq \hbar/2$ for which $\mathcal{X}(t) < 0$, which implies that $v(t)$ goes through a maximum at the zero crossing. Thus, overshoot arises in the systems for which there are two time constants, provided that energy relaxation is slower than momentum relaxation. In Figure 3.1, the autocorrelation function for the velocity is shown for n-Si for several values of the electric field at 300 K. It is clear that for low fields, only momentum relaxation is important, but for higher fields behavior like (3.7) begins to occur [18]. Thus, velocity overshoot and its effect in devices can be expected in short channel semiconductor devices. The critical time scale is the inelastic (or energy) relaxation time. The effect is much larger in GaAs devices, since the overshoot is connected with the transfer of electrons from one valley to another in the conduction band.

3.2.3 Measurements on Submicron Devices

We have fabricated a series of ultra-submicron MESFET devices using electron-beam lithography [19], for the purpose of studying in these struc-

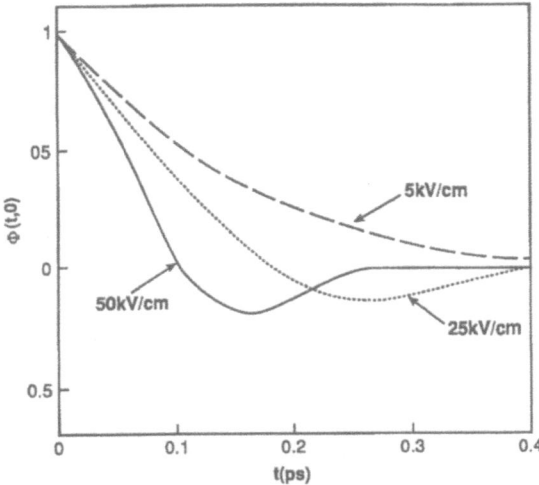

Figure 3.1: The velocity autocorrelation function for n-Si, for several values of the electric field. The function is calculated by an ensemble Monte Carlo technique.

tures the effects of the inelastic mean free path discussed in the previous section. People have discussed the appearance of ballistic transport and the velocity overshoot effect in devices for some years. These two effects are just equivalent statements of the role which non-equilibrium transport plays in these devices. However, there has been no clear evidence of the appearance of these effects in normal devices, primarily because the gate lengths have been too long. It is to be expected that for a clear observation of velocity overshoot, it will be necessary for the entire high electric field region, over which the velocity overshoot occurs, to be completely under the gate and to be reduced in length to below the inelastic mean free path. The overshoot length is that over which the energy relaxes, or the carriers lose memory of the initial energy (phase). This is just the quantum mechanical inelastic mean free path, which has been estimated to be only about 50-75 nm in GaAs at 300 K. If the gate region is longer than this, charge is redistributed within the device, leading to inhomogenous distribution of the charge under the gate. Where the velocity is high, the density will be low. Where the velocity is low, the density will be high, which is in keeping with Kirchhoff's current law. Thus, truly short gate length devices are required in order to explore this effect.

The devices we have made have the gate length as short as 25 nm. In Figure 3.2, such a gate structure is shown. For gate lengths below about 50

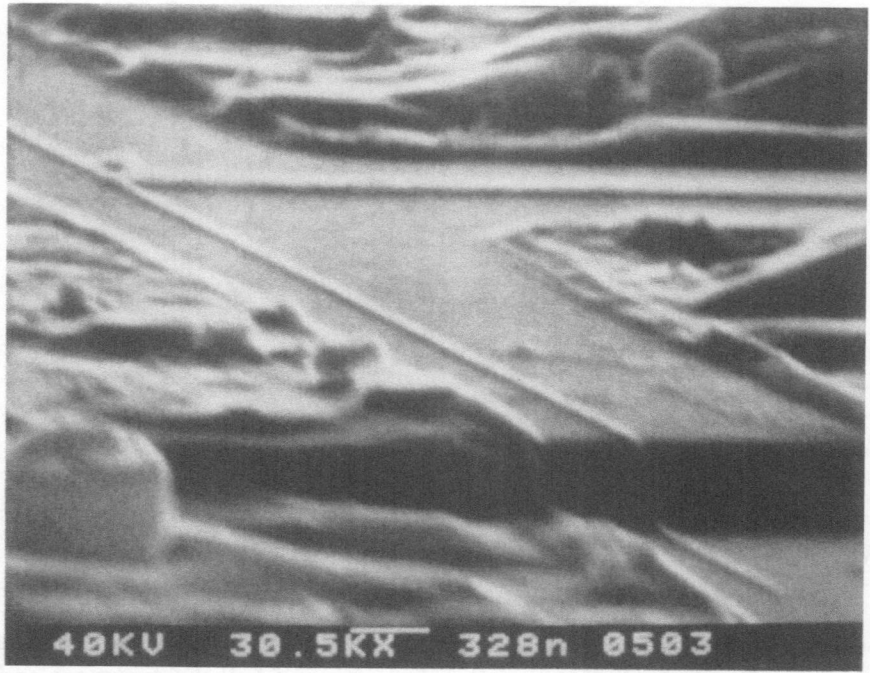

Figure 3.2: A photomicrograph of one of the ASU short channel MESFETs which exhibits velocity overshoot in its operation.

nm, we see an increase in the transconductance, when all other parameters (doping, channel thickness and width, etc.) are maintained at the same values. Normally, with the doping we use, $n = 2 \times 10^{17}$ cm^{-3}, we expect (and models incorporating the complete energy transport process also predict) that the transconductance will peak, as the gate length is reduced, near that length which gives an aspect ratio between 2 and 3 (gate length to channel thickness). For smaller gate lengths, the transconductance drops and can only increase again if some new physical process causes the carriers to transit the gate region faster. In our case, the aspect rato is below 0.16 for a gate length of 100 nm, so that the rise we observe can reasonably be attributed to the onset of velocity overshoot in these devices. In Figure 3.3, we plot the effective saturation velocity that is achieved in these devices. While these results are for GaAs MESFETs, similar results for MOSFETs with gate lengths as short as 70 nm have been obtained by IBM [20].

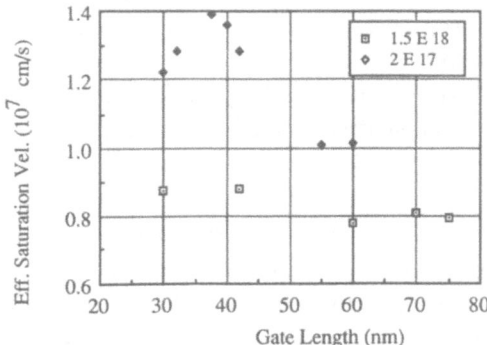

Figure 3.3: The effective saturation velocity determined from the transconductance of several ultra-short channel MESFETs for two different dopings.

3.2.4   Inter-Device Interactions

Many people have examined the limit to which semiconductor devices can be scaled downward, and while devices as small as 0.025 μm gate length have been made, problems such as interconnections, electromigration and thermo-migration of metallization, and power density within the device strongly affect the packing density and device size that can be achieved. Yet no one has really looked carefully at the problems of arrays of devices with this scale of gate length. The interactions within arrays of such devices is such that the performance of the device itself cannot be treated in isolation. Because of the size of such a very-small device, it is coupled strongly to the environment in which it is located [21].   The basic transport equations cannot be separated from their causal boundary conditions and both of these factors must be modified to account for the influence of the device environment.

In conventional descriptions of VLSI circuits, each device is assumed to behave in the same manner within the total system as it does when it is isolated. The full function of the system is determined solely by the interconnection metallization specified to join the individual devices together. A different function can only be assigned to the system by redesigning the interconnection metallizations – a practical impossibility for most systems, but in practice accomplished in some PLA modules. The conventional clear separation of device design from system design thus depends ultimately on being able to isolate each individual device from the environment of other devices except for planned effects occurring through the interconnection matrix. This gross over-simplification is likely to be seriously in error for ultra-submicron dimensioned ULSI systems, such as the billion transistor chip envisaged above, where the isolation of one device from another will be difficult to achieve.

The possible device-device coupling mechanisms are numerous and include such effects as capacitive coupling, of which line-to-line parasitic capacitance is one example [22], and wave-function penetration (tunneling and charge spillover) is another. The former is significant already in VLSI, and one cannot limit device-device interactions to just those size scales of the order of the wave function or the inelastic mean free path. The parasitic interaction arising from this line-to-line coupling leads to a direct device-device interaction outside the normal circuit or architectural design [23]. The constraints imposed by device-device interactions will have to be included in future architectural design of compact ULSI systems, and this will most easily be accomplished if these constraints are reflected in the system theory description of the architecture itself. It is found that the pair-wise nearest neighbor interaction dominates the device-device effects, which suggests two important points. First, the architecture begins to resemble neural networks or cellular automata in format, and these latter system descriptions hold some usefulness in architectural design [24]. Secondly, the nearest neighbor interactions suggest that arrays of devices will begin to look like superlattices of devices [22], and such lateral surface superlattices can be made generically to look at possible cooperative effects. The former is beyond the scope of this article, but cellular automata and neural networks possess a morphism to each other, and are different constraints on a general interactive cooperative network [25].

In the next section, we begin to discuss the role of this device-device interaction by introducing concurrent processing. This suggests that the best way to accommodate the interactions is to use them as part of the architectural construct of the total VLSI chip.

3.3   Concurrent Processing

The combination of down-scaling to minimum feature size and upscaling in integrated chip area has dramatically increased the complexity of monolithic integrated circuits. However, as these chips become more complex, they become more sensitive to yield reducing single defects or faulty gates in the processed circuitry. One way of enhancing the degree of defect and fault tolerance is to apply the strategies of redundancy. The use of synthetic neural networks has become a method of trying to implement various distributed, and therefore robust, architectural implementations of circuits to accomplish a variety of different tasks. In the neural architecture, robustness is gained by the use of a distributed data representation in which information is not stored in a discrete local node or interconnection [26]. These networks are certainly useful for optimization problems such as associative memories and optimal control problems (e.g. the traveling salesman problem and the digital-to-analog converter) [27]. Indeed, to our knowledge, there still does not exist a systematic procedure for mapping a general computational problem onto a synthetic neural architecture, and therefore no sequential programming procedure to implement a computational task with one of these networks.

In this section, we describe a procedure that allows the programming of a general purpose, *digital* synthetic neural network to implement an algorithm for general purpose computation. It also constitutes a theory for reliable computation using unreliable components, in which the reliability or degree of fault tolerance is quantifiable. We consider those tasks that are definable in terms of a finite state machine and its directed graph representation in terms of a state transition matrix [24]. We find that the concept of robustness in the neural network is analogous to the concept of signal coding, with additional circuit constraints (described below). While we discuss the approach in terms of digital networks, we will mention at the end the manner in which these networks can be representative of the general analog neural network. Finally, we will point out how these networks can be made reconfigurable to new tasks so that the system's performance is improved by a better match between the data structure of the algorithm and the connection topology among the processing elements. We begin by matching the general neural summation to a digital framework.

3.3.1 Basic Architectural Model

In this section, we will describe a dynamically reconfigurable architecture which is intended for parallel processing a class of problems which can be represented by directed graphs (digraphs). The proposed architecture is made up of a network of boolean McCulloch-Pitts neuron-like cells, each dedicated to one vertex of a digraph and its associated edges. By partitioning each cell and integrating the neural-like network into several functional blocks, a highly regularly structured reconfigurable processing unit is achievable. Such a processing unit is capable of storing symbolic assertions and performing parallel search and deduction within its collection of knowledge. Potentially this architecture can be realized by the VLSI technology and the design approach also exploits an application for on-chip expert systems.

Since the work of McCulloch and Pitts [28], the function of the nerve cell (or so-called neuron) has generally been formulated as

$$r_i(n+1) \;=\; f_W\left(\sum_{j=1}^{N} r_j(n) \cdot W_{ji}(n) - \theta_i(n)\right) \tag{3.8}$$

$$=\; f_W(H_i(n)),$$

where W_{ij} is the connection weight from neuron j to neuron i; r_j is the output of neuron j; θ_i is the threshold in neuron i; and f_W may be a hard limiter function, a threshold logic function, or a sigmoid function. For example, if f_W is a threshold logic function, the firing status of a neuron is determined by $r_i(n + 1) = 1$ (firing) if $H_i \geq 0$, or $r_i(n + 1) = 0$ or -1 (not firing) if $H_i < 0$.

For an interesting class of neuronal equations, we can connect this equation with VLSI-like structures in two ways. First, we can restrict ourselves to a binary case, where r_i takes a value of 0 or 1 and all arithmetic operations are performed modulo 2. That is,

$$r_i(n+1) = f_W\left(\sum_{j=1}^{N} r_j(n) \cdot W_{ji}(n) - \theta_j(n)\right) \; (mod\ 2). \tag{3.9}$$

Now, we define f_W to be a unit step function, f_u, and θ_i a constant threshold whose value lies on the interval $(0, 1)$. Then, since $0 \leq \theta_i \leq 1$ and $f_u(x - \theta_i) = x$ if $x = 0$ or 1, we can rewrite (3.9) as

$$r_i(n+1) = \left(\sum_{j=1}^{N} {}_\mathbf{v}r_j(n) \cdot W_{ji}(n)\right) \; (mod\ 2). \tag{3.10}$$

Now that the threshold subtraction has been brought into a redefined f_W, we could then use a Boolean interpretation, in which r_i takes truth values and the arithmetic operations are replaced by Boolean equations. We thus express (3.10) in the following Boolean form:

$$r_i(n+1) = \left(\sum_{j=1}^{N} {}_\mathbf{v}r_j(n) * W_{ji}(n)\right). \tag{3.11}$$

where the summation symbol "$\sum_\mathbf{v}$" stands for the ORing of terms "$r_j * W_{ji}$,,

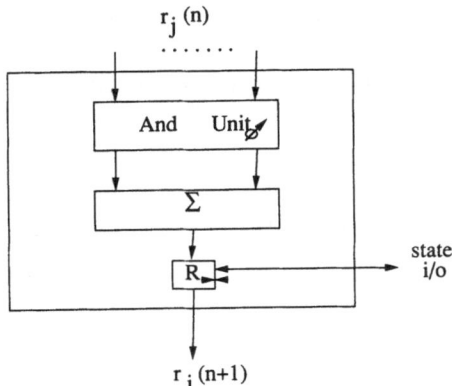

Figure 3.4: Data-path of a BMPN characterized by (3.4)

for $j = 1, 2, \ldots, n$, and the symbol "$*$" represents a logic-AND operator. Since (3.11) falls into a subclass of formulae that model the signal processing of a nerve cell, we therefore refer such a reconfigurable cell to as a Boolean McCulloch-Pitts neuron (BMPN) [29]. The corresponding data path of this Boolean processing element is depicted in Figure 3.4.

Let us now consider a network, which is composed of N such BMPNs, and ascertain the function that the network is able to perform. To see this, we first rewrite (3.11) in the following vector forms:

$$
\begin{aligned}
r_i(n+1) &= \sum_{j=1}^{N} {}_\mathbf{v} r_j(n) * w_{ji}(n), \\
&= r_1(n) * w_{1i}(n) \vee r_2(n) * w_{2i}(n) \vee \ldots \vee r_N(n) * w_{Ni}(n), \\
&= [w_{1i}(n) \; w_{2i}(n) \; \ldots \; w_{Ni}(n)] \circ [r_1(n) \; r_2(n) \; \ldots \; r_N(n)]^t, \\
&= [w_{ji}(n)]_j \circ \mathbf{R}(n), \; (j = 1, 2, \ldots, n) \tag{3.12}
\end{aligned}
$$

where the symbols '$\vee$' and '$\circ$' represent the logic-OR and the Boolean scalar product operators, respectively. The transformation process occurred in a BMPN network can then be expressed by a set of equations, each of which is in the form of (3.12), as follows:

$$
\begin{aligned}
r_1(n+1) &= [w_{j1}(n)]_j \circ \mathbf{R}(n) \\
r_2(n+1) &= [w_{j2}(n)]_j \circ \mathbf{R}(n) \\
&\vdots \\
r_N(n+1) &= [w_{jN}(n)]_j \circ \mathbf{R}(n). \tag{3.13}
\end{aligned}
$$

We can further combine the equations in (3.14) into the following vector-matrix form:

$$\mathbf{R}(n+1) = \mathbf{W}(n) \circ \mathbf{R}(n),\qquad(3.14)$$

where

$$\mathbf{W}(n) = \begin{vmatrix} W_{11}(n) & W_{21}(n) & \cdots & W_{N1}(n) \\ W_{12}(n) & W_{22}(n) & \cdots & W_{N2}(n) \\ & \cdot & & \\ & \cdot & & \\ & \cdot & & \\ W_{1N}(n) & W_{2N}(n) & \cdots & W_{NN}(n) \end{vmatrix}\qquad(3.15)$$

Now, the problem of determining the function of the BMPN network is reduced to the interpretation of (3.14). One way of interpretation is to view abstractly the BMPN network as a directed graph (or digraph) $G = (V, E)$ where V is the set of vertices v_i, each represented by a BMPN, and E is the set of edges e_{ij} which can be thought as the interconnection pattern among BMPNs in the network. The matrix $\mathbf{W} = [w_{ij}]$, shown in (3.15), then corresponds to the adjacency (or Boolean connection) matrix of a digraph G such that $w_{ij} = 1$ if there exists an edge $e_{ij} \in E$ which directs the data-flow from vertex v_i to vertex v_j, and $w_{ij} = 0$ otherwise. Accordingly, (3.14) simply implies that the cell v_j will be fired at time n (i.e., $r_j(n) = 1$) iff $\exists\, e_{ij} \in E$, and also $\exists\, v_i \in V$ which has been activated at the previous time unit.

An alternative way is to treat the BMPN network as a finite-state automaton [30] and (3.14) as its corresponding state-transition function. Accordingly, $\mathbf{W}$ and $\mathbf{R}$ in (3.14) are interpreted as the transition matrix and the state vector, respectively. For a k-state automaton M, the state vector $\mathbf{R} = (r_1\ r_2\ \ldots\ r_k)$ contains k bits in which r_i represents the i-th state, and $\mathbf{W}$ is a square matrix that is composed of k rows and k columns in which the entry $w_{ij} = 1$ iff there is an input which takes M from state r_i to state r_j. Note that the state representation defined here is different from the conventional scheme by which each state of a k-state automaton M is often represented as a pattern of $\log 2k$ bits. We instead represent the state of M as a k-bit vector in which each bit denotes a different state of M and is represented by a BMPN. The advantage of this scheme is its capability of representing multiple states and thus nondeterminism in one vector. For example, let us consider a 4-state automaton. By the conventional scheme, we represent the state $S = \{s_1 \ s_2 \ s_3 \ s_4\} = \{00, 01, 10, 11\}$ which is in essence a deterministic representation. However in the BMPN network denotation, we represent S as $S = \{0001, 0010, 0100, 1000\}$. Accordingly, the state vector $R = (1010)$ is interpreted as the network is in both the state s_4 and s_2.

Thus, the behavior of a BMPN network can be completely determined by the content of its associated connection-matrix W. In general, if every column of the adjacency matrix W contains one and only one entry 1 then such a BMPN network will behave as a deterministic finite-state automaton (DFSA). Otherwise a BMPN network is said to be a nondeterministic FSA (NFSA) since it permits more than one possible BMPNs to be fired at time n for a given activated BMPN at time $n-1$. The BMPN network described above is suitable for modeling the system that can be represented by a digraph. In what follows we further describe a modified BMPN network, that will be referred to as connection-addressable network (CAA), by which edge-labeled digraphs can be mapped and manipulated. The CAA network is a collection of identical processing elements (PEs) where the activities of each PE is defined as

$$[w_{ji}(n)]_j \quad = \quad f_{ai}(s_n) \tag{3.16}$$

$$r_i(n+1) \quad = \quad f_u\left(\sum_{j=1}^{N} r_j(n) * W_{ji}(n) - \theta_i(n)\right)(mod\ 2) \tag{3.17}$$

where (3.17) is equivalent to (3.11) that defines a BMPN cell, and the function f_{ai}, shown in (3.17), performs an associative mapping which in turn produces an effective connection vector in which the element $w_{ji} = 1$ if the input s_n has been associated with the link between $PE-j$ and $PE-i$ before time n, otherwise f_{ai} produces a zero vector. Figure 3.5 illustrates the internal structure of such a PE that constitutes the CAA network.

Following the same derivation shown earlier, we can obtain the formula that determines the state transition of a CAA network. That is,

$$R(n+1) = W_{s_n} \circ R(n) \tag{3.18}$$

where W_{s_n} represents the effective state-transition matrix that corresponds to the input at time n. We note that the architecture based on (3.14) or

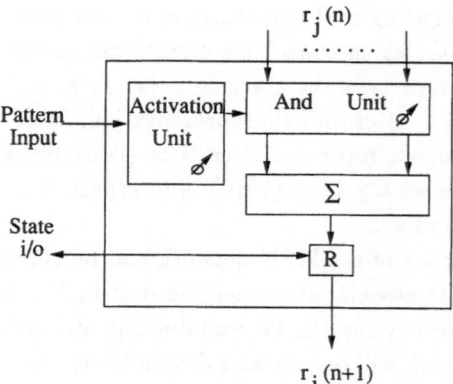

Figure 3.5: Data-path of a PE that constitutes the CAA network.

(3.18) is in a function-partitioning form that offers the feasibility of VLSI implementation.

In summary, we have described the basic architectural model for developing a neuron-embedded digital system for the parallel processing of digraph-structured problems. The model of computation we proposed can indeed be viewed as a novel computational technique for parallel symbolic processing as opposed to the conventional method which is a sequential process of unifications. In general, this model first applies the technique of reconfiguration in converting the system's configuration into a form of uniformly labeled digraph, and then performs parallel search for all of the possible next states. Speedup is obtained by initiating simultaneously the operations from all of the active BMPN-cells within the network.

3.3.2   Achieving Fault-Tolerance

A state representation vector can be cast in two forms. We can either treat it as an $N \times 1$ vector in which each element represents the state of a single gate in the network (the vector $\mathbf{R}$ above), or we can represent it as a second $2^N \times 1$ vector $\mathbf{S}$ in which only a single entry differs from zero and this entry represents the single state in which the network is found. There, each entry in $\mathbf{S}$ corresponds to a specific selection from the 2^N possible choices for the vector $\mathbf{R}$. In fact it is the $\mathbf{S}$-vector representation in which the standard finite state machine is describable by the directed state transition graph. This graph describes the trajectory an algorithm will follow as it proceeds from one state to the next. In fact, we can write this process as

$$\mathbf{S}(n+1) = \mathbf{M}(n)\mathbf{S}(n)$$

where $\mathbf{M}$ is the state transition matrix, and is a representation of the directed graph of the finite state machine [31]. We note that $\mathbf{M}$ is one of a set of possible state transition matrices that exist for a given directed graph and its possible input vectors. The choice of how much of the input vectors to include directly in $\mathbf{S}$, and how much to leave in a selector that picks the appropriate matrix $\mathbf{M}$, is one of personal preference usually. The reduction of $\mathbf{M}$ to $\mathbf{W}$ is well known in system graph theory, and is essentially the process of introducing a cut-set matrix, which describes the connections of individual circuit nodes (gates) to each state of the system. This cut-set matrix is denoted by $\mathbf{T}$, so that

$$\mathbf{R} = \mathbf{TS}.$$

It is then simple to show that

$$\mathbf{W}^T = \mathbf{TMT}^T$$

under the condition that $\mathbf{T}^T\mathbf{T} = 1$. We note that there is in fact no requirement that the finite-state machine operate in a synchronous or a deterministic fashion, and many suggestions for how such asynchronous and/or non-deterministic automata may be implemented have appeared in the past [32,33].

The cut-set reduction contained in the matrix $\mathbf{T}$ must be interpreted, and evaluated, in the Boolean fashion introduced for (3.11), e.g. as an ORed set of AND functions in the matrix product. The reduction (3.11) can be expressed as a multi-branched directed graph in its own right, and each node is then represented by a BMPN cell. This approach can be extended to the representation not only of Boolean variables, but also of semantic or symbol processing networks. Once the directed graph, represented by $\mathbf{M}$, is generated for a desired algorithm, the cut-set matrix defines the reduction onto the normal set of gates. The general reduction, common in computational hardware today, is to use a minimal set of gates; i.e., if the size of 2^N is set by the directed graph, then only N gates are used to represent the logic network. However, if we use only N gates, we cannot achieve the robustness promised in a neural network.

How then are we to map the above ideas into the synthetic neural network paradigm? Coding theory offers a way out of this dilemma. In a neural network, if we destroy a single synapse, the net still generally functions correctly. For example, in memory applications, the stored information can still be reproduced. There is nothing fundamentally new about this sort of redundancy. When an error correcting code is used, a single bit can be destroyed and then later corrected. In both cases, the robustness comes from the distribution of a single information bit over many bits or synapses. In both cases, redundant "hardware" is needed in order to allow this non-localized representation to be formed. Hence, redundancy is mapped into the Boolean network through the use of multiple gates to over-specify the individual states of the system. In the minimal basis set described above, a simple boolean word (e.g., 1001101 . . .) is used to describe the state of the system. By using more gates than this minimal number, we build robustness and redundancy into the network. The method of chosing these gates is given directly through one of the many techniques in the field of coding theory, just as in the use of error-correcting codes for memories. The additional circuit constraint that must be imposed here is distribution of the added error-correcting gates throughout the network architecture in order to fully distribute the information throughout the network. If we chose to use $2N$ gates, rather than N gates, to implement the actual network for the directed graph of $2N$ states, then the optimal coding of the $2N$ states onto the $2N$ "bits" is given by a coding process.

An analog equivalence of the above network can be recovered by chosing the decode algorithm to be a unary summation of a set of output lines chosen to represent a given state. The unary summation process can be made to provide the sigmoidal transfer function, with the transition region set by the threshold and gain of the switching gate in the summing network. If this latter network computes the unary sum of K inputs, and the transition region is traversed for $L < K$ inputs, then the sigmoid is not truly smooth, but is simulated by approximately L steps. For L large, the transition is effectively smoothed out, and true analog behavior is of course recovered for $L \to \infty$. For finite L, though, each analog neural "cell" satisfying an equation like (3.9) can be coded into a digital representation, in which the digital cells satisfy (3.11).

3.3.3 Programmability

The formulation of the transition matrix $\mathbf{W}$ in terms of the state transition matrix $\mathbf{M}$, and the appropriate cut-set matrices, allows us to at the same time introduce the concept of reconfiguration of the network, i.e. programmability. Computation, in the general sense of a Turing machine, proceeds by the introduction of a sequence of state transition matrices, each of which arranges the states in the order necessary to carry out a prescribed sub-computation. This can be accomplished by using an activation function to set the weights in the transition matrix, as

$$\mathbf{W} = f_a(\mathbf{U})$$

where f_a is an activation function in which $\mathbf{U}$ represents the symbolic input matrix, which replaces the general product $\mathbf{TS}$ as an additional processing level between the cut-set reduction and the transition matrix. The activation function f_a basically generates an effective weight matrix, in which each element is set to 1 if the input pattern is associated with a connection between the cells i and j at or before time n. Otherwise, the weight is 0. This approach has been named previously as a function alterable recognizer (FAR) [34] owing to its utility in modifiable connectivities and in pattern storage processes. We note in passing that the reprogrammability can also be applied in the decode process, rather than in the weights, owing to the equivalence of employing the nonlinearity prior or post synaptic summation [35], represented by (3.9) or (3.11).

Let us summarize the main results presented here. First, we have shown a procedure whereby a computational algorithm, describable by a finite state machine and its directed state transition diagram, can be mapped onto a digital implementation of a synthetic neural network through the use of an over-specified cut-set reduction matrix. The use of an over-specified set of gates to implement the desired state transition graph results in built-in redundancy and overall robustness of the network, just as in the use of error-correcting coding schemes, which is a major goal of the neural system. The actual computational network can be mapped onto a PLA, which provides a regular scheme in which the gates now occupy the central and major portion of the integrated circuit, in direct contrast to most electronic neural nets in which the vast majority of the chip area is devoted to interconnection wiring. Finally, the digital network is a finite level simulation of a true analog synthetic neural network, with the latter being implemented through the decoding, or output, step. The overall computational network is programmable through the modification of the PLA level architecture, either through an activation network or a post-processing modification of the decode network. This programmability allows the network to operate as part of a true implementation of a Turing machine, and also allows one to actually program desired responses into the network when implementing associative memories. The reconfiguration can be dependent upon the output of the system and carried out by an adaptive decision processor running externally to the synthetic neural network, thus providing the complete simulation of a Turing machine.

3.4   Neural Architectures

3.4.1   Introduction

Synthetic neural systems (SNS), also called artificial neural networks, connectionist networks, or parallel distributed processing networks, is the engineering discipline concerned with the synthesis, design, fabrication, training, and analysis of neuromorphic, i.e. brain-inspired, electronic systems. These systems achieve high performance by having dense interconnections of simple switching elements processing information in parallel. SNS process information by its state response to an input (relaxation), or under certain restricted conditions by computation. Neuromorphic systems offer the potential of processing information in a manner similar to the methodology developed by nature.

Modern digital computers are excellent at storing and retrieving bits of data in precise locations, and at performing complex calculations involving thousands of numbers and millions of operations. These are skills a human brain can not hope to match. But, as powerful as today's computer are, they are very limited in their abilities. For example, computers are not good at extracting information from the data that they store. Hence, they are not good at generalizing from information stored in memory, self-organization, autonomous acquisition of knowledge, and learning associations. There are skills a human baby acquires within a few weeks of birth, such as being able to recognize its mother, that requires pattern recognition skills far beyond the current capabilities of computers. While no definitive proof exist which rules out the possibility of computers performing this task or exhibiting other higher cognitive functions such as consciousness, no computer so far has been able to demonstrate such behavior.

SNS is a rapidly growing field primarily because of the promise of solutions to problems that has continued to confound computer science and artificial intelligence. In the next few years neuromorphic systems will provide solutions to problems requiring parallel searches though spatial and spatial-temporal information, allow implementation of self-organized associative memories, and permit systems to autonomously collect knowledge from observations of it's environment. Applications of these systems to problems of sensor processing, knowledge processing, natural language, vision, and real time control offer new markets for VLSI and ULSI circuits.

The neuroscience community is still very unclear on the exact nature used by the brain to process information. Researchers in neural modeling, psychology, cognitive science, and computer science have used a variety of models to simulate and study how the brain processes information. Many of these models are closely guided by experimental results and in some cases have offered predictions of human behavior. In all cases the models are constrained by neural biology. SNS is not constrained by neural biology, but by VLSI technology. While SNS models can be used to study many of the functions of the brain, the SNS model is self-consistent and does not require the correctness of neural theory to validate their operation. They are only inspired by the tremendous potential, highly parallel operation, and fault tolerant nature of the brain, and are not constrained by the exact details.

3.4.2 Biological Neural Networks

A brief discussion of biological neural networks will be presented only to describe the terminology and to illustrate the source of the inspiration for the SNS architecture. The signal processing element in the brain is the nerve cell or neuron. There are hundreds of different types of neurons, but most of them have certain signal processing characteristics in common, and hence we will represent these properties with an ideal neural model. The internal state of the neuron is characterized by an electrical potential difference across the cell membrane. This voltage is called the membrane potential or activity of the cell. External inputs produce deviations in this voltage from a resting voltage of approximately -70 mV. When the activity level exceeds a certain threshold voltage, a pulse or action potential is transmitted along the output line, called an axon. Each pulse is a large depolarizing signal with a peak-to-peak amplitude of 90 mV and a pulse width of 1-10 ms. The pulse travels along the axon with a constant amplitude and velocity of typically between 10 and 100 m/s and terminates at the synaptic knob. The neuron emits trains of evenly spaced pulses with a frequency in the range of 2 and 400 Hz. Single pulses do appear to be able to be generated, but are random and are not believed to carry information. It is believed that the information resides in the pulse train frequency. Hence, this frequency will be represented by a positive real number. The axons terminate on a very important part of the system, the synapse. The synapse connects to the inputs of the neuron, the dendrites. The synapse is an extremely complex structure and has critical effects on the behavior of the system. When an incoming signal traveling along the axon reaches the synapse, an electrical to chemical conversion takes place. The input signal causes the release of a substance called a neurotransmitter from small storage vesicles. The released neurotransmitter diffuses across the synaptic cleft to the postsynaptic region where it alters the potential and causes a signal to be transmitted down the dendrite to the neuron.

The neuron will be assumed to perform a temporal summation of the dendrite signals. Changes in the dendrite voltage are additive and depend on the pulse frequency of the incoming pulse train. Synapse are either excitatory or inhibitory. An synapse is excitatory if it increases the voltage on the dendrite, and inhibitory if it decreases this voltage. The neuron then sums the all the individual inputs, in some cases over 100,000, and on the average 10,000, and causes the neuron to fire if the cell threshold voltage is exceeded. The human nervous system consist of over 100×10^9 neurons, with over 10^{15} synapses. While in local regions the neurons are highly interconnected, full global interconnectivity does not occur.

To model the nervous system, let the i-th neuron be represented by the node v_i, connected to the j-th neuron at node v_j. The path between nodes v_i and v_j, is denoted by e_{ij}, and has a transmittance value z_{ij}. A signal, S_{ij}, propagates along e_{ij}. S_{ij} is a function of the activity level, x_i, of the node v_i. The magnitude of the signal when it reaches the synapse is

$$S_{ij}(t) = f(x_i(t - \tau_{ij}))b_{ij},$$

where τ_{ij} is a delay constant, and b_{ij} is a path strength constant. In general $f(x_i)$ is any monotonicly increasing threshold function, such as,

$$f(x_i) = [x_i - \Gamma_i]U_o(x_i - \Gamma_i),$$

where Γ_i is an internal noise parameter and U_o is the Heavyside step function defined by $U_o(x) = 1$ for $x \geq 0$, and $U_o(x) = 0$ for $x < 0$. Thus, the node v_i emits a signal only when the activity level at the cell exceeds Γ_i. Notice that we have transformed the burst of pulses into a voltage level which represents the average firing frequency of the neuron. For a network with n nodes, the time evolution of the activity level of node j can be modeled by

$$\partial x_j/\partial t = -A_j x_j + \sum_{k=1} S_{kj} z_{kj} + I_j(t). \tag{3.19}$$

A_j can be interpreted as a short term memory decay rate, and $I_j(t)$ is an input from either sensory inputs or networks outside the local network. The transmittance term, z_{ij}, which can be interpreted as storing long term memory, changes on a slower time scale and is modeled by

$$\partial z_{ij}/\partial t = -B_{ij} z_{ij} + S'_{ij} f[x_j], \tag{3.20}$$

where $B_i i$ can be interpreted as a forgetting term or long term memory decay rate, S'_{ij} is the presynaptic learning signal, and x_j is the postsynaptic activity of node v_j. Notice to change z_{ij}, both S'_{ij} and x_j must be positive simultaneously.

3.4.3 Neural Architectures for ULSI

Hardware implementation of equations (3.19) and (3.20) span a wide range of approaches. At one end of the spectrum are hardware accelerators which enhance the processing speed of the host computer. The hardware for this method is easy to install and use, relatively inexpensive, and offers 2 to 3 orders of magnitude of enhanced processing speed. The other end of the spectrum is the design and use of custom Very Large Scale Integrated (VLSI) chips. This approach contributes an additional 3 to 4 orders of magnitude of enhanced processing speed over accelerator boards. These VLSI systems have low power consumption, are small in size, and are inexpensive in large volumes. Only the VLSI chips offer the potential of matching the processing speed, high density, and low power consumption of complex biological systems.

Two disparate groups of workers are presently engaged in VLSI chip implementations of neural networks. The first is committed to electronic-based implementations of neural networks, and use standard or custom VLSI chips. The driving force for this group is to implement the neural system equations, not to design novel integrated circuits. The electronic systems are only a vehicle to obtain the desired system behavior and through-put. The second group desires to build fault-tolerant, adaptive VLSI chips, and are much less concerned with whether the design rigorously duplicates the neural models. This group is composed of VLSI designers who realize the opportunities of obtaining biological behavior in hardware. They see numerous problems for VLSI designers on the horizon, and recognize that nature has found solutions to many of these problems. As will be discussed later, VLSI technology currently has the capability of fabricating systems which border on biological complexity. The central problem in the construction of a VLSI neural network is that the design constraints of VLSI differ from those of biology [36]. In particular, the high fan-in/fan-out of biology imposes connectivity requirements such that the VLSI chip implementation of a highly interconnected neural network of just a few thousand neurons would require a level of connectivity which exceeds the current or even projected interconnection density of Ultra Large Scale Integrated (ULSI) systems [25]. Fortunately, highly-layered, limited-interconnected networks can be designed that are functionally equivalent to highly-connected systems [37].

3.4.4   Training Limited Interconnect Architectures

Interconnections in VLSI technology are very expensive in terms of die area. As the number of synthetic neurons are scaled to large numbers, fully-connected architectures will require significant amounts of area for interconnects. Our objective is to design highly-layered, limited-interconnect synthetic neural architectures that are functionally equivalent to highly-connected systems, and develop training algorithms for systems made from these chips.

Several algorithms for training networks of binary threshold elements have been proposed. The topic of network synthesis for threshold elements goes back to the sixties when it was believed that the way to obtain more powerful computers was to increase the power of the processing elements. All methods considered during this period were for the synthesis of complex boolean, i.e. linear functions. Methods in this section are for multi-layered networks implementing nonlinear functions. The earliest method is the training algorithm for Widrow's ADELINE, which employed a single layer of neurons, called perceptrons in early work, followed by a single second layer node which employed a simple function such as majority voting [38]. The single layer is essentially a linear filter and can therefore be adapted using any linear filter algorithm, including least mean squares (LMS) learning. Widrow's latest method for multilayered binary networks is to employ a method he calls least disturbance, which basically involves a search through network space, modifying only those connections which most contribute to the reduction of output error [39].

Back propagation is a powerful algorithm for adapting layered networks, but this method typically requires a continuous, differentiable activation function such as a sigmoid in order to determine the error gradient at every node in the network. This problem may be circumvented by determining a "desired" state for every node in the network. Le Cun [40] has described a simple procedure for determining the desired states working backwards beginning with the desired responses in the output layer. With desired states determined, any learning algorithm for single layer systems can be employed.

In Backward Error Propagation (BEP), the output error is defined as

$$E = \frac{1}{2} \sum_C \sum_J (y_j - d_j)^2 \tag{3.21}$$

where C is an index over the number of input-output pairs, J is the index of the output units, y_j is the actual output value and d_j is the desired output value at each output unit. The output of each processing element is a nonlinear function of its input, x_j,

$$y_j = \frac{1}{1 + \exp(-x_j)} \tag{3.22}$$

where the input x_j is a weighted sum of the outputs of units in the previous layer. The weighted transmittance value between the previous output y_i and the next input x_j is w_{ij}. x_j is expressed as

$$x_j = \sum_i y_i w_{ij}. \tag{3.23}$$

The use of a differentiable node transfer function allows the use of the chain rule to determine the change in the output error resulting from each transmittance value change. The procedure for adaptation using the Delta Rule involves applying input vectors at the input layer and accumulating the difference between the actual and desired output vectors for the entire example set. The change for each transmittance value as a function of total output error is

$$\Delta w(t) = -\epsilon \frac{\partial E}{\partial w(t)} + \alpha \cdot \Delta w(t-1) \tag{3.24}$$

where t is incremented by 1 for each sweep through the whole set of input-output cases, ϵ is a proportionality constant which determines the magnitude of transmittance adjustment at each step, and α is a momentum factor which determines the contribution of the previous gradients to the transmittance change. This procedure is repeated until the total accumulated error falls below some minimum value.

Since the networks described above employ binary threshold elements, additional considerations are necessary. For this type of network, desired values for the states of the internal processing elements as well as the output nodes must be defined. A procedure has been described [41] in which internal desired states are calculated,

$$d_i = 1, \text{ if } \sum_j w_{ij}(2d_j - 1) > \mu_i \tag{3.25}$$

$$\text{else } d_i = 0 \tag{3.26}$$

where j is the index over the succeeding layer of processing elements and i is the index of the layer under consideration. μ_i is an arbitrary threshold for the generation of the backward-propagated desired state. Plaut has modified this procedure to generate a "criticality" term for each desired state associated with each hidden unit. This ratio is a numerical representation of the "confidence" associated with the desired state selected for each hidden unit and is used to modify the weight update. The transmittance change for any connection then becomes

$$\Delta w_{ji}(t) = \epsilon(d_j - y_j)c_j y_i + \alpha \cdot \Delta w_{ij}(t-1), \qquad (3.27)$$

where c is the criticality of any node in a given layer, defined by

$$c_i = \frac{\text{abs}\left[\sum_j w_{ij}(2d_j - 1)c_j\right]}{\sum_j \text{abs}\left[(2d_j - 1)c_j\right]}. \qquad (3.28)$$

In this way, desired states which have a high criticality will exert the greatest influence on the modification of a given connection.

Each weight in this type of network develops in a way that not only converges on the training set, but also constrains all units to the saturated endpoints of their activation functions. In addition, since all units are forced to the endpoints, each unit ends up acting as a simple threshold element implementing a boolean function. For this reason, binary threshold elements may be used to replace the continuous sigmoids in feedforward operation after training has completed.

Additional considerations are required for sparsely connected networks adapted with BEP [42]. Efficient internal network representations are necessary for generalization of a given problem in a perceptron network. A general rule for accurate generalization in perceptrons with full interconnection between layers is that they must contain a minimum number of hidden units necessary to encode the invariant properties of the input training set. In a similar fashion, sparsely connected perceptrons which generalize have a minimum number of active internal units. Learning algorithms for these networks must not only develop internal abstractions with a minimum number of processing elements, but must also route required signals to the proper locations within the network. Low fan-in and the use of random initial weight values serves to reduce the probability that a signal necessary for a given hidden unit to generate a required abstraction will be routed in. For this reason, the generation of a "high" desired state within a hidden unit must be made artificially difficult. In this way, the majority of connections will be eliminated from the forward signal path unless they are needed. Fortunately, the presence of a positive threshold value in each processing element means that each node is hard to turn on and easy to turn off. Another necessary *a priori* consideration required is that the inputs must be arranged in a way that ensures that they can be connected to all of the correct output nodes with the number of layers provided.

Sparsely connected perceptrons are generally more prone to local minima during training. Fully-connected perceptrons providing more signal paths and a richer, more redundant set of internally formed abstractions more easily find a near-optimal solution (in the LMS sense) in weight space. Since gradient descent is basically a shortcut through an NP-complete search in weight space, greater redundancy and overlapping of internal representations of information improve the probability of convergence to a near-optimal solution of the training set. It is well known however, that networks which have an over-specified layer of hidden units converge quickly, but generalize untrained cases poorly.

Sparse networks provide less redundancy and have a more difficult time forming the necessary internal abstractions since now routing of signals to the correct hidden unit forming a needed abstraction becomes important. An advantage however, is that since fewer points in weight space are available to converge on the given training set, the probability is higher that the given weight set has captured the invariant properties of the desired network function.

3.4.5 Electronic Implementations

Hopfield [43] is generally credited with clearly articulating the fascinating possibilities of neuromorphic architectures to VLSI designers. While many of his ideas and approaches have been previously reported in the literature, Hopfield presented this information in the terminology and in the journals read by circuit designers (see for example [44]). Hopfield also inspired the first chip implementations of these architectures. He promoted the view that highly interconnected networks of nonlinear analog switching elements fabricated on a die could be extremely efficient in generating a good, but not necessary optimum, solution to computationally complex problems.

One classical problem solved by these types of networks is the retrieval of a complete vector from partial knowledge of the vector, hence an associative or content addressable memory. The initial condition represents part of the complete set of information to be retrieved, and the system will relax to the closest complete set. Other problems which have been implemented with this type of network are optimization problems. Examples are the traveling salesman problem [27], and an analog-to-digital converter [44].

Inspired by Hopfield's work, a team at Bell Laboratories [45] has designed, fabricated, and tested a number of neural network electronic circuit implementations. These circuits include a thin-film array of read-only resistive synapses [46], an associative memory with 256 neurons on a single chip using a combination of analog and digital VLSI technology plus custom microfabrication process [47], and an array of programmable synapses and amplifiers serving as electronic neurons [48].

Connections between neurons, or the synapses, forms a major component of an electronic neural network. A virtue of resistive synapses is that they can be packed very densely. Using layered thin films, Bell-Lab have made resistors considerably smaller than the smallest state-of-the-art transistor and is VLSI process compatible. A 22×22 array of microfabricated resistors was fabricated and programmed to serve in a Content Addressable Memory (CAM) mode. The resistive array was made by sandwiching amorphous silicon between tungsten as shown in Figure 3.6.

The upper tungsten layer served as the dendrites; the amorphous silicon served as the resistive synapses material since current from axons (the lower tungsten layer), to dendrites, had to pass through this silicon. The array had only two synaptic strength, no connection or connection through the amorphous silicon of about 100 $k\Omega$. The array was coupled to an array of twenty-two CMOS inverters to form the complete network. The network was coded to store four 22-bit words in a distributed fashion. The network was able to find the best match in hamming distance for a test word to memory word that differed from the test word by 4 or less bits.

Another chip fabricated which uses the microfabricated resistors is the Electronic Neural Network (ENN) memory with 256 neurons. Amplifiers with inverting and noninverting outputs are used for the neurons to make

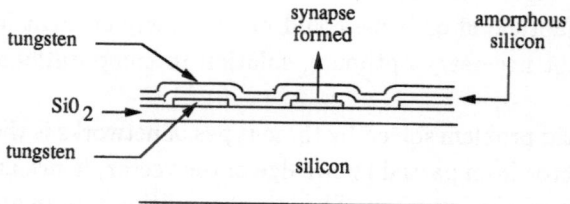

Figure 3.6: Microfabricated resistor.

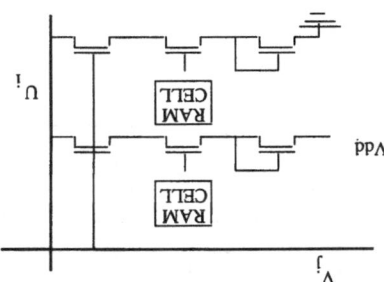

Figure 3.7: Bell-Lab's programmable synapse.

inhibitory and excitatory connections. The ENN consists of fully connected array of amplifiers and therefore the reduction in the connection area by using microfabricated resistor is critical.

The disadvantage of the resistive array is that once it is fabricated, the synaptic strength cannot be changed. Graf, from Bell Laboratories, designed a self contained VLSI chip with fifty-four neurons and about 3000 programmable synapses. The synapses can either be excitatory, inhibitory or open (no connection). A novel aspect of the design is that each synapse actively drives the axon, reducing the drive requirement of the neuron amplifiers as compared to a circuit with simple resistive synapses. Figure 3.7 shows a programmable synapse connecting the output of neuron j to neuron i.

The two RAM cells control whether the connection is inhibitory (gate towards ground enabled), excitatory (gate towards VDD enabled), or open (both gates disabled). When the *out* of neuron j is high ($out = 1$, $\overline{out} = 0$) current flows into or out of the input line of neuron i, depending on how the two RAMs are loaded. The best configuration of this chip for performing associative recalls [48], is the one shown in Figure 3.8.

The neurons are partitioned into vector neurons, that accept the input keys, and label neurons, that identify the best-match memory. The input key passes through the vector neurons and then is tested by the label neurons whose synapses are templates for the memories they represent. The label neurons are excited in proportion to their template match to the input vector. The label neurons are connected through a matrix to the input vector. The label neurons are connected through a matrix of mutually inhibitory connections that act as a winner-take-all circuit, that is the label whose template is the best match to the input vector is turn on, all the

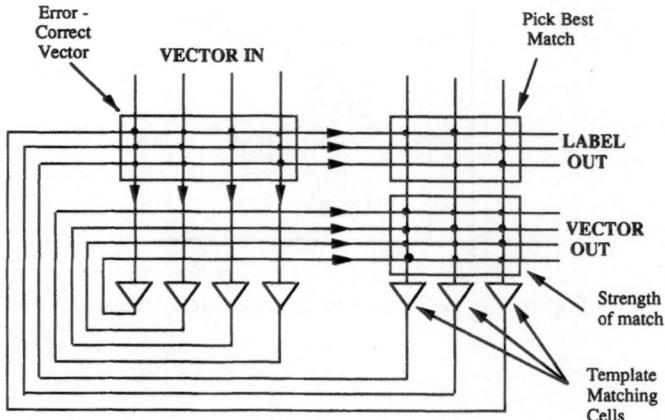

Figure 3.8: Configuration for associative recall.

others are turned off. The label neuron, in turn, feeds back to the vector neurons through a template that impose that cell's memory word on the vector neurons, accomplishing associative recall. The chip uses standard 2.5 μm CMOS fabrication technology, but the calculation is a mixture of analog and digital processing.

Inspired by the biological neural nets models, California Institute of Technology, or Caltech, has fabricated a set of VLSI chips called RET10, RET20 and RET30, using large scale analog circuits, which performs real time visual processing [49]. Analysis of images, static or dynamic, requires vast parallel computations of informations which cannot be efficiently performed on a digital computer. Artificial digital vision systems are further disadvantaged by the early sampling performed by cameras. A vision system intended for operation in an unconstrained environment must include AGC (Automatic Gain Control) with respect to absolute ambient light level. Taking the logarithm of the incident light intensity is a simple local AGC mechanism. An integrated photoreceptor, which is the basis of the RET10 chip fabricated, has an output that is logarithmic over 5 order of magnitude in light intensity is shown in Figure 3.9.

Motion is perceived when a point in an image displays non-zero spatial and temporal derivatives. In other words, an edge that is moving causes a change in brightness at that point in the image. Thus a local time derivative is the simplest computation to highlight areas of an image that are moving. Since this computation is purely local, no inter-pixel communication is required. The derivative can be approximated by comparing the

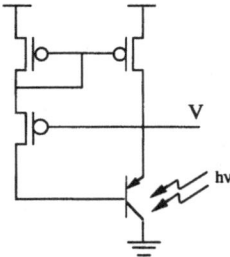

Figure 3.9: Integrated photoreceptor by Caltech.

current photoreceptor output with some suitable delayed version of itself.

The RET20 chip fabricated performs the discrete time derivative based on the circuit shown in Figure 3.10. Capacitor $C1$ stores the previous state of the system and is compared with the present state to obtain the time derivative.

The RET30 chip consists of an array of receptors, R, interconnected by a hexagonal resistive network as shown in Figure 3.11. It is inspired by the biological retinas which contain horizontal cells. These horizontal cells provide lateral conductance and can be loosely thought of as providing an average of the signal values in the neighborhood with which local signals can be compared. The RET30 has a capacitor to ground located at each junction of 6 neighboring horizontal resistors, to provide temporal smoothing. Each local processing element takes the difference between the potential of the horizontal network and the receptor output and drives the local potential of the horizontal network toward the local receptor output potential. The "derivative" computed is the difference between the input signal and a spatially and temporally smoothed version of the signal. To obtain a time of the same order of magnitude as the time scale of motion, without enormous area of capacitors, large horizontal resistors value are re-

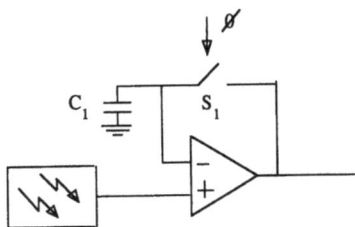

Figure 3.10: Caltech's discrete time derivative circuit.

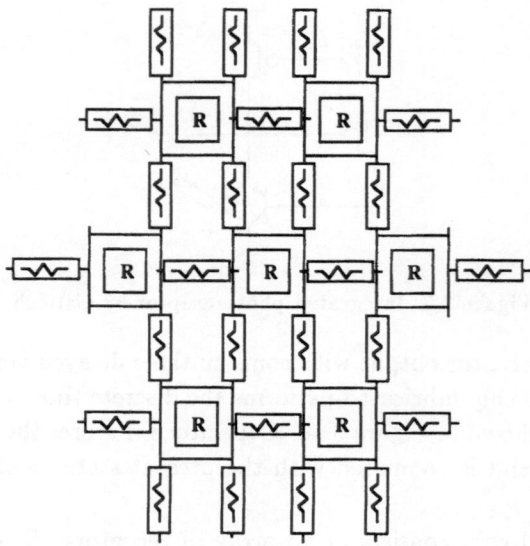

Figure 3.11: RET30 - horizontal resistive network.

quired. To implement the large resistor value, the circuit shown in Figure 3.12 is used. V_1 and V_2 represent potential V_i at two neighboring locations in the network.

In an investigation at Arizona State University on the usefulness of neural networks in performing computation, a digital SNS capable of varying its interconnection neighborhood and interconnection weights has been designed by the authors, and fabricated at MOSIS [37]. The custom designed

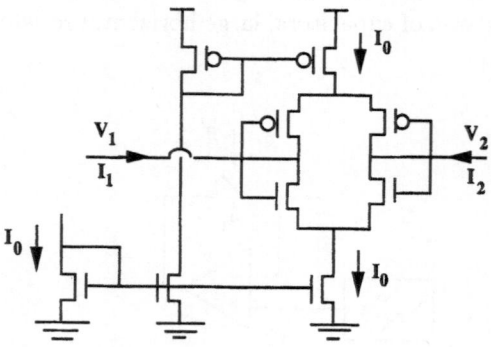

Figure 3.12: Large resistor implementation.

VLSI chip was among the first implementations of a digital neural networks based on a programmable interconnection pattern. The digital SNS consists of 12 neurons in a systolic array architecture. Each neuron performs the evaluation function, as in the Hopfield model, with a programmable threshold. All weights are limited to the range ±1, with a resolution varying between four and eight bits of representation. Each processing element contains four sections: the router, the memory, the accumulator, and the control unit. Figure 3.13 is a block of one cell. All actions are synchronized by an external clock and control signals. The router is responsible for routing each neuron's output state to its neighbors. A neuron has four connections to each of its four physical neighbors. The router is composed of flip-flops, which implement a two-dimensional shift matrix. The input to the flip-flops is controlled by a four-input multiplexer. This allows each cell to direct its own output to any one of its four nearest neighbors. The selection of the neighbor receiving the signal is controlled by direction control signals. All flip-flops of the shift matrix are controlled by the same signals. On each cycle of the shift clock, information moves in any one of four directions. This signal routing scheme is similar to that found in Hillis' connection machine [50]. Each cell is designed to be autonomous, except for the external clock and control signals. Many cells can be connected together to form a matrix of neurons. The edges of the matrix may be connected to latches that can be read or written by a microprocessor. This test vehicle is being used to study the effects of interconnectivity on the transition from local to distributed data storage, digital learning algorithms, and system robustness against individual device failure. The chip was fabricated using 3 μm CMOS double metal technology and packaged in a 84 Pin Grid Array.

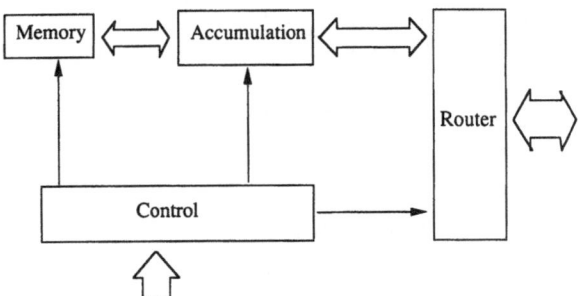

Figure 3.13: Simplified functional block of a neural cell.

SNS are limited by VLSI constraints, and not neural constraints. A principal VLSI constraint is cost, and the cost of a chip is directly related to it's die area. By exploiting the natural functions available with analog circuits, like summation, less die area is consumed than with a digital implementation of the same function. Of course, analog VLSI designs have additional problems not found in digital systems. For example, power dissipation can be a serious problem for large chips. While digital circuits are relatively insensitive to varying device parameters, in most cases analog circuits are very sensitive to these variations. Analog neural-like circuits must be designed not to rely on the absolute behavior of each individual transistor, but on the cooperative behavior of large numbers of devices.

To take advantage of the compactness of analog circuits, and the device process tolerance associated with digital circuits, a hybrid analog-digital circuit has been developed [51]. This cell is designed for use in limited-interconnect architectures, so tens of thousands of neurons can be fabricated on a die. Figure 3.14 is the circuit diagram of the limited-interconnect analog neural cell and Figure 3.15 is the timing diagram. The operation of the cell is as follows. Weights, $W1$, $W2$, and $W3$, are stored dynamically

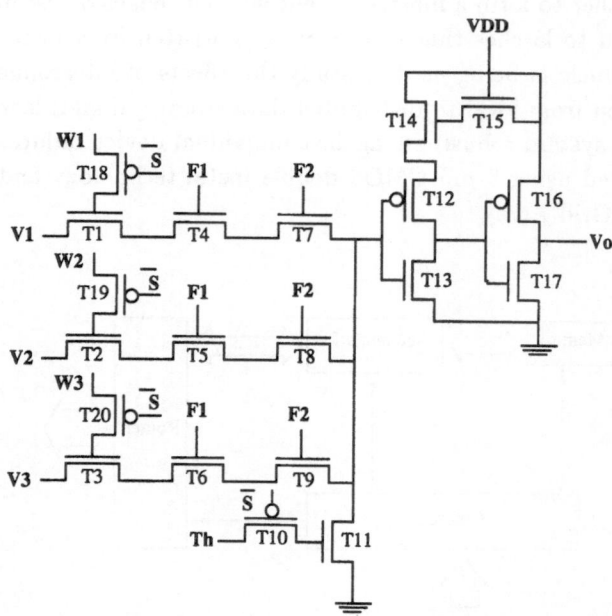

Figure 3.14: Analog synthetic neural cell.

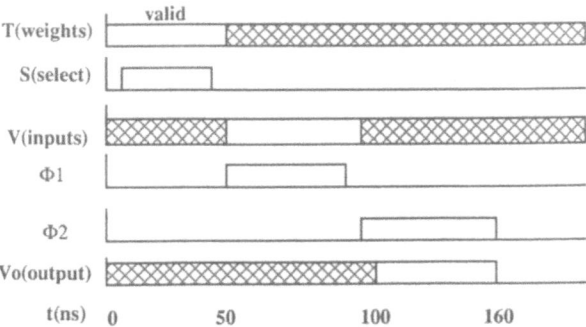

Figure 3.15: Timing diagram for analog neural cell.

on the gates of transistors $T1$, $T2$ and $T3$. Notice only PMOS transistors ($T18$, $T19$, and $T20$) are used to pass and isolate the weights instead of transmission gates. This is allowable since only weights above the device threshold are important, and hence a degraded low state voltage has no effect on circuit performance. For inputs of 5 volts, the drain parasitic capacitors of $T7$, $T8$, and $T9$ are charged by current flowing through the pass transistors $T4$, $T5$, and $T6$, to a voltage equal to the weight minus the device threshold voltage. For inputs of 0 volts, the pass transistors will allow the capacitors to discharge. While exact multiplication of the input and the weight is not done, shifting of the circuits' logical threshold voltage and modifying the training algorithm compensates for this behavior. In fact, one of the very useful characteristics of neural networks is exact generation of products are not necessary. Once the storage capacitor in each branch is charged, clock $\Phi1$ is turned off to isolate the signal from the input. Turning on $\Phi2$ allows the signals to be analog summed and compared to the logical threshold of the first inverter. The first inverter needs to be of minimum size to allow acceptable charge transfer. The circuit on top of the PMOS pull-up device allows the logical threshold and hence the neural threshold to be set at a voltage lower than $0.5V_{dd}$. The output inverter restores the output voltage level and drives the next stage. Since this circuit uses only positive weights, a shunting transistor $T11$ is used to provide inhibition. Arrays made with this cell can perform as a complete logic family. Figure 3.16 shows a circuit simulation of the cell.

A system formed by replicating the analog cell operates in the following manner. To keep the number of I/O pins at reasonable numbers as the system is expanded, we share the input, weights, and output pins. For the implementation of 512 neurons in an array 32 wide by 16 long, 32 lines are

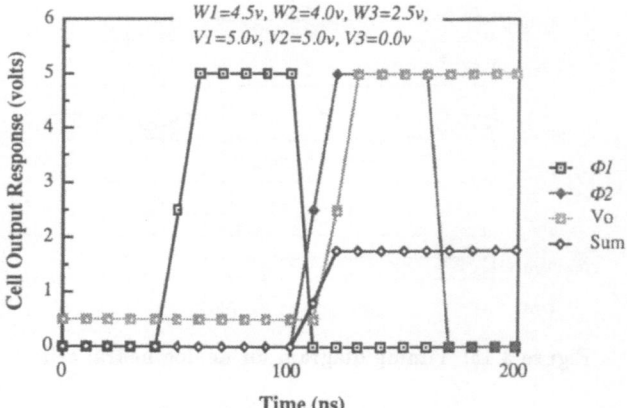

Figure 3.16: Circuit simulation of cell.

used for the weights, and I/O. The four unique weights are multiplexed to the single line running to each cell. Hence, a row is selected for a write, then weights for each cell are written. This continues for four cycles after which all weights for the row addressed have been written. The next row can then be selected for weight loading. The whole array can be loaded in approximately $10\mu s$, an order of magnitude faster than the discharge time constant for an individual gate. Figure 3.17 shows the block diagram for the chip. For efficient data flow through the layers, the clock lines are interchanged in every other row. After the weights have been loaded, the inputs are loaded, and the output vector ripples through the layers. Using this architecture, a 512-element, feedforward neural IC has been designed [52].

3.5 The Future: The Ultimate Integrated Circuit

To end this chapter, we discuss our vision of the ultimate integrated circuit. A combination of wafer scale integration and ultra-large scale integration will culminate in a "chip" containing several billion transistors. The central dilemmas are first, that it is unlikely that all of these devices will work, second that we will never be able to test this system, and last that we do not know what it is that we will do with all of these devices. We would suggest that techniques that answer the first two of these dilemmas will almost certainly lead to an answer to the last.

The chip must be based on a regular array of regularly connected elements, or it is unlikely that we will ever be able to complete the initial

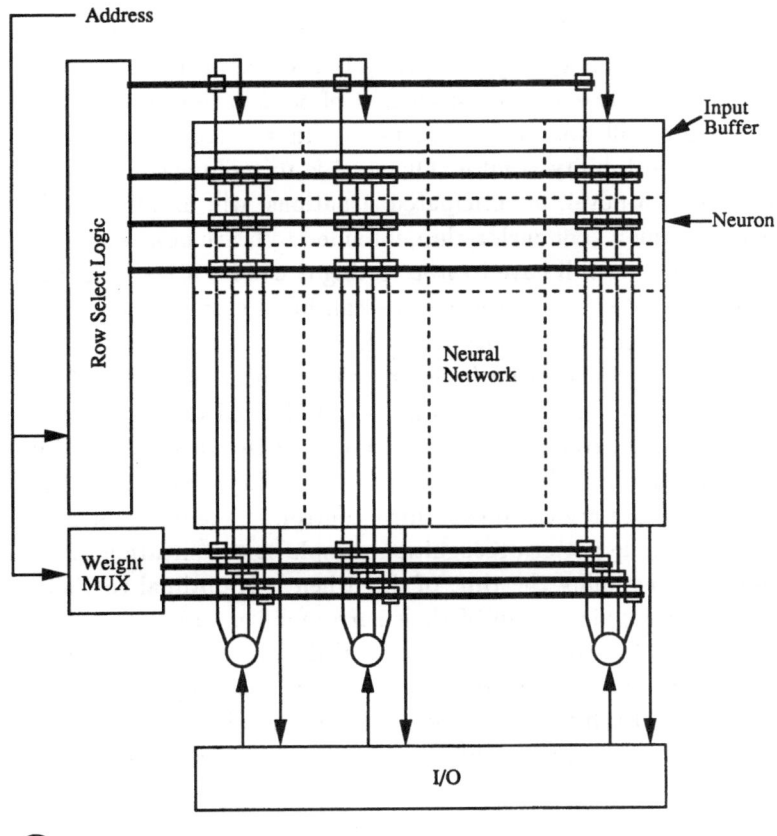

Figure 3.17: Chip architecture.

design. These elements and connections however will be plastic. We will be able to reconfigure the system locally to solve any problems posed by a poorly functioning chip. We can even envision systems in which we handle problems such as the tendency of threshold voltages to vary as one moves across a wafer by allowing various regions of the chip to "learn" that the voltages of the next region are a little low. In short, our chip may contain regional dialects and accents. This type of adaptability and insensitivity to parameter fluctuations will be essential if our yield is to be greater than zero. What is sometimes not mentioned is that they also play a role in long term reliability as well. Where one is concerned about temporal variations in device parameters through effects such as oxide charging.

While obviously a significant amount of on-chip testing will occur, even then the chip will not be fully testable. In a certain sense though the worry about testability is false. Our goal is to build systems which when confronted with novel, unanticipated situations, will usually function in a reasonable fashion. For such a chip, intended to brave new worlds, the time will come when we will have to stop testing it and let it leave the nest. Our challenge therefore is to learn how we can build systems capable of being "parented" rather than quality-assured.

The neural system of an insect may contain of the order of a million neurons. While a neuron is much more complicated than a transistor, our ultimate chip has several orders of magnitude more transistors and it seems to not be totally unrealistic to anticipate achieving similar complexity. Insects such as a bee are capable of flight control, fine motor control, genuine navigation, simple pattern recognition, simple communication (the famous bee dance), scheduling the time of day when it is optimal to visit certain locations, developing a map of their surroundings and a large number of tasks that no robot today can imitate. Attaining similar behaviors as these depends critically on developing adaptability, learning capabilities and a large measure of self-testing. These, whether obtained through an SNS, a pipelined CAM, or some reconfigureable automata, are where the frontiers of ULSI will be found.

Acknowledgements

The central role of our students Larry Clark, Jennifer Wang, Mark Walker, L. C. Shiue, Mary Snyder, Paul Hasler, W. Fu, Ataru Shimodaire, Wen Looi, C. C. Goh, Siamack Haghighi, Jerome Brandt, and Aron Rao in formulating many of these ideas and correcting our mistakes must be acknowledged. M. Walker and C.C. Goh are also thanked for contributing part of the Neural Architecture section.

References

[1] G. Bernstein and D. K. Ferry, *Electron beam lithographic fabrication of ultra-submicron GaAs MESFETs,* Superlatt. and Microstruc. **2**, 147 (1986).

[2] Y. Jin, D. Mailly, F. Cercenac, B. Etienne, and H. Landis, *Nanostructures in GaAs TEGFET*, Microelectr. Engr. **6**, 195 (1987).

[3] J. R. Barker and D. K. Ferry, *On the physics and modeling of small semiconductor devices*, Sol.-State Electr. **23**, 519 (1981); **23**, 531 (1981).

[4] J. M. Mikkelson, L. A. Hall, A. K. Malhotra, S. D. Seccombe, and M. S. Wilson, *An NMOS VLSI process for fabrication of a 32-bit CPU chip*, IEEE J. Sol. State Circuits **16**, 542 (1981).

[5] G. Baccarani, M. R. Wordeman, and R. H. Dennard, *Generalized scaling theory and its application to a 1/4 micrometer MOSFET design*, IEEE Trans. Electron Dev. **31**, 452 (1984).

[6] R. Troutman, *VLSI limitations from drain-induced barrier lowering*, IEEE Trans. Electron Dev. **26**, 461 (1979).

[7] J. Sinkkonen, S. Eranen, and T. Stubb, *Linear conductance of short semiconductor structures*, Phys. Rev. B **30**, 4813 (1984).

[8] G. Lewicky and J. Maserjian, *Oscillations in MOS tunneling*, J. Appl. Phys. **46**, 3032 (1975).

[9] M. V. Fischetti, D. J. DiMaria, L. Dori, J. Batey, E. Tierney, and J. Stasiak, *Ballistic electron transport in thin silicon dioxide films*, Phys. Rev. B **35**, 4404 (1987).

[10] K. Lehovec and R. Zuleeg, *Voltage-Current characteristics of GaAs J-FETs in the hot electron range*, Sol.-State Electron. **13**, 1415 (1970).

[11] J. R. Ruch, *Electron transport in short channel field-effect transistors*, IEEE Trans. Electron Dev. **19**, 652 (1972); D. K. Ferry and H. L. Grubin, *The role of transport in very small devices for VLSI*, Microelectr. J. **12**(2), 5 (1981).

[12] D. K. Ferry, *High-field transport in wide-band-gap semiconductors*, Phys. Rev. B **12**, 2361 (1975).

[13] D. K. Ferry, *Fundamental aspects of hot electron phenomena*, in Handbook on Semiconductors, Vol. 1, Ed. by W. Paul (North-Holland, Amsterdam, 1982) pp. 563-598.

[14] R. Zwanzig, *Elementary derivation of time-correlation formulas for transport coefficients*, J. Chem. Phys. **40**, 2527 (1966).

[15] H. Mori, *Transport, collective motion, and Brownian motion*, Prog. Theor. Phys. **33**, 423 (1965).

[16] J. Zimmermann, P. Lugli, and D. K. Ferry, *Non-equilibrium hot-carrier diffusion phenomenon in semiconductors. I. A theoretical non-Markovian approach*, J. Phys. Coll. **42**-C7, suppl. 10, 95 (1981).

[17] R. Kubo, *Statistical-mechanical theory of irreversible processes*, J. Phys. Soc. Jpn. **12**, 570 (1957).

[18] P. Lugli, J. Zimmermann, and D. K. Ferry, *Non-equilibrium hot-carrier diffusion phenomenon in semiconductors. II. An experimental Monte Carlo approach*, J. Phys. Coll. **42**-C7, suppl. 10, 103 (1981).

[19] D. K. Ferry, G. Bernstein, and W.-P. Liu, *Electron-beam lithography of ultra-submicron devices*, in Physics and Technology of Submicron Structures, Ed. by H. Heinrich, G. Bauer, and F. Kuchar (Springer-Verlag, Heidelberg, 1988) pp. 37-44.

[20] G. A. Sai-Halasz, M. R. Wordeman, D. P. Kern, S. Rishton, and E. Ganin, *High transconductance and velocity overshoot in NMOS devices at the 0.1 5m gate-length level*, IEEE Electron Dev. Letters **9**, 464 (1988).

[21] J. R. Barker and D. K. Ferry, *Physics and modeling of submicron semiconductor devices*, Sol.-State Electr. **23**, 531 (1981).

[22] D. K. Ferry, *Materials considerations for submicron VLSI*, in Adv. in Electronics and Electron Phys. **58**, 311 (1982).

[23] D. K. Ferry, *Device-device interactions*, in The Physics of Submicron Semiconductor Devices, Ed. by H. L. Grubin, D. K. Ferry, and C. Jacoboni (Plenum, New York, 1988) pp. 503-520.

[24] D. K. Ferry, L. A. Akers, and R. O. Grondin, *Two-dimensional automata in VLSI*, in Physics of VLSI at the 0.5 to 0.05 Micron Dimension, Ed. by R. K. Watts (Academic Press, New York, 1989) pp. 377-412.

[25] D. K. Ferry, L. A. Akers, and E. W. Greeneich, *Ultra-Large Scale Integrated Microelectronics* (Prentice-Hall, Englewood Cliffs, NJ, 1988).

[26] J.J. Hopfield, *Neural Networks and Physical Systems with Emergent Collective Computational Abilities*, Proc. Natl. Acad. Sci. U.S.A. **79**, 2554 (1982).

[27] J.J. Hopfield and D.W. Tank, *Neural Computation of Decisions in Optimization Problems*, Biol. Cybernet. **52**, 141 (1985)

[28] W.S. McCulloch, and W. Pitts, *A Logical Calculus of the Ideas Imminent in Nervous Activity*, Bulletin of Mathematical Biophysics, 5 (1943).

[29] L.C. Shiue, R.O. Grondin, *Neural Processing of Semantic Networks*, International Joint Conference on Neural Networks, Washington, D.C. (1989).

[30] J.E. Hopcroft, J.D. Ullman, *Introduction to Automata Theory, Language, and Computation*, (Addision-Wesley 1979).

[31] We and others have participated in an "apples vs. oranges" argument of the physical limits to computation. One position insists on the primacy of invertibility, while we have taken the position for the primacy of a physically deterministic evolution. Invertibility (in a logical sense) requires that each row of M contain one and only one non-zero element, while determinism here means that each column of M has one and only one non-zero element. If both requirements are implemented simultaneously, the system state space consists of "garden-of-eden" states and states which are part of complete rings. Therefore, the invertible system cannot pass the standard "halting" definition of a computational automaton, as discussed in [24].

[32] R.O. Grondin, W.Porod, C.M. Loeffler, and D.K. Ferry, *Synchronous and Asynchronous Systems of Threshold Elements*, Biological Cybernetics, **49**(1), 1 (1984).

[33] P. Peretto and J.J. Niez, *Long Term Memory Storage Capacity of Multiconnected Neural Networks*, Biol. Cybernet. **54**, 53 (1986).

[34] L.C. Shiue, R.O. Grondin, *An Automata Approach to Reconfigurable Learning Network Design*, in *Neural Networks from Models to Applications*, Ed. by L. Personnaz and G. Dreyfus (E.S.P.C.I., Paris, France 1988).

[35] M. Snyder and D. K. Ferry, *Open-loop Stability Criteria for Layered and Fully-Connected Neural Networks*, in *Neural Networks from Models to Applications*, Ed. by L. Personnaz and G. Dreyfus (E.S.P.C.I., Paris, France 1988).

[36] M. Walker and L. A. Akers, *A Neuromorphic Approach to Adaptive Digital Circuitry*, Proc. IEEE Conf. Computers and Comm. Phoenix 19 (1988).

[37] L. A. Akers, M. Walker, D. K. Ferry, and R. O. Grondin, *Limited Interconnectivity in Synthetic Neural Systems* in *Neural Computers*, Ed. by R. Eckmiller and C. v.d. Malsburg (Springer-Verlag, Berlin, 1988) pp. 407-416.

[38] B. Widrow, in *Self-Organizing Systems*, Ed. by M. Yovits, G. Jacobi, and G. Goldstein (Spartan, New York 1962) pp. 435-461.

[39] B. Widrow, and R. Winter, *Neural Nets for Adaptive Filtering and Adaptive Pattern Recognition*, IEEE Computer **21**, 25 (1988).

[40] Y. Le Cun, *Learning Process in an Asymmetric Threshold Network* in *Disordered Systems and Biological Organization*, Ed by E. Bienenstock (Springer-Verlag, New York 1985).

[41] D. Plaut, S. Nowlan, and G. Hinton, *Experiments on Learning by Back Propagation*, Computer Science Tech. Rep. (Carnegie-Mellon 1986).

[42] M. Walker, and L. A. Akers, *Training of Limited-Interconnect Feedfordward Neural Arrays*, Abst. First Annual INNS Meeting, Boston 372 (1988).

[43] J. Hopfield, *Neural Networks and Physical Systems with Emergent Collective Computational Abilities*, Proc. Nat. Acad. Sci. **79**, 2554 (1982).

[44] D. Tank and J. Hopfield, *Simple Neural Optimization Networks: An A/D converter, Signal Decision Circuit, and a Linear Programming Circuit*, IEEE Trans. Cir. Syst. **CAS-33**, 533 (1986).

[45] H. P. Graf, L. Jackel, R. Howard, B. Howard, B. Stranghn, J. Denker, W. Hubbard, D. Tennant, and D. Schwartz, *VLSI Implementation of a Neural Network Memory with Several Hundreds of Neurons*, AIP Conf. Proceeding, Snowbird **151** 182 (1986).

[46] W. Hubbard, D. Schwartz., J. Denker, H. Graf, R. Howard, L. Jackel, G. Straughn,, and D. Tennant, *Electronic Neural Networks,* in *Neural Networks for Computing,* J. S. Denker Ed., AIP Conf. Proc. 151 (1986).

[47] L. D. Jackel, H. P. Graf and R. E. Howard, *Electronic Neural Network Chips,* Applied Optics, December **26**(23) (1987).

[48] H. P. Graf and P. DeVgar, *A CMOS Implementation of a Neural Network Model,* in *Advance Research in VLSI: Proceedings of 1987 Stanford Conference,* Ed by Paul Losleben (MIT Press, Cambridge, MA 1987).

[49] M. A. Sivilotti, M. A. Mahowald and C. Mead, *A Real Time Visual Computation using Analog CMOS Processing Arrays,* in *Advance Research in VLSI : Proceedings of 1987 Stanford Conference,* Ed by Paul Losleben (MIT Press, Cambridge, MA 1987).

[50] D. Hillis, *The Connection Machine,* (MIT Press, Boston 1985).

[51] L. A. Akers, M. Walker, D. K. Ferry, and R. O. Grondin, *A Limited-Interconnect, Highly Layered Synthetic Neural Architecture* in *VLSI for Artificial Intelligence,* Ed by J. Delgado and W. Moore, (Kluwer Academic, Norwell, MA. 1989) pp. 407-416.

[52] L. A. Akers and M. Walker, *A Limited-Interconnect Synthetic Neural IC,* Proc. IEEE Neural Net. Conf., San Diego, **III**,151 (1988).

CHAPTER 4

HYBRID WAFER SCALE
INTERCONNECTIONS

Dennis Herrell and
Hassan Hashemi
Microelectronics and Computer Technology Corp.
12100 Technology Blvd.
Austin, Texas 78727

4.1 Introduction

Because of the speed of light limit to signalling between the chips, smaller and smaller electronic assemblies are being used to satisfy the high speed demands of today's computers. This has long been true for super-computers and mainframes and is now becoming a driving force with engineering workstations. The requirement for very compact, highly integrated interconnect systems is fueling a worldwide interest in electronic packaging and interconnect technologies to find ways of inexpensively packaging chips with high area or volume efficiency: "wall-to-wall" semiconductor (area efficient) and floor to ceiling semiconductor (volume efficient).

Gate delays in silicon ICs have reduced remarkably in recent years to less than 100 ps, promising a further order of magnitude improvement in system speeds [1]. A well designed high performance computing system divides the cycle time into 1/2 logic delay on chip and 1/2 delay between the chips. Additionally, a typical cycle in a general purpose processor is 10 logic gate delays (= 10×100 ps = 1 ns), so machines with an overall cycle time of 2 ns will soon be seen. This is a clock frequency of 500 MHz. In 1 ns, light in free space travels 30 cm, and in electronic packages no more than 15 cm with a dielectric constant (ϵ) of 4.

In order to fully utilize the advancements in integrated circuit fabrication technologies, the interconnect delays between chips has to be reduced by an equivalent degree. Otherwise, the future supercomputer speeds can at most only double being limited by the interchip delays. One possible solution that has received significant attention is the concept of **Wafer Scale Integration** (WSI) where all the chips remain as part of the wafer and the good ones are interconnected together.

Wafer scale integration is not a straightforward extension of very large scale integration (VLSI) fabrication processes. In order to achieve a cost effective process, the tolerable manufacturing defect level needs to be two orders of magnitude below current very large scale integration circuit processes [2]. Different parts of an integrated system have differing requirements: it is the solution of these differing requirements that makes the classical idea of monolithic wafer scale integration untenable for general applications. Logic, memory, interconnect as well as other active and passive elements all have their own specific requirements for an optimized design. These requirements are in terms of the basic transistor types, diffusion profiles, metal and dielectric thicknesses, etc. No cost-effective, single-wafer process technology has been found that provides optimized operation for this demanding set of differing requirements.

The best approach to achieve a satisfactory cost-effective optimization of these differing requirements is through the concept of **Hybrid Wafer Scale Integration** (HWSI). Hybrid wafer scale integration (or Wafer Scale Assembly [5]) refers to ways where chips, and all the special support components and devices, can be effectively assembled into a small volume. Hybrid wafer scale integration promises dramatic improvements in system density and performance. Different chips (logic, static and dynamic memory, power regulation) and chip technologies (CMOS, Bipolar, GaAs) can be closely interconnected with specialized interconnect. This approach can surpass the classical wafer scale integration objective of very high percentage of semiconductor usage, since the yield and reliability redundancy built into the wafer scale integration approaches can be circumvented with hybrid wafer scale integration through component test and rework: techniques not readily adopted by wafer scale integration.

The challenges for hybrid wafer scale integration are to cost effectively solve the interconnect, assembly, test, placement, routing, powering and heat removal problems associated with chips densely packaged into a small volume. In past systems it was possible to treat these challenges relatively independently because there was a clear priority of one discipline over the next. With hybrid wafer scale integration all of these disciplines compete equally for attention (signal fidelity, ease of assembly, cooling, powering, etc). The design team has to find efficient ways to span this multi-disciplinary field: Computer aided design tools are essential, and those with the best integrated set of tools will have a significant advantage in the time-to-market race.

The main component of the hybrid wafer scale integration approach is the Multi-Chip Module (MCM). Two objectives must be met for multi-chip modules to find widespread application: time to market and low cost. Time to market will be controlled by the development of fast turn-around-time tools and technologies for the design and fabrication of multi-chip modules. A multi-chip module technology that takes months to years to design, fabricate, assemble and test will not be effective. The lumbering first steps in multi-chip modules that can presently be seen in very costly high end mainframes will be replaced by nimble designs and technology in the hands of workstation and PC manufacturers or their suppliers. A design to manufactured module goal of one or two weeks (or at most a month) is essential for advanced electronics and computers.

The second objective is to find ways to substantially reduce the cost of the multi-chip module technology. This is now becoming recognized as a supply and demand problem. To get low cost requires high volume for the manufacture of multi-chip modules, yet the start up cost of multi-chip module manufacture can be prohibitively high (equivalent to semiconductor manufacturing facilities) such that few will venture into this area until large volumes of customer orders can be foreseen.

We believe that new technology breakthroughs in our laboratory will be one way by which these two main objectives can be met. Our technology has the capability of producing computers that are fast (3 ns cycle time), large (10 million gate) and low cost ($5000). The design to market critical path will be dominated by the design and fabrication cycle of the semi-conductor devices. However, in many applications, existing chip designs will be used in new machine designs. Provided the supply issues associated with these existing chip designs can be solved then multi-chip module design and manufacturing based on our technology can be reduced to less than four weeks. In this time we believe it is possible to go from design start to completed multi-chip module hardware, including chip placement, inter-chip routing, power delivery, cooling technology, chip connection, inter-connect manufacture, sub-part testing, assembly, connectors, sealing and finally, testing.

The remainder of this chapter is organized as follows. We discuss the conventional interconnect structures such as printed circuit board and multi-layer ceramic along with several examples of the very high performance systems using these technologies. We address the need for wafer scale integration and discuss the issues with the classical approach. This is followed by a discussion of the potential of thin film multichip packaging as a hybrid wafer scale integration giving as an example our work in developing copper/polyimide interconnect. We then consider the signal fidelity of thin film interconnect and develop some thoughts on the extension of this technology to smaller linewidths and faster risetimes. We next consider the performance of both the signal and power connections to the chip. Following this we discuss a number of areas of importance including module connectors, cooling technology, thin film reliability, alternate materials for thin film interconnect and the test challenges that hybrid wafer scale integration presents. We conclude with some comments on the availability of the technology.

4.2   Printed Circuit Board Technology

Traditionally Printed-Circuit Boards (PCB) have been used to interconnect chips that are packaged in Single-Chip Packages (SCP). State-of-the-art printed circuit boards can achieve down to 100 μm (4 mil) line widths and pitches. The limits of low cost printed circuit board technology are fast approaching as the interconnect requirements increase, driven by the quest for more and more powerful processors and faster cycle times. The inherent characteristics of how lines and through-board vias are made in printed circuit board technology dictates a relatively large separation between the chips. The relatively large printed circuit board pad pitch means a typical area as large as ten times the chip is required to get the connections to the chip. This reduces the silicon coverage on low cost printed circuit boards to less than 10%.

Printed circuit board technology has been used not only for low end computers, but also in supercomputer applications. The number of metal layers can reach up to 40 in the most advanced applications. The difficulties that advanced printed circuit board technology faces is illustrated with two examples: the Fujitsu M-780 computer and the CDC ETA-10 supercomputer. The first design needed an interconnect for 338 LSI packages each with 180 terminals. It was found necessary to design and manufacture a 42 layer printed circuit board to solve this interconnect problem. The effective interconnect density with this board design is of the order of 315 cm/cm^2 and the resultant board costs over \$10,000 to manufacture [3].

The ETA-10 supercomputer [4,5] is a liquid nitrogen cooled **Very Large**

Scale Integration (VLSI) Complementary Metal-Oxide-Silicon (CMOS) machine which operates at approximately 1000 MFLOPS with a single processor. The processor is contained on a single board. The design uses 240 chips, each with 284 connections, 238 of which are for signals. ETA's solution to the interconnect challenge posed by this array of chips was an advanced printed circuit board technology. The chips are directly mounted onto the printed circuit board ($55\times40\times0.6$ cm^3). The board has 44 conductor layers, 20 of those for signal interconnect, 20 layers for power and ground distribution. The line width is 100 μm and the average line pitch is 0.75 mm yielding an interconnect density of 13 lines per cm per layer and a total interconnect density of 266 cm/cm^2. (The actual line pitch alternates between 0.25 mm and 1.25 mm in order to accommodate the vias through the board.) The board has space for 260 integrated circuits, but only 240 of the sites are occupied. The cycle time is 7 ns at 77K [6]. Again this massive and complex multilayer board costs tens of thousands of dollars to fabricate.

4.3 Wafer Scale Integration

In order to take advantage of the advances in integrated circuit logic designs and reduce the interconnect delays and parasitic effects on signal propagation, it has been proposed to integrate all the functions of a required computing system on a single wafer. Since the devices are physically closer together, the performance is expected to increase because of the shortened signal path lengths. The reliability of the system will increase since a number of non-permanent connections such as pins, connectors, cables, and packages are eliminated. The size and the weight of the system is also reduced. The overall system power requirement is reduced by fewer and lower power signal driving transistors required to drive the shorter signal paths.

These benefits attracted companies such as Trilogy to pursue this interconnection scheme. However, their efforts along with a number of others have been crippled by a number of problems that have proved to be very difficult to overcome. One problem is that a variety of chip types, each with their own unique chip technology, are required for the design of general computers: logic chips, both fast and medium speed, memory such as DRAM, SRAM, together with an expanding arsenal of Application Specific Integrated Circuits (ASICs). A relatively low cost wafer processing technology cannot provide the best of characteristics for each of the differing chip types: a performance, density, cost, yield and reliability compromise has to be made.

A second problem with wafer scale interconnect comes from the resistance and the complexity of the interconnects since many levels of interconnect need to be added to the wafer. These require additional process steps, reducing further the already yield-burdened semiconductor process. Thirdly, the typical narrow and thin metallizations developed for silicon chips have insufficient current handling capability for the long distance communication of power and signals needed with wafer scale integration. The resistive losses have been found to limit the expected performance of wafer scale integration that houses high pin count, high power chips.

There is a niche for this wafer scale integration technology: applications that require a large number of chips with very few chip types (ideally only one) that are interconnected with short, nearest neighbor, chip-to-adjacent-chip connections. Structures that can reorganize around non-functioning chips will be an attractive application for wafer scale integration. Image processing and neural network systems are possible applications that can take advantage of classical wafer scale integration.

4.4   Hybrid Wafer Scale Integration

A more evolutionary interconnection scenario is being adopted where several elements of the computing system are mounted on an intermediate substrate. These smaller, denser, higher performance MultiChip Modules (MCM) are integrated onto a motherboard that requires only a modest level of interconnect. This approach eliminates interconnect levels such as chip packages, sockets, and cables. A good pioneering example of this approach is the thermal conduction module used in the IBM 3090 computer. This liquid cooled MultiLayer Ceramic (MLC) module houses 133 chips that are flip chip attached to the ceramic substrate. Nine thermal conduction modules are mounted on a modest 20 layer motherboard to complete the system. The NEC SX-AP computer adopts its own version of the thermal conduction module which requires a 16 layer motherboard. The wiring density on the second level is reduced to a manageable 32-64 cm/cm^2 [3].

These were the first attempts at replacing single chip packages with multi-chip module, but the thick film multilayer ceramic approach is very costly and limited in performance. The dielectric constant of ceramic is in the order of 8-10 times that of the free space limiting the propagation speed of signals launched across the ceramic module to one third that of the speed of light. The high resistivity of tungsten/molybdenum traces (cf. copper) causes significant attenuation in the signal as it propagates along the line.

The increased integration levels on integrated circuit chips demand ever greater number of layers from the thick film multi-layer ceramic technologies (cf. The number of layers in IBM 3090 Thermal Conduction Module is 33 layers [7]). The increased number of interconnect layers will adversely affect the yield and reliability of the already expensive multi-layer ceramic process. The vias required to interconnect between the many layers become longer and more inductive. The more inductive paths increase the transient noise from switching currents and deleteriously affects the performance of the power and signal distribution networks.

Multi-layer ceramic technology has evolved remarkably; however, limitations such as electrical characteristics at high performance and increased cost to achieve more layers in the multilayer module have led to the development of "thin-film" processes [8]. Over 50 companies and research institutions worldwide are now pursuing thin-film alternatives to multi-layer ceramics.

The most cost effective approach to the hybrid wafer scale integration problem is a thin film interconnect of multilayer copper or aluminum embedded in an organic or inorganic dielectric. Thin-film interconnect refers to a process where the conductors and insulators are fabricated using deposition and patterning techniques similar to those used for fabricating integrated circuit chips. What distinguishes thin film from thick film is the method of deposition of the film. Thin-films are typically 1 to 5 μm thick with metal patterns 5 to 25 μm wide. The metal and dielectric layers are deposited by sputtering, evaporation, chemical vapor deposition, and similar processes. This compares with thick-film processing with 150-200 μm thick ceramic layers [8] patterned with 100-200 μm wide conductors that are deposited by a screen printing process.

The thin film technology can be used to increase the wiring density of chip carrying modules. Similar to the multi-layer ceramic on printed circuit board example, the thin film multi-chip module on printed circuit board allows the number of layers in the printed circuit board motherboard to be reduced since the functionality of the board is now divided into smaller high performance multichip modules. A variety of integrated circuit chips such as logic, memory, or passive elements can be mounted on a single module. In this case, the space demanding, performance limiting, cost and reliability burden single chip carriers are replaced with direct chip-on-module attachments.

4.4.1   Performance Potential of Thin Film Multi-Chip Packaging

The goal is to improve system performance and reliability at reduced cost. Improved chip technologies are an increasingly costly way to improve system performance and density, and they do not address the major reliability factors. The main reliability limiting parts have usually been in the interconnection and packaging of the chips into electronic systems. A substantial improvement in performance and reliability can be achieved with high density chip-on-board packaging. Instead of the chips being inches apart when in single chip packages on printed circuit boards, they can be placed only 0.1 inch apart when directly attached to high density interconnect.

The performance is improved with shorter nets and lower capacitance chip interconnect. Reliability is improved by reducing the number of conductor to conductor bonds needed to connect between chips (chip-to-board rather than chip-to- package and then package-to-board) together with the better control of the bonding processes and overall lower mass systems that are more robust under extremes of temperature variation and mechanical acceleration and vibration.

4.4.2   Copper/Polyimide: An Example of a Thin Film Interconnect Technology

A number of companies are developing process technologies for the manufacture of high density interconnect based on the use of copper or aluminum conductors immersed in polyimide or a similar organic material used as the dielectric. We have developed a copper/polyimide substrate process whose fabrication flow is illustrated in Figures 4.1(a)-(f).

An alumina, silicon, or metal substrate is used as the base substrate material.

(a) A layer of polyimide is coated on the substrate, and mechanically polished to provide a planar and smooth starting surface.

(b) Next the plating interconnect and adhesion layers are sputter deposited on the polyimide surface. Photoresist is coated, exposed, and developed to form the plating mask for pattern plating. Copper electroplating forms the first layer of reference or signal level.

(c) Then, the resist mask for reference or signal layer plating is stripped with wet resist stripper. A thicker layer of resist is coated, exposed, and developed to form the plating mask for pattern plating of copper to form the first pillar layer.

(d) The resist is then stripped and a nickel layer is coated over all copper features to protect copper from oxidation and corrosion.

(e) Polyimide dielectric layer is spin coated over all copper features and fully cured. Partial planarization is achieved through the polyimide coating.

(f) Finally, the mechanical polish is carried out to achieve true planarization and to expose the tops of all the copper pillars at the surface to make contact to the next layer of conductor [9].

In a typical design, the complete copper/polyimide multilayer interconnect consists of two reference layers (ground and a power), two signal layers and a bonding pad layer on the top surface, and four pillar layers to interconnect between the layers. The process steps (b) through (f) are repeated for each layer deposition. For repair and rework of the layers, should this be necessary, the higher layers can be polished away to remove the defective layer.

This patterning process typically achieves lines that are 5 μm thick, 15 μm wide at a pitch of 50 μm. The dielectric layers are 15 μm thick. This stripline geometry has a characteristic impedance of 50 ohms with a loss below 3 ohms per cm. This geometry is ideal for signal connections between chips with well-managed crosstalk for risetimes as fast as 100 ps.

At 50 μm line pitch, a layer pair of interconnect represents 400 cm/cm^2 (1000 in/in^2) of interconnect and is sufficient to satisfy all present wiring requirements. The chips can be attached to the surface by wire-bonding, TAB, flip chip solder or adhesive bonding technology. Figures 4.2 and 4.3 illustrate scanning electron microscope micrographs of pattern plated conductors and pillars, and cross-sectional view of a four layer copper/polyimide interconnect on alumina substrate.

An example of the application of copper/polyimide technology can be seen in the NEC SX2 supercomputer [10,11]. This machine is a water cooled Large Scale Integration (LSI) Emitter Coupled Logic (ECL) machine designed to achieve up to 1,300 MFLOPS. It consists of 12 modules mounted on a printed wiring board (541x457x4.9 mm^3). The board has 8 planes for

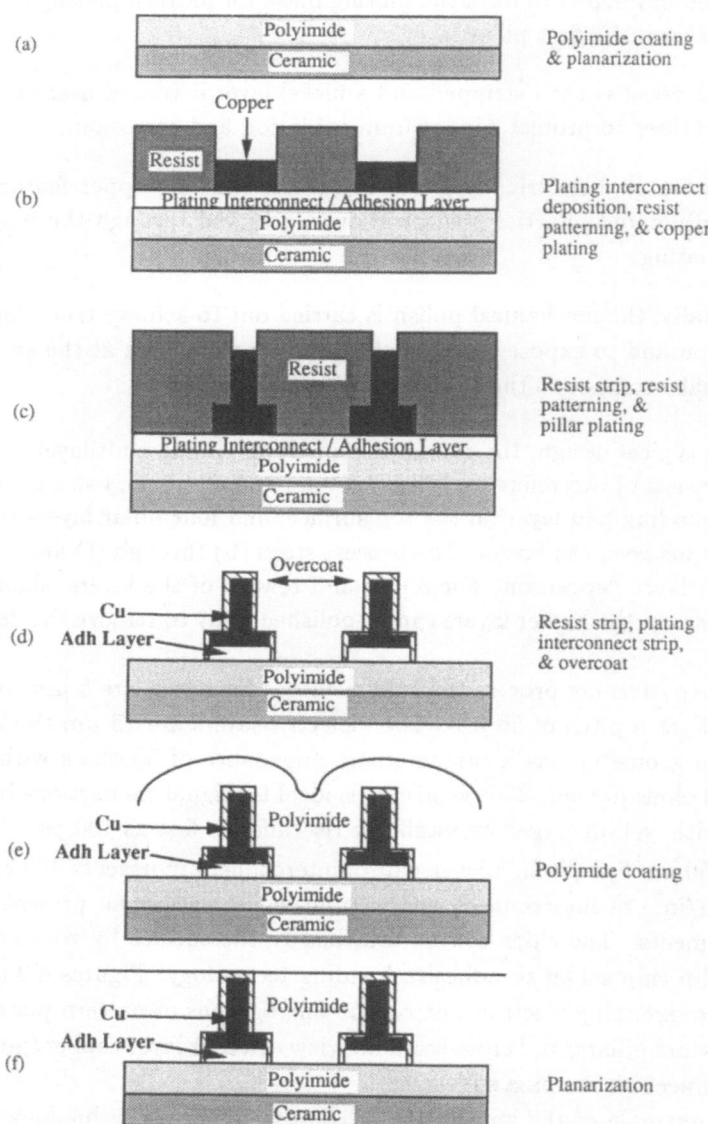

Figure 4.1: Process sequence of the multilayer interconnect fabrication.

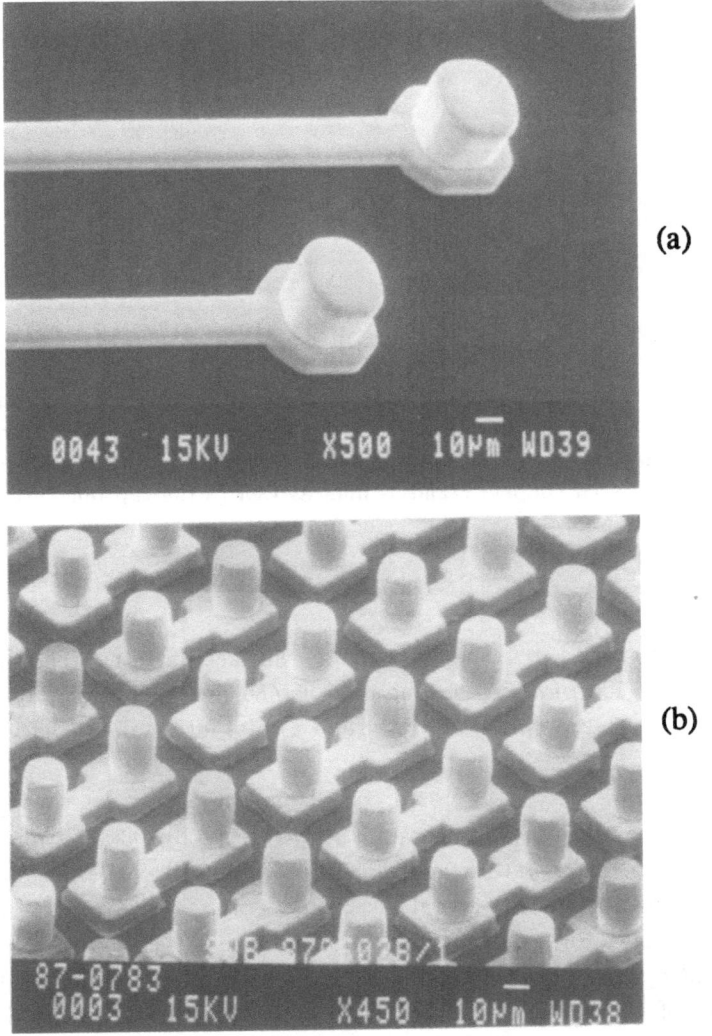

Figure 4.2: SEM micrograph of pattern plated conductors and pillars, (a) two signal lines with pillars, (b) dense array of circular pillars of 15 micron diameter.

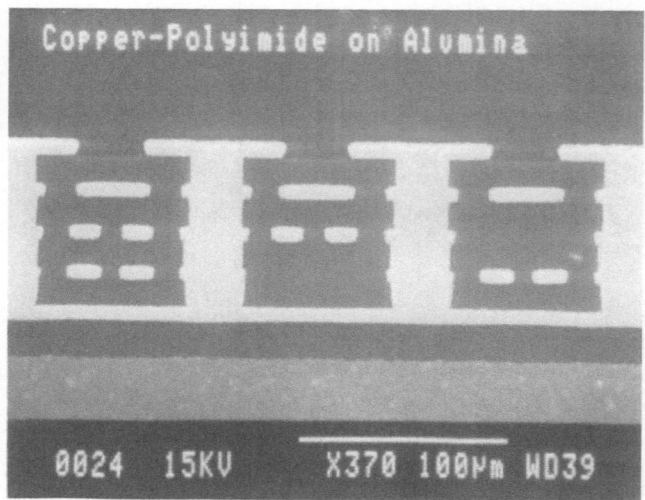

Figure 4.3: Cross-sectional SEM micrograph of a 4 layer copper/polyimide inter-connect on alumina substrate. The stacked pillar structures are fabricated on a reference plane which resides on an adhesion layer on top of an alumina substrate. The nickel coated copper X and Y lines as well as the top reference plane are also demonstrated.

power and ground, 6 for signal and 2 for surface patterns. The line width on board is 100 μm and the line pitch is 485 μm, corresponding to a line density of 21 lines per cm per layer and a total interconnect density of 124 cm/cm^2.

The copper/polyimide liquid cooled multichip modules that plug into this board are based on a ceramic substrate (100x100x2.75 mm^3). The multi-chip modules have several power and ground layers embedded in the ceramic together with 5 metal layers and polyimide on top: 2 for signal interconnect, 2 for ground layers and a top layer for chip attachment. The line width is 25 μm and the line pitch is 75 μm, corresponding to a line density of 133 lines cm/cm^2 per layer and a total interconnect density of 266 cm/cm^2. Each multi-chip module has 36 packaged chips attached to it. Each chip is packaged in flip TAB (Tape Automated Bonding) carrier with 169 I/O's, 128 of which are for signals. There are two sizes of 12x12 mm^2 and 14x14 mm^2. The off-chip driver impedance is about 10 Ω. The gate delay is 250 ps and the resulting clock cycle time is 6 ns. The SX2 chip interconnect is designed to operate in the time-of-flight regime.

4.4.3 Signal Fidelity of Copper/Polyimide Thin Film Multi-Chip Modules

A controlled impedance line structure is necessary to enable propagation of fast signals with a minimum cross-talk. Either a microstrip, stripline, or coaxial transmission line structure can be fabricated in a copper/polyimide interconnect. The conductor geometry and the insulating layer dielectric properties determine the characteristic impedance of the structure.

We find that the signal and power distribution capability of the copper/polyimide interconnect is excellent. For example, Figure 4.4 shows a measurement of signal risetime and crosstalk for long parallel lines. The launched signal has a risetime of approximately 50 ps, which degrades to 150 ps after travelling along 6 cm of a 5×15 μm copper line. The degradation in the risetime and the attenuation of the amplitude are characteristic of the propagation of fast pulses along lossy lines. Most of this degradation comes from the ohmic losses of the line, although a small amount of rounding comes from the skin effect and the protective overcoat of Ni.

To evaluate the performance of lossy interconnect we conservatively define the delay as the time it takes the signal to reach 90% of the input step amplitude at an open termination. There are a number of criteria that decide the method and impedance of the termination of the off-chip signal net such as reflections, net topology, resources for termination (where the resistors are), or active versus passive termination. For this simplified study we assumed an approach, that is increasingly being used for high performance systems, to not terminate the net, but rather leave it open.

We assume a high impedance open termination where the signal amplitude will be doubled by the reflection at the end. This follows from equations (4.1) and (4.2),

$$\rho = \frac{Z_L - Z_o}{Z_L + Z_o} \tag{4.1}$$

$$V_r = V_i(1 + \rho) \tag{4.2}$$

where, ρ is the reflection coefficient, Z_L is the load impedance, Z_o is the line characteristic impedance, V_r is the reflected signal voltage amplitude, and V_i is the incident signal amplitude. The signal in a well designed systems is established after a single time-of-flight. An open termination yields a steady-state signal voltage independent of the lossy line length together with the advantage of zero remote power dissipation. A matched termination would result in different steady-state voltages for different lengths of lossy line and the matching criterion dependent on lossy net length. If the

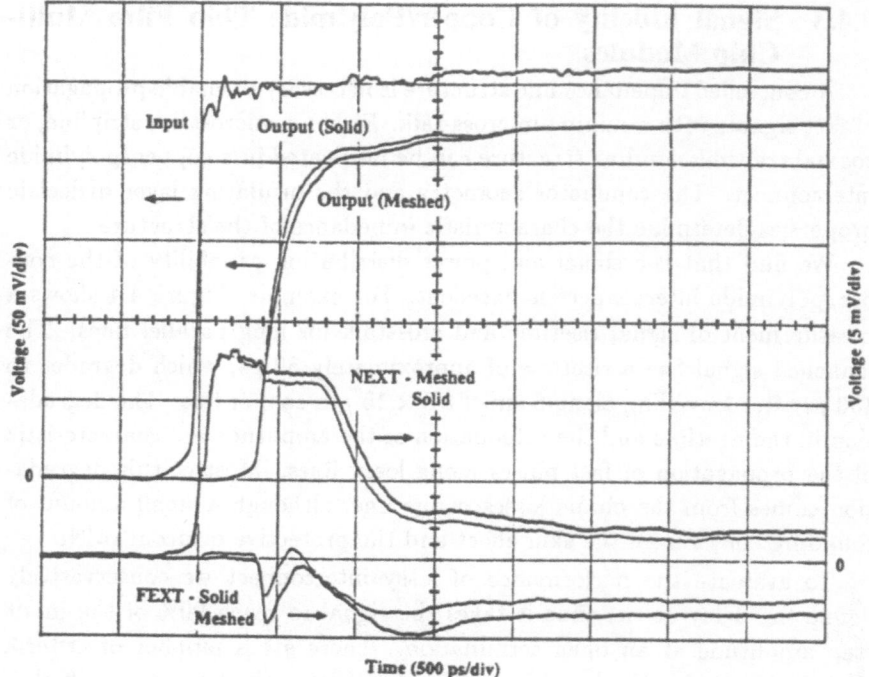

Figure 4.4: A comparison of crosstalk between two 6 cm long 50 Ω terminated microstrip lines on meshed and solid ground planes. FEXT is the far end crosstalk, and NEXT is the near end crosstalk. The tails of NEXT and FEXT traces are due to the ground loop in the probes. FEXT and NEXT are in 10X scale.

interconnect is to be operated in the time-of-flight regime, it is preferable to have a matching termination at the source which will eliminate long term reflections bouncing back and forth.

We have used a relatively simple approach to study the scaling of copper/polyimide multi-chip module interconnect. We assume the thickness of the interconnect line is half of the line width. The thickness of the dielectric can be chosen so as to yield $Z_o = 50\Omega$, which for polyimide with $\epsilon = 3.5$ yields a thickness of approximately 1.14 times the line thickness. This yields a propagation speed of $v = 1/\sqrt{LC} = c/\sqrt{\epsilon}$ of 1.6×10^8 m/s for the propagation of electro-magnetic waves along the lines giving a time-of-flight delay of 62 ps/cm, assuming a TEM mode. The capacitance per unit length is $1/vZ_0 = 1.25$ pF/cm.

To evaluate the pulse performance of this interconnect, we assume the driver is a voltage source of 1V amplitude with a rise time which equals

10% of the time-of-flight for the line length under consideration. We use this definition since we wish to explore the pulse propagation limits. As we develop our argument, it is readily apparent that this is also reasonable way to model the charging of a "capacitance load" representation of the line suitable for CMOS circuits.

As depicted in Figure 4.5, two different regions describe the received pulse: the first region is a fast rising edge corresponding to the time of flight propagation of the signal step along the lossy line. The amplitude of this step decreases exponentially with length of the line.

We define V_1 as the voltage reached on the first hit.

$$V_1 = \left[\frac{2Z_o}{R_s + Z_o}\right] \, exp \left(\frac{R}{2Z_o}\right) \tag{4.3}$$

with the DC resistance given by

$$R = \frac{2rd}{w^2}$$

where

> r is the line resistivity,
> d is the line length,
> w is the line width.

The time-of-flight regime is defined as the regime where this voltage V_1 is greater than or equal to 90% of the input signal. The second region is a long slow rise (RC-like tail) where the signal finally charges up to the launched voltage.

The exact behavior and number of back-and-forth reflections depends on the line losses, line length, and the source impedance compared with the line characteristic impedance.

We find that the skin effect rounds off the transition between the two regions. At signal threshold levels set at 90% of the step, there is less than 15% difference between the propagation without skin effect to that with skin effect. The skin depth scales as the square root of the resistivity. The skin effect increases in importance when the skin depth is small compared to the line size. Equation (4.4) shows the high frequency skin impedance per unit length for a given interconnect.

$$Z_{sn} = G\sqrt{\frac{j\omega\mu}{\sigma}} \coth \sqrt{j\omega\mu\sigma}GWt \tag{4.4}$$

where

> G is geometric factor, $G \approx 0.05 \, (\mu m^{-1})$ for nominal geometry,

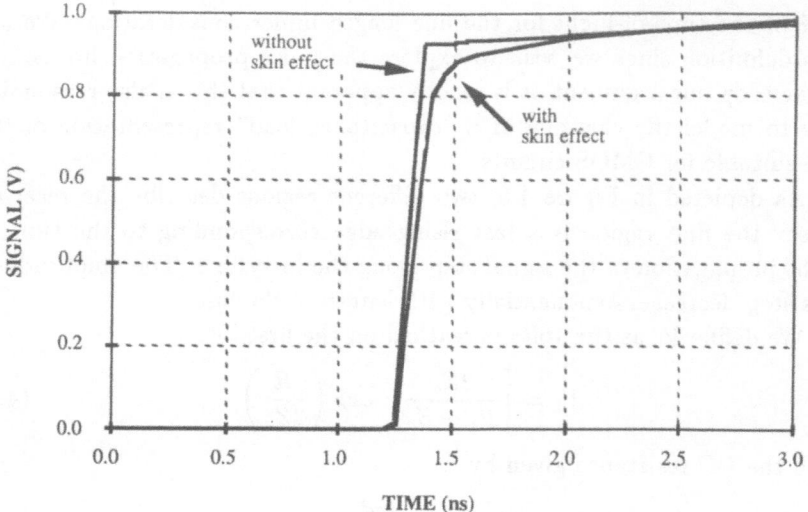

Figure 4.5: SPICE results for 10×5 μm^2, 20-cm-long copper line at 77 Kelvins showing signal voltage across 1 MΩ load resistor. The skin effect is of secondary importance as far as the absolute delay is concerned. It only rounds the signal step due to the frequency-dependent attenuation of the line.

> ω is 2π times the frequency,
> μ is permeability of material,
> σ is electrical conductivity of the conductor,
> W is the width of the conductor,
> t is the thickness of the conductor.

which approximates to $R_{sn} = G/\sigma\delta$ as $\omega \to \infty$. Here R_{sn} is the skin resistance and $\delta = \sqrt{2/\omega\mu\sigma}$ is the skin depth [24].

Consequently we find that the skin effect becomes less important as we scale to smaller lines, remain at relatively high temperatures (> 300K) and use normal conductors (Cu, Al, etc). We have concluded that the skin effect can safely be disregarded for small line digital applications at or above 77K without risk of major error [13,14].

From these studies we conclude that the copper/polyimide interconnect structure has excellent high frequency characteristics. Signals with edge rates as fast as 100 ps can be launched over a fairly long distance (5-10 cm) without significant degradation. The transmission line medium for wave propagation provided by multiple metal layers creates a matched impedance environment where signal reflections are minimized. Although the copper lines are lossy and there is some attenuation together with waveform rounding from the skin effect we find that the copper/polyimide structures can be operated well into the GHz clock rate regime.

4.4.4 Off-Chip Interconnection with TAB, Wire Bond, or Flip Chip

Usually the poorest link for signal fidelity is at the connection from the chip to the interconnect. The problem is the mutual coupling between adjacent lines and not the impedance discontinuity represented by the short TAB or wire bond leads.

Consider the three bonding technologies:

1. Flip chip bonding offers the shortest interconnect lengths, and highest signal fidelity. The mutual coupling between the interconnects is small due to very short electrical paths. An example of its use with copper/polyimide substrate is in a Toshiba Corp. image processing module. Sixteen silicon chips are flip chip bonded to the module. The 150 μm diameter copper cored solder bumps with a minimum pitch of 180 μm are formed on the chips initially, and the ICs are in turn bonded to the copper/polyimide substrate [15].

   Flip chip bonding allows a large number of bonding pads on the integrated circuit since they are not restricted to the periphery of the chips. Another advantage is the integrated circuit bonding area under the chip is equal in area to the integrated circuit, allowing chips to be placed side by side with very little gap, thereby maximizing the ratio of the silicon coverage on the multi-chip module. The area of this module is equal to $\leq 20\%$ of conventional dual in line packages placed on printed circuit board. Issues such as testability, rework, alignment, and more expensive cooling technologies associated with flip chip bonding, have made wire bonding and TAB technology more appealing.

2. Wire bonds introduce a transmission discontinuity for the signals traversing the integrated circuit boundary. The inductance of thin wires, of diameter 0.025-0.032 mm (0.001-0.00125 in) and length 1.9-2.5 mm (0.075-0.100 in), is of the order of 2 nH. Wire Bonding can be done down to a wiring pitch of 0.1 mm (0.0045 in). The inductive mutual coupling between the wires is significant (1 nH cumulative mutual inductance and 1 pF of mutual capacitance). The inductance terms scale logarithmically with distance and so their coupling values

do not drop very rapidly as one moves away from a signal line. It is necessary to have ground wires placed among every few signal wires in order to keep the crosstalk within reasonable bounds.

3. TAB offers a denser and lower resistance interconnect compared to wire bonding (larger cross section Cu cf. Al wire). We have developed TAB processes for peripheral bond pads down to 0.05 mm (0.002 in,) wide on a 0.10 mm pitch (0.004 in.). The connection length from chip to thin film interconnect can be reduced to less than 1.27 mm (0.050 in) by maintaining the outer lead bonding pitch the same as the inner lead bonding pitch. A flip (face down) TAB in contrast to face up TAB bonding reduces the interconnect lengths even further. Figures 4.6 and 4.7 illustrate a top view of a customized copper/polyimide substrate with bonding pads laid out for 6 devices and a micrograph of four devices TAB bonded to the substrate.

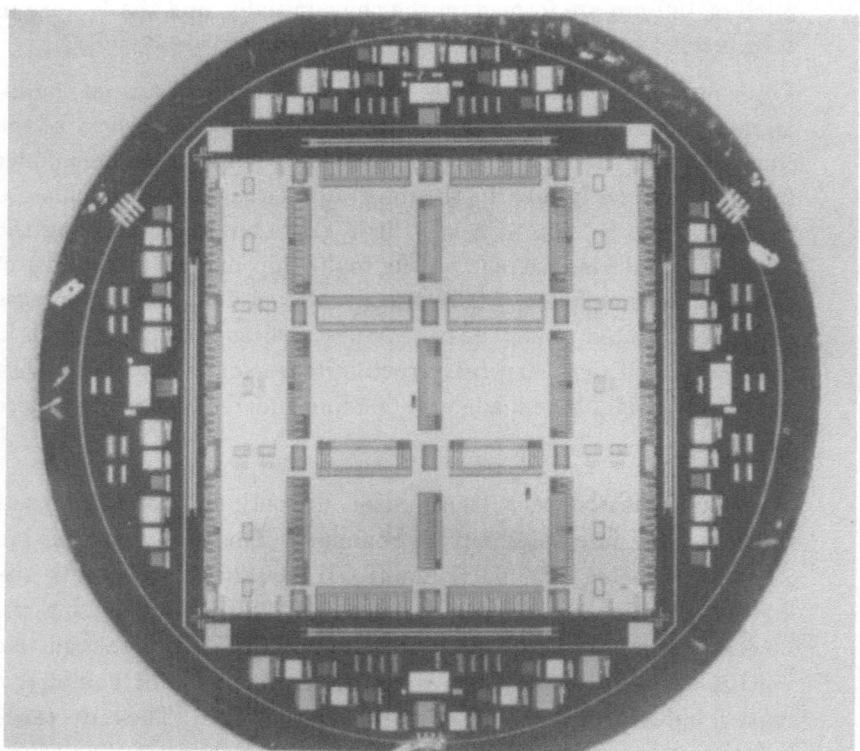

Figure 4.6: Top view of the bonding layer of a copper/polyimide substrate.

The more controlled spacing between adjacent leads (due mainly to a narrow 0.05 mm thick polyimide support ring) together with the shorter lead capability gives TAB a significant performance advantage over wire bonding. TAB is an excellent chip connection technology for high performance systems characterized by off-chip edge rates greater than 60 ps. For example, consider a TAB lead with a typical inductance $L = 1000\ pH$ inserted into a matched system with characteristic impedance $Z_o = 50\ \Omega$. Under these conditions the signal will not be distorted if its rise time $T_r \gg 3 \times T_d \approx 60$ ps, and will be delayed through the TAB lead by $T_d = L/Z_o = 20\text{ps}$.

The coupling between signal I/O, by either mutual inductance between leads (matched terminated line case) or mutual capacitance between leads (open terminated line) can be reduced using shorter line lengths and smaller signal to ground ratios. This may demand more off-chip pads. Alternatively, a two metal layer (groundplane) TAB tape with a lower impedance (i.e. lower inductance) can be used.

We find that the groundplane tape is preferable for high speed systems where a fanout or radial trace pattern is needed as a "space transformer" for connecting the chip to the relatively coarse feature sizes of conventional PCB's. However, with high speed systems based on higher density interconnections such as copper/polyimide, the outer lead bond pitch can be

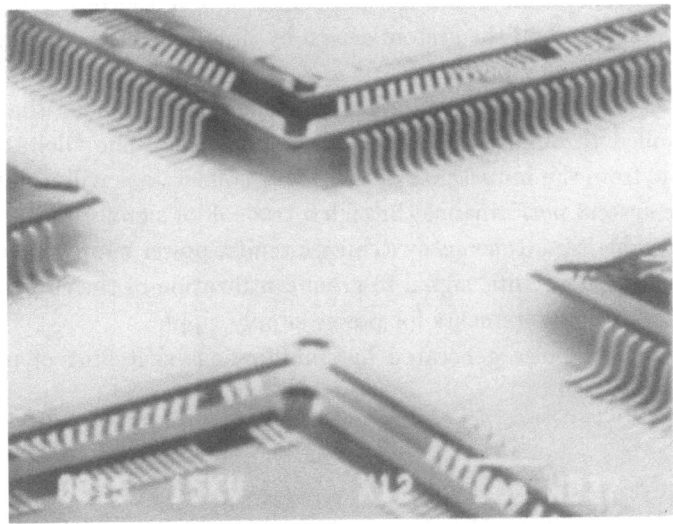

Figure 4.7: High I/O devices TAB bonded to a copper/polyimide substrate.

the same as the inner lead bond pitch, thus the controlled impedance environment provided by a two metal layer TAB tape is not required [16]. The very short interconnect length made possible by this technology combination (TAB on copper/polyimide substrate) permits interconnection of state of the art logic families with switching rates above 1 GHz with edge rates below 100 ps.

4.4.5 Termination of Signal Nets

The copper/polyimide hybrid wafer scale integration approach can be modified where off-chip termination of signal nets is required. Termination resistors may be needed to minimize the signal reflections and achieve acceptable signal fidelity. For instance, ECL typically requires a 50 Ω system matched with far-end termination. The copper/polyimide interconnect technology offers the possibility of fabricating active and passive devices in either the metal layers of the interconnect or in the carrier substrate. For example, Gigabit Logic has fabricated diffused termination resistors and reverse biased p-n junction decoupling capacitors in a silicon substrate used in a single chip GaAs package [4].

4.5 Power

We have seen that the main performance limiting links in the communications chain from chip-to-chip are associated with the impedance discontinuities of the connections to the chip. However, it is not the signal risetime or fidelity that limits the performance, but the power regulation requirements placed on the system design by simultaneous switching events that take place during operation.

Off-chip driving signals require sudden surges of current that are to to be supplied through the power leads to the chip. The "delta-I noise" that results from the inductance of the power connections will usually limit achievable system performance through a tradeoff of signal risetimes, number of allowable simultaneous switching circuits, power supply bounce tolerance of internal circuits, signal to ground utilization of the chip I/O, and critical damping requirements for power supply ripple.

The transient noise generated by simultaneous switching of n output drivers is expressed by

$$\delta v = \frac{Ln\delta i}{\delta t} \tag{4.5}$$

where

δv is the amplitude of noise,

L is the inductance of interconnect,

δi is the current demand per driver at the time of switching,

δt is the rise (fall) time of the signal.

This transient noise needs to be handled rapidly. Assuming that a series RLC circuit that represents the network components between the current demanding chip and current supplying bypass capacitor, the parameters of this RLC network need to be optimized to critically damp the induced noise. The value of the bypass capacitor in this case has to be $\geq 4L/(R/n)^2$, where L is the interconnect inductance plus the capacitor self inductance, and R is impedance of one output driver at the time of switching. The amplitude of the initial noise needs to be minimized by reducing the interconnect inductance, and the duration of oscillation needs to be damped out before the next edge (clock) arrives. In addition, the bypass capacitor needs to have a very low self inductance so that its resonant frequency is greater than the highest frequency associated with the signal edge rate.

These problems can be ameliorated in copper/polyimide substrate technology by including thin film decoupling capacitors in the interconnect or in a silicon carrier substrate. The location of the decoupling capacitor compared with the inductance of the interconnect between the chip and the power plane, along with the self inductance of the capacitor are the two most important parameters concerning the suppression of delta-I noise.

AT&T has fabricated a large area decoupling capacitor in their advanced very large scale integration Packaging (AVP) system [4]. We have developed assembly techniques to closely-attach thin film de-coupling capacitors in the vicinity of the chip. We find this in association with low impedance power planes in the copper/polyimide interconnect provides adequate control of the delta-I noise problem for off-chip signal risetimes above 200 ps. Below 200 ps, on-chip regulation and complementary driving techniques will be needed for higher inductance chip interconnect techniques such as TAB or wire bonds.

4.6   Connectors From Multi-Chip Module to Board

Multichip substrates require several thousand interconnects to the next higher level in a packaged system. The present state-of-the art connector has approximately 2000 I/O for a 100 chip substrate of about 100 cm^2 (16 in^2) in area. For example, 2177 brazed pins are used in each processor multi-chip module of the NEC-SX2 supercomputer. Connectors are needed that will transmit signals with with very fast rise times and keep crosstalk magnitudes between neighboring lines low compared to the threshold characteristics of the off-chip driver-receiver circuits.

Conventional connector technologies are not easily adapted for use with high density copper/polyimide multi-chip module. A low cost connector is needed that will allow off-substrate edge rates of the order of 200 ps with minimized crosstalk ($\leq$ 5%-10% cumulative) with a connection density of 160 contacts/cm^2 (1000 contact/in^2).

One approach is to use a multiple layer controlled impedance flexible tape. This high density, high performance connector is an extension of TAB tape technology with the addition of raised vias in the form of gold plated pads that are used for a demountable connection at one end. The other end of the tape can be permanently attached to a substrate by thermosonic or laser bonding. Figure 4.8 illustrates a connector that has 80 connections per centimeter and can be fabricated in a tape format with sections that are 5 cm or longer.

Figure 4.8: High density connector based on a multiple layer flexible tape. Upper and lower parts of the connector are illustrated to depict the miniature conductor features. The gold plated raised pads are designed in the upper section of the connector which through pressure contact mounts on the lower section and provides electrical interconnection.

The electrical connection between the copper-polyimide tape and the substrate, whether permanent by thermosonic bonding or demountable by pressure contact must survive a variety of environmental tests. The bond strength at a 0.12 mm (0.005 in) effective bonding pitch with a thermosonic single point bonding process with gold/gold interface has yielded pull tests with an average force of 20 grams per contact.

The high frequency properties of this tape connector have been characterized by time domain reflectometry and transmission line techniques. The designed tape incorporated a microstrip transmission line geometry where 50 μm wide, 18 μm thick patterns were separated from the ground plane by a 50 μm thick layer of polyimide. The characteristic impedance of this configuration was measured to be 69 ± 5 Ω. We have observed less than 10% cumulative crosstalk for active line edge transitions as fast as 100 picoseconds. The results indicate that the microstrip trace array geometry is suitable for a wide variety of high speed signal applications in addition to just a connection from multi-chip module to the next level of the package.

4.7 Thermal Issues

The high density interconnect capability of copper/polyimide interconnect technology allows a compact electronic assembly, but the heat generated from high power chips mounted within small area could be prohibitive. The quest for high speeds has increased the power dissipation levels of the state-of-the-art chips: Removing that heat to enable the operating temperature of the system to remain within safe limits requires a careful thermal design.

Individual CMOS chips produce 1-2 W/cm^2, and state of the art ECL chips produce as much as 35-40 W/cm^2. The power density can go higher, for example, at an integration level of 32000 gates per 1 cm^2 die with 5 mW of heat generated per gate, an overall dissipation level of 160 W/cm^2 might be expected. On the other hand, board power density for conventional printed wiring boards such as the one used in the Apple computer is about 0.10-0.15 W/cm^2. The IBM thermal conduction module which contains 100 chips in an area of 81 cm^2 provides a heat dissipation of approximately 500 W or 6 W/cm^2 [8], while Trilogy was expecting 12.4 W/cm^2 using wafer scale integration [5].

The lowest cost heat removal method that satisfies these goals needs to be designed: The device temperature must be maintained below maximum allowable limits while allowing the reliability goals to be achieved (typically

≤ 55 °K above ambient). The heat transfer mechanism should be reliable and designed to allow the system to be exposed to a variety of operating environments. The designed heat transfer mechanism may have to meet acoustic noise limits (e.g. ≤ 50 dBA for office environment), weight and volume limits, hermeticity and many other criteria that depend on the cooling medium and the technology used.

In general, there are two paths for cooling a chip on a multi-chip module, either through the substrate or away from the substrate from the back of the chips. For through-substrate cooling, the chips are typically wire or TAB bonded in a face-up orientation. The thermal path to the heat exchanger includes the chip, the chip-to-substrate interface, the interconnect multilayer structure, the substrate-to-heat-sink interface, and the heat-sink. On the other hand, for face-down TAB bonded or flip-chip attached chips, the heat transfer includes the chip, the chip to heat sink interface, and heat sink. Both techniques have advantages and disadvantages.

The advantage of backside cooling is the more direct, potentially shorter, thermal path. However, the thermal interface between the chip and the heat sink is difficult to design since it has to be thermally efficient while maintaining contact between a heat exchanger and the chip's back surface. This contact problem needs to account for assembly tolerances as well as changes in usage, but it is less severe if one heat exchanger is dedicated to each chip. The heat sinks have to be structurally supported, which in the case of one heat exchanger per chip requires a complicated design and assembly. If hermeticity is required, the design becomes even more complicated. In summary, backside cooling is difficult to design. However, a well-designed structure can solve these problems, and backside cooling may be necessary to achieve thermal performance expectations for high power modules (i.e. ≤ 60 W/cm^2 of chip or substrate area).

Through-substrate cooling is simpler, and offers hermeticity and ease of repair, but it also has its share of concerns, namely, a more complicated fabrication process to include thermal vias in the design, and it usually yields a higher thermal resistance path to that of direct backside cooling.

We have found that without thermal vias the limit on cooling through substrate is about 6 W/cm^2 of silicon chip area for both force air and liquid conduction cooling. This limit is based on conduction resistance of the copper/polyimide interconnect layers without assuming thermal spreading. The substrate thermal performance is dominated by the "sea of polyimide" in the copper/polyimide multilayer structure (K of Pi $\leq 1/2500$ K of Cu).

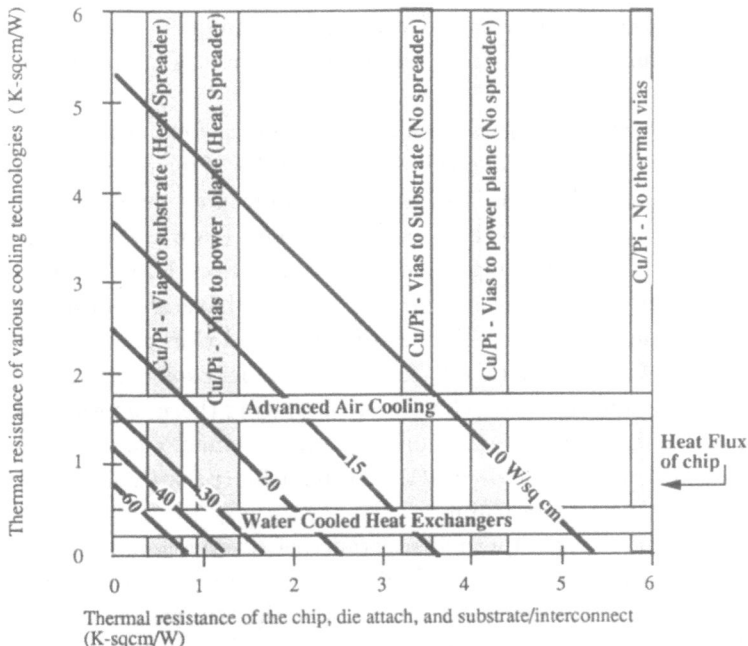

Figure 4.9: First-order upper and lower bounds of through substrate cooling for copper/polyimide substrate with and without thermal vias. Thermal vias are made of copper. No spreading in the signal or power/ground planes is considered for any of the calculations. The die attach used is 50 μm of thermal epoxy. Acceptable solutions lie within the triangle created by two axes and the heat flux lines.

The cooling limit can be further improved to 10 and 15 W/cm² of chip area for air and liquid cooling, respectively, if 8-10% of the substrate area is allocated to thermal vias. The via diameter can range from 30-100 μm diameter copper pillars on 75-200 μm pitches. If these vias are used in conjunction with a 5-10 μm thick copper heat spreader in the bonding layer, or a 50 μm thick high conductivity die attach (thermal conductivity ≤ 0.02 W/cm°K), these cooling limits can be extended to 20 and 30 W/cm² for the same air and liquid cooling technologies, respectively.

For higher performance through-substrate cooling, we recommend extending the thermal vias through the smoothing layer between the interconnect and the supporting substrate. Chip power densities of the order of 40-60 W/cm² (per chip area) for liquid cooling and about 25 W/cm² for air cooling can be successfully cooled with these techniques. For higher power densities, cooling from the chip backside away from the interconnect has to be used.

Compact heat exchangers have been developed for both backside-chip and through-substrate cooling [19]. The principles of microlaminar heat exchange design have been used to develop advanced air cooling techniques, which can be used to cool as high as 25-30 W/cm^2 (chip area). The thermal resistance of these air cooling technologies range from 1.25 - 1.8 K-cm^2/W for heat exchanger volumes below 5 cm^3. We have also developed microchannel liquid cooling techniques that can cool chip power densities as high as 40-60 W/cm^2. With a 1 cm^2 microchannel cooler we have lowered the pressure loss by a factor of 3 without sacrificing thermal performance as compared to Tuckerman-Pease's original microchannel coolers [20]. Thermal resistances of 0.2-0.5 K-cm^2/W can be achieved with reasonable cost and system pumping constraints.

Figure 4.9 illustrates thermal resistance of several cooling technologies vs. thermal resistance in (K-cm^2/W) of the chip, die attach, and substrate/interconnect (K-cm^2/W) for a copper/polyimide interconnect design. The total thermal resistance is split into two components for different thermal designs: the thermal resistance of the compact heat exchanger and thermal resistance from the chip, through the die attach, copper/polyimide interconnect, silicon substrate, and heat exchange attach. Thermal epoxy is assumed to be used to attach the heat exchanger directly to the back of the substrate. For a given chip heat flux, the heavy lines represent the maximum total thermal resistance from chip to cooling fluid that limits the chip temperature rise to 55 °C above the fluid temperature. Intersections of the heat exchanger resistance and the path resistance to the heat exchanger that lie beneath a heavy diagonal line toward the origin are capable of meeting the temperature restriction for that chip heat flux. From the figure one can assess the through substrate cooling limit for different systems.

4.8   Thin Film Hybrid Wafer Scale Integration Reliability

As the intermediate interconnection levels, such as packages, pins, sockets, and cables are deleted in a copper/polyimide chip on board approach we can expect substantial improvements in the reliability of the packaged system. This is being explored in a number of companies.

As we remove one source of poor reliability, we potentially can add new ones. For example, most polyimides absorb a significant amount of water and this moisture absorption affects both the substrate process and its long term reliability. Further, the coefficient of thermal expansion mismatch between the polyimide and copper features as well as between the polyimide and substrate generate high shear stresses. So the selection of a low expansion rate, low moisture absorbing polyimide and the use of precautionary steps in baking the moisture out of polyimide are essential to obtain a reliable process. In addition, we find that the copper features need to be nickel plated in order to protect them from the corrosive medium introduced by moist polyimide.

The usual procedure for establishing the reliability of a process is to expose a statistically significant number of samples to several forms of environmental stress. The number of reported HWSI multi-chip modules undergoing stress tests is still rather small: most have been developed at laboratory levels. There is no historical record for hybrid wafer scale integration multi-chip modules, so it is difficult to establish absolute reliability figures for this process at present.

The critical part of characterizing the multilayer interconnect is to determine whether environmental stresses cause degradation on either electrical or physical/mechanical properties. In our labs, we have recently stressed a group of 81 copper/polyimide substrates. They have been exposed to five different stress tests and no test related failures have been detected. These tests include:

1. Temperature Cycling according to MIL-STD-883C, 10 minute dwell at -65°C and 10 minute dwell at 150°C;

2. Autoclave-Accelerated Aging, where the parts are exposed for relatively long durations to 121°C, 15 psig steam atmosphere with 97% to 99.9% RH;

3. Moisture Resistance, which consists of successive exposure to temperature and humidity variations (-10°C to 65°C with humidity 80-100% RH);

4. Liquid to Liquid Thermal Shock which is a successive cycle of immersion in hot bath of FC70 at 150°C for 5 minutes, followed by immersion in a cold bath of FC77 at -65°C for 5 minutes; and

5. 85/85 Temperature/Humidity Bias Test which consists of exposure to 85°C and 85% RH atmosphere while circuits are electrically biased.

The testing scheme is such that the material is subjected to one or more (sequential) environmental stresses. At specified readpoints, the substrates were evaluated for various possible changes. We analyze the DC electrical test results for opens and shorts and significant parametric shifts. In addition, we have biased the copper/polyimide interconnect and monitored the performance during the tests. At the last readpoint, the wafers are evaluated for their high frequency characteristics and compared with starting conditions.

No test related failures in copper/polyimide substrates have been found after 1500 hours of temperature cycling, 384 hours of autoclave, 116 cycles of moisture resistance, 500 cycles of liquid-to-liquid thermal shock, and 1000 hours of biased 85/85 testing. DC electrical tests performed at each readpoint indicate less than a 1% shift in resistance occurs for via and serpentine test structures. The built-in capacitors in the copper/polyimide substrate exhibited an increase in capacitance when wafers were exposed to the Autoclave and moisture resistance tests. This was related to absorption of water at the surface. The changes observed in the high frequency characteristics before and after moisture resistance, air-to-air temperature cycling, and autoclave were very small. Figure 4.10 illustrates the changes in attenuation characteristics of a 6 cm line after it was subjected to moisture

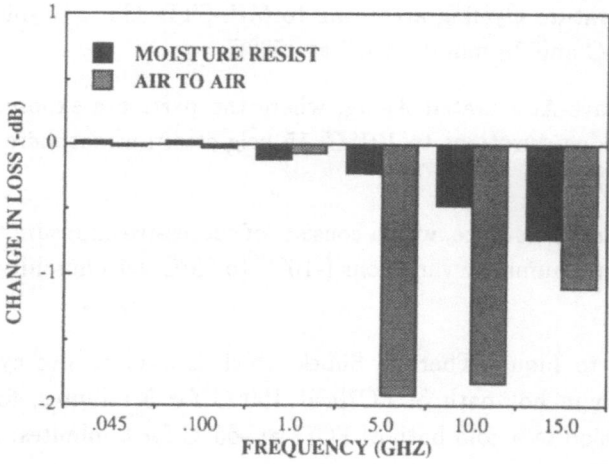

Figure 4.10: **Changes in the attenuation characteristics of the 6 cm copper lines after moisture resistance and air-air temperature cycling.**

resistance and air-to-air temperature cycling. The line showed an added loss of approximately 2 dB between 5 GHz and 10 GHz.

The integrity of the other components required for a thin film multi-chip module with TAB'd or wire bonded devices has been independently established. The gold bumps plated on ICs, inner lead bond and outer lead bond TAB bonds, or wire bonded chip to boards have also been individually (environmentally) tested. Similar to the copper/polyimide process, reliability data was obtained for these integral components of the technology, with the difference that the samples prepared for establishing the wafer bumping and TAB reliability were orders of magnitude greater than the numbers tested to date for the copper/polyimide wafers.

In summary, these results so far promise excellent mechanical integrity and long term reliability for this approach to multi-chip packaging where we use encapsulated and silicon nitride passivated integrated circuit chips bonded with TAB to a high density hybrid wafer scale integration multi-chip module fabricated of nickel overcoated copper interconnect in polyimide on either silicon or ceramic substrates.

4.9 Alternate Materials and Processes for Hybrid Wafer Scale Integration

The copper/polyimide process that we have described uses a fully planarized pillar approach for the multilayer fabrication, (Hitachi L110) low temperate coefficient of expansion polyimide as the primary dielectric material, alumina ceramics as the primary base material, and self-aligned electroplated nickel as the copper overcoat. There are alternate materials and processes that we expect will simplify the process, reduce the processing cost, and improve the substrate performance.

Material vendors are constantly working on improving materials and creating new dielectrics. We have successfully polished dielectrics such as BCB of Dow Chemical and Parylene of Union Carbide. The biggest concern with many new material is the high temperate coefficient of expansion values which result in high film stresses [9].

The choice of dielectric material can substantially affect the overall process. A dielectric that has good adhesion to copper and has a low water absorption would eliminate the need for any overcoat and hence simplify the process. Alternatively, a photo-imagable dielectric can be applied after conductor level patterning to define the vias. If successfully implemented, this would eliminate the need for polish planarization and thus simplify the process. There are, however, two primary concerns with this class of materials. First is the low aspect ratio of the dielectric thickness to via diameter that can be obtained. The second concern is the high temperate coefficient of expansion for photoimagable materials that are generally an order of magnitude higher than the baseline polyimide being used.

The base material of a thin film copper/polyimide substrate may also vary depending on the process and its end use application. Silicon and ceramic alumina are the most generally used base materials. The stresses induced by the mismatch between the thermal coefficient expansion of (copper/polyimide) multilayered features and the base material, its thermal conductivity as well as electrical and mechanical properties determine which base material is used. Silicon substrates have been used by Rockwell international in developing a 1750A multi-chip module using Polycon's aluminum/polyimide substrate process. In this work the multi-chip module was packaged in an aluminum nitride package. The excellent thermal conductivity of the aluminum nitride provides for efficient heat removal and is particularly important for avionic applications where cooling is by lateral conduction to cooled "side rails" in the electronics box. Thermal conductivity depends on purity, particularly oxygen content. The low expansion rate of aluminum nitride (2.1 ppm/°C at -55°C to 3.8 ppm/°C at 125°C) is very close to that of silicon at 3 ppm/°C [17]. With smaller grain size and uniformity, good heat conduction and favorable temperate coefficient of expansion, silicon carbide (SiC) and aluminum nitride are more suitable than alumina ceramic for the interconnect base substrate.

However, aluminum nitride has it own share of problems that need to be addressed. Good adhesion of films to aluminum nitride is a problem which is probably due to the formation of weak aluminum hydroxide at the surface. Toshiba recommends its customers re-fire aluminum nitride in oxygen to make a dense oxide coating that can be reliably adhered to. The thermal conductivity of aluminum nitride varies from lot to lot. SiC has variations in electrical insulation resistance. It has a high dielectric constant and it needs to be coated with polyimide or silica before the film circuits can be deposited, but it appears that the roughness of SiC can cause pinholes in the coatings [17,18].

4.10   Test

Testing is a major bottleneck to design and produce low cost systems. Test methods and test technology solutions are needed. Hybrid wafer scale integration has a significant advantage over wafer scale integration in that the single chips and the interconnect can be independently tested prior to assembly: Good chips can be attached to good interconnect.

This highlights one of the main advantages of TAB technology versus wire bonding or C4 (controlled collapse chip connection – flip chip). The convenient TAB format allows high speed chip testing as well as safe chip shipping from semiconductor manufacturer to assembly house. The 35 or 70 mm tape frame used to attach the bonding leads to the chips is patterned to fanout the connections to a larger footprint to enable convenient probing for chip on tape testing. This "space transformer" is very important particularly for high lead count chips where the I/O pads have $\leq 100\mu m$ pitch. Probing of single die or wafers at these dimensions with controlled impedance high performance probes is very difficult, time consuming, and costly. In contrast, Chip On Tape (COT) testing is relatively straightforward with COT down to risetimes as fast as 100 to 200 ps. Below these risetimes, special design guidelines need to be followed for the space transformer fanout on the tape. Another advantage of COT is that neither the die pads themselves nor the outer lead bond locations are probed and therefore are not damaged by the probes, so that subsequent bonding yield is not adversely affected.

Testing the high density interconnect before chips are attached presents some new problems. The high density of interconnections and the relatively small bonding pads (e.g. 50×150 μm) means that new, high-precision shorts and open test tools have to be developed. Consider a multi-chip module interconnect substrate that has 5000 nets (a typical number). To exhaustively test for any shorts and opens requires approximately $0.5 \times 5000 \times 5000$ resistance measurements. If each of the 10 million tests can be done in 1 second it will take nearly three hours to test each hybrid wafer scale integration substrate, which will be too costly on a relatively expensive tester (say \$100,000 + operator costs). We have to find testing methods that can reduce the time per test to at least 100 ms and preferably 1 ms.

One tool that is being used is a capacitance tester [21] which can be used to probe each pad and measure the net capacitance. This is compared to the expected value based on net geometry. Deviations may indicate shorted or open nets.

We are developing an interconnect shorts and opens tester based on the voltage contrast in an electron beam system (VCEB) [22]. By charging each net with the electron beam, which is a very small diameter current probe, we can measure the charging rate and hence deduce the net capacitance. Additionally, the secondary electrons emitted from the probed surface can be energy analyzed to yield the voltage developed on the first net node. Vectoring the primary electron beam to another node on the net allows the net continuity to be checked by observing the energy of secondary electrons from the second node and hence the voltage of the second node.

4.11   Other Issues Regarding Hybrid Wafer Scale Integration

There are a number of CAD/CAM tools, testing algorithms, bonding and assembly processes that need to be developed to fully utilize HWSI technology. Routing thousands of wires to meet a prescribed functionality needs the development of automated and intelligent software that can maximize the percentage of available resources (wiring channels). We have found that extensions of either printed circuit board or multi-layer ceramic routing algorithms do not necessarily achieve the required improvements in resource utilization and efficient automatic completion. We are developing some very successful new routing algorithms [23].

Other tools need to be developed to evaluate the tradeoffs between interconnection, cooling, powering, and stress in addition to component and system reliability at an early part of a design cycle. Quick turn around of the design will be essential component of the widespread utilization of the HWSI technology. We believe that direct extensions of printed circuit board and single chip packaging alone are not satisfactory. Improved tools based on *knowledge based systems* and *design advisors* are needed to guide the designers through the multi-disciplinary decisions needed for hybrid wafer scale integration designs.

4.12   Conclusions

Packaging and interconnection plays a major role in overall performance of computing systems. Hybrid wafer scale Integration promises the high density and high performance interconnection capability required for the next generation of computing systems packaging. Thin film hybrid wafer scale integration is an extensible interconnection and packaging technology that is applicable to the high performance computing systems. This technology builds on integrated circuit fabrication processes in order to achieve fine line interconnection and low dielectric medium for signal propagation.

Hybrid wafer scale integration offers the ability to mix chip technologies on one multichip module. Pretested dies can be mounted on pretested interconnect substrate, while bulky packages and expensive testing fixtures are avoided. In comparison with competing technologies used for multichip modules such as multilayer ceramic, monolithic wafer scale integration, or conventional printed circuit board technology, hybrid wafer scale integration offers a lower cost per function alternative. Thin film hybrid wafer scale integration has higher levels of integration made possible by fault tolerance and has higher performance due to smaller interconnect lengths and signal delays. Since a number of interconnect levels such as packages, pin, sockets, and cables are eliminated we expect the reliability of systems will improve substantially with the introduction of hybrid wafer scale integration technology. The wire, TAB, or flip chip bonded integrated circuit dies can be removed from the hybrid wafer scale integration for repair, and the hybrid wafer scale integration interconnect substrate can be removed layer by layer to access and repair defective parts.

As yet there are no extensive manufacturing and assembly records for hybrid wafer scale integration multichip module. However, we believe that upon maturity, this technology can be less costly, lighter, and smaller than surface mounted packages on printed circuit boards.

We now face a significant challenge: the establishing of an open approach to standardized hardware and software interfaces, so that these modules can be used as easily as the single chip packages of today. For the hardware standards we need to agree and define certain footprints for I/O module size, weight, cooling, etc. For the software interfaces we need to define approaches to the design of the modules, and the efficient development of computer aided design and *computer undergirded manufacturing* tools.

There are three phases of technology development that have to co-exist for rapid utilization of multi-chip modules in the electronics industry: toys, prototypes, and production. Initial interest on the part of companies in this technology is in the development of "toys" which are demonstration vehicles to test out the technology. Some are exploring prototypes that are the next stage test vehicles, designed with the idea of identifying and debugging the technology in order to rapidly scale up to production. For the technology to be credible, production level capability has to be nearly available before many will commit funds to try out toys.

In many areas of integrated circuit endeavor we have found that toys and prototypes need to be fabricated and assembled by taking advantage of a well-operated production line. This, for example, has been a key finding with the MOSIS project [25]. This poses an additional demand to the design and production of the emerging multi-chip module technology based on hybrid wafer scale integration: the ability to rapidly turn out toys and prototypes from a production facility. Quick turn-around of designs will make or break new ventures into this technology arena.

Acknowledgments

The authors would like to thank Tom Dolbear for his input on the thermal management section. They would like to thank Claude Hilbert for his editorial comments, and the whole MCC packaging team for the data on fabrication, bonding and assembly, and reliability.

References

[1] *Integrated 84 ps ECL with I2L*, IEEE ISSCC Digest of Technical Papers, Vol. XXVII, p. 154, 1984.

[2] B. McWilliams and D. Tuckerman, *Wafer Scale Integration*, Energy and Technology Review, Lawrence Livermore National Laboratory, pp. 3-4, Dec. 1985.

[3] George Messner, *Price/Density Tradeoffs of Multichip Modules*, ISHM Proceedings., pp. 28-36, 1988.

[4] R. Wayne Johnson and T. Phillips, *Multilayer Thin Film Hybrids on Silicon*, ISHM Proceedings., pp. 365- 373, 1988.

[5] Richard C. Landis, *Electronic Packaging for the Year 2000*, IEPS Journal, Vol. 11 No.1, pp. 3-7, 1989.

[6] Personal Communication, D. Carlson (ETA).

[7] Albert Blodgett, Jr., *Microelectronic Packaging*, Scientific American, pp. 86-96, July 1983.

[8] Rao R. Tummala et al., *Microelectronics Packaging Handbook*, Van Nostrand Reinhold Publications, New York 1989, pp. 475-480 and 673-684.

[9] J. Tony Pan et al., *A Planar Approach to High Density Copper-Polyimide Interconnect Fabrication*, IEPS Proceedings., pp. 174-184, 1988.

[10] T. Furukatsu, T. Watanabe, and R. Kondo, *NEC Supercomputer SX System*, Nikkei Electronics, Vol. 11-19, pp. 237-272, 1984.

[11] T. Watari and H. Murano, *Packaging Technologies for the NEC SX Supercomputer*, Proc. IEEE Electronics Components Conf., pp.192-198, 1985.

[12] R.E. Matick, *Transmission Lines for Digital and Communication Networks*, McGraw-Hill, New York, 1969.

[13] H. Kroger et al., *Application of Superconductivity to Packaging*, IEEE Circuits and Devices Journal, pp. 16-21, May 1989.

[14] Hilbert et al., *A Comparison of Lossy and Superconducting Interconnect for Computers*, IEEE Transactions on Electron Devices, Vol. 36, No. 9, pp. 1830-1839, Sept. 1989.

[15] Susumu Kimijima et al., *High-Density Multichip Module by Chip-on-Wafer Technology*, ISHM Proceedings, pp. 314-319, 1988.

[16] R.T. Smith and H. Hashemi, *Electrical Analysis of TAB tape in Bonding High I/O Chips to High Density Boards*, IEPS Proceedings, 1989.

[17] John Hagge, *Ultra-reliable Hwsi with Al/Nitride packaging*, Nepcon West Proceedings, pp. 1271-1283, 1989.

[18] Daniel Shanefield,*Comparison of Ceramics for Multichip Hybrids*, Nepcon West Proceedings, pp. 937-943, 1989.

[19] Claude Hilbert et al., *Advanced Air Cooling Techniques*, submitted to IEEE CHMT Journal, 1989.

[20] D. B. Tuckerman, *Heat Transfer Microstructures for Integrated Circuits*, Stanford University, Feb. 1984.

[21] Teledyne TAC SCT-1000 capacitive probe system data sheet.

[22] Ollie C. Woodard et al., *Voltage Contrast Electron Beam Testing Experiments on Very Large Scale Integrated Chip Packaging Substrates*, Journal of Vaccum Science & Technology B, pp. 1966-70, Nov./Dec. 1988.

[23] Kei Suzuki et al., *A Gridless Router: Software and Hardware Implementation*, International Federation for Information Processing, VLSI 1987 Proceedings.

[24] U. Ghoshal and L. Smith, *Skin Effects in Narrow Copper Microstrip at 77 K*, IEEE Transactions on Microwave Theory and Techniques, Vol. 36, No. 12, Dec. 1988.

[25] C. Tomovich, *MOSIS - A Gateway to Silicon"* IEEE Circuits & Devices Magazine, Vol. 4, No. 2, pp. 22-23, Mar. 1988.

CHAPTER 5

PHOTONIC SWITCHING ARCHITECTURES AND THEIR COMPARISON

N. K. Ailawadi
AT&T Bell Laboratories
Middletown, NJ 07748

Abstract

This paper reviews various architectures for photonic switching that have been proposed in the literature. The paper presents only the routing aspects of photonic switching, and in particular, the lithium niobate technology of the directional coupler. The paper:

1. provides the motivation for photonic switching, describes the various photonic switching elements, and discusses different control mechanisms required for photonic switching;

2. explains the principles of an electro-optic switch;

3. enumerates the architectural considerations involved in a photonic switch design;

4. discusses several space division switch architectures and compares their characteristics;

5. describes time division switching and different basic time division switching architectures.

[1] This chapter is published with permission of AT&T Bell Laboratories. It is also published by the Kelly Education and Training Center of AT&T with accompanying video cassettes (Kelly Education and Training Center, AT&T Bell Laboratories, 200 Laurel Ave., Middletown, NJ 07748). ©1989 AT&T.

5.1 Introduction

5.1.1 Background

Photonic switching is of considerable interest in communications and in computing systems. Although currently there are no photonic switches or photonic cross-connect systems in telecommunications networks, intensive studies on photonic switching are under way in several research laboratories. For example, research laboratories of a number of telecommunications vendors (such as AT&T, Ericsson, GTE Corporation, British Telecommunications plc, NEC Corporation, Nippon Telegraph & Telephone Corporation, and GEC/Plessey Telecommunications Systems Ltd.) have reported 8 × 8 prototype photonic switches. Because photonic switching will be a leading edge technology for perhaps the next generation of telephone switches and computers, general interest articles about it have also appeared in popular trade magazines and newspapers.

A complete discussion of the subject of photonic switching requires a study of two competing technologies — lithium niobate and self-electro-optical effect device (SEED). Lithium niobate technology provides unlimited throughput (10s of Gb/s or even Terabit/s), while the switching control must be provided externally. SEEDs, on the other hand, perform switching functions by reading the incoming photonic bit stream, and are therefore logic devices which do not need external switching control. SEED devices thus do not provide an unlimited throughput. SEED-based systems have the potential for free-space interconnections and parallel processing in optical computing, while lithium niobate-based systems have primary application in communication by providing a high bit rate switching function. Since lithium niobate technology is the most advanced, and most likely to be commercially available in the near future, we shall consider the lithium niobate based architectures in this paper.

We shall use the term *photonic switch* to include photonic cross-connects as well as photonic switches, and discuss photonic switching from a communications perspective. (The only difference from our perspective is in the switching speed, which might vary from microseconds to picoseconds.) In discussing the motivation for photonic switching, we begin by addressing the state of the present telecommunications network and describe the need for photonic switching systems and photonic cross-connect systems from the planner's perspective. We then discuss basic principles and the theoretical basis of photonic switching devices. Next, we present the architectural considerations involved in designing a photonic switch, and describe several photonic switch architectures, space division, and time division. These architectures have been designed or proposed in research laboratories, and could form the basis for commercial optical switches. Finally, we shall discuss the limitations of optical switching.

5.1.2 Motivation for Communications — Why Photonic Switching?

Status of the Current Network

As traffic on the current telecommunications network increases, high-capacity fiber optic transmission systems (such as the FT Series G with a bandwidth of 1.7 Gb/s) are being installed not only in the AT&T network, but also in other Inter-Exchange Carriers' networks (U. S. Sprint, MCI, etc.). In addition, the local Bell Operating Companies (BOCs) are installing fiber optic transmission systems for inter-office traffic in their metropolitan areas. Figure 5.1 illustrates the concept of how fiber optic transmission systems work in the present telecommunications network.

As shown in Figure 5.1, we need to first multiplex the digital electronic signals in central office A, convert the electronic signals to optical signals, and then provide a transmitter to send optical signals out of office A. At the receiving office B, the optical signals are terminated, converted back to electronic signals, and demultiplexed before the traffic can be switched.

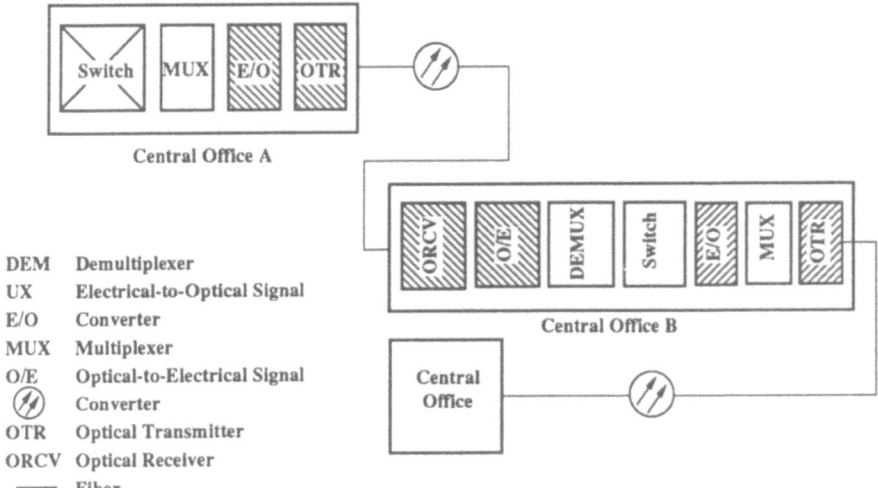

DEM	Demultiplexer
UX	Electrical-to-Optical Signal
E/O	Converter
MUX	Multiplexer
O/E	Optical-to-Electrical Signal
(//)	Converter
OTR	Optical Transmitter
ORCV	Optical Receiver
——	Fiber

Figure 5.1: Current state of telecommunications network.

The outgoing traffic from the switch in office B must again be multiplexed, converted to optical signals from electrical signals, and then transmitted to office C. Thus, we need to convert, in each office, electrical signals to optical signals and back again to electrical signals. In addition, because of the need to regenerate and amplify the signals every 25 to 40 miles, this back-to-back conversion from optical-to-electrical and then from electrical-to-optical signals is required at each repeater station. The situation is analogous to the early 1960s when the telecommunications network was entirely analog and digital transmission was being introduced into the network. At that time, analog-to-digital and digital-to-analog conversion was needed in every central office. Similarly, the present network does not allow the full synergy of the fiber optic transmission systems to be exploited.

New Services

For local telephone companies to provide new services, such as video, transmission bandwidth of 500 Mb/s and higher is required in the loop. Copper-based twisted pair technology can provide sufficient bandwidth for services such as Integrated Services Digital Network (ISDN), which provides 144 kb/s to the customer. However, twisted pair technology will never be able to provide the bandwidth necessary for high-quality entertainment video [1]. Cable TV companies, which provide the majority of video services to the residential market, do not have the capability to provide enough bandwidth for some of the future services, such as enhanced

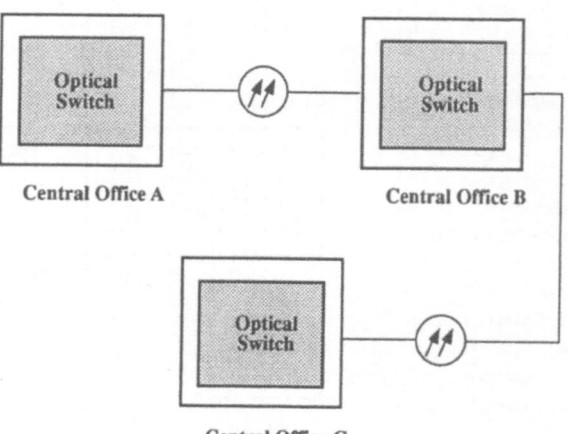

Figure 5.2: Optical network of the future.

definition (EDTV) or high definition (HDTV) television. These new services could require the telephone companies to provide high bandwidth on the order of 500 Mb/s or higher to all customers. At present, the vehicle for providing large bandwidth is fiber in the loop. With fiber in the loop, conversion from optical-to-electrical signals and back from electrical-to-optical signals will begin right at the local office instead of at a tandem or toll central office, thereby complicating the existing networks even further. Similar complexity occurs when fiber is used for local area networks (LANs) and metropolitan area networks (MANs). In addition, to provide high bandwidth at the local office, switching must be provided at a much higher signal rate, such as 500 to 600 Mb/s, than at the current rate of 64 kb/s.

5.1.3 Motivation for Computing Systems — Why Photonic Switching?

Speed is a primary consideration in designing a computer system. For example, a measure of computer processing power is the number of millions of instructions per second (MIPS). Currently, the fastest electronic devices are in the nanosecond (10^{-9} second) range. For any faster processing, we need optical switching. In fact, with the generation of ultrashort laser pulses of a few femtoseconds (10^{-15} second), optical switching at the rate of 0.1 picosecond (10^{-12} second) may be within reach. Moreover, optical interconnects can be used for parallel processing.

5.1.4 Use of Photonic Switching

Photonic switching is being developed to provide large bandwidths and will replace repeated optical-to-electrical and electrical-to-optical signal conversions. As illustrated in Figure 5.2, The network is greatly simplified with a photonic switch in the central office. The term *photonic switching* is loosely defined as the switching of optical signals from the 500 Mb/s range and higher, and may or may not have the intelligence of the current electronic digital switches [2], such as 4ESS^{TM} or 5ESS$^{\text{(R)}}$. Thus, photonic switching includes cross-connect functionality as well as switching intelligence.

A photonic switch in the central office provides the following benefits:

- Large bandwidth of 500 Mb/s and higher.

- Bit-rate independence where the same switch fabric can switch 200 Mb/s or 500 Mb/s and higher bit rate signals.

- No need for optical-to-electrical and electrical-to-optical signal conversions.

- The ultrafast (picosecond and less) switching property of optical switches will be useful in designing high-speed optical computing.

By using a suitable parallel processing architecture, high-speed optical computers will find applications in telecommunications and data processing. This technology could also prove quite useful in future weapons systems, such as *Star Wars*.

5.2   Photonic Switching Elements

5.2.1   Definition

An *optical switching element* is a device that allows incoming optical signals to be routed to one or more outgoing optical paths without any electronic conversion of the optical signals inside the device. The controlling signals may, however, be mechanical, electrical, magnetic, acoustic, or optical, as shown schematically in Figure 5.3.

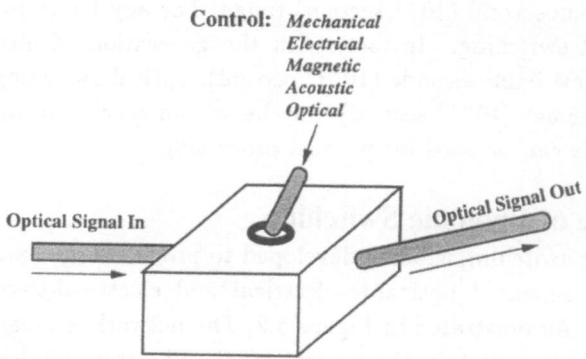

Figure 5.3: Concept of an optical switching element.

5.2.2   Switching Element Types

There are four types of basic switching elements: 1×1, 1×2, 2×1, and 2×2.

1 × 1 Switching Element

The 1×1 switching element is an on-off device, such as an optical modulator. We can envisage a 1×1 switching element where, for example, an

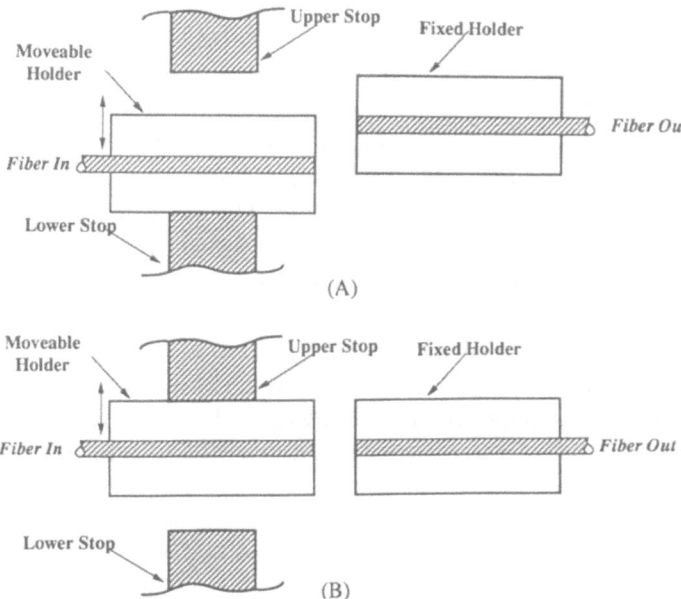

Figure 5.4: Example of a 1 x 1 mechanical/electromechanical optical switching element. (A) Off state. (B) On state.

input fiber is physically moved either mechanically or electromechanically to connect and disconnect with an output fiber, as shown in Figure 5.4. An alternate example of a 1 × 1 switching element consists of two mirrors illustrated in Figure 5.5. (Two mirrors ensure that practically no unwanted light enters the output fiber.) The mirrors can be moved mechanically to either transmit the incident beam or block the transmitted beam. The mirrors thus act as on-off switches [3]. Such 1 × 1 optical switching functions can also be obtained by using a range of different liquid crystal shutter devices, which are light valves controlled by incoming light intensity.

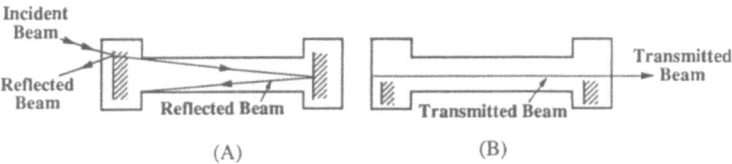

Figure 5.5: Example of a 1 x 1 photonic switching element using mirrors. (A) Off state. (B) On state.

1 × 2 and 2 × 1 Switching Elements

The 1 × 2 and 2 × 1 mechanically activated optical switching elements are shown in Figure 5.6. In the 1 × 2 optical switching element shown in Figure 5.6(a), a mechanical force moves an incoming fiber to connect to one of the two outgoing fibers. The switching element has hermetically sealed tubes with a square internal cross section. The switching is performed by a mechanical force generated by an electrically activated solenoid, which moves the tube from upper to lower stop and vice versa, thereby allowing the incoming fiber to couple to one of the outgoing fibers [2,4]. This type of 1 × 2 switching element can be used to split an optical beam and thus functions as an active splitter. The 2 × 1 optical switching element shown in Figure 5.6(b) is the opposite of the 1 × 2 optical switching element (Figure 5.6(a)) and can be used to combine two different optical beams and acts as an active combiner.

In contrast to the active splitter, the passive splitter is composed of one fiber that connectorizes to two outgoing fibers in a Y-geometry, illustrated in Figure 5.7(a). In the same way, the 2 × 1 element shown in Figure 5.7(b)

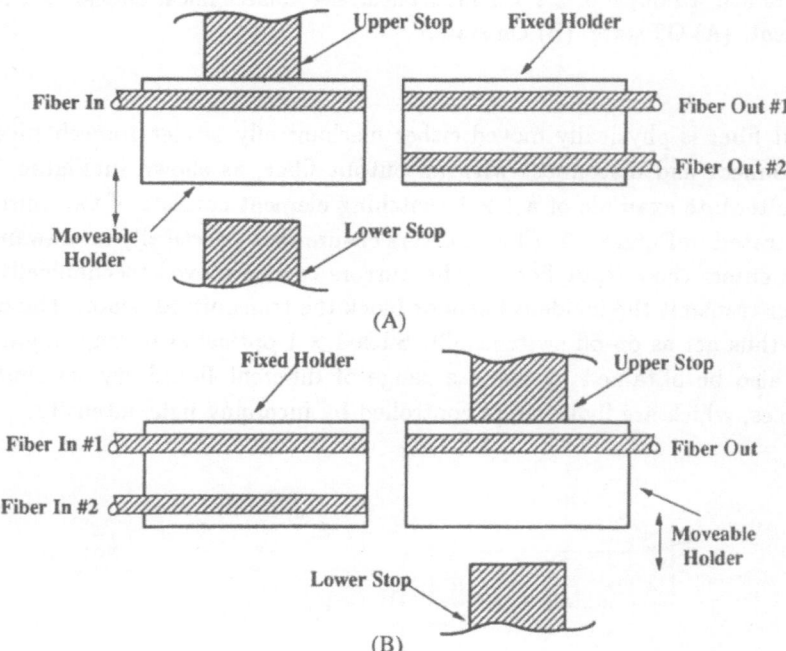

Figure 5.6: Principle of a 1 x 2 and 2 x 1 electromechanical photonic switching element. (A) 1 x 2 switching element. (B) 2 x 1 switching element.

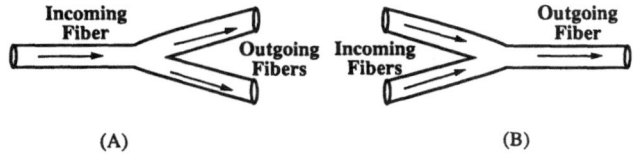

Figure 5.7: Illustration of 1 x 2 and 2 x 1 passive optical switching devices. (A) 1 x 2 device. (B) 2 x 1 device.

is made up of the two incoming fibers connectorized to one outgoing fiber; it is known as the passive combiner.

The 1×2 and 2×1 electromechanical optical switching elements shown in Figure 6 can be used in a fiber local area network for protection switching either to place a spare laser into operation by remote control or to bypass a failed station. 2×1 electromechanical optical switching elements have been used as building blocks in constructing the 4×1 electromechanical optical switch for TAT-8 repeaters to provide 4×1 redundancy in laser transmitters [5].

2×2 Switching Element

In a 2×2 optical switching element, any one of the two input light beams can be switched to any of the two outputs. The two functional states of a 2×2 switching element are shown in Figure 5.8. The cross state refers to the case when input lightbeam A is switched as output beam C, and lightbeam B is switched to output beam D. The bar state denotes the state of the switching element in which input lightbeam A is output as lightbeam D and beam B as output beam C. The 2×2 switching element, known as the "beta element", was considered to be the basic building block of the switching network more than 20 years ago [6].

Both the 1×2 active splitter and 2×1 active combiner can be considered special cases of a 2×2 optical switching element. The 1×2 optical switching element is obtained when only one input is used, and the 2×1 switching element is realized by using only one output. An example of a 2×2 optical switching element is shown in Figure 5.9, where the center part can be moved either mechanically or electromechanically to bring the switch in the cross state or the bar state.

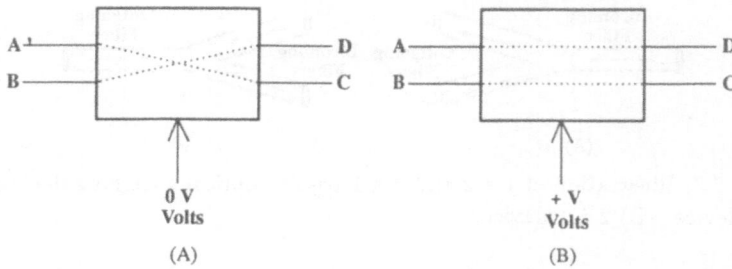

Figure 5.8: Two functional states of a 2 x 2 optical switching element. (A) Cross state. (B) Bar state.

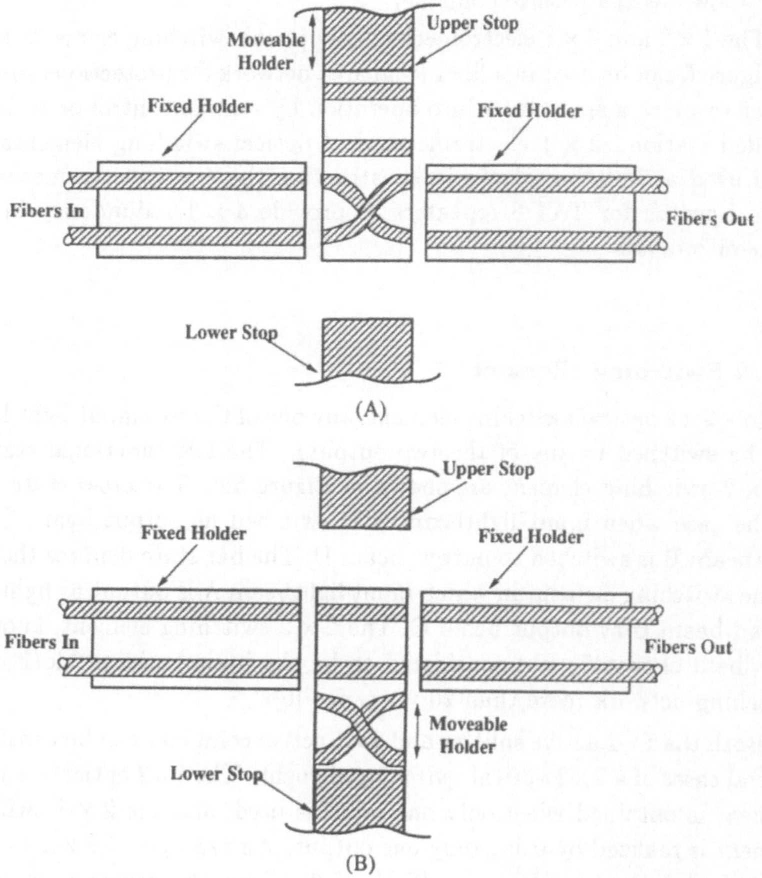

Figure 5.9: An example of a 2 x 2 mechanical/electromechanical optical switching element. (A) Cross state. (B) Bar state.

Higher Dimension Switching Elements

Higher dimension optical switching elements are conceivable but difficult to realize, and none has been made so far. For example, a 4 × 4 switch is made from 2 × 2 switching elements as building blocks.

5.2.3 Control Mechanism

As shown in Figure 5.3, a control mechanism is required to switch an incoming optical signal to the outgoing path. This control mechanism can be mechanical or electromechanical (see Figures 5.4, 5.5, 5.6, 5.9). Alternatively, for a 2 × 2 optical switching element, the control mechanism is based on the ability to dynamically manipulate the index of the refraction of the switch material. One such mechanism is the incoming optical beam itself. Thus, a switching device could be an optical logic gate, controlled by a threshold intensity of light. Such devices operating at ultrafast speeds could be very useful in optical signal processing and computing. This type of control mechanism is called opto-optic. Such switching elements are known as self electro-optic effect devices (SEED), and are the subject of intense study [7]-[11].

A completely different type of control mechanism is provided by means of external stimuli. The external stimuli considered thus far are acoustic vibrations (acousto-optic effect) [12], applied stress or strain (elasto-optic effect), magnetic field (Kerr effect) [13], and electric field (electro-optic effect) [14]-[16]. The amount of the change in the refractive index depends on the type of material and the strength of the applied stimulus. Of these control mechanisms, the electro-optic effect appears to be the most promising. In fact, lithium niobate-based switching elements and architectures are controlled by external electric fields using the electro-optic effect as the switching mechanism, and are most likely to find commercial application for routing. Therefore, for the rest of this unit, we shall consider a 2 × 2 optical switching element controlled by the electro-optic effect as the basic building block of a photonic switch.

5.3 Principles of a 2 x 2 Electro-Optic Switching Element

The 2 × 2 electro-optic switching element is based on a material whose index of refraction can be changed by the application of an external electric field (a thin piece — approximately 1 cm × 6 cm — of such a material is known as a chip or a substrate). Highly accurate regions of refractive index are formed in the substrate by diffusion of a different substance into the substrate. The refractive indices of these regions are controlled by an applied electric field.

Initially, the substrate used was lithium tantalate (LiTaO$_3$), in which electric fields of 400 V to 500 V were needed to switch incoming light to the output path. However, the current work focuses on a lithium niobate (LiNbO$_3$) substrate, in which titanium (Ti) is diffused because it requires smaller voltages and is cheaper [2]. Lithium niobate is an anisotropic material that exhibits different refractive indices along two of its three crystallographic axes. Its index of refraction can be changed by application of 10 V to 50 V, and is different for the ordinary and extraordinary (z-direction) axes. Thin slices of z-cut single LiNbO$_3$ crystals are the wafers or the substrates used for waveguide processing.

We shall discuss two types of 2 × 2 electro-optical switching elements based on LiNbO$_3$: Total Internal Reflection (TIR or X-switch) and the Directional Coupler.

5.3.1   Total Internal Reflection Device or X-Switch

Two pairs of horn-shaped channel waveguides are connected to an LiNbO$_3$ substrate. These channel waveguides are tilted symmetrically in relation to the X-axis of the substrate, and function as input and output arms of the substrate [14]. A pair of parallel electrodes, aligned with the X-axis, are located in the middle of the intersection region as shown in Figure 5.10. Ti atoms are diffused in the intersection region containing the electrodes. In the absence of an electric field, there is no change in the refractive index and the incident light in Channel Waveguide 1 will travel straight to Channel Waveguide 4, while incident light from Channel Waveguide 2 will be transmitted through Channel Waveguide 3. When an electric field is applied in the intersecting region, there is a reduction in the refractive index in the region between the two electrodes due to the electro-optic effect, and the incident light from Channel Waveguide 1 is reflected to Channel Waveguide 3, thus giving rise to a bar state.

We now have two separate refractive index interfaces – an interface to Regions I and II, and a second one at Regions II and III. Light coming from Channel 1 will be partially reflected at the interface of Regions I and II and will be partially transmitted. Total internal reflection will occur at this interface when the incident angle is equal to or greater than the critical angle. (Note that the critical angle is a function of the refractive indices of the two media forming the interface.) As a result, a portion or all of

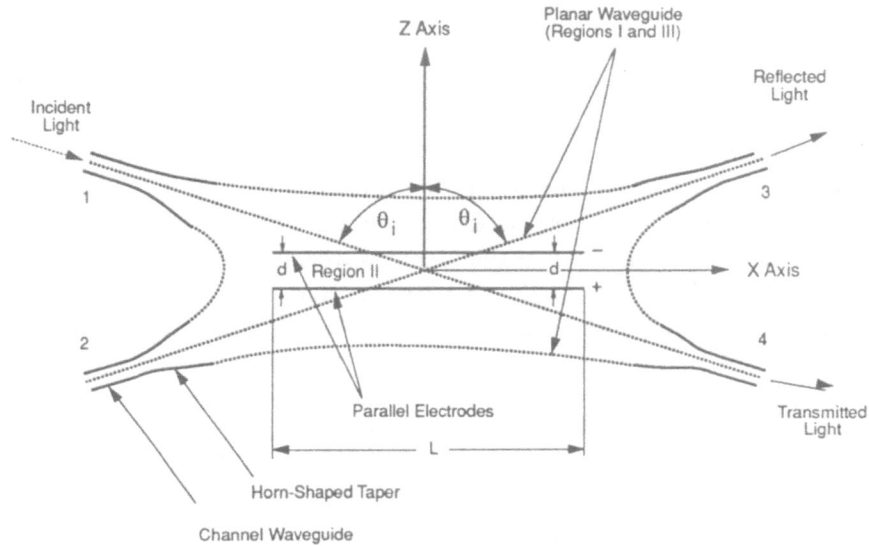

Figure 5.10: Illustration of a total internal reflection device.

the incident light will be switched to Channel 3. Similar results will occur when light from Channel 2 is incident on the interface of Regions II and III. This critical angle, θ_c, at the interface separating Regions I and II can be expressed in terms of applied voltage, V, as [14]

$$\sin \theta_c = 1 - \frac{1}{2} n_1^2 r_{33} \frac{V}{d} \qquad (5.1)$$

where

$n_1 = $ refractive index of Region I and Region III
$r_{33} = $ electro-optic coefficient
$d = $ separation between electrodes.

For the LiNbO$_3$ substrate, we have $n_1 = 2.2$, $r_{33} = 30.8 \times 10^{-10}$cm/V, and $\theta_c = 87.8°$ at an electric field intensity of 1×10^5 V/cm or 10 V/μm. Clearly, the angle decreases as the applied voltage is increased. If the tilt angle of the channel waveguides and, consequently, the incident angle θ_i of the light beam are chosen to be close to the critical angle, the ratio of the reflected (switched) light power to the transmitted (nonswitched) light power becomes a sensitive function of the applied electric field intensity. For $\theta_i \approx \theta_c$, the total internal reflection (TIR) is encountered for the electric field intensity given by

$$\frac{V}{d}\bigg|_{tir} = \frac{2(1 - \sin\theta_1)}{n_1^2 r_{33}} \simeq \frac{1}{n_1^2 r_{33}} \left(\frac{\pi}{2} - \theta_i\right)^2. \tag{5.2}$$

This approximation is valid because for all practical purposes, θ_c and, thus, θ_i are very close to $\pi/2$. The closer the tilt angle is to $\pi/2$, the smaller the applied electric field intensity needed for total internal reflection.

Let us now assume that in the planar waveguide, Region II, a change in refractive index is induced by Ti diffusion. Now, with the application of an electric field, the peak change in the refractive index can be as much as a few percent, and there is a gradual lateral change in the refractive index in Region II. This change results in a critical angle approaching 90°, and will result in a reduced drive voltage (voltage required for total internal reflection).

5.3.2   Directional Coupler

A directional coupler is composed of two single-mode optical waveguides formed by diffusing titanium into a lithium niobate substrate. These waveguides are brought close together for a distance L, as shown in Figure 5.11.

This distance L can range from a few millimeters to several centimeters. In the coupling region, where the distance d between the waveguides is closest, electrodes are placed over the waveguides. The electrodes are separated from the titanium diffused $LiNbO_3$ waveguide by a buffer and insulating layer, typically silicon dioxide (SiO_2). With the two waveguides

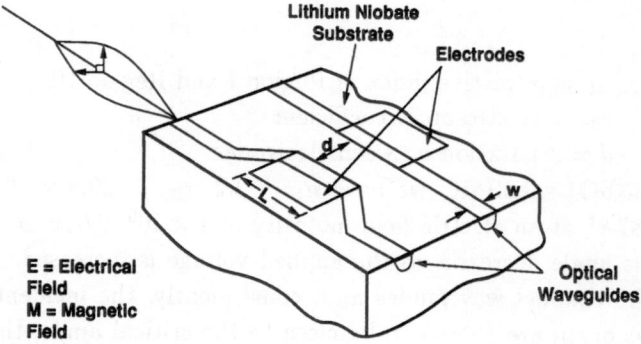

Figure 5.11: A directional coupler with two waveguides diffused into a lithium niobate substrate. (TM polarization is perpendicular to the plane of the crystal, and the TE polarization is parallel to the plane of the crystal.)

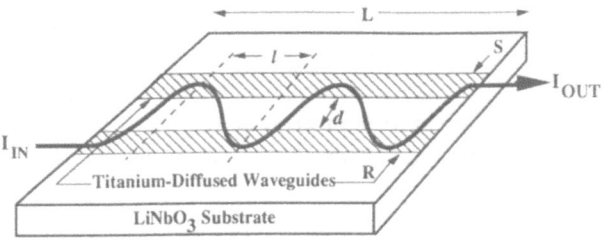

Figure 5.12: Illustration of the transfer of optical energy from one waveguide to the other in a directional coupler. (This figure illustrates the case when $L/\ell = 5$ where $\ell = $ transfer length.)

placed close to each other, the optical energy in one waveguide can couple to the other [15] due to the overlap in the evanescent electric fields of the two waveguides. Light entering one waveguide will couple completely from one waveguide to the other if the propagation constants of both waveguides are equal. As illustrated in Figure 5.12, the incoming light is periodically coupled between the input and output waveguides. When the length L is an odd multiple of the transfer (or coupling) length ℓ, then the light in the input waveguide is transmitted through the output waveguide; here, the transfer length ℓ is the length required for the optical energy in one waveguide to transfer completely to the other waveguide. When an electric field E is applied, the refractive index and propagation constant change. These changes result in a change in the transfer length ℓ, so that the light in one waveguide will not pass completely through the second waveguide.

The theory of directional coupler switching is based on coupled two state systems [17,18] and is discussed by Hinton [15]. As illustrated in Figure 5.12, transfer of optical energy from one waveguide to another will occur if:

1. The propagation constant given by

$$\beta = 2\pi\mu/\lambda \tag{5.3}$$

   is the same for both waveguides, where μ is the effective refractive index of the optical mode traveling in the waveguide and depends on the direction of the propagation, and λ is its free-space wavelength.

2. The interaction length L of the waveguides in the coupling region (Figure 5.11) is an odd multiple of the transfer length ℓ (Figure 5.12),

i.e.,

$$L/\ell = (2n + 1), \ n = 0, 1, 2, \ldots . \tag{5.4}$$

3. For light in the same phase in both waveguides (phase-matched operation), which is the case if the waveguides are identical, the transfer efficiency is given by

$$\eta = \sin^2(\kappa L + 2\phi) \tag{5.5}$$

where κ is the coupling coefficient and the phase term 2ϕ arises due to coupling in the bend regions where κ is not constant.

The parameters influencing transfer length ℓ are: interguide spacing d, difference $\Delta\mu$ in waveguide refractive indices, waveguide dimensions, wavelength λ, and refractive index μ of the waveguide. When the electric field E is applied, the change in the index of refraction is given by

$$\Delta\mu \propto \mu^3 r E \tag{5.6}$$

where r is the electro-optic coefficient for the substrate crystal orientation in use and the optic mode (TE or TM) of the incoming light. A change in the effective index of refraction produces a change in the propagation constant β of each waveguide: in one waveguide, β will increase; in the other waveguide, it will decrease. Because the propagation constants of the two waveguides are unequal, the coupling from one waveguide to the other is no longer 100%. The change in the propagation constant

$$\Delta\beta = \frac{2\pi\Delta\mu}{\lambda} \tag{5.7}$$

leads to a phase change

$$\Delta\beta L = \frac{2\pi\Delta\mu L}{\lambda} \tag{5.8}$$

in the light propagating through one waveguide as compared with the other waveguide. Let R and S be the complex electric field amplitudes in the two waveguides. The optical intensity in the two waveguides is denoted by RR^* and SS^*, respectively, where the asterisk denotes the complex conjugate. The relationship between the electric fields in the two waveguides after the incoming signals have traversed the coupling region, L, is given by the coupled mode equations [15,17,18]

$$\frac{dR}{dx} - j\delta R = -j\kappa S \tag{5.9}$$

and

$$\frac{dS}{dx} - j\delta S = -j\kappa R \qquad (5.10)$$

where x denotes the direction of propagation and

$$\kappa = \pi/2\ell, \quad \delta = \frac{\Delta\beta}{2}. \qquad (5.11)$$

Assuming that the light is input into the R waveguide, the optical intensity in the S waveguide is given by

$$SS^* = 1 - RR^*. \qquad (5.12)$$

We show in Appendix A that for the case $\delta = 0$ and $\kappa L = (2n + 1)\pi/2$, the optical energy is completely transferred to the S waveguide. We also show in the appendix that the switching in a directional coupler can be represented by rotations in three-dimensional space [18].

Reversed $\Delta\beta$ Electrodes

Directional couplers are generally designed in the cross state when applied voltage $V = 0$ ($\delta = 0$). As a consequence, the length of the coupling region L must be an exact odd integral multiple of the coupling length ℓ. This limitation requires precise fabrication tolerances [16]. The cross state can be made electrically tunable by using two pairs of electrodes of length $L/2$ instead of a single pair of length L, as shown in Figure 5.13. For the cross state, each pair of electrodes has opposite voltages applied across them and, for the bar state, the same voltage is applied across both sets of electrodes. The electrode configuration is known as the reversed $\Delta\beta$ electrode configuration [19,20]. Unlike the single-pair electrode configuration (uniform $\Delta\beta$) of the directional coupler discussed earlier, both the cross and bar states are now electrically tunable.

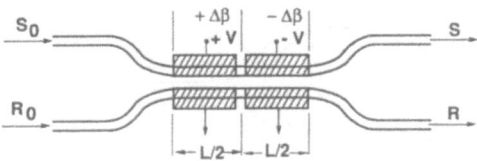

Figure 5.13: The $\Delta\beta$ electrode structure of a directional coupler.

5.4   Architectural Considerations in Designing a Photonic Switch

A limited size (8 × 8, or perhaps, 16 × 16) photonic switch may be designed on a single LiNbO₃ substrate with several 2 × 2 electro-optical switching elements such as directional couplers. These 2 × 2 switching elements can be interconnected by waveguides consisting of Ti diffused into the LiNbO₃ substrate. To construct larger optical switches, this process must be repeated on several substrates, and different substrates must be interconnected by single-mode fibers. Because of the interconnect problem on the same substrate and among different substrates and the number of 2 × 2 switching elements required on each substrate, a number of architectural considerations have emerged in designing such systems. In particular, in the design of large commercial size optical switches, attenuation (optical path loss) and signal-to-noise ratio are particularly important [21-23] because the receiver must be able to accept the output signal and distinguish it from the accumulated noise.

5.4.1   Attenuation

Attenuation of light passing through a switching network has several components. The first is the propagation loss through the waveguide in a directional coupler, including absorption and scattering effects.

The second loss mechanism is associated with waveguide bends. Waveguides having S-bends are used to connect directional couplers on the same substrate. Figure 5.14 shows typical S-bends connecting two directional couplers.

The loss occurs because the difference in the refractive index between the titanium diffused waveguide and the surrounding LiNbO₃ is not large enough to completely confine the light as the waveguide bends. Bend loss is proportional to a^2/h, where h is the vertical offset and a is the total length

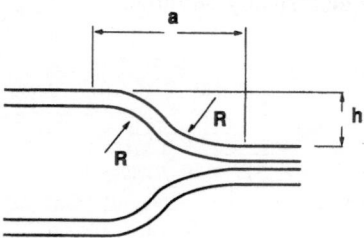

Figure 5.14: S-bends used to interconnect directional couplers on a substrate.

of the bend as shown in Figure 5.14. The smaller the radius of curvature R, the larger the loss per bend. However, a large radius of curvature will make a waveguide bend consume a large amount of substrate real estate.

The next two mechanisms, fiber-to-switch and switch-to-fiber coupling loss, are associated with getting the optical signal onto and off of the substrate. These losses occur because of the differences in refractive indices of the fiber and the LiNbO$_3$ substrate, and also because of the mode mismatch between the diffused waveguide channel and the fiber core. The losses due to waveguide bends can be reduced to 0.1 dB per bend and the losses due to fiber-to-switch coupling and switch-to-fiber coupling are about 1 dB each, whereas the propagation loss in the directional coupler varies from 0.1 dB/cm to 0.5 dB/cm, depending on the fabrication process.

Since in any optical switch design the optical path will have to pass through several directional couplers, the propagation loss through the directional couplers is considered the primary design criterion and is directly proportional to the number of couplers the optical path passes through. An accepted measure for the optical attenuation is the *worst case attenuation* for the highest path loss. It is a direct function of the number of couplers that the optical path passes through [21-23].

5.4.2   Signal-to-Noise Ratio (SNR)

Signal-to-noise ratio is a measure of the optical crosstalk that occurs when two signals interact with each other. There are two ways in which optical paths can interact in a photonic switch. (1) The channels or waveguides carrying the optical signals on a given substrate can cross each other to embed a particular topology. This occurrence is called *channel or optical waveguide crossover.* (2) Two paths sharing a switching element will experience some undesired coupling of one path to the other because of the non-zero transmission of light. This occurrence is called a *switch crossover.*

Channel or Optical Waveguide Crossovers

A topology that does not require waveguide channels to intersect is referred to as "planar". We shall discuss several planar architectures in Section 5.5. However, many other switching networks, such as Clos, Benes, Banyan, and shuffle networks, require interconnecting paths to cross. In addition to increased attenuation, each waveguide crossover couples the light beams passing through it, thus introducing noise or crosstalk from the other channel. The coupling between intersecting waveguides is strongly dependent on the intersecting angle and decreases as the interaction angle increases.

Generally, then, the number of *channel crossovers* should be minimized, and furthermore, design of the channel crossover should be such that crosstalk is minimized by keeping the insertion angles above a certain minimum value. Recent experimental results [3] indicate that it is possible to make *crosstalk from channel crossover negligible.*

The *worst case signal-to-noise ratio* is an important parameter. It is based on *switch crossover*, if the design criteria for channel crossovers are adhered to. The more the number of switching elements in a path, the worse the SNR. The *worst case signal-to-noise ratio (SNR)* is based on the number of switching elements the longest path takes and is considered to be a good measure of SNR [21-23].

In addition to attenuation and SNR, the following architectural problems should be considered in the design of commercial optical switches [21,22].

5.4.3   Blocking Characteristics

The total number of switching elements required for a given switch architecture depends on the blocking probability desired for the switch fabric. There are, in general, four types of switch fabrics that should be considered.

Strict- and Wide-Sense Nonblocking Networks

A switching network is *nonblocking* if any desired input port can be connected to any unused output port without interference from connections that may already be established in the network. If this property is independent of any switching algorithm, then the switching network topology is known as *nonblocking in the strict sense.* If the nonblocking property holds true under some particular switching algorithm, i.e., under this algorithm no rearrangement of paths is needed to provide the desired input/output connection, then the switching system is *nonblocking in the wide sense.* As an example, the three-stage nonblocking symmetric array known as Clos Network and generally used in designing electronic switches, is a switching network that is nonblocking *in the strict sense* when $k = 2n - 1$, where n is the number of inputs and k is the number of outputs of an $(n \times k)$ switching module.

Rearrangeably Nonblocking and Blocking Networks

A switching network is *rearrangeably nonblocking* if any desired connection between two idle ports that are temporarily blocked by connections already established in the network can be completed after some established connections are possibly moved to different paths. Such topologies are known as *parallel nonblocking*, whereby any set of input/output pairs can be connected without blocking if the network is initially idle and the set is known in advance. In contrast, the topologies discussed in the Strict and Wide-Sense Nonblocking Networks Section are known as *serial nonblocking*, whereby arbitrary sequences of input/output pairs can be connected and disconnected without blocking.

A switching network is blocking if some permutations of the network cannot be realized, even with rearrangement of the established network.

5.4.4 Point-to-Point/Broadcast Architecture

In a point-to-point architecture, one input goes to one and only one output channel at a given time. In a broadcast architecture, every output can listen to any input, even if other output channels are simultaneously listening to the same input. The input optical power in a broadcast architecture must be divided among several output channels [22].

5.4.5 Number of Switching Elements Per Substrate and Number of Substrates

The number of switching elements necessary to implement a switching network [21,22] is a good measure of the cost of the network. The more directional couplers on a substrate, the harder it is to design and the lower the manufacturing yield – resulting in higher cost. Having more directional couplers end-to-end on a single substrate requires a longer substrate or shorter directional couplers. Shorter directional couplers will require a higher voltage to put incoming light in the bar state. In addition, if the switching network design requires more than one substrate, more real estate, power, and cost are involved.

5.4.6 Number of Electronic Drivers

Electronic Drivers are needed to change the applied electric fields across various 2 × 2 switching elements of an optical switch. The amount of control and driving circuitry needed to implement a given architecture has an impact on the real estate requirements. If an architecture does not require one driver per switching element, the control and driving circuitry is less complex in terms of the number of pins required on the board and will occupy less real estate.

5.4.7 Number of Optical Fibers Required

Some architectures require a large number of optical fibers to interconnect the various stages. More fibers imply higher cost and difficult switching system interconnections.

5.5 Architecture for Space Division Optical Switches

Several architectures for space division optical switches have been studied in the literature [15,21-28] In this section, we shall discuss a number of those architectures.

5.5.1 Crossbar Architecture

The crossbar architecture has been widely studied and implemented as 4×4 and 8×8 optical networks on a single substrate. It is a square or rectangular matrix switch, as shown in Figure 5.15, where each of the rectangles is a 2×2 directional coupler. The crossbar architecture is nonblocking in the wide sense; the required algorithm is to allow all inputs to continue along the horizontal lines corresponding to their input locations. That is, all the directional couplers associated with a given input row are initially in the cross state. To connect an input to an output, the directional coupler at the intersection of the input row and output column is put in the bar state. Putting the rest of the directional couplers associated with a given output column in the cross state allows the input information to reach the desired output port.

The crossbar architecture is point-to-point and planar so that no waveguide channel crossovers occur. An $N \times N$ crossbar architecture requires N^2 crosspoints, as in the electronic domain, and the number of directional couplers is N^2. Furthermore, the number of drivers is N^2 since each directional coupler requires its own separate control lead and driver. The number of switching elements encountered along various optical paths through the switch are unequal. The shortest possible path is just one switching element, whereas the largest path passes through $2N - 1$ switching elements and each switching element adds additional attenuation and crosstalk into the signal. Therefore, attenuation or insertion loss in the worst case is $(2N - 1)$ switching elements $\times$ L dB/switching element, where L dB is the

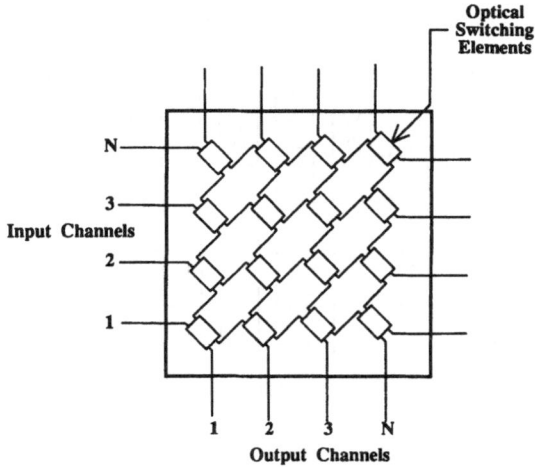

Figure 5.15: The classical rectangular crossbar matrix switch.

characteristic loss of each switching element. The signal-to-noise ratio similarly occurs, in the worst case, when input N is connected to output 1 and must pass through $(N - 1)$ switching elements, each carrying a full power signal (and a potential source of crosstalk). Part of this full power signal will enter the channel carrying the desired signal as noise, and appears as crosstalk. If the crosstalk isolation per switching element is given by X (typically -20 to -30 dB), for crossbar architecture

$$SNR = X - 10\log_{10}(N - 1) \quad \text{dB}$$

5.5.2 N-Stage Planar Architecture

The number of switching elements and drivers can be substantially reduced by using the N-stage planar architecture, shown in Figure 5.16. It requires N stages of switching elements [24] and the topology requires $N(N - 1)/2$ switching elements. The algorithm used for this switch shows the various switching elements set at bar and cross states with input 1 at output π_1, input 2 at output π_2, etc. For example, the 8 × 8 switch shown in Figure 5.16 is comprised of 28 switching elements. This network is rearrangeably nonblocking, per the definition given in Section 5.4.3. This architecture requires $N(N-1)/2$ switching elements and $N(N-1)/2$ drivers for an $N \times N$ switch.

As in the crossbar architecture (Section 5.5.1), this architecture is planar and there are no waveguide channel crossovers. The worst-case optical path length is now N-switching elements. If the optical attenuation is L dB per

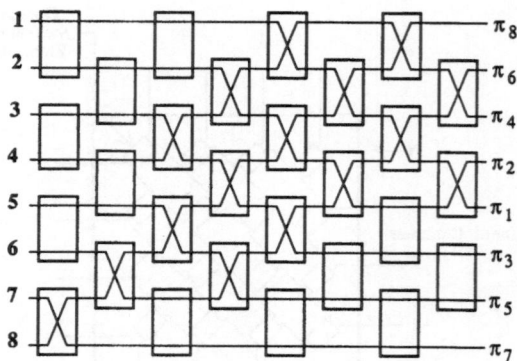

Figure 5.16: 8 x 8 N-stage planar architecture.

switching element, the optical path loss $= NL$ dB. The worst-case signals pass through N directional couplers that can leak noise (crosstalk) into the desired signal channel. The worst-case SNR is given by [24]

$$SNR = X - 10\log_{10} N \quad \text{dB}$$

Thus, SNR is slightly worse than the crossbar architecture discussed in Section 5.5.1.

Larger switch architectures of this type would require the partitioning of the N-stage planar crossbar network into several identical subnetworks, with each subnetwork on a separate substrate and optical fibers interconnecting various subnetworks, as shown in Figure 5.17.

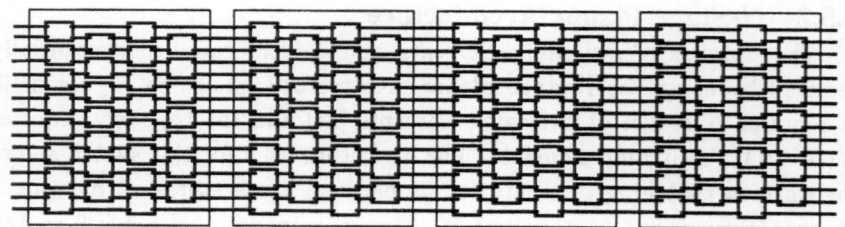

Figure 5.17: Partitioned 16 x 16 N-stage planar architecture.

5.5.3   Double Crossbar Architecture

The double crossbar architecture was introduced by Kondo et al. [25]. It is constructed with two crossbar-like architectures placed on top of each other and has interconnectivity as shown in Figure 5.18.

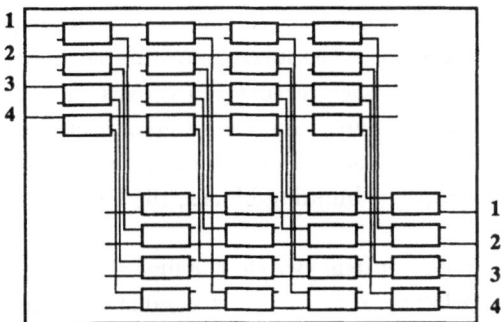

Figure 5.18: The double crossbar architecture.

This architecture is point-to-point and nonblocking in the wide sense. It also requires $2N^2$ crosspoints, which is twice the number of crosspoints needed in the crossbar architecture. The number of switching elements required for the double crossbar architecture is $2N^2$, and the same number of drivers is needed. The additional switching elements are used to obtain a significant increase in the signal-to-noise ratio. In this architecture, the desired signal is selected in the first matrix and then selected again in the second matrix, thereby giving the double crossbar "squared" signal-to-noise ratio.

All the possible paths in this architecture pass through $(N+1)$ switching elements; hence, the attenuation is equal to $(N+1)L$ dB, where L dB is the optical path loss per switching element. The SNR for the double crossbar architecture is given by

$$SNR = 2X - 10\log_{10}(N-1) \quad \mathrm{dB}$$

However, in addition to switch crossovers, the double crossbar architecture requires significant waveguide channel crossovers. The number of channel crossovers is given by

$$\text{channel crossovers} = N^2(N-1)$$

which would adversely affect the SNR of the system.

5.5.4 Clos Architecture

The Clos architecture [26], is a three-stage network designed for virtually nonblocking electronic switching networks, and provides a method of obtaining larger architectures by interconnecting several smaller nonblocking substrates. Clos architecture is point-to-point and is used to reduce the number of crosspoints for large $N \times N$ ($N > 23$) switching systems. Three stages of substrates are used; the interconnection is shown in Figure 5.19.

Each stage of the Clos architecture can consist of any nonblocking architecture fabricated on a substrate; the interconnections between various stages are made by optical fibers. In particular, if we use the crossbar architecture on the substrates as building blocks, the Clos crossbar architecture is obtained.

For an overall $N \times N$ optical switch, the first stage requires r substrates of dimension $n \cdot m$, where $r \cdot n = N$. The second stage requires m substrates of dimension $r \cdot r$, and the third stage consists of r substrates of dimension $m \cdot n$. The Clos architecture [26] is strictly nonblocking if $m \geq 2n - 1$, and rearrangeably nonblocking if $m \geq n$. The rearrangeably nonblocking Clos network with crossbar architecture on each substrate is considered in computing insertion loss and SNR characteristics. The Clos network requires

$$r \cdot m \cdot n + m \cdot r^2 + m \cdot n \cdot r = 2r \cdot m \cdot n + m \cdot r^2$$

switching elements, and the same number of drivers is needed. It requires more than one substrate. The number of substrates is $2r + m$, and the interconnections between different substrates are made by fibers. The attenuation or insertion loss for this architecture is $(2n + 2m + 2r - 3)L$ dB, where L dB is the insertion loss per switching element. Because of the

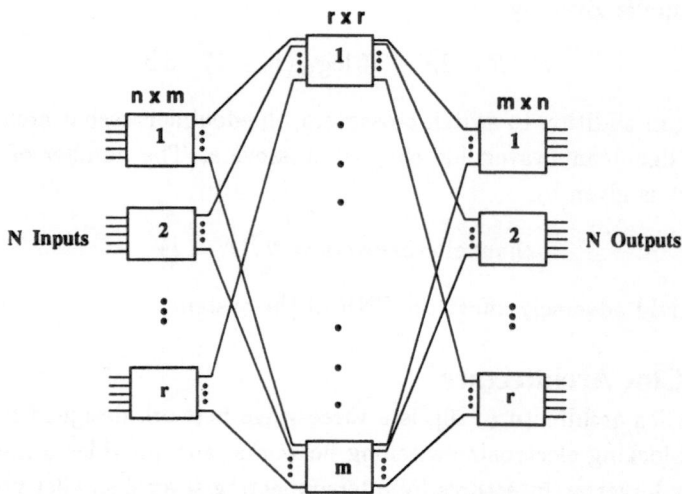

Figure 5.19: Three stage Clos network.

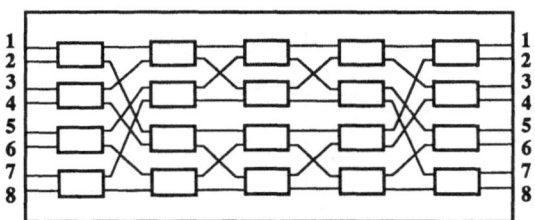

Figure 5.20: The Benes architecture.

planar architecture within each substrate and also because the interconnections between different substrates are fibers, there are no waveguide channel crossovers. All of the possible signal paths in this architecture pass through the same number of switching elements. The signal-to-noise ratio is given by

$$SNR = X - 10\log_{10}(n + m + r) \quad \text{dB}$$

5.5.5 Benes Architecture

The Benes architecture [27], shown in Figure 5.20, is rearrangeably non-blocking and can be implemented on a single substrate for small switch sizes in which a significant number of crossovers occur. It is more suitable for multi-substrate implementation when the switch size is $N \times N$ (N large), because then the crossovers can be replaced by fiber optic interconnections. It requires the fewest number [27] of switching elements, $(2\log_2 N - 1)N/2$. The number of drivers is the same as the number of couplers. If the Benes architecture is implemented on a single substrate, the number of waveguide channel crossovers is given by $2^{2k-1} - (2k + 1) \cdot 2^{k-2}$, where $k = \log_2 N$.

All of the possible paths in the Benes architecture pass through the same number of switching elements. The worst-case attenuation or insertion loss is given by $(2\log_2 N - 1)L$ dB, where L dB is the attenuation for a single switching element. The signal-to-noise ratio is given by

$$SNR = X - 10\log_{10}(2k - 1) \quad \text{dB}$$

where $k = \log_2 N$ and X is the extinction ratio for one switching element.

5.5.6 Architectures Based on Active and Passive Splitters and Combiners

Two additional multiple substrate architectures merit discussion: they are based on active and passive splitters and combiners [28]. An active

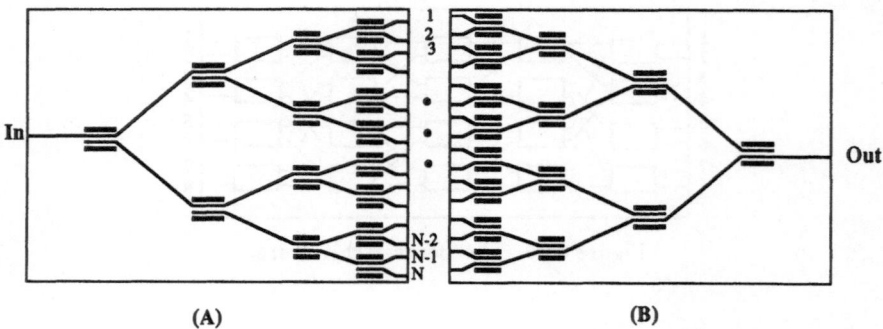

Figure 5.21: (A) 1 × N active splitter. (B) N × 1 active combiner.

splitter is a tree-structured optical switch made from 2 × 2 switching elements. A 1 × N active splitter requires $(N-1)$ directional couplers. An $N \times 1$ active combiner is just the opposite of an active splitter and also requires $(N-1)$ directional couplers. A 1 × N active splitter and an $N \times 1$ active combiner are shown schematically in Figure 5.21.

A 1 × N passive splitter is simply an even power split and can be performed on an LiNbO$_3$ substrate or with fiber splitters. The two architectures we will discuss are (1) Active Splitter and Active Combiner (AS/AC), and (2) Passive Splitter and Active Combiner (PS/AC).

Active Splitter and Active Combiner (AS/AC) Architecture

The active splitter and active combiner architecture, shown in Figure 5.22, is a strictly nonblocking point-to-point architecture and requires a total of $2N(N-1)$ switching elements. It requires multiple substrates, even for the small switch sizes. The number of substrates required is $2N$.

However, an advantage of this type of switch architecture is that every switching element does not need individual control and driving circuitry. All switching elements in each vertical column of the splitter and combiner can be tied together electrically so that only $\log_2 N$ control leads and drivers are needed for each 1 × N active splitter and for each $N \times 1$ active combiner. Thus, the number of drivers for this architecture is $2N \log_2 N$.

All of the possible signal paths in the AS/AC architecture have the same path length and are equal to $2 \log_2 N$ switching elements. If the insertion loss per switching element is L dB, the total attenuation for this architecture is $2(\log_2 N)L$ dB. To calculate the signal-to-noise ratio, it should be noted that no noise or crosstalk is introduced in the splitter part

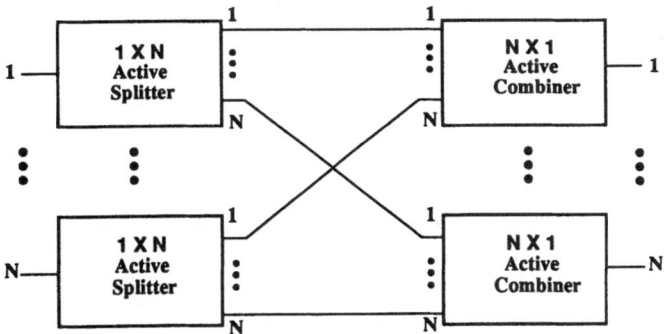

Figure 5.22: N × N active splitter and active combiner (AS/AC.) architecture.

of the architecture. The crosstalk is introduced into the desired channel only in the active combining stage.

The desired signal will pass through $k = \log_2 N$ switching elements with a crosstalk of X dB per element. The signal-to-noise ratio for this architecture is

$$SNR = 2X - 10\log_{10} k \quad \text{dB}$$

The SNR in this architecture is doubled, similar to the double crossbar architecture discussed in Section 5.5.3.

Passive Splitter and Active Combiner (PS/AC) Architecture

Unlike all the other architectures discussed so far in Section 5.5, the passive splitter and active combiner architecture shown in Figure 5.23 is a broadcast architecture, i.e., any output can listen to any input, even if other outputs are listening to the same input. The PS/AC architecture is strictly nonblocking. Since the passive splitter portion of the architecture does not require switching elements, the number of switching elements required for the active combiners is $N(N-1)$. Like the AS/AC architecture, the PS/AC architecture is also a multiple substrate architecture requiring $2N$ substrates if each $1 \times N$ passive splitter is on an LiNbO$_3$ substrate. If passive splitting is performed with fibers, then only N substrates are sufficient.

Similar to the AS/AC case, in the PS/AC architecture each switching element does not require a separate driver. Only $\log_2 N$ drivers are required for each $N \times 1$ active combiner, giving rise to a total of $N \log_2 N$ drivers. The path length in this architecture is the same for all possible connections and passes through $\log_2 N$ switching elements. Assuming fiber splitters with a 50/50 power split, there is a 3 dB loss at each splitting point and

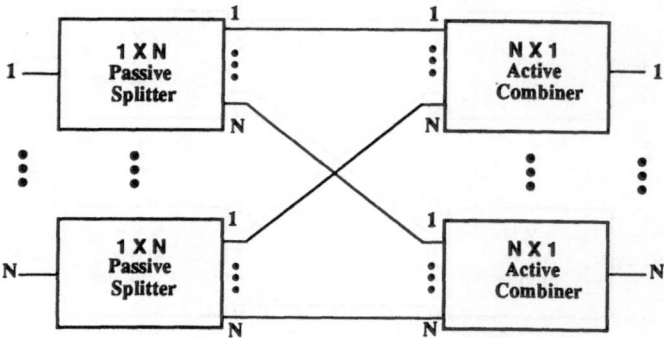

Figure 5.23: N × N passive splitter and active combiner (PS/AC) architecture.

the attenuation or insertion loss is given by $(3 + L) \log_2 N$ dB, where L dB is the attenuation in a switching element.

No noise is introduced into the signal path in a passive splitter. The only crosstalk noise in this architecture is introduced in the active combining stage. All inputs to the active combiner have the same signal power. The desired signal will pass through $\log_2 N$ switching elements with a crosstalk of X. The SNR for the PS/AC architecture is given by

$$SNR = X - 10 \log_{10} k \quad \text{dB}$$

where $k = \log_2 N$. The attenuation and SNR characteristics in the PS/AC architecture are not as good as the AS/AC or double crossbar architectures.

5.5.7 Dilated Benes Architecture

The Dilated Benes architecture, proposed recently [23], uses one input and one output of each switching element in the Benes network. In general, the dilated network architecture is based on the requirement that no switching element carry more than one active path at a given time, i.e., each 2×2 switching element is a 1-active device, as opposed to a 2-active device in which both inputs and both outputs are active simultaneously. Figure 5.24 shows an 8×8 Dilated Benes architecture, with fixed inputs and outputs.

The Dilated Benes architecture consists of $2 \log_2 N$ stages, with N switching elements in each stage. Thus, the total number of switching elements becomes $2N \log_2 N$. With one driver per switching element, we shall need an equal number $(2N \log_2 N)$ of electronic drivers for the Dilated Benes architecture. Under the requirement that no switching element carry

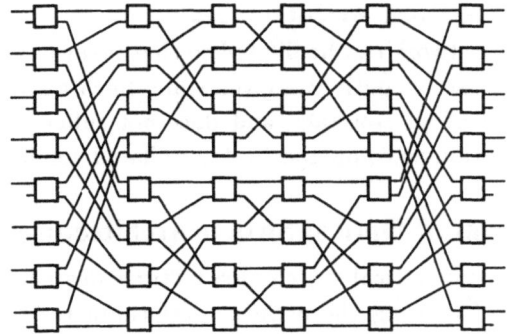

Figure 5.24: An 8 × 8 dilated Benes architecture.

more than one active path, the simplest 2-active × 2-active switch is shown in Figure 5.25. It switches two pairs of inputs, each containing one active input to two pairs of outputs, each containing one active output. Thus, when no 2-active switching elements are permitted, the minimum number of switching elements is $2\log_2(N!)$. The Dilated Benes network is optimal under these conditions.

The great advantage of this architecture is that there are no switch crossovers at any stage and, consequently, there is no crosstalk. However, attenuation and the total number of switching elements are greater than the simple Benes architecture discussed in Section 5.5.5. The path length of the Dilated Benes architecture is $2\log_2 N$, which is one more than the Benes architecture. It has an optical path loss given by $(2\log_2 N)L$ dB, where L dB is the attenuation per switching element. Thus, the optical path loss is approximately the same as the Benes architecture.

Partially Dilated Benes Architecture

To reduce the number of switching elements proposed in the Dilated Benes architecture, we allow some switching elements for which 2 inputs and 2 outputs are simultaneously active. Networks may, thus, be constructed to obtain uniform crosstalks and have, at the same time, an optimum number of switching elements.

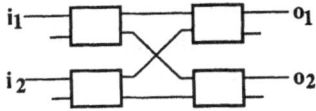

Figure 5.25: 2 × 2 photonic switch in dilated Benes architecture.

Other Dilated Network Architectures

Note that any network can be dilated so that no switching element carries more than one active path at a given time. Such a switch architecture has the advantage of no crosstalk, and does not suffer significantly from additional attenuation as compared to its undilated counterpart.

5.6   Comparison of Optical Switch Architectures

The space division optical switch architectures described in Section 5.5 are compared [22,23] using the architectural characteristics discussed in Section 5.4. The following sections summarize the differences among these architectures.

5.6.1   Attenuation

Attenuation (or insertion loss) is directly dependent on the number of switching elements that an optical signal travels. As discussed in Section 5.4.1, the measure of attenuation is the worst-case optical path loss incurred for the longest path. Assume that each switching element has a characteristic loss, L dB, associated with it. This loss budget includes material absorption, scattering losses that a signal incurs as it traverses a switching element, losses associated with waveguide bends as the signal enters and leaves the switching element, and incomplete coupling. (For a directional coupler, L is in the range of 0.5 to 1.0 dB.) The attenuations for the longest path for the architectures [22] discussed in Section 5.5 are shown in Table 5.1.

The optical path loss characteristics of the various architectures for the $L = 0.5$ dB switching element loss are shown in Figure 5.26.

5.6.2   SNR Characteristics

As discussed in Section 5.4.2, each switching element that the signal passes through introduces a small amount of crosstalk from the other channel into the desired signal channel. The better the extinction ratio of a given switching element, the lower the crosstalk will be. The extinction ratio of a single switching element in dB is represented by X. (Typical values for X can vary from 10 dB up to 40 dB, depending upon the type of switching element and fabrication characteristics.) The SNR for an optical switch architecture can be estimated by determining the largest number of switching elements that the signal channel passes through and the power that will be leaked into the signal channel at each point. The amount of

Table 5.1: Attenuation characteristics for various optical space division architectures

ARCHITECTURE	OPTICAL PATH LOSS	
Crossbar	$(2N - 1)L$	dB
N-Stage Planar	NL	dB
Double Crossbar	$(N + 1)L$	dB
CLOS	$(2n - 1)L + (2r - 1)L + (2m - 1)L$	dB
Benes	$(2\log_2 N - 1)L$	dB
AS/AC	$(2\log_2 N)L$	dB
PS/AC	$(\log_2 N)(3 + L)$	dB
Dilated Benes	$(2\log_2 N)L$	dB

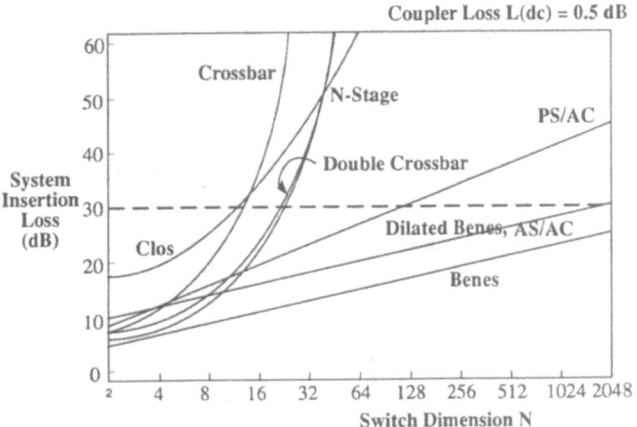

Figure 5.26: Optical path loss characteristics for various space division optical switch architectures ($L = 0.5$ dB).

Table 5.2: SNR characteristics for various optical space division architectures

ARCHITECTURE	SNR	
Crossbar	$SNR = |X| - 10 \cdot \log_{10}(N-1)$	dB
N-Stage Planar	$SNR = |X| - 10 \cdot \log_{10}(N)$	dB
Double Crossbar	$SNR = 2|X| - 10 \cdot \log_{10}(N-1)$	dB
CLOS	$SNR = |X| - 10 \cdot \log_{10}(n+m+r)$	dB
Benes	$SNR = |X| - 10 \cdot \log_{10}(2k-1)$	dB
AS/AC	$SNR = 2|X| - 10 \cdot \log_{10}(k)$	dB
PS/AC	$SNR = |X| - 10 \cdot \log_{10}(k)$	dB
Dilated Benes	$SNR = \infty$	dB

power crossed over depends on whether the other channel was carrying a full power signal or a signal already attenuated by one or more extinction ratios.

The worst-case SNR characteristics have been calculated for each of the architectures [22,23] and are given in Table 5.2. These equations take into account only the noise terms associated with the switching elements, and represent a first-order approximation to SNR.

As can be seen from Table 5.2, the Benes architecture has SNR that decreases on the order of k rather than on the order of N, and the Dilated Benes architecture shows no crosstalk because only one path is active per switching element at any time.

SNR characteristics of these architectures are plotted in Figure 5.27. (For comparison, the extinction ratio X is assumed to be -20 dB.) Note that SNR for the Dilated Benes architecture is infinite.

5.6.3 Blocking Characteristics

All of the architectures under consideration are nonblocking. However, they exhibit different degrees of nonblocking, as shown in Table 5.3.

Furthermore, all the architectures, except the Passive Splitter and Active Combiner (PS/AC) architecture, have point-to-point interconnectivity. Note that the PS/AC is a broadcast architecture, where multiple outputs can listen to the same input channel.

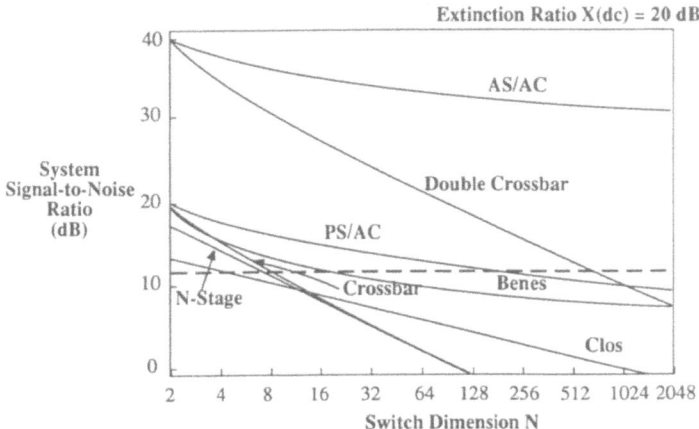

Figure 5.27: Signal-to-noise ratio (SNR) characteristics for various space division optical switch architectures ($x = -20$ dB). Note that SNR for dilated Benes architecture is infinite (zero noise).

Table 5.3: Blocking characteristics for various optical space division architectures

ARCHITECTURE	BLOCKING CHARACTERISTIC
Crossbar	Wide-Sense Nonblocking
N-Stage Planar	Rearrangeable Nonblocking
Double Crossbar	Wide-Sense Nonblocking
CLOS	Strictly Nonblocking if $m \geq 2n - 1$
	Rearrangeable Nonblocking if $m \geq n$
Benes	Rearrangeable Nonblocking
AS/AC	Strictly Nonblocking
PS/AC	Strictly Nonblocking
Dilated Benes	Rearrangeable Nonblocking

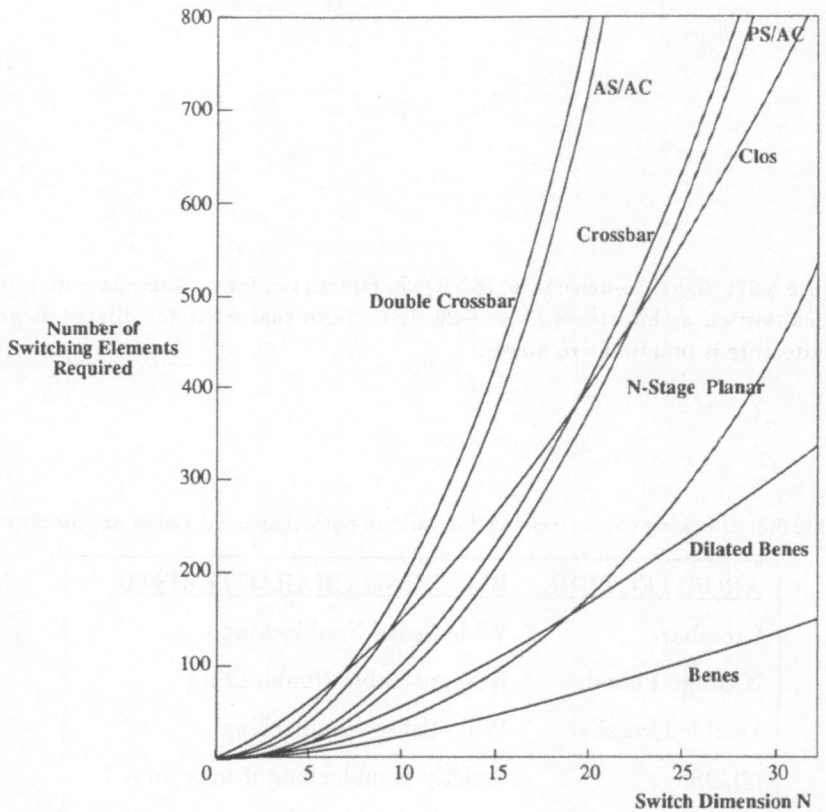

Figure 5.28: Number of switching elements required for various space division optical switch architectures.

Table 5.4: Number of switching elements for various optical space division architectures

ARCHITECTURE	SWITCHING ELEMENTS
Crossbar	N^2
N-Stage	$N \cdot (N-1)/2$
Double Crossbar	$2N^2$
CLOS	$2 \cdot r \cdot m \cdot n + m \cdot r^2$
Benes	$(N/2) \cdot (2\log_2 N - 1)$
AS/AC	$2N(N-1)$
PS/AC	$N(N-1)$
Dilated Benes	$2N log_2 N$

5.6.4 Switching Element and Driver Characteristics

The architectures discussed in Section 5.5 require a different number of switching elements to implement an $N \times N$ optical switch. The number of switching elements required for each of the architectures is given in Table 5.4 and, for comparison, is plotted in Figure 5.28.

Most architectures require a separate driver circuit for every switching element. In AS/AC and PS/AC architectures, many of the switching elements can be electrically tied together and driven from the same driver [28]. This procedure significantly reduces the number of drivers required for these architectures. The number of drivers required for each of the architectures is given in Table 5.5 and is plotted in Figure 5.29.

5.6.5 Switch Dimension Limits

An estimation of switch dimension limits assumes the following values: $L = 1$ dB and $X = -20$ dB, a maximum acceptable system attenuation of 30 dB, and a minimum acceptable system SNR of 11 dB (for a bit error rate of 10^{-9}). Within these limits, the largest size of the eight architectures discussed can be estimated [22]. They are tabulated in Table 5.6.

The *crossbar* architecture can grow to 8×8, yielding a system insertion loss of 19 dB and an SNR of 11.5 dB. The *N-stage planar* architecture can grow to 8×8, yielding an insertion loss of 12 dB and an SNR of 11 dB. The *double crossbar* architecture can grow to 25×25, yielding an insertion

Table 5.5: Number of electronic drivers for various optical space division architectures

ARCHITECTURE	DRIVERS
Crossbar	N^2
N-Stage	$N \cdot (N-1)/2$
Double Crossbar	$2N^2$
CLOS	$2 \cdot r \cdot m \cdot n + m \cdot r^2$
Benes	$(N/2) \cdot (2\log_2 N - 1)$
AS/AC	$2 \cdot N \cdot \log_2 N$
PS/AC	$N \cdot \log_2 N$
Dilated Benes	$2 \cdot N \cdot \log_2 N$

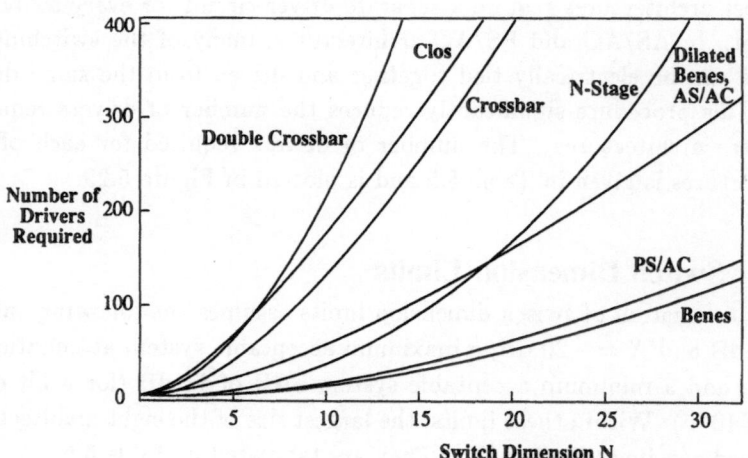

Figure 5.29: Number of electronic drivers required for various space division optical switch architectures.

Table 5.6: Switch dimension limits for various space division architectures

ARCHITECTURE	SIZE	OPTICAL PATH LOSS	SNR
Crossbar	8 × 8	19	11.5
N-Stage	8 × 8	12	11
Double Crossbar	25 × 25	30	26.6
CLOS	9 × 9	27	10.5
Benes	16 × 16	11	11.5
AS/AC	2048 × 2048	30	29.5
PS/AC	32 × 32	29	13
Dilated Benes	2048 × 2048	30	∞

loss of 30 dB and an SNR of 26.6 dB. The *Clos* architecture can grow to 9 × 9, with an insertion loss of 27 dB and an SNR of 10.5 dB. The *Benes* architecture can grow to 16 × 16, with an insertion loss of 11 dB and an SNR of 11.5 dB. The *PS/AC* broadcast architecture can grow to 32 × 32, with an insertion loss of 29dB and a 13dB SNR. Both the AS/AC and Dilated Benes architectures could theoretically grow up to 2048 × 2048, with an insertion loss of 30 dB and an SNR of 29.5 dB for AS/AC. However, channel waveguide crossovers (for the Dilated Benes architecture), number of substrates, interconnection fibers, and fibers leaving a substrate edge now become limiting factors.

As the values for L decrease or X increase, or the acceptable limits for attenuation or SNR improve, the obtainable sizes for all of the architectures will increase.

5.7 Time Division Optical Switching

The time division switching in an electronic digital switch consists of a time-slot interchanger as a basic element. The order of time slots in a time multiplexed signal is changed from input to output sides of a time-slot interchanger. In electronic systems, this procedure is done by reading the input signals stored in a temporary input buffer and writing the signals in a different order in the output temporary buffer (the order in which input signals are written into the output buffer is determined by external processors that contain the intelligence of the switch).

In electronic digital switching, time division switching technology is implemented with a very large scale integrated (VLSI) circuit, called elastic store. Input data is stored as it is received and goes to the output by random access, according to the switching assignment. Since the development of a photonic elastic store is not expected in the near future, storage and synchronization of data require alternate and more primitive means, simply because the technology is less mature. We shall first discuss the memory element and then the basic architectures.

5.7.1 Memory Element

The memory element [29-31] consists of a fiber delay line that acts as a buffer where the photons continue to be held until they are ready to be switched. A fiber delay line, which is one time slot in length, will store an entire block of photons contained in one time slot. Inherent in time division switching is a serial photonic signal as input organized as a sequence of frames, where each frame consists of a sequence of words arranged as time multiplexed signals. Each time slot in the frame may consist of a block of from 100 to 1000 bits belonging to the same subscriber. The frame structure shown in Figure 5.30 is thus block interleaved in a fashion similar to the byte-interleaved DS1 frame, rather than bit-interleaved higher rate signals such as the DS2 or DS3. Furthermore, some gap between time slots is left to allow time for electro-optical switching of the photons. The SYNTRAN [32] and SONET standards are block interleaved and are examples of the optical signals, which can be used in time division optical switching.

There are two types of memory elements: constant length re-entrant fiber loop and variable length fiber delay line.

Constant Length Re-Entrant Fiber Loop as Memory Element

In this type of memory element, the fiber delay line is a loop connecting one of the outputs of a 2 × 2 directional coupler to one of its inputs [29], as shown in Figure 5.31.

A block of photons is switched into the loop and recirculated continually around the loop until required, at which time it is switched out. A per block time-slot interchanger [29,30] can be realized by circulating groups of photons into and out of the loops at the required times. This memory element is called a re-entrant loop.

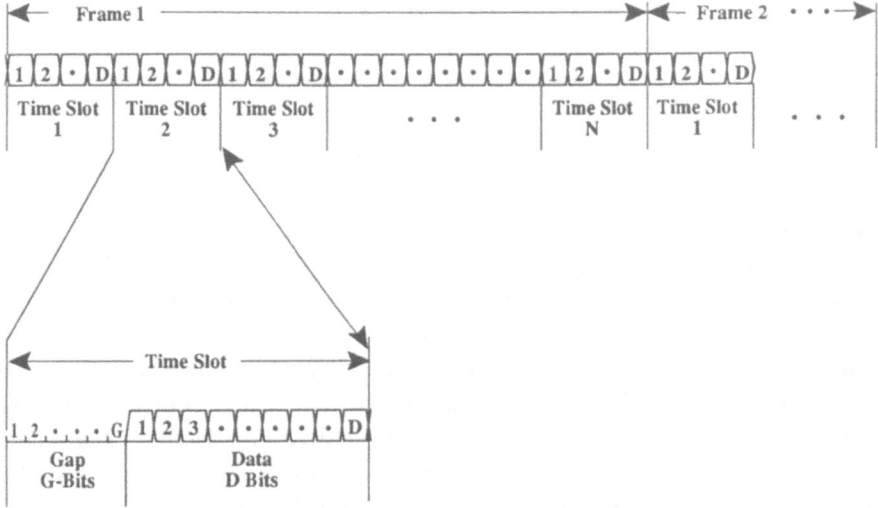

Figure 5.30: Optical data format for time division switching.

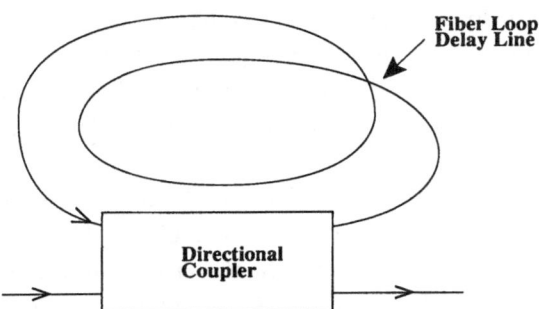

Figure 5.31: Schematic diagram of a constant length re-entrant fiber loop memory element.

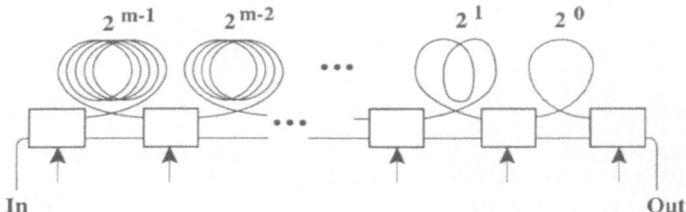

Figure 5.32: Series feedforward structure as memory element.

Variable Length Fiber Delay Line

Two different types of variable length fiber delay lines have been proposed. In the first architecture, straight fiber lines of different lengths, which are integral multiples of one time-slot length [31], have been proposed; in such delay lines, the length of the fiber is cut such that the time it takes a block of photons to reach the 2 × 2 switch is equivalent to one time slot, two time slots, etc. Thus, the time division switching is a result of different delay times in arrival rate at the switching element. In the second architecture, the series feed forward structure [30], shown in Figure 5.32, is proposed as the memory element. The fiber lengths between two consecutive switching elements in the memory element are given by 2^{m-1}, 2^{m-2}, 2^{m-3}, ... , 2^2, 2^1, 0, where $m = [\log_2(number\ of\ time\ slots)] + 1$.

5.7.2   Basic Architecture: Constant Length Fiber (Re-Entrant Loop)

The basic architecture [29,30] is shown in Figure 5.33. It contains three equal-length fiber loop elements for a system with three time slots in the input and output data streams. The implementation uses the 2 × 2 LiNbO₃ directional couplers. Referring to Figure 5.33, photonic data is input at IN in preassigned time slots, and the output at OUT is rearranged into different time slots.

As data in a given time slot arrives at IN, it is steered to the memory element that is emptying its current data to OUT. The switch controlling the loop in this memory element is in the cross state, and all other loop control switches are in the bar state. Since all loops are exactly the correct length to hold one time slot, the first bit in this time slot reaches the end of the loop when the last bit in this time slot enters the loop. At this moment, the switch is put in the bar state and the photons recirculate. The photons are effectively stored, each recirculating once per time slot until its assigned output time slot when the switch element goes into the cross state.

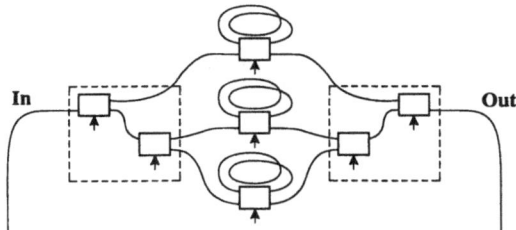

Figure 5.33: Time slot interchanger using re-entrant fiber loops.

If N is the number of time slots in a frame and the data in the i-th input time slot is to appear in the j-th output time slot, this data is delayed by

$$k = N - i + j \qquad (5.13)$$

time slots. Maximum delay k_{max} occurs when i is the first time slot and j is the last time slot N,

$$k_{max} = 2N - 1. \qquad (5.14)$$

Also, the number of memory elements is equal to the number of time slots N. Thus, this basic architecture requires N loops of fiber for N time slots; depending on the rearrangement needed, a time slot can be delayed anywhere from 1 to $2N - 1$ time slots. For each travel through the fiber loop, the data in the time slot suffers L dB optical path loss as it travels through the 2×2 switching element (such as a directional coupler). The architecture requiring a maximum delay of $2N - 1$ time slot maintains the integrity of the frame, i.e.,

1. Data in one frame in the input stream appears in the same frame in the output stream. Data is generally in a different order in going from input to output, but no data moves across a frame boundary.

2. The delay between an input and the corresponding output frame is fixed, typically a delay of one frame.

3. A given time slot in different input frames will enter *different* memory elements (and different delay lines) because the *only* available delay line is the one that is currently being emptied to the output channel. The delay-line selection algorithm is thus nontrivial.

SNR in a Re-Entrant Loop

Suppose the input signal intensity S is attenuated by a factor r as it traverses the switching element once. Further, let us assume that cross talk

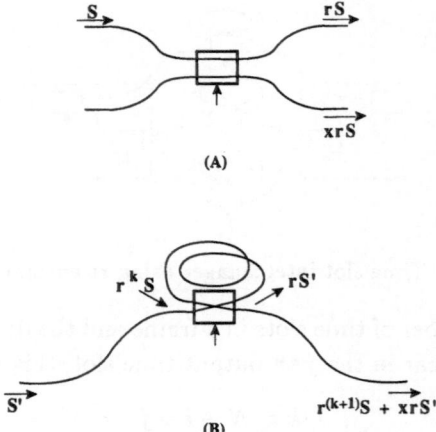

Figure 5.34: SNR in a re-entrant loop. (A) Signal intensities at switch ports before switching. (B) Signal intensities in a re-entrant loop at the critical instant.

is x, implying that a fraction x of the intensity arrives at the unintended output channel. This concept is illustrated in Figure 5.34A for a 2×2 switching element.

With the re-entrant loop serving as a memory element, the signal S is recirculated through the fiber loop k times before it is switched. Since each time the signal traverses the switching element its intensity is reduced by r, the signal intensities at the critical instant when one signal is being switched to the output channel and another signal S' is being switched into the loop are as shown in Figure 5.34B. The signal S has circulated around the re-entrant loop k times and the switching element has just been put in the state in which S is unloaded from the loop and signal S' is loaded on. Because S has recirculated k times, it has been attenuated $k + 1$ times by loss r when it reaches the output of the switching element. At the same instant of time, S' corrupts S by the crosstalk factor xr. Let S and S' have the same original intensity, and let S' be considered noise in the presence of S. The signal-to-noise ratio for the signal in this instant is given by

$$signal - to - noise\ ratio = \frac{coefficient\ of\ S}{coefficient\ of\ S'} = \frac{r^{k+1}}{xr} = \frac{r^k}{x}. \qquad (5.15)$$

When $k = k_{max} = 2N - 1$, then, we have the SNR in the worst case:

$$SNR = \frac{r^{2N-1}}{x}. \qquad (5.16)$$

5.7.3 Basic Architecture: Variable Fiber Delay Lines

The architecture discussed in Section 5.7.2 consisting of constant length re-entrant fiber delay lines, has two drawbacks. First, the signal is attenuated each time it traverses the switching element associated with the fiber loop. Second, the signal is contaminated by crosstalk due to new signals entering the re-entrant fiber delay line while the original signal is being switched out of it. The SNR thus tends to be lower [30]. To avoid this problem, two different solutions have been proposed, and will be discussed below.

Straight Fiber Delay Lines

We could use straight fiber lines of different integral multiples of one time slot length [31]. For the three time slot basic architecture discussed in Section 5.7.1, we shall now need fiber delay lines of lengths corresponding to 1, 2, 3, 4, 5 time slots under the constraint of having to maintain the frame integrity. If the frame integrity requirement is slackened, the delay is reduced to a maximum of $N-1$ time slots. If a block is to move forward in a frame, it is delayed to the new position in the following frame. If a block is to move back in a frame, it is delayed only to that new position in the same frame. Thus, a move forward of one time slot requires a delay of $N-1$ times, and a move backward of one time slot requires a delay of only one time slot. If the block is to remain in the same time slot, there is no delay at all. Therefore, the shortest delay is 0 and the longest delay is $N-1$ time slots, giving a total of N discrete delays required if the frame integrity is not maintained. Furthermore, N discrete delays are introduced by having fiber loops of different lengths from 0 to $N-1$ time slots. The basic architecture [31] of Figure 5.33 is now modified as shown in Figure 5.35.

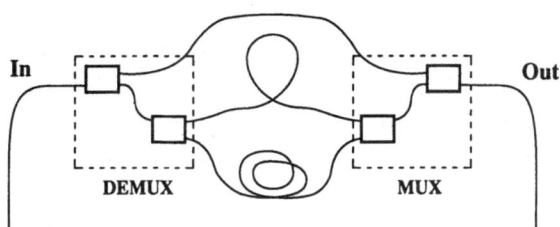

Figure 5.35: Time slot interchanger using variable length straight fiber delay lines without maintaining frame integerity.

Consider a three time-slot input signal where time slots 1 and 3 are interchanged and time slot 2 remains unchanged. The three time slots are demultiplexed, with time slot 1 going to the memory element having a fiber loop of length equal to 2 time slots, and time slot 3 to the memory element with a fiber loop of 1 time-slot length. There is no delay in time slot 2, which is switched as soon as it arrives. The first time slot in the first output frame is empty, and the data in input time slot 1 is now in output time slot 3; output time slot 2 contains data from input time slot 2. The next output frame contains data in all three time slots, with data in input time slots 3 and 1 reversed in order in the output frame.

The architecture ensures that a given input time slot goes to the same fiber delay line. Since there is no switching element involved in such a time-slot interchanger, the only attenuation is due to fiber-switch coupling, since the fiber attenuation is relatively small. However, for a large N time-slot interchanger, the fiber lengths could be several kilometers long; then the fiber attenuation could become significant. For large N, either multiple stage time-slot interchangers or architectures using the series feed forward structure of Figure 5.32 as a memory element have been proposed.

Series Feed Forward Structure

A single memory element in the series feed forward structure [30] consists of several fiber delay loops and several switching elements, as shown in Figure 5.32. However, for the same delay, this structure uses less fiber than the straight fiber delay lines discussed earlier and passes through a fewer number of switching elements than the re-entrant fiber loop delay lines discussed in Section 5.7.2. In this design (Figure 5.32), a structure requiring a delay of m time slots requires $m+1$ switching elements. The fiber delay loops between the switching elements have different lengths equal to $2^{(m-1)} \times$ the unit delay of one time slot. An optical signal (moving from left to right across Figure 5.32) either enters the i-th fiber loop or bypasses it by putting the i-th switching element in the cross or bar state respectively, as appropriate. The delay for a single memory element of Figure 5.32 can be from 0 to 2^{m-1} time slots. The signal passes through each switching element only once.

The basic architecture for the three time-slot interchanger is now shown in Figure 5.36(a) when the frame integrity is maintained.

With frame integrity maintained, the maximum delay required for a

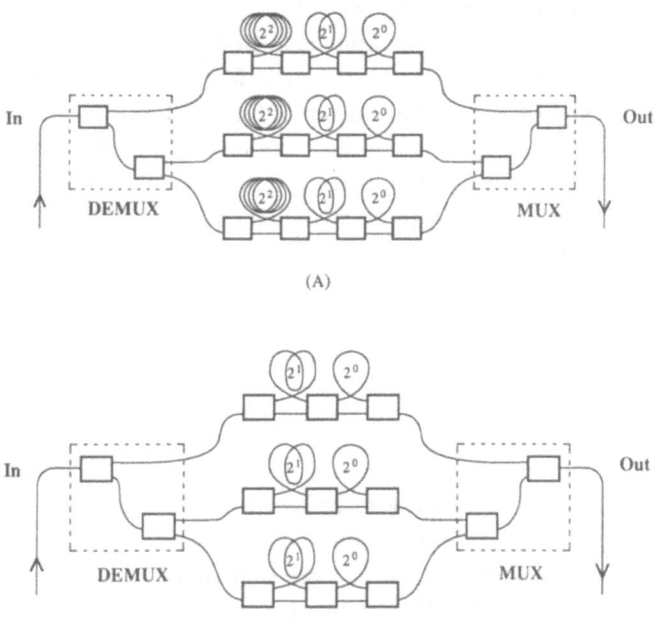

(A)

(B)

Figure 5.36: Time slot interchanger using series feedforward structure as memory element. (A) Frame integrity maintained. (B) No frame integrity.

time-slot interchanger with s time slots is given by

$$m = \log_2 2s = \log_2 s + 1$$

and the required number of switching elements is $\log_2 s + 2$. For a time-slot interchanger with three time slots, we have $m = 3$ with fiber loop lengths of 2^2, 2^1, and 2^0, spread between four switching elements. For time slot 1 on the input side of the time-slot interchanger (TSI) to be switched to the position of time slot 3 on the output side of the TSI, time slot 1 on the input side has to be delayed by $2s - 1 = 5$ time slots, which is obtained by sending time slot 1 on the input side first to the fiber loop of length equivalent to 4 time slots and then to the fiber loop of length equal to 1 time slot, thereby making a total delay of 5 time slots. On the other hand, for time slot 3 on the input side to be switched to time slot 1 on the output side, there is a delay corresponding to only one time slot. The photons contained in this time slot will be switched to a fiber loop of length equal to 1 time slot only. The photons in all the three time slots must traverse all four switching elements of the series feed forward structure. However, if the requirement of frame integrity is relaxed, the three time slot interchanger architecture shown in Figure 5.36(b) is simplified with

$$m = \log_2 s$$

where s is the total number of time slots and the required number of switching elements reduces to $\log_2 s + 1$. Relaxation of frame integrity results in reduction of fiber lengths and a reduction in traverses of switching elements of the series feed forward structure. Note that there is no crosstalk in either the variable length straight fiber delay line or the series feed forward structure. However, the signal would be somewhat weaker in this architecture compared to the straight fiber delay line architecture because of the need to traverse switching elements in the series feed forward structure. The advantage of this structure, however, is the ability to provide a fault-tolerant architecture because all the memory elements are identical.

5.8 Conclusions and Summary
5.8.1 Limitations of Optical Switching

We have discussed several optical space division and time division architectures. However, any commercial application is some time away. We conclude the unit with a discussion on the limitations and possible applications of optical switching.

Electro-optic guided wave switching offers many potential advantages, especially where very high throughput (10s of gigabits and terabit range) is desired. However, there are practical limits of using this technology in a switching product.

One major constraint is the physical size of the optical devices. The directional coupler (one of the most promising switching elements) is very long and can range from 2 to 10 mm in length. In addition, a significant amount of room must be left between devices for waveguide interconnections, since the diffused channel waveguides are limited to gradual curves with radii greater than about 4 cm. Today's best densities are about 10 to 100 couplers on a standard $LiNbO_3$ crystal (1 × 6 cm) size.

Another constraint is the control voltage, typically in the range of from 10 to 50 volts. Special driver circuits must be used to provide the required voltages. With the addition of driver circuits, an optical switch requires even more physical space. High voltage tends to increase the cost of the drivers and decrease the switching speed and reconfiguration rate of the switch. Maximum reconfiguration rates for a reasonable-sized switch matrix (that is, 8 × 8) may be confined to 10s to 100s of MHz if 10 to 50 volts must be switched. The 2500 picosecond reconfiguration rates that have been reported for an 8 × 8 Dilated Benes switch matrix [33] may be the maximum achievable rate. Once configured in a state, however, the optical switch has a virtually unlimited data throughput rate. The third major constraint is the problem of synchronization. Care must be taken that no data bitstream is lost during the configuration change of the switching element from bar to cross state and vice versa.

Finally, given the attenuation and SNR limits discussed in Sections 5.6.1, 5.6.2, and 5.6.5, there is a limit on the dimensionality of an optical switch without requiring regeneration and amplification within the switch. Even with the best architectures, an $N \times N$ switch can approach dimensions of only a few hundred before becoming seriously limited by attenuation or SNR. However, it may not be a serious limitation with the use of time division switching because optical switches and electronic switches have different applications.

Several other technological problems must be addressed before optical switches are likely to be commercially successful. Some problems are:

1. Voltage sensitivity and drift. The 2 × 2 directional coupler, which is the basic component of the architectures discussed here, is highly sensitive to applied voltage for switching from the cross to the bar

state. Furthermore, the voltage needed to switch from cross state to bar sate and vice versa changes with time. Thus, the crosstalk would increase with time for a given voltage setting.

2. Polarization.   Polarization of light generally changes as it travels through the fiber. Although polarization-maintaining fibers are available, such special-purpose fibers are expensive. Furthermore, the applied voltage required for switching depends somewhat on the polarization of light. In addition, there is a change in polarization when the fiber couples to the diffused titanium waveguide because of the differences in waveguide cross-section from circular to elliptical. This change in polarization as the light from the fiber enters the titanium waveguide is an additional source of attenuation and crosstalk.

3. Format. As noted in Section 5.7.1, time division switching depends on block multiplexing rather than bit multiplexing. However, only recently a standard format (SONET) has emerged for optical signals using block multiplexing.

4. Wave division multiplexing (WDM). Proposed time division switching architectures use wave division multiplexing to extract clock data from incoming signals to synchronize the switching function of the directional coupler. Questions similar to B8ZS and B3ZS coding schemes for electronic digital signals DS1 and DS3 arise so that clock data can be extracted.

5. Additional issues, such as automatic gain control, need to be also addressed.

Dilated networks, discussed in Section 5.5.7, are promising because by carrying only one active path per switching element at a given time, crosstalk problems associated with voltage drift and polarization changes become irrelevant. For large $N \times N$ networks, optical signals may require some amplification for a reasonable level of output signals.

Future research should improve the characteristics of the basic optical devices, as well as bring new devices and architectures to this emerging field. We are looking at a young technology, continually developing with a lot of potential for the future.

5.8.2 Optical Switching Applications

While Ti : LiNbO$_3$ guided wave optical switching technology is the most advanced, there are constraints as discussed in Section 5.8.1. It may very well be the case that this is not the ultimate solution for all switching needs. the ultimate solution could combine the logic aspects of the SEED technology with the unlimited throughput of the guided wave technology. However, until such systems become available, we ask ourselves how and where this optical switching technology might best fit into the overall switching framework. The first consideration is defining the type of environment that is best suited for optical switching.

Optical switching fits into high data rate environments, especially those situations where the data rates are faster than can be handled in a large electronic switch matrix (above several 100s of MHz). Because the reconfiguration rates are relatively slow (10s to 100s of MHz) compared with the possible data throughput rates (10s of GHz to THz), optics should be used for slow-speed switching of very high-speed signals. One example is a very high-definition TV channel that is switched only when the customer changes stations. Other possible applications may be high throughput protection switching, high throughput optical cross-connect systems, and local area or metropolitan area networks. At present, size, power, attenuation, SNR, and cost tend to limit optical switching applications to small switching networks. We can envision the size of these networks to reach several hundred by several hundred, but not several thousand in the foreseeable future.

Acknowledgements

I thank Richard A. Thompson and Ronald A. Spanke for providing me access to their published and unpublished material, for reviewing several of my drafts and for their invaluable suggestions on improving the material contained in this paper.

APPENDIX A: Directional Coupler – Three-Dimensional Representation

In this appendix, we show that the cross state of a directional coupler occurs if the interaction length L of the waveguides in the coupling region, is given by

$$L = (2n + 1)\ell, \quad n = 0, 1, 2, 3, \ldots$$

and the propagation constants in the two waveguides are equal, i.e., $\delta = \Delta\beta/2 = 0$. Here, ℓ is the transfer length. We also show that switching in a directional coupler can be expressed mathematically by three-dimensional rotations.

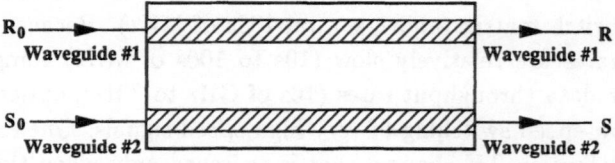

Figure A.1: Representation of input and output light beams for a directional coupler.

Let R_o and S_o be the electric fields of the incoming light beams and let R and S represent the same quantities in the outgoing light beams, as shown in Figure A.1. Note that the quantities R_o, S_o, R, and S are complex, and can be represented as complex vectors:

$$C = \begin{bmatrix} R_o \\ S_o \end{bmatrix} \text{ and } C' = \begin{bmatrix} R \\ S \end{bmatrix} \tag{A.1}$$

where

$$R_o R_o^* + S_o S_o^* = 1 \tag{A.2}$$

and

$$RR^* + SS^* = 1. \tag{A.3}$$

The transfer matrix D, describing the modified relative amplitude and phase of light in the two outgoing waveguides, is given by [15,17,18]

$$C' = D \cdot C \tag{A.4}$$

where

$$D = \begin{bmatrix} A & -jB \\ -jB & A^* \end{bmatrix} \tag{A.5}$$

and where A is complex and B is real. In terms of the coupling coefficient κ and phase difference δ, A and B can be written as

$$A = \cos\psi + j\delta L\frac{\sin\psi}{\psi} \tag{A.6}$$

$$B = \kappa L\frac{\sin\psi}{\psi} \tag{A.7}$$

where

$$\psi = L\sqrt{\kappa^2 + \delta^2} \text{ and } \delta = \frac{\Delta\beta}{2}, \quad \kappa = \pi/2\ell. \tag{A.8}$$

Consider the case when light is incident only from waveguide 1, i.e., $S_o = 0$ in Eq. (A-1). Substituting $S_o = 0$ in Eq. (A-3) and using Eqs. (A-4), (A-5), and (A-6), output electric field vectors are given by

$$R = \left(\cos\psi + j\delta L\frac{\sin\psi}{\psi}\right)R_o \tag{A.9}$$

$$S = -j\left(\kappa L\frac{\sin\psi}{\psi}\right)R_o. \tag{A.10}$$

The power output is given by

$$SS^* = \kappa^2 L^2\left(\frac{\sin\psi}{\psi}\right)^2 R_o R_o^*. \tag{A.11}$$

From Eq. (A-2), we get

$$R_o R_o^* = 1 \tag{A.12}$$

and

$$RR^* = 1 - SS^*. \tag{A.13}$$

When the propagation constants in the two waveguides are equal, $\Delta\beta = 0$, and hence $\delta = 0$. Eq. (A-10) now reduces to

$$SS^* = \kappa^2 L^2\left(\frac{\sin\kappa L}{\kappa L}\right)^2 = \sin^2\kappa L. \tag{A.14}$$

Note that Eq. (A-13) is maximum when

$$\kappa L = (2n+1)\frac{\pi}{2}, \quad n = 0, 1, 2, 3, \ldots \tag{A.15}$$

as discussed in the text. Substituting from Eq. (A-7), where $\kappa = \pi/2\ell$ from Eq. (A-14), we get

$$L = (2n+1)\ell. \tag{A.16}$$

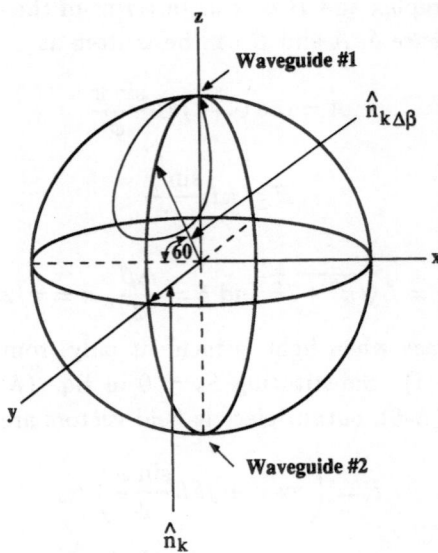

Figure A.2: Three dimensional rotational representation of switching in a directional coupler.

To derive a three-dimensional rotational representation of the directional coupler [18] we consider the properties of the transfer matrix D in Eqs. (A-3) and (A-4).

The 2×2 matrix D in Eq. (A-12) is complex, preserves the vector dot product, and conserves the norm. Such a matrix is a unitary matrix satisfying

$$U^+ U = 1 \tag{A.17}$$

and has a determinant,

$$\det U = 1 \tag{A.18}$$

This unitary matrix can be represented as rotations in 3-dimensional space, given by

$$
T(D) = \begin{bmatrix}
\frac{1}{2}(A^2 + A^{*2}) + B^2 & -\frac{i}{2}(A^2 - A^{*2}) & jB(A - A^*) \\
\frac{i}{2}(A^2 - A^{*2}) & \frac{1}{2}(A^2 + A^{*2}) - B^2 & -B(A + A^*) \\
jB(A - A^*) & B(A + A^*) & AA^* - B^2
\end{bmatrix}.
\tag{A.19}
$$

In the case of a directional coupler shown schematically in Figure A-1, light crosses over completely from waveguide 1 to waveguide 2 in the absence of an applied voltage. In the cross state (see Figure 5.8), when no voltage is applied, the input state vector points at the north pole and is rotated about the Y-axis to the south pole, as shown in Figure A.2. When a voltage is applied to induce a phase difference, $\Delta\beta = \sqrt{3}\pi/\ell$, the axis of rotation in Figure A.2 is no longer the Y-axis or the Z-axis but is in the Y-Z plane at 60°. The initial state vector is rotated about this axis in Figure A.2 starting at the north pole by 360° and ends at the starting point. This rotation results in the bar state shown in Figure 5.8.

References

[1] Hewitt, L., and Pitchford, M., *Making the Transition: Fiber Winds Its Way Home,* Telephony, Feb. 15, 1988, p 34.

[2] Elion, H. A., and Morozov, V. N., *Optoelectronic Switching Systems in Telecommunications and Computers,* Marcel Dekker, Inc., New York & Basel, 1984.

[3] Pyykkonen, M., *Optical Switching and Computing,* Telecommunications, Dec. 1986, p. 32.

[4] Personick, S. D., *Photonic Switching: Technology and Applications,* IEEE Communications Magazine, Vol. 25(5), p. 5, May 1987.

[5] Kaufman, S., Reynolds, R. L., and Loeffer, C., *Optical Switch for the SL Undersea Lightwave System,* in *Undersea Lightwave Communications,* P.K. Runge and P.R. Trischitta (Editors), IEEE Press, New York, 1986, p. 487.

[6] Joel, A. E., Jr., *On Permutation Switching Network,* Bell System Technical Journal, Vol. 47, p. 813, 1968.

[7] Hinton, H. S., *Photonic Switching Connects to the Future,* Telecommunications, p. 79, May 1987; Prucnal, P. R., Blumenthal, D. J., and Perrier, P. A., *Self-Routing Photonic Switching Demonstration with Optical Control,* Optical Engineering, Vol. 26(5), p. 423, May 1987.

[8] Huang, A., *Architectural Considerations Involved in the Design of an Optical Digital Computer,* Proceedings of the IEEE, Vol.72(7), p. 780, July 1984.

[9] Jewell, J.L., Rushford, M.C., and Gibbs, H.M., *Use of a Single Nonlinear Fabry-Perot Etalon as Optical Logic Gates*, Applied Physics Letters, Vol. 44(2), p. 172, Jan. 1984.

[10] Miller, D. A. B., et al., *The Quantum Well Self-Electro-Optical Effect Device: Optoelectronic Bistability and Oscillation, and Self-Linearized Modulation*, IEEE J. Quantum Electronics, Vol.QE-21(9), p. 1462, Sept. 1985.

[11] Streibl, N., et al., *Digital Optics*, Proceedings of the IEEE, Jan 1990 (to be published); Miller, D.A.B., *Optics for low-energy communication inside digital processors: quantum detectors, sources, and modulators as efficient impedance converters*, Optics Letters, Vol. 14(2), p. 146, Jan 15, 1989; Friberg, S.R., et. al., *Femtosecond switching in a dual-core-fiber nonlinear coupler*, Optics Letters, Vol. 13(10), p. 904, Oct 1988.

[12] Ohmachi, Y., Node, J., *LiNbO₃ TE → TM Mode Converter Using Collinear Acousto-Optic Interaction*, IEEE J. Quantum Electronics, Vol. QE-13, p. 43, 1977.

[13] Tien, P. K., et al., *Switching and Modulation of Light in Magnetoptic Waveguides of Garnet Films*, Applied Physical Letters, Vol. 21, p. 394, 1972.

[14] Tsai, C. S., Kim, B., and El-Akkari, F. R., *Optical Channel Waveguide Switch and Coupler Using Total Internal Reflection*, IEEE J. Quantum Electronics, Vol. QE-14(7), p. 513, 1978.

[15] Hinton, H. S., *Photonic Switching Using Directional Couplers*, IEEE Communications Magazine, Vol. 25, p. 16, May 1987; Bergmann, E. E., McCaughan, L., and Watson, J. E., *Coupling of Intersecting Ti : LiNbO₃ Diffused Waveguides*, Applied Optics, Vol. 23(17), Sept. 1, 1987.

[16] Schmidt, R. V., and Alferness, R. C., *Directional Coupler Switches, Modulators and Filters Using Alternating Δβ Techniques*, IEEE Transactions on Circuits and Systems, Vol.CAS-26, p.1099, Dec.1979.

[17] Miller, S. E., *Coupled-Wave Theory and Waveguide Applications*, Bell System Technical Journal, Vol. 33, p. 661, May 1954.

[18] Korotky, S. K., *Three-Space Representation of Phase-Mismatch Switching in Coupled Two-State Optical Systems*, IEEE J. Quantum Electronics, Vol.QE-22(6), p. 952, June 1986.

[19] Kogelnik, H., and Schmidt, R. V., *Switched Directional Couplers with Alternating $\Delta\beta$*, IEEE J. Quantum Electronics, Vol.QE-12, p. 396, July 1976; Schmidt, R. V., and Kogelnik, H., *Electro-Optically Switched Coupler with Stepped $\Delta\beta$ Reversal Using Ti-Diffused $LiNbO_3$ Waveguides*, Applied Physical Letters, Vol.28(9), May 1, 1976.

[20] Alferness, R. C., Schmidt, R. V., and Turner, E. H., *Characteristics of Ti-diffused Lithium Niobate Optical Directional Couplers*, Applied Optics , Vol. 18,(23), p. 4012, Dec. 1979.

[21] Thompson, R. A., *Traffic Capabilities of Two Rearrangeably Non-Blocking Photonic Switching Modules*, AT&T Technical Journal, Vol. 64(10), p. 2331, Dec. 1985.

[22] Spanke, R. A., *Architectures for Guided-Wave Optical Space Switching Systems*, IEEE Communications Magazine, Vol. 25(5), p. 42, May 1987.

[23] Padmanabhan, K., and Netravali, A., *Dilated networks for photonic switching*, IEEE Trans. Communications, Vol. COM-35(12), p. 1357, Dec. 1987.

[24] Spanke, R. A., and Benes, V. E., *N-Stage Planar Optical Permutation Network*, Applied Optics, Vol. 26(7), April 1987.

[25] Kondo, M., Takado, N., Komatsu, K., and Ohta, Y., *32 Switch Elements Integrated Low-Crosstalk $LiNbO_3$ 4×4 Optical Matrix Switch*, IOOC-ECOC 1985, Venice, pp. 361-364, 1985.

[26] Clos, C., *A Study of Non-Blocking Switching Networks*, Bell System Technical Journal Vol. 32, p. 404, March 1953.

[27] Benes, V. E., *Mathematical Theory of Connecting Network and Telephone Traffic*, Academic Press, New York, 1965.

[28] Spanke, R. A., *Architectures for Large Nonblocking Optical Space Switches*, IEEE J. Quantum Electronics, Vol. QE-22, p. 964, June 1986.

[29] Thompson, R. A., and Giordano, P. P., *An Experimental Photonic Time Slot Interchanger Using Optical Fiber as Re-Entrant Delay-Line Memories*, IEEE Journal of Lightwave Technology, Jan.1987.

[30] Thompson, R. A., *Architecture for Improved Signal-to-Noise Ratio in Photonic Systems with Fiber-Loop Delay Lines*, AT&T Bell Laboratories Report (1987), and *Architectures with Improved Signal-to-Noise Ratio in Photonic Systems with Fiber-Loop Delay Lines*, IEEE Journal SAC, Vol. 6, p. 1096, Aug. 1988.

[31] Kondo, M., et al., *High Speed Optical Time Switch with Integrated Optical* 1 × 4 *Switches and Single-Polarization Fiber Delay Lines*, presented at the International Conference of Integrated Optical Fiber Communications, June 1983.

[32] G. R. Ritchie, *Syntran - A new direction for digital transmission terminals*, EEE Communications, Nov. 1985.

[33] Watson, J.E., Milbrodt, M.A., Bahadori, K., Dautartas, M.F., Kemmerer, C.T., Moser, D.T., Schelling, A.W., Murphy, T.O., Veselka, J.J., and Herr, D.A., *A Low Voltage Low Crosstalk* $8 \times 8\ Ti : LiNbO_3$ *Switch for a Time-Multiplexed Switching System*, Optical Fiber Communication Conference Digest, Optical Society of America, Houston, Texas, Feb 6, 1989, p. 135.

CHAPTER 6

SYNCHRONIZATION IN HARD
REAL-TIME SYSTEMS

Satish K. Tripathi and **Vivek M. Nirkhe** [1]
Computer Science Department
University of Maryland
College Park, MD 20742

Abstract

Maruti is a testbed for the design of distributed, hard real-time systems and is based on object-oriented philosophy. In such an environment, synchronization among concurrently executing objects is an important issue. Apart from providing mutual exclusion and conditional synchronization, we need to maintain the required order among threads and to characterize the timing behavior of the primitives. In this paper we have specified real-time synchronization requirements, reviewed various approaches, and evaluated them with respect to the requirements. We have proposed a set of primitives which are integrated into Maruti object-oriented programming. They are designed to be efficient and with low overheads. Separate primitives for each function makes programs more readable. They also help in pre-scheduling the application to guarantee that the deadlines will be met.

This work is supported in part by contract DSAG60-87-C-0066 from the U. S. Army Strategic Defense Command to the Department of Computer Science, University of Maryland. The views, opinions, and/or findings contained in this report are those of the authors and should not be construed as an official Department of Defense position, policy, or decision, unless so designated by other official documentation.

[1] This author was supported in part by a fellowship from the UMIACS, Department of Computer Science and Institute for Advanced Computer Studies, University of Maryland, College Park, MD 20742.

6.1   Introduction

Embedded real-time systems are being used for control in a number of complex applications. Due to the critical nature of such applications, the functional correctness, reliability, and temporal behavior of real-time systems are of utmost importance to the application. The applications range from simple home appliances, laboratory instruments to more complex process control, robotics, flight control and tactical control in military applications. It is evident that such systems need high safety and reliability. The correct behavior of these applications is entirely dependent on that of real-time systems.

With ever increasing automation in different applications, real-time systems will continue to play a vital role in every aspect of our lives. The next generation of real-time systems will add further complexities with the need for distributed and parallel processing. In a recent article Stankovic [1] claims about real-time systems that "They will be distributed and capable of exhibiting intelligent, adaptive, and highly dynamic behavior. They will also have long lifetimes. Moreover, catastrophic consequences will result if the logical or timing constraints are not met.".

The two reasons, that have brought about these changes in the way we view real-time systems, are the following. Firstly, newer applications have put increasing demands on real-time systems. Secondly, the advances in hardware technology have made it possible to use a number of inexpensive processors to build multiprocessors and distributed systems to support such applications. The software technology and theory of real-time systems have failed to keep pace with such advances in applications and hardware.

This paper deals mainly with one aspect of real-time systems, namely, synchronization. In the second section, we introduce real-time systems and pinpoint the issues that are central to them. We describe the traditional approaches towards building real-time systems and show how they fall short of their goals. In the third section, the problem of synchronization is introduced. We describe the goals of concurrent programming and enumerate the aspects of synchronization in real-time systems. In the fourth section, we have reviewed different synchronization primitives. We have also given the pros and cons of each solution. In the fifth section, we describe the desirable features of synchronization primitives for a hard real-time, distributed environment. We have also compared the traditional synchronization primitives for their merits. This is also a motivation for the design decisions for the synchronization primitives presented in Section 6.6. In Section 6.6, we have presented the design philosophy of Maruti, a hard real-time distributed testbed being developed at University of Maryland. We introduce object-oriented programming, the approach taken in Maruti. Thereafter we have described the Maruti synchronization primitives. In the end we have some comments on the shortcomings of our approach. The paper concludes with directions towards future research.

6.2 Real-Time Systems

There is no single definition of real-time systems on which experts agree, but the following definition captures the essence. Young [2] claims that "the term *real time* can be used to describe any information processing activity or system which has to respond to externally generated input stimuli within a finite and specifiable delay ". Thus, the aspect that sets real-time systems apart from usual systems is that their total correctness depends on both the logical correctness and timely responses. Failure of any of the aspects is a failure of the system. A real-time system must *guarantee* correct response within some specified time under all anticipated load and fault conditions.

Real-time systems can be partitioned into two classes, hard real-time systems and soft real-time systems. The term *hard real-time* (HRT) is used to specify the systems where there are strict bounds on the response times to all stimuli [3,4,5,6]. The responses that do not come within their time-bounds are invalid or of no use. In *soft real-time* systems, some deadlines may be missed or some responses that come outside the time bounds are still useful. Northcutt [7] defines the terms *hard* and *soft* to indicate the value in continuing the specified computation after it is determined that its deadline cannot be met. In the former case there is none whereas in the latter one there is some. We restrict ourselves to the study of hard real-time systems. Though HRT may be too restrictive, it is easier to study.

Traditionally, fast response time has been used as a remedy for predictability. Estimation of program timing is also used as a technique. Such techniques include use of an assembly language [8], use of extensive simulation [9], or testing [10]. Often priorities are used; and higher priorities are assigned to real-time tasks to ensure timely and quick responses to critical applications. Small and dedicated systems that process sensory data provide low level device (sensor) interfacing and fast interrupt handling to ensure that critical applications are processed in time.

These traditional techniques have often been used for small and simple systems and have been found useful. They do not seem sufficient for complex applications which are dynamic and adaptive for the following reasons. Any changes in the system can lead to changes in its timing characteristics and a complete reevaluation of its behavior is necessary. They fall short in uncovering logical incorrectness, or complete timing characteristics, which are a must in case of the critical applications described above.

If the execution times of machine instructions are known, assembly language programs can be analyzed to determine their completion times. Deadlines of applications are ensured by interleaving unrelated tasks or using busy waits. Assembly language programming is very awkward and error-prone. It is a primitive concept for the complex systems of today. Timing characteristics of assembly programs are very rigid, making the system inflexible and difficult to extend.

Simulation too is undesirable since it fails to model all aspects of the system and does not give a precise idea of the behavior under all conditions. It is impossible to test all possible execution paths in the system and those untested paths make the system vulnerable.

Use of static priorities is also incapable of meeting the process requirements. There is no proper policy or algorithms for allocating priorities. Mostly the task of assigning priorities is left to the user, which involves a lot of tuning [7]. Arrival of a higher priority interrupt can disrupt an ongoing task. It does not guarantee the absence of a higher priority, and hence the correct behavior.

Thus, newer and better techniques are needed to design real-time systems and to better understand the underlying fundamental problems [11]. In the words of Duanne Northcutt [7] " Most so-called real-time operating systems today have relatively little that separates them from other types of operating systems. For the most part, they provide minimal functionality, preferring instead to pass the time, space, and intellectual complexity burdens of the system resource management to the application programmer." Therefore, we need theories to reason about correctness, timeliness and reliability of these systems to construct systems that will meet demands of the future applications.

Real-time systems are affected by a number of aspects of computers: processor, system architecture, operating system, programming environment (language, compiler, and run-time libraries), run-time kernel, network architecture, and communication mechanism. Each of the above components - its logical correctness and temporal behavior - is of crucial importance to the correctness of the real-time systems. These aspects make real-time software development a very complex task. Fault tolerance requirements add further complexities. Changes or failure of the any components of the system can lead to changes in the behavior of the system; it may not satisfy the application constraints any longer. Any modification of the system can involve high costs [12]. These aspects make real-time software development complex and expensive. It is also true that the current software development techniques will not be sufficient to meet the requirements of next generation real-time systems.

To overcome such problems, many attempts have been made to incorporate ideas that were developed in the other areas of software development. They include use of modular programming [13], top-down design, use of abstract data types [14], program verification [15,16], and object-oriented programming [17,18,19,20].

6.3 Synchronization

Most of the traditional real-time systems are static and are dedicated to particular applications. In future the HRT systems will be expected to perform a variety of unrelated tasks. The software development for such systems is handled by treating each task separately. This issue of *separation of concern* has led to the development of problem decomposition, stepwise refinement [21,22], and data abstraction [14]. This technique makes it easier to understand, maintain and modify the software [4,23]. It is also used for development of real-time software of AE-7 aircraft in order to reduce timing dependencies among unrelated tasks [3,4]. The software for AE-7 is developed as a set of cooperating processes, each of which deals with one task.

A *sequential program* is a list of statements that are executed in sequence. It's execution is called a *process*. A sequential program consists of a single thread of control in one address space. A *concurrent program* is a multi-thread, one address space entity, whereas a *distributed program* is a multi-thread, multi-address space entity [24,39]. In a multi-thread execution, different threads execute as *parallel processes*. Since we are interested in the program invocations, henceforth we will use the term "process" in our discussion. An example of concurrent processes is one of *readers and writers*, where both readers and writers (separate processes) are trying to access the same file [26]. We can allow multiple readers to read in parallel, whereas only one writer can write at a time, in order to prevent lost updates or inconsistency in the data.

Concurrent processes can be considered to be independent for the purpose of scheduling their execution. They can be designed and executed with a view that they have their own processor. In practice, processes are not completely independent since they share common resources with other processes. They depend upon each other, if the output produced by one may be used as input to another or if they have timing dependencies.

Processes which share resources or are cooperating with each other in some computation are called *cooperating processes*, (e.g. readers and writers). Such processes can execute in parallel with certain restrictions which are imposed due to the nature of the shared resource. Since, no assumptions can be made regarding the relative speeds of such processes, they need to synchronize with each other to cooperate.

Concurrent programming provides high level constructs for writing programs that have concurrent processes. A number of languages have been developed and used for concurrent programming. The objectives of concurrent programming are [23]:

- To hide the sequencing of operations. Concurrent programming constructs (e.g. cobegin, fork-join) provide explicit means to express the situation wherein two statements do not have any sequence and can be executed in any order. The actual sequence may depend upon the number of processors, the compiler, system architecture etc. Use of such constructs facilitates recognition of parallelism and parallel execution of operations.

- To provide tools for problem decomposition. The technique can be used to decompose complex problems into smaller unrelated or loosely related problems. The smaller problems can in turn be decomposed or solved independently and modeled as independent processes. Any data and order dependency among the processes is reflected in their synchronization; programmers do not have to worry about the exact sequencing of individual processes.

- To make efficient use of hardware. Especially in operating systems, concurrent programming has been used to allow i/o overlap for an efficient use of available processors. A multiprocessor system can also be utilized efficiently by running different processes on different processors.

Real-time programming differs from concurrent programming in the first goal discussed above. In real-time systems, the programmer has to control the order of execution of processes. The order may be needed to control some physical processes and meet their timing constraints. Unlike concurrent programming, ordering may be necessary even if the processes do not share any resources. Consider the following example of two processes which control operation of an automobile: a process controlling the running of the car and another process which monitors whether any door is open. Though they do not share anything tangible, the safety of the passengers requires a sequence that the door be closed before the automobile runs. In order to operate the car, the two processes need to execute in a certain order and in particular, the latter has to be completed before the former.

Synchronization has the following aspects in real-time programming.

1. **Interprocess Communication (IPC)**

   IPC allows one process to influence the outcome of another process and is usually achieved using shared variables or message passing. Since processes can execute at unpredictable speeds, they need to synchronize to communicate. For example, if processes communicate via shared variables, then the process that is going to read the variable has to synchronize with the process that is modifying the variable. One process needs to detect some action performed by another process for IPC to take place. Thus, their execution must be ordered in that way. This is usually done by delaying one process until the event for which it is waiting takes place. Instead of delaying the process by busy waiting, the process sleep-waits and a synchronization mechanism is used to awaken it. Thereafter, the communication takes place using the appropriate means.

   Normally, processes that are waiting for the arrival of a message are in a *ready* state, that is they can be scheduled for execution any time afterwards. The synchronization mechanism wakes the process and the process is put in the queue of ready processes in the scheduler. In real-time systems, they may do so only if the application demands it. The following example illustrates the point. Consider a robot, which is sorting blocks of different colors off an assembly line. A sensor informs the robot of the color of the coming block. Even after the robot gets a communication from the sensor regarding the color of the block, the robot has to wait until the block comes within its reach. This shows that execution speeds and timings of real-time processes are determined by the application and the external events. Hence processes may not be awakened up by the synchronization mechanism.

2. **Process Ordering**

Some process which do not share any data may still have to be synchronized due to the precedence requirements of the events of the real-time processes it is controlling. Consider an example of process control, where two valves have to be opened simultaneously or within some fixed time of each other. It may be the case that the liquids released from the valves may have to be mixed some time later and hence the timing restriction. In this example, even if the processes do not share any data or communicate, they have to be synchronized to follow a particular order. It is possible to synchronize their actions and get the required order by making one process send unnecessary signals or messages to another. Such use of synchronization (messages) here is misleading since its purpose is not clear. As we shall see later, processes need not signal or communicate if the system can schedule the respective processes, appropriately recognizing their mutual ordering requirement. Implicitly, time itself can be used for synchronization.

3. **Mutual Exclusion**

Since computing resources are scarce, we would like to keep them busy to increase the throughput and reduce response time. This manifests in process interleaving for sharing the resources. However, such interleaving can give rise to problems. Consider the following two processes that are updating the same account. They are depositing money by executing the following statements:

```
process 1 :                      process 2:
...                              ...
 local1 := balance;               local2 := balance;
 local1 := local1 + 100;          local2 := local2 + 200;
 balance := local1;               balance := local2;
```

Under normal circumstances, the total deposit should be 300 dollars. But, consider the following order of execution. If the order was, in terms of (process : statement), (process 1:1), (process 2:1), (process 1:2), (process:1:3), (process 2:2), and (process 2:3) the result would be 200. This phenomenon is called *lost updates*. Thus processes sharing some resource like data, devices, or processors, need some synchronization in order to ensure resource integrity. *Mutual exclusion* is one such mechanism which allows a process to execute a number of statements in an indivisible manner. This also ensures that no more than one process can access the same resource at the same time.

4. **Conditional Synchronization**

The actions of two processes need to be synchronized when the state of the shared data is not suitable to be used by one of the processes. The process that needs the system to reach some state has to wait for the other process to cause the required transition.

Consider the problem of producers and consumers. A producer can continually produce data and fill buffers until the all buffers are full. Thereafter, the producer needs to wait for the consumer to consume some data and free some buffers. These buffers can then be used to store more data. Similarly a consumer can consume all the data that is produced but needs to wait for the producer to produce some more data after all buffers are empty. Thus each process has to wait on some condition that can be set by the other. A process cannot proceed unless the system reaches some state, or unless some condition becomes true, or until the system makes a required transition [3]. Such synchronization is referred to as *conditional synchronization.*

6.4 Synchronization Primitives

In this section a number of synchronization primitives are described. We divide these primitives into two classes: the ones based on shared memory and the ones based on message passing. There are a number of primitives of each kind and we will not be able to consider all of them. We will not describe the constructs used to express the parallelism in the language either.

6.4.1 Synchronization Based on Shared Variables

These techniques can be used efficiently where processes share the memory. By shared variables, we mean some address space that can be addressed by both processes.

Busy-Waiting

In this method, one process performs an infinite loop to check the value of a shared variable that is used to synchronize. It can be used to provide mutual exclusion by controlling access to the critical section. The access is controlled using an entry protocol and an exit protocol. The entry protocol is used to monitor if any process is in the critical section and allows only one process to enter if no other process is there. The process that wants to access the shared variable busy waits at the entry protocol. The first correct solution to this problem was presented by Dekker [27] followed subsequently by a much simpler solution by Peterson [28]. These protocols are the basis of software implementation of semaphores, the topic of the next section. Busy waiting can be implemented with indivisible assembly instructions such as *test-and-set* or *compare-and-swap* [29]. Conditional synchronization can be implemented by making the process check the required condition periodically. The variables of the condition are accessed using mutual exclusion.

The drawbacks of these primitives are that they waste processor cycles and are difficult to design and understand, since they are not structured. Protocols for mutual exclusion of n processes have also been developed, namely Lamport's Bakery algorithm [30] and Dijkstra's generalization of Dekker's algorithm [31,32]. These algorithms need not know the identities of processes but need to know the exact number of processes. The best complexity of these algorithms is $O(n)$, where n is the number of processes taking part in synchronization. The other drawback of these algorithms is that a high level programmer has to worry about the details of loops, condition evaluation, use of a proper protocol to evaluate the conditions etc., making the code unreadable.

Semaphores

Recognizing the difficulties of low level programming, Dijkstra [33] developed semaphores. A *semaphore* is an abstract data type, which takes non-negative integer values and has only two operations defined on it, namely, **P** and **V**. For a semaphore s, a process executing **P**(s), gets delayed until $s > 0$, and then s is decremented by 1. **V**(s) increments s by 1. Both these operations are executed as indivisible operations.

Mutual exclusion is implemented using semaphores with the entry protocol replaced by **P** and exit protocol by **V** on the same semaphore by all concerned processes. A conditional synchronization can be implemented by representing the condition by a semaphore. The process that wants to wait on the condition performs **P**, whereas the process flagging the condition performs **V**. Processes can synchronize with each other simply knowing the name of the shared semaphore. They do not need to know the identities of each other.

Semaphores can be implemented using methods mentioned in the previous section which are not efficient. An efficient implementation uses calls to kernel by which the processes performing **P** are put into a *wait queue*. A wait queue is a queue of processes that are waiting for some event to take place and thus, are not ready to execute. The wait queue is maintained in the scheduler. The responsibility of waking a process is entrusted to the kernel. The process itself does not recognize the condition.

The drawback of semaphores is that they do not constitute a structured mechanism. It is difficult to understand the purpose of a particular semaphore, whether it is used for synchronization or for mutual exclusion. Since the semaphore operations are distributed over different processes, it is also difficult to follow the logic of the program. All processes sharing a common resource have to follow the same constructs; a single mistake such as reversing the order of **P** and **V** or missing an operation, can lead to unpredictable results. The translation of higher level synchronization requirements into semaphores can be cumbersome since it can require a large number of semaphores. It is not possible to differentiate between processes without using multiple semaphores and some auxiliary information (e.g. *readercount* in readers and writers [33]). Since a V on a semaphore increments its value by 1, semaphores cannot be used to synchronize with a number of processes. Belpaire and Willmotte [3] provide another set of primitives which solve the above problem.

Critical Regions (CR)

Critical region is a structured construct for synchronization, proposed by Brinch Hansen [37] and Hoare [35]. It is a systematic and reliable protocol to access shared variables. Shared variables are divided into different groups called *resources*. The resource variables can be accessed only from within a critical region. The resources are explicitly declared and made known to the compiler, which ensures that the variables are not accessed outside the CR. The CR construct is translated and the statements accessing the resources are enclosed by a proper access protocol. The statement below declares a variable *buffer* of type *array* that is shared by number of processes. The access to the variable by means of **region** construct is also illustrated.

> **var** *buffer* : **shared** *array[10] of Int*;
> **region** *buffer* **do**
>   **begin**
>   ...

shared resource access

...

end;

The compiler creates the necessary code for the access protocols. This ensures that there are no mistakes and that every process follows the same protocol. The implementation of critical regions may employ any method including semaphores.

The CRs do not provide any mechanism for conditional synchronization. A naive solution with busy wait does not work if the conditions involve shared variables. If a process already in the CR has to wait for some condition involving the variables from the same resource then no other process can enter the region to set the condition leading to a deadlock. To remedy this problem, Brinch Hansen [36] proposed another construct called *Conditional Critical Regions*(CCR),[2] in which processes can wait on conditions. A process executing a wait on a condition gets suspended on the queue associated with that condition and releases the region. This way the process inside the CCR does not block other processes from entering. When a process setting the condition leaves the CCR, the suspended process is awakened.

CCRs guarantee synchronization, but do not ensure that all operations on the resources will be legal. The programmer can circumvent the CCR construct and access the shared resource using lower level mechanisms. CCRs are also expensive to implement because the conditions can involve local variables of processes and may involve context switches to evaluate the condition. In CCRs, the code manipulating the resources is distributed over different processes, making it difficult to follow the logic of the program. CCRs have a large exclusion granularity and thus can be inefficient. Though it is possible to use CCRs to synchronize a number of processes, it is not possible to distinguish between different kinds of processes.

Monitors

In order to remedy the objection that the CCR operations are distributed over different processes, *Monitors* [31,34,38] were proposed. Monitors encapsulate the shared resources and the operation manipulating them, by putting them syntactically together. Monitors provide a uniform way

---

[2]Hoare [35] proposed a variant of CCR, **region** *var* **when** *condition* **do**. This construct allows processes to wait only at the beginning of the CR.

for exclusive access to the resources. This abstraction lets the user ignore the details of the implementation of mutual exclusion and access methods.

Syntax and Synchronization

The syntax of the monitors is described below [38]:

monitorname: **monitor**
    declarations of data local to the monitor ...
    procedure *procedurename* (... formal parameters ...);
        begin ... procedure body ... **end;**
    procedure ...;
    ...
    declarations of other procedures local to the monitor ...
    begin ... initialization of the data local to the monitor ... **end;**

The data local to the monitor is static and constitutes the state of the monitor. It can be manipulated only by the monitor procedures. An operation of the monitor can be invoked by giving the name of the monitor and the name of the procedure as follows:

$$monitorname.procedurename(... \text{actual parameters} ...);$$

At a time only one call to the monitor can succeed in entering the body whereas remaining calls get blocked, providing the required mutual exclusion. Conditional synchronization is provided using *condition variables* [38] which are queues of processes. A process executing *wait* on a condition is suspended and removed from the monitor, and enqueued on the condition queue. A *signal* on a condition causes the process waiting the longest[3] in the queue, if any, to be awakened. The process executing signal gets blocked on another condition called *urgent*. It needs to be ensured that the condition the queued process is waiting on is satisfied. This obviates the need for repeated evaluation of conditions as needed in CCR. No other process should intervene between the signaling and waking of the waiting process to ensure that the corresponding condition is not nullified. Hoare [38] gives a axiomatic proof method to prove the correctness of monitors.

The drawback of monitors is that they implicitly provide mutual exclusion between all operations and thus have a a large exclusion granularity. The other problem of *nested monitor calls* has received attention and a

---

[3] There is a provision to implement a more complex scheduling processing policy using scheduled waits [38].

number of solutions have been proposed [39]. Since condition variables do not directly correspond to the logical conditions for which processes wait, the program can be difficult to understand unless the logical conditions are well documented.

Path Expressions

Path expressions [40] provide a solution to the above problem by separating the functional description and mutual exclusion constraints. In this method, a module which is similar to a monitor encapsulates the data and procedures that operate on the data. A *path* in the header of a module specifies the restrictions on the operations and is specified as follows:

   path *path_list* **end**

A path_list contains the list of operations and a number of sequencing operators called *path operators*. Path operators specify a variety of sequencing between operations. For example, it is possible to specify that two operations need to be sequential, or that they can be concurrent, or that one can go n invocations ahead of the other etc. Using path expressions all meaningful sequences of process interleavings can be specified.

Path expressions are based on the operational semantics of synchronization. One of their advantages is that the implementation is separate from their description and the path operators can be implemented in any manner. They can provide fine granularity of concurrency and differentiate between types of processes. Their major limitation is that they can only capture the synchronization based on the history of the operations and not on the state of the data or on the parameters of the procedures. Due to the separation of the logic of the program and synchronization requirements programs become unreadable and difficult to design.

6.4.2   Synchronization Based on Message Passing

The primitives described here use *message passing* for synchronization. Message passing is used for inter-process communication as well. One of the most important advantages of message passing systems is that they work similarly in centralized and distributed systems. On the other hand methods based on shared variables (memory) can be very expensive, inefficient and slow when used in distributed systems as they use message passing at lower level.

A message is a collection of information that can be exchanged among processes. It can contain data, signals, commands, addresses, or code. A message usually consists of two parts, namely, the *header* part, containing sender and receiver identifications and other control information, and the *data* part. A variety of message passing primitives are possible depending upon the nature of communication: synchronous or asynchronous, and blocking or non-blocking. Different choices in specifying source and destinations can also give rise to different primitives. We will elaborate on these aspects below in detail.

Synchronization among processes can be achieved by the fact that a message can be received only after it is sent by the sending process. For processes that do not use shared memory, mutual exclusion is of no concern[4]. Thus we shall consider only conditional synchronization.

Naming

There are two ways of naming: direct and indirect. In direct naming, the sender and receiver both know the identities of each other and are specified in the message. An advantage of such communication is that it is symmetric and easy to implement. This addressing paradigm is not helpful for *client and server* interaction. A server needs to accept a request from any client without knowing his identity. In reality, a server would not know the identity of each client as clients of each server can change. A scheme that solves the above problem is called *indirect* naming. Indirect naming schemes use *mailboxes*, which are essentially global names and hence can appear in send or receive statements of any process[5]. Conceptually a message is sent to a mailbox and anyone can receive it. Thus the sender need not know the name of the receiver. This method is quite versatile and can provide communication between one-one, one-many, many-one, or many-many processes. Implementation of mailboxes can be expensive since every message must be sent to all sites where a potential receiver can exist. These methods are illustrated in Figure 6.1

In another indirect naming scheme called *port naming*, the name of a mailbox, called *port*, can appear in the receive statements of only one process. Many processes can send messages to a port but only one can receive. This is more efficient than the previous method for one-one or many-one communication. An explicit form of *broadcast* or *multicast*[6]. mechanism is needed to provide one-many communication.

---

[4] For other shared resources, a number of other algorithms have been devised [41,42].

[5] Only processes with capabilities to access the mailboxes can name them, but, we shall ignore the issue of protection here.

[6] A variant of broadcast where the recipients can be chosen by the sender.

```
process A;
   ...
   send(B, message);
   ...


process A;
   ...
   send(mailbox, message);
   ...


              process B;
                 ...
                 receive(A, message);
                 ...


              process B;
                 ...
                 receive(mailbox, message);
                 ...
```

Figure 6.1: Direct and indirect naming.

Synchronization

The other important issue in message communication is whether the execution of a message passing statement causes delay. In *synchronous message passing* the sender and receiver have to wait for each other to execute the corresponding send and receive statements. Both processes can proceed when the message gets transferred and hence processes may be delayed. In *asynchronous message passing* the sender need not wait for the receiver to receive a message. Unread messages are simply stored in a buffer and later accessed by the receiver. Usually the number of buffers are limited and in such systems the sender can only get a limited amount ahead of the receiver. A statement is called *blocking* if it causes delay to the invoker, else it is called *nonblocking*. In a blocking send, a sender trying to send more messages than the capacity of the buffer gets blocked. Similarly, in a blocking receive, the receiver gets delayed until at least one buffer is full. In the nonblocking method, both send and receive return immediately, possibly with an error.

```
process A;                              ...
   ...                           begin  /*initialization*/
   receive(mutex, message);            create_mailbox(mutex);
   critical section;                   send(mutex, null);
   send(mutex, message);               ...
   ...                           end;
end;   /* process A */

   ...
   other processes
   ...
```

Figure 6.2: Mutual exclusion using message passing.

Some systems provide another primitive to test if any messages are present for a process and if there are to *select* one of the available ones. Dijkstra's guarded commands [43] is an example of primitive of this kind. Hoare proposed a communication primitive based on guarded commands which forms the basis of CSP [44]. It has the following form:

$$guard \rightarrow statement$$

where the guard is a boolean expression possibly with an I/O statement. The statement succeeds if the guard is true and any communication that is specified at the right side of the guard does not cause delay.

Figure 6.2 illustrates an example of the use of message passing for mutual exclusion using mailboxes. It uses blocking receive and asynchronous non-blocking send. This scheme is conceptually similar to semaphores. A single message, along with a shared mailbox, is used as a token to ensure mutual exclusion. Figure 6.3 demonstrates the use of messages for conditional synchronization and is based on guarded commands of CSP. In the above example, the guards provide the means to accept certain messages and delay others depending upon the state of the process. Similar ideas form the basis of synchronization in POOL-T [45] and ABCL-1 [46].

Synchronization using Higher Level Message Passing

Though the above primitives are sufficient to program any kind of process interaction and synchronization, a number of higher level language constructs based on the above ideas have been developed. These constructs are described below.

```
process producer;                    process consumer;
    ...                                  ...
    while(true) do                       while(true) do
        send(buffer, message);               receive( buffer, message);
    end;                                 end;
    ...                                  ...


process buffer;
    data store[0..MAX];
    int in,out = 0;
    do
        in < out + 10; receive store[in mod 10] from producer;
            → in := in + 1;
    []
        out < in; receive from producer
            → send(consumer,out mod 10);
    od;
    ...
```

Figure 6.3: Conditional synchronization using message passing.

Remote Procedure Call (RPC)

Remote procedure call [47,48,49] provides the same semantics as a procedure call, except that the caller and callee belong to different processes. The caller sends the parameters of the call to the callee and gets blocked until results are received. The callee, after receiving the parameters, performs the necessary action and then sends the result.

RPC is an ideal mechanism for client/server interaction, since the client needs to know the identity of the server but the server need not. There is no notion of conditional synchronization in RPC. RPC has been extended to a replicated (remote) procedure call [48,50] to handle one-many communication.

Rendezvous

Ada provides a variant of RPC called *rendezvous* [25]. It uses direct naming, and is blocking and synchronous in nature. Ada tasks (processes) have their own ports, called *entries*, which are the names of the remote procedure calls. A Client can invoke the server entries using the *call* statement. In the body of the server, *accept* is used to accept the calls and *select* to choose between the outstanding invocations. The select statement provides support for conditional synchronization where a particular entry can be selected for execution.

Asynchronous Remote Procedure Call

This is a generalization of the RPC mechanism where neither caller nor callee block on the RPC. After sending an invocation message, the sender can resume other activities and wait for the reply at some other point in the program. After receiving the message, the callee performs requested operations and sends a reply in the form of a *no-wait send* and continues its activities. Thus, in this mechanism there is very little synchronization between caller and callee. ABCL-1 provides this kind of communication along with a facility to *select*. Asynchronous procedure calls give maximum freedom to the programmer; all forms of communication and synchronization are possible in this framework. It is possible to use select statement to provide conditional synchronization. A process can synchronize with a number of processes by sending multiple invocations to each of them and thereafter waiting for replies from each of them.

One-Way Invocations

This mechanism is useful where invocation replies are of no importance. The invocations only bring about change in the receiving process. A caller simply sends a message to the callee which, upon receipt, carries out the required computation. The callee can in turn send messages to other processes, including the original caller. Some other process later in the sequence of messages can send a message (reply) to the original invoker. Thus this mechanism can be used for implementing pipelines or where the reply need not come from the receiver of the invocation. Conditional synchronization can be provided using any of the above techniques. One way invocations provide only one part of synchronization; the sender and the receiver meet only when the message is sent. Thereafter their speeds are unpredictable. Actors [51] and Maruti [52] provide such communication.

6.5 Real-Time Synchronization

In this section we describe the synchronization requirements of real-time concurrent programs. Though most of the requirements of real-time programs and concurrent programs are similar, the emphasis is on meeting the real-time deadlines of applications. Later in the section, we shall evaluate different primitives that were described earlier, using these yardsticks. In section 6.3, we enumerated the important differences between the constructs for concurrent programming and constructs for real-time programming. Here we describe the synchronization requirements of real-time systems.

6.5.1 Synchronization Requirements

- The most important objective of real-time programming is to meet the time constraints of the application. Different language constructs, including synchronization primitives, should be designed to meet the above criterion. The synchronization primitives should facilitate the scheduling and interleaving of processes so that their timings are satisfied. Synchronization primitives should not be used where their use can reduce the predictability of the timing.

- There is a need for separation of synchronization mechanisms at different levels of abstraction. At a higher level, the synchronization should be in terms of application variables or system state. This provides portability to upper level code, better abstraction, and readability. The lower level mechanism should worry about efficiency and machine dependency. It can be used to build the complex synchronization requirements of the higher levels. The lower level mechanism can use any implementation, and the system should deal with translation between the higher and lower levels, as the logic of the program and actual implementation need not be directly related. The high level programmer need not worry about the lower level mechanisms since it is difficult to develop and maintain low level programs.

- It is also desirable that separate constructs be provided for different functions of synchronization. Such use can improve the readability of programs. An appropriate implementation of each primitive can also be more efficient. Use of a primitive where some other effect (and another primitive) is intended can lead to different behavior. Consider the use of mutual exclusion to correctly order two processes, one of which should begin processing before another. Mutual exclusion can be used to achieve the required effect but will also cause the processes to exclude each other. Thus, mutual exclusion should not be used to achieve another effect if processes need not mutually exclude each other. Such use can in fact hinder the progress of the processes.

Separate constructs also have the benefit that the implementation of any one of the primitives can be changed without affecting the timing properties of others.

- Synchronization primitives should be efficient. The amount of code executed by the primitives themselves should be small and predictable. The processes waiting for synchronization should not consume system resources.

- Processes should have as little information as possible about the processes it wants to synchronize with [3]. This principle is in keeping with modular decomposition, where the interfaces should be as small as possible [19]. Any change in one process should minimally affect the process with which it is interacting. We have seen that the direct naming form of message passing requires a processes to know the identities of its peer whereas indirect naming does not. We have also seen the drawback of the former method. If it is possible to synchronize with a number of processes then a process need not know the number and identities of all processes that are waiting to synchronize with it since processes die, fail, or are created anew. It should be possible for the synchronization to distinguish between different kinds of processes since synchronization requirements with different kinds of processes may be different. For example, in the problem of readers and writers [26], a reader has to exclude another writer, but not another reader. Thus a reader has to be differentiated from a writer.

- Processes need to synchronize to communicate with each other, in the sense that one process needs to wait until the other has produced the required information. A different construct for communication can make programs readable. The programmer can thus ignore the details of the synchronization and communication, and concentrate on how such information can be used.

We are advocating that the synchronization primitives have different levels of abstraction. The higher level mechanisms should be in terms of program logic, should be machine independent, portable, and readable. On the other hand, the lower level should handle the machine dependent idiosyncrasies and efficiency. The function of each primitive should be well defined to avoid their improper use, which in turn leads to unreadable and complicated programs. The timing properties of all primitives should be deterministic to facilitate proper scheduling. The system should provide translation between different levels.

6.5.2 Evaluation of Primitives

In this section, we evaluate the properties of the synchronization primitives that were described in the previous section. We look at the desirable features of each of them in the light of the measures mentioned in the previous section.

We have seen that message passing based mechanisms offer one advantage over shared memory based mechanisms, namely, a separate means for IPC. The message based IPC is attractive since it works similarly in a distributed environment. In a message passing environment, synchronization is simpler as it does not have to support an added feature of communication. Regarding the higher level mechanisms based on message passing, RPC is very useful and easy to program. Similarly, one-way communication is useful in real-time systems. Many real-time systems involve a pipeline of processes, where data gets processed in stages. Such pipelined architectures also provide higher concurrency. One-way communication is also general enough to support any kind of communication mechanism on top of it. Thus both kinds of communication seem desirable for real-time systems.

Another desirable feature of the synchronization mechanism is the provision of different primitives for different functions of synchronization. Conditional critical regions, with the clear separation between conditional synchronization and mutual exclusion, provide a good example of this kind. In addition to such clear separation, monitors provide an elegant abstraction for system resources. In fact, such encapsulation of resources is a step towards object-oriented programming. The encapsulation of data and operations make the program readable which is a desirable feature. We would like to do away with the shortcoming associated with monitors, namely, the large granularity of concurrency. The concurrency should be controlled according to the properties and constraints of the resource and not by the limitation of the synchronization mechanism. For example, if some data is read only and can be accessed simultaneously by multiple processes then it should be possible to achieve the required effect using the synchronization primitives. Monitors as well as CCRs do not allow a user selectable granularity of concurrency. We feel that such a feature is essential.

Path expressions do away with this restriction, providing finer granularity of concurrency. The separation of synchronization and program logic as provided by them, is not a very desirable feature, since it reduces program readability. Hence, program logic, process timing, and different synchronization requirements should be in terms of program variables and physical constraints.

One important requirement of real-time systems is the ordering of processes. Though it is possible to use any of the above synchronization primitives for this purpose, they do not provide a natural solution to the problem. The natural solution should allow the programmer to specify the requirements in terms of program variables and application constraints. Similarly, in order to control process timing, a separate clock process can be used, but does not seem an attractive solution. The programmer has to worry about clock implementation, setting of alarms, the interaction of processes and clocks, etc. Instead, the timing requirements should be expressed naturally in terms of physical constraints. None of the above primitives provide a satisfactory solution for this purpose.

Semaphores provide an efficient solution for synchronization. They are not suitable for higher level mechanism but are attractive for lower level implementation. Thus it is possible to have higher level synchronization construct for programming and performing necessary translation of the constructs to the semaphore based implementation. Knowing the timing of assembly instructions, busy looping can be used to exercise proper control over process timings and ordering. However, it leaves the responsibility for synchronization to the programmer. A high level programmer has to worry about the the details of loops, condition evaluation, use of proper protocol to evaluate the conditions, etc. The timing of the loop depends upon the implementation, on the speed of the hardware and the instruction set of the system. These features make the code unreadable as well as unportable.

In summary, synchronization mechanism chosen for real-time programming should have clear separation between higher level constructs and implementation. The mechanism should be abstract enough, so that it can be implemented over a number of systems efficiently. The mechanism should provide different primitives for different objectives making the programs readable. Above all, it should be possible to characterize the timing behavior of the primitives to make the programs predictable.

6.6 Proposed Primitives for Real-Time Synchronization

In this section we describe the proposed primitives for inter process communication and process synchronization. These primitives are aimed at a distributed hard real-time environment. We feel that such an environment represents the next generation of real-time systems. These primitives are designed for Maruti, a distributed real-time environment. Maruti is based on an object-oriented philosophy which provides the benefits of abstraction, modularity, extensibility and software reuse.

To begin with, we introduce Maruti and fundamentals of object-oriented programming. Thereafter the communication and synchronization primitives of Maruti are described. We show how our approach fits real-time programming and describe how it solves many problems associated with earlier designs.

6.6.1   Introduction to Maruti

Maruti is a testbed for research in distributed hard real-time systems, being developed at University of Maryland [53,54,55]. We are studying major aspects of real-time systems including fault-tolerance and reliability. These issues are important for the critical applications described earlier. Maruti is based on the philosophy of validation and verification of real-time programs, pre-allocation of resources, and pre-scheduling of all tasks. We feel that this is the most promising approach to guarantee the execution of real-time programs within constraints of the applications.

A Maruti real-time task consists of a number of objects, written in the Maruti programming language, interacting with each other [56]. Objects model the entities of the application and invocations of objects by others model external actions or operations on such entities. Real-time systems require a strict bound on the invocation time, and execution time and hence, the language provides natural constructs to express such time constraints [57]. A program written in the Maruti programming language is analyzed by the system to estimate the execution times of object operations. Time constraints and temporal (precedence) relations between object invocations are also extracted from the program. The operating system uses these times to schedule the object invocations. The resource requirement of each object is analyzed and appropriate resources are allocated and reserved.

Active research is under progress in the area of the design of a programming language which will facilitate easier program development, program readability, execution time estimation and extraction of temporal relations. There is a focus on resource allocation, timely communication, scheduling, and fault-tolerance of real-time systems. Details of the language and the above aspects are outside the scope of this paper. We should mention that currently the programs are preprocessed and translated to C [58]. The process of gathering time constraints and execution time analysis is not fully automated.

6.6.2 Object-Oriented Programming

Why Object-Oriented Programming

One of the goals of object-oriented programming is to increase programmer efficiency by reusing software and by controlling the complexity of software. Object-oriented programming is an outcome of the following techniques which also have similar goals: modularity, top-down design philosophy, and data abstraction.

An *object* consists of some private data (the state of the object) and operations which are the only means to access the data [59,20]. Every operation can be treated as a service provided by the object when the object is viewed as a server. In the object-oriented approach, a problem is decomposed in terms of data as opposed to functions in the traditional approach [19]. The interface provided by the operations defines the properties of the object completely, thus providing abstraction. Information hiding or encapsulation is provided by the restriction that the data and the implementation are not open to inspection. The operations are the only means of interaction. Since the functions on objects are side effect free the effects of changing the implementation of an *object* are localized. The clients of the objects remain unaffected if the implementation is changed while keeping the interface the same.

Definitions

In addition to abstract data types, object oriented programming provides the class and inheritance mechanisms [60]. A *class* is a description of the object variables and operations of a set of similar objects. Strictly, these operations are the only means to interact with an object[7]. An object of a particular class is called an *instance* of that class and is *created* by *instantiation* of that class. A class is a way to define a new type of objects or a way to generalize the behavior of similar objects. For example, a class 'automobiles' can be used to define vehicles with four wheels and are motorized. Another useful concept analogous to class is that of *type* [61,62] which pertains to type checking, but we will not describe it here.

---

[7]Some languages [19] make the object variables accessible using a construct called *attributes*.

It is possible to define a new class in terms of one of the already defined classes. If a new class is similar to an existing class in many aspects but differs in others, then the new class can be defined as a specialization of the old class. This mechanism is called *inheritance*. The new class is called a *subclass* and is a specialization of the old class called *superclass*. A subclass inherits the variables and operations of its superclass[8] and it may extend or modify them as well. Using this mechanism, new classes called 'trucks' and 'cars' can be defined which are specializations of 'automobiles'. In addition to its use for software reuse, inheritance is a natural means to model real objects.

Object operations are invoked by sending a *message*, which consists of a *message selector*, which specifies the operation to be invoked, along with a set of arguments. The operations can access local object variables that constitute the state of the object. While executing the operations, the object can in turn send messages to other objects and invoke operations on them. The operations may return values in response to messages. This depends upon the method of communication offered by the system. Maruti provides both *one-way* and RPC communications but referred to as *message passing* in this paper.

Figure 6.4 describes the essential form of an object[9] and its use in another class. It describes a class called **Node** of a binary tree. The class description consists of variables and operations of its instances. Two variables **leftNode** and **rightNode** form the state of any such object. An instance of **Node** replies to message selector **left** by sending the node from its left subtree whereas in response to **assignleft: aNode**, it changes its left subtree to point to new argument **aNode**.

A new node is created by sending a message **new** to **Node**[10]. Its subtrees can be initialized by sending **assignleft** and **assignright** messages to the newly created object.

6.6.3   Communication

In this section, we describe the implementation of Maruti objects and the communication primitives.

---

[8]Some languages do not allow subclasses to see all variables/operations of superclass but only a subset in order to provide better encapsulation.

[9]This example is illustrated in a pseudo language which is influenced by Smalltalk and Trellis/Owl.

[10]Not documented here.

```
class Node;                              class dummy;
var leftNode : Node;                     var temp, root : Node;
    rightNode : Node;                    operation foo();
operation left();                        begin
begin                                         ⋮
    return (leftNode);
end;                                     temp = Node.new();
operation assignleft(aNode);             temp.assignright(NIL);
begin                                    temp.assignleft(NIL);
    leftNode = aNode;
end;                                     root = Node.new();
operation right();                       root.assignleft(temp);
begin                                    root.assignright(NIL);
    return (rightNode);
end;                                          ⋮
operation assignright(aNode);
begin                                    end;
    rightNode = aNode;
end;
```

Figure 6.4: Example of an object node and its use

Object Implementation

Currently Maruti objects are implemented as processes[11]. Maruti objects are large grain or heavy weight objects. The address space of the process constitutes the state of the object and threads can access this address space and execute. The ports represent the operations of the object and different objects can send messages to them.

At a conceptual level, a new thread is generated to handle the service invocation contained in a newly arriving message. The invoking thread may suspend or continue depending upon the kind of communication used. The thread services the incoming message by executing the code of the operation. Though conceptually every thread dies at the end of the service, a fixed number of threads can be used. They continually execute a loop wherein they receive a new message and service it. Objects may have one more thread representing the initial processing. The initial threads may die after initialization or exist forever performing independent actions. This organization ensures that in the absence of any contention, an object can provide maximum concurrency. The off-line scheduler in Maruti schedules every object invocation separately such that the deadline of each of them as

---

[11] In the sense of Mach [63].

well the overall application deadlines are met. The schedule is represented as a calendar and used by a dispatcher to dispatch threads.

In Maruti, each object is represented by a unique *object id* which is created by the system. The object id is the means to address the object uniquely. Instantiation of an object consists of a creation of a unique id, along with the object structure itself.

Maruti Communication Structure

Higher Level Communication Primitives

Operation invocation on an object from another involves communication between two objects. Maruti provides both remote procedure call and one-way communication at the Maruti programming language level. Message passing has been used in Maruti in keeping with the object paradigm and since it is attractive in distributed systems. A message consists of the name of the object, the name of the operation and actual parameters. The parameters are passed by value. The objects themselves are not passed via messages but their ids are.

Maruti programming language is a strongly typed language and uses typed messages. This provides type checking at compile time which can save erroneous message exchange, unnecessary operation execution, and unpredictable error-recovery. These savings are of considerable importance to the real-time systems. Similarly, it provides exception handling in case of erroneous messages at run time.

If a reply is expected, the caller gets blocked for the reply; else it can service one of its invocations or continue other actions. After receiving the message, the callee performs the action specified in the message. If needed, it sends the reply or forwards the processed message.

Implementation of the Communication Primitives

The higher level primitives are not bound to a particular implementation at the lower level. Depending upon efficiency and other issues, message passing can be implemented using shared memory or message communication provided by the lower level protocols. Thus we have separated the issues of implementation and efficiency from that of functionality.

In a message based implementation, an object owns a set of ports that can be addressed by the name of the operation. The caller packs the parameters of the call in a message and sends it to the port of the callee, which represents the particular operation that it needs to invoke. The port addresses are public and any object can send a message to another.[12]. After receiving a message on a port, a new thread is created, which processes the code of the associated operation.

In a shared memory system, the messages are deposited by the sender in a memory shared by the sender and the receiver. Each operation has its own memory where messages for that operation are deposited. A thread monitors the arrival of a message, and then services it. The access to this shared memory is controlled using semaphores or some other synchronization mechanism.

One-Many Communication

We have seen that the port based addressing does not provide a solution for one-many communication and hence a separate mechanism for broadcast or multicast needs to be provided. The simple approaches are either to explicitly address all recipients or to send a separate message to each of them. In another approach, the system takes care of addressing multiple processes and delivering messages. Number of processes can be addressed by grouping them together and using a single name for communication. Such an approach is used in V-kernel [50] and ISIS [64].

Maruti uses a similar idea and provides a mechanism by which objects can be grouped together[13]. The groups form addressable entities and an object can be a member of a number of groups. The semantics of group communication is an extension of the simple one-one communication. Transparency is also one of the aims of Maruti group communication [65], and thus the client need not know the number and identities of objects receiving the message. Though it is possible to specify the number of objects within a group that should receive the message, the number of objects that need to reply to a procedure call, or how to combine their results.

6.6.4 Synchronization

In this section we describe Maruti's proposed synchronization primitives. We have evaluated them with respect to objectives that were mentioned earlier. If an object (or a process that does not share memory with others) allows only one thread at a time, there is no need for mutual exclusion. Since Maruti objects have multiple threads sharing the common data, there is need for mutual exclusion among threads.

---

[12] It is also possible to use capability based addressing for ports to provide protection.
[13] In Maruti, objects can be grouped together for a number of reasons.

every *time-period* do

   ...

from *begin-time* to *end-time* every *time-period* do

   ...

after *some-time* do

   ...

within *time-interval* do

   ...

parallel *obj1.op1(...)* ∥ *obj2.op2(...)* ∥ ...;

Figure 6.5: Language constructs to express timing.

We have stated the desirability of expressing synchronization in terms of conditions and variables pertinent to the problem for the ease of programming and readability. Thus, the higher level synchronization primitives should be in terms of the state of the system and related transitions. Parnas [3,4] also considers this as one of the most important design criteria. For instance, in the problem of readers and writers, mutual exclusion between readers and writers should be in terms of problem variables, i.e. in terms of the number of readers and writers requesting the service. Such expression is natural and in accordance with the problem specification.

Process Ordering

We have seen that the processes that have some external order constraints and those that do not communicate with each other, may have to be synchronized to assure that the processes follow required precedence.

In Maruti such precedence constraints can be expressed in the program itself. The programming language provides constructs to express these relations [57]. They in turn place constraints on the order in which different invocations take place and on the time at which each operation can be executed. In Figure 6.5 such language constructs are illustrated. The first two constructs can be used to invoke an operation, or execute some code, periodically. They provide natural ways to specify periodic operations along with their periodicity. This approach can be contrasted with the approach taken in the Alpha kernel [7] where processes have to be declared periodic or aperiodic explicitly. The third one gives a usual precedence relationship whereas the fourth one provides a start-time and a deadline. Using this set it is possible to express different temporal relations. The statements

```
...
valve1.open(full);
after( inter-valve-time)
    valve2.open(half);
```

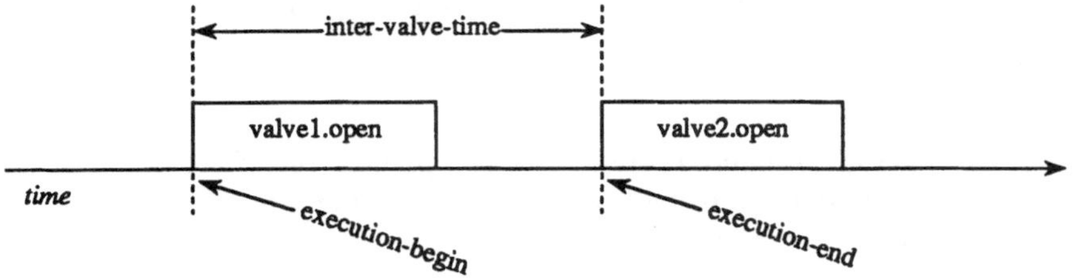

Figure 6.6: Maruti program and corresponding schedule.

that are written sequentially have a simple order between them. The last primitive called *parallel* denotes a parallel execution of a number of invocations. Currently only object invocations can be executed in parallel and not blocks. For a complete description of primitives see [57].

It is also possible to provide such ordering among processes using some synchronization primitives and a clock. In Maruti, such constraints are enforced using scheduling. The Maruti scheduler schedules operation invocations (the message transfer to objects and operation execution) appropriately such that invocations satisfy the precedence relations and time constraints. While compiling, these relations are extracted from the source code and are provided to the scheduler as directives for scheduling. Consider the example of two valves that need to be opened within some time of each other. The program and the corresponding output of the scheduler are shown in Figure 6.6.

This example illustrates the time driven scheduling and use of scheduling for enforcing precedence relations. Using such an approach it is possible to guarantee that the order and the time-constraints will be followed. If there is no precedence between operation executions, the scheduler is free to choose any order. Some of the aspects that can affect the schedule are application dependent time constraints, order constraints, synchronization, and resource requirements.

Conditional Synchronization

The Maruti approach regarding conditional synchronization is similar to that in ABCL-1 [46] and Pool-T [45]. The approach is based on CSP guarded commands and ADA select statements. In Maruti, a Boolean condition can be attached to the declaration of each operation of an object (class). The operation gets invoked only when the given condition is met. Thus a condition can be used to block a thread until it is satisfied. The syntax of operation declaration is is as follows:

> **operation** *op-name (para-1: type-1 , para-2: type-2, ...)*
>   [**returns** *(ret-type)]*[**when** *boolean-condition*]
>   [**do** ... *exclusive code* **end**;]
> **begin**
>   ... *operation body*
> **end**

The *When* statement provides control over acceptance of an invocation using the Boolean condition. After a message is received, the *when* condition is evaluated in a mutually exclusive manner. If the condition is met then the optional *do* block is executed. This block is also executed in a mutually exclusive manner, without releasing the exclusion. This ensures that no other thread executes in between to nullify the condition. If the condition is not met, the exclusion is released and the condition is evaluated reevaluated. If the *when* condition is absent then it is treated as *true*.

Mutually exclusive access for evaluating the condition can prevent two or more threads, that satisfy their respective conditions, from entering the object body simultaneously. After the first thread enters the body, it can allow or disallow other threads from entering the object depending upon its mutual exclusion requirement. It is possible to perform any actions within the *do* block. The *do* block is provided in order to access the variables that are used in the *when* condition. It provides a mechanism for a thread to prevent other threads from entering the object after it starts execution, if needed. It can do so by nullifying the conditions of the operations (and hence, the threads) that it needs to mutually exclude.

Shared Data and Mutual Exclusion

The *when* can also be used for mutual exclusion among different threads at the entrance to the body. Since multiple threads can be active within the object, there is a need for mutual exclusion among them while in the body. Hence, we provide a construct called *region*, to control access to the shared data, the syntax of which is described below:

region *region-name* **do**
   ...
   critical section statements;
end

The region is a named critical section, and only one thread may be active within regions with the given name. If one thread is within a region, then another thread cannot enter any region with the same name. This does not put restriction on the regions with different names. Different threads can be present in critical sections with different names. This facilitates division of program statements into groups, each of which requires mutually exclusive variables used in statements of that group. If the variables are read-only, then no statements need to be mutually exclusive. This approach may be contrasted with monitors where the granularity of synchronization is very coarse. Thus we have provided separate primitives for mutual exclusion and for conditional synchronization.

Examples

Consider the implementation of read and write operations on object "file" from Figure 6.7. It solves the readers and writers problem and illustrates the above points. A mutually exclusive access to an object can also be provided if such synchronization is necessary. Figure 6.8 shows an implementation of semaphores illustrating the use of the primitives for mutual exclusion.

Conditional Synchronization within Operation

As described earlier, *when* synchronization is used to block threads at the entrance of the operation for some condition to become true. However, it is not always sufficient to block the thread at the entrance of the operation. There are situations when synchronization must be placed anywhere in the body [33]. Waiting inside the body of the operation can increase efficiency or may be imperative in some cases. The condition variables of monitors as well as CCR as proposed by Brinch Hansen provide such facility [33]. In Maruti, such facility is not provided as we feel that it can be implemented by semaphores. Since a number of threads can be active within an object, another thread can enter and wake such thread. As we

```
class shared_file : file;
operation read () when no_writers = 0
     do no_readers += 1; end
     read the file ...
     region readers do no_readers -= 1; end;
   ...
operation write () when no_writers = 0 and no_readers = 0
     do no_writers += 1; end
     write the file ...
     no_writers -= 1;
```

Figure 6.7: Solution to Readers and Writers.

have seen earlier, semaphores can be easily implemented in terms of previously defined primitives. Semaphores can also be provided as a class in the library. If a condition is complex, then the user can optimize it and use semaphores cleverly.

Implementation Issues

In Maruti, process ordering is enforced by scheduling processes appropriately. The precedence relations are derived automatically from the program. They are used by the allocator to create a computation graph which is later used by the allocator and off-line scheduler to create the schedule. In the next phase, we plan to extract execution times and time constraints also automatically. We have provided a framework in the Maruti operating system to implement and evaluate a variety of scheduling algorithms. Different algorithms have been evaluated with respect to their complexity and the classes of problems for which they can be used [66,67].

The evaluation of the *when* condition is done in a mutually exclusive manner. Similarly the *do* block associated with the operation, if any, is also evaluated in an exclusive manner. These mechanisms are based on semaphores. Initially every thread waits on a mutual exclusion semaphore. After getting an access the condition is evaluated and, if the condition is met, the do block is also executed followed by release of the semaphore. If the condition is not met the semaphore is released. Threads are prescheduled using analysis as described in [68].

```
class semaphore;
int s = 0;
operation p() when s > 0
    do s -= 1; end
operation v()
    do s += 1; end
```

Figure 6.8: Implementation of semaphore.

Regions are also implemented using semaphores. For each named region, one semaphore is created. The region construct is translated by enclosing the statements by a p and v on the corresponding semaphore.

Synchronization between number of processes

Typically there can be more than one process waiting for some condition to take place. In a dynamic system this number can change over time. In Maruti, both conditional synchronization and mutual exclusion primitives do not depend upon the number of threads that are synchronizing; neither do they have to know the identity of each other.

A process waiting for the some event (condition) gets blocked until the *when* condition becomes true. It does not have to know the identity of the process that caused the condition to become true. Similarly a process that makes some condition true need not know the processes waiting. After waking up all of them, they can progress depending on their mutual exclusion requirements with respect to each other. The synchronization mechanism does not hinder their progress.

Mutual exclusion requires that at most one thread can be active in a named region. All threads need to know the identity of the semaphore guarding the mutual exclusion but not of each other. Thereafter only one thread can progress which is what is required by the application. When a thread enters or leaves the exclusion region is independent of the number of threads waiting. Out of the threads waiting to enter, one is chosen to enter the region according to the schedule; which depends on their deadlines.

6.6.5 Comments and Shortcomings

One of the drawbacks of the CCRs was that the condition evaluation can be expensive if it involves the local variables, since it involves a context switch. In our implementation, each of the contending entities is a thread and thus a context switch does not pose a problem. The actual parameters are copied from the messages and are local to the thread. The problem that we face is the possibility of some *when* condition getting evaluated repeatedly. Such evaluation can be expensive and detrimental to the real-time system. We plan to remedy this problem by pre-scheduling the operations and hence the evaluations of conditions. In our current approach, the operations with conditions involving history variables can be pre-scheduled [68]. A complete schedule may not be possible if other conditions (that are based on parameters to the operation or the object state) are involved. We are currently investigating means to schedule threads with such conditions. Our aim in this direction is to schedule the operations so that either the conditions are not evaluated repeatedly or we get an upper bound on the evaluations.

Another potential problem that can arise is the deadlock due to incorrect nesting of regions. Different solutions have been proposed for nested monitor calls which are applicable here. One approach disallows nested calls [69], whereas other allows only lexical nesting of monitors [70]. Another optimistic approach does not restrict nesting but prescribes detection of a deadlock and breaking it, once it occurs. In such approach the application needs to be restarted again which may not be possible for a real-time system. We do not propose any solution to this problem and leave it to the user. We feel that unlike different processes which are developed by different users, the threads (operations) are part of the same object and developed by the same programmer. Thus the user needs to write safe programs.

We are also taking an easier approach for the problem of access to private variables of the object. This problem is similar to that of accessing shared variable in critical regions [37,35]. We do not require that variables be declared to be part of the resource and be accessed in the region with the same name. We do not divide the variables into groups. Again, we believe that it is the programmer who develops all operations, and would exercise care and develop safe code. We do not provide the same level of protection as in critical regions.

As pointed out by a number of designers, we also recognize the limitations of the pre-scheduling [3,71]. The aim of Maruti is not to completely schedule the execution, since a general scheduling problem is NP-hard [6]. We feel that a large portion of problems that are in the realm of real-time systems are in a special class problems and our approach will apply in those cases. A large class of real-time problems are repetitive in nature and are quite deterministic in nature. We are investigating the class of problems where our ideas would be applicable.

6.7 Conclusions

In the early stages of the Maruti project, observing that current techniques of software development would not suffice for the complex applications of the future, it was felt that advances in the area of software engineering need to be applied to the area of real-time systems.

Accordingly, we decided to apply the object-oriented philosophy to real-time programming. One of the aims of the Maruti programming language was to provide a natural way to program real-time systems. Separate primitives for communication and all aspects of synchronization are provided to increase the readability of the programs. For portability and efficiency, a clear separation is made between higher level mechanisms and their implementation. The other major requirements of these primitives are that they should facilitate in estimating the execution times of various operations, deriving restrictive time constraints, and extracting precedence relations among object invocations. Thus it would be possible to pre-schedule the execution of the complete system and guarantee the deadlines.

In this paper, we have enumerated requirements of next generation real-time systems. In this light, we studied different aspects of synchronization in real-time systems. Different synchronization mechanisms presented in the literature are reviewed. We have described how we have combined their attractive aspects and integrated them with object-oriented programming.

Currently, we are also working on other aspects of real-time systems, namely, resource allocation, scheduling, timely communication, and fault tolerance. Preliminary versions of these subsystems have been designed and implemented. We have prototyped a single machine as well as a multi-machine version of Maruti. A few non-trivial examples have been programmed in the language and executed successfully on these platforms. Our experience to date in using the system has been very satisfactory.

In future, we would like to use the features of the language and the synchronization primitives to derive execution times, temporal relations among invocations, and deadlines of individual invocations. The temporal relations and execution times would be used by scheduling algorithms to derive schedules to ensure the application deadlines. We need to experiment with a number of scheduling algorithms for different classes of problems. It is necessary to integrate fault-tolerance schemes into every aspect of the system. We would like to use the techniques of exception handling, n-version programming, recovery blocks, check-pointing, among others. These (especially n-version programming and exception handling) would have impact on language including synchronization and communication. We would like to extend our scheduling technique for different classes of problems and investigate limitations of our approach.

We feel that our approach is promising and that it will be a valuable tool for studying real-time systems. Maruti will be a useful testbed to experiment and examine different aspects of real-time systems. It will also give us more experience in building real-time systems. In the end, the success of the approach will depend upon its actual use itself.

Acknowledgements

We would like to thank Scott Carson, Ken Salem, and Dipak Ghosal for carefully reading this manuscript and providing valuable comments.

References

[1] John A Stankovic, *Misconceptions About Real-Time Computing,* IEEE Computer Magazine, pp. 10–19 (Oct. 1988).

[2] S. J. Young, *Real Time Languages: Design and Development,* Ellis Horwood Publishers (1982).

[3] Stuart R. Falk and David L. Parnas, *On Synchronization in Hard-Real-Time Systems,* Communications ACM, **31**(3), pp. 274–298 (March 1988).

[4] Stuart R. Falk and David L. Parnas, *On the Uses of Synchronization in Hard-Real-Time Systems,* Proc. IEEE Real-Time Systems Symposium, pp. 101–109 (1983).

[5] E. Kligerman and A.D. Stoyenko, *Real-Time Euclid: a Language for Reliable Real-Time Systems,* IEEE Transactions on Software Engineering, pp. 941–949 (Sept. 1986).

[6] Al Mok, *Fundamental Design Problems for the Hard Real-Time Environment,* PhD thesis, Computer Science Department, M.I.T., MA (1983).

[7] J. Duanne Northcutt, *Mechanisms for Reliable Distributed Real-Time Operating Systems: The Alpha Kernel*, in *Perspectives in Computing*, Vol. 16, Academic Press (1987).

[8] David Cheriton, Michael Malcolm, Lawrence Melen, and Gary Sager, *Thoth, a Portable Real-Time Operating System*, Communications ACM, **22**(2), pp. 105–115 (Feb. 1979).

[9] D. F. Palmer and R. L Stone, *Real-Time System Design, Sizing, and Simulation using DSIGNR*, Proc. IEEE Real-Time Systems Symposium, pp. 205–210 (1982).

[10] A. B. Quirk, *Verification and Validation of Real-Time Software*, Springer Verlag, Berlin (1985).

[11] Karsten Schwan and Rajiv Ramnath, *Adaptable Operating Software for Manufacturing Systems and Robots: A Computer Science Research Agenda*, Proc. IEEE Real-Time Systems Symposium, pp. 255–261 (1984).

[12] R. L. Glass, *Real-time: The 'Lost World' of Software Debugging and Testing*, Communications ACM, **23**(5), pp. 264–271 (May 1980).

[13] N. Wirth, *Algorithms + Data Structures = Programs*, Prentice Hall, Englewood Cliffs, N. J. (1976).

[14] J. V. Guttag, E. Horowitz, and D. R. Musser, *Abstract Data Types and Software Validation*, Communications ACM, **21**(12), pp. 1048–1064 (Dec. 1978).

[15] C. A. R. Hoare, *An Axiomatic Basis for Computer Programming*, Communications ACM, **12**(10), pp. 576–583 (Oct. 1969).

[16] Susan Owicki and David Gries, *Verifying Properties of Parallel Programs: An Axiomatic Approach*, Communications ACM, **19**(5), pp. 279–285 (1976).

[17] Adele Goldberg and David Robson, *Smalltalk-80: The Language and its Implementation*, Addison-Wesley, Reading, Mass. (1983).

[18] Barbara Liskov and Robert Scheifler, *Guardians and Actions: Linguistic Support for Robust, Distributed Programs*, Proceeding of the Ninth ACM Symposium on the Principles of Programming Languages, pp. 7–19 (Jan. 1982).

[19] Bertrand Meyer, *Object-oriented Software Construction*, in International Series in Computer Science, C. A. R. Hoare (Ed), Prentice Hall (1988).

[20] B. J. Cox, *Object-Oriented Programming*. Addison Wesley Publishing Company, Reading, MA (1986).

[21] E. W. Dijkstra, *Notes on Structured Programming*, A.P.I.C. studies in Data Processing, pp 1–81 (1972).

[22] N. Wirth, *Program Development by Stepwise Refinement*, Communications ACM, **14**(4), pp. 221–227 (April 1971).

[23] Virgil D Gliogor and Gary L Luckenbaugh, *An Assessment of the Real-Time Requirements for Programming Environments and Languages*, Proc. IEEE Real-Time Systems Symposium, pp. 3–19 (1983).

[24] Jurgen Nehmer, *A Structuring Framework for Distributed Operating Systems*, Technical Report CS-TR-2007, Department of Computer Science, University of Maryland, College Park (April 1988).

[25] ANSI/MIL-STD 1815a-1983. *Reference Manual for The Ada Programming Language*, U.S. DOD (Feb. 1983).

[26] P.J. Courtois, F. Heymans, and D. L . Parnas, *Concurrent Control with Readers and Writers*, Communications ACM, **14**(10), pp. 667–668 (Oct. 1971).

[27] A. C. Shaw, *The Logical Design of Operating Systems*, Prentice Hall, Englewood Cliffs, N.J. (1974).

[28] G. L. Peterson, *Myths about the Mutual Exclusion Problem*, Information Processing Letters, **12**(3), pp. 115–116 (June 1981).

[29] Milan Milenkovic, *Operating Systems: Concepts and Design*, McGraw Hill Computer Science Series (1987).

[30] L. Lamport, *A New Solution of Dijkstra's Concurrent Programming Problem*, Communications ACM, **17**(8), pp. 453–455 (Aug. 1974).

[31] E. W. Dijkstra, *The Structure of 'THE' Multiprogramming System*, Communications ACM, **11**(5), pp. 341–346 (May 1968).

[32] M. A. Eisenberg and M. R. McGuire, *Further Comments on Dijkstra's Concurrent Programming Control Problem*, Communications ACM, **15**(11), p. 999 (Nov. 1972).

[33] J. Peterson and A Silberschatz, *Operating System Concepts*, Addison Wesley Publishing Company, Reading, MA (1983).

[34] Per Brinch Hansen, *Structured Multiprogramming*, Prentice Hall, Englewood Cliffs, N.J. (1973).

[35] C. A. R. Hoare, *Towards a Theory of Parallel Programming*, in *Operating Systems Techniques*, C. A. R. Hoare and R. H. Perrott (Eds), pp. 61–71. Academic Press (1972).

[36] Per Brinch Hansen, *Concurrent Programming Concepts*, ACM Computing Surveys, **5**(4), pp. 223–245 (Dec. 1973).

[37] Per Brinch Hansen, *Structured Multiprogramming*, Communications ACM, **15**(7), pp 574–577 (July 1972).

[38] C. A. R. Hoare, *Monitors: An Operating System Structuring Concept*, Communications ACM, **17**(10), pp. 549–557 (Oct. 1974).

[39] Gregory R. Andrews and Fred B. Schneider. *Concepts and Notations for Concurrent Programming*, ACM Computing Surveys, **15**(1), pp. 3–43 (March 1983).

[40] R. H. Campbell and A. N. Habermann, *The Specification of Process Synchronization by Path Expressions*, Lecture Notes in Computer Science, Vol. 16, pp. 89–102 (1974).

[41] G. Ricart and A. Agrawala, *An Optimal Algorithm for Mutual Exclusion in Computer Network*, Communications ACM, pp. 9–17 (Jan. 1981).

[42] K. M. Chandy and J. Misra, *The Drinking Philosophers Problem*, ACM Trans. on Programming Languages and Systems, **6**(4), pp. 632–646 (Oct. 1984).

[43] E. W. Dijkstra, *Guarded Commands, Nondeterminancy, and Formal Derivation of Programs*, Communications ACM, **18**(8), pp. 453–457 (Aug. 1975).

[44] C. A. R.Hoare, *Communicating Sequential Processes*, Communications ACM, **21**(8), pp. 666–677 (Aug. 1978).

[45] Pierre America, *POOL-T: A Parallel Object-Oriented Language*, in *Objet-Oriented Programming*, Akinori Yonezawa and Mario Tokoro (Eds.), pp. 199–220, The MIT Press (1987).

[46] A. Yonezawa, E. Shibayama, T. Takada, and Y. Honda, *Modelling and Programming in an Object-Oriented Concurrent Language ABCL/1*, In *Objet-Oriented Programming*, A. Yonezawa and M. Tokoro (Eds), pp, 55–90, The MIT Press (1987).

[47] A.D. Birell and J. Nelson, *Implementing Remote Procedure Calls*, ACM Trans. on Computer Systems, **2**(2), pp. 39–59 (1984).

[48] Eric C. Cooper, *Replicated Procedure Call*, 3rd PODC Conference Proceedings, ACM, pp. 44–55 (1984).

[49] B. N. Bershad, D. T. Ching, E. D. Lazowska, J. Sanislo, and J. Zahorjan, *A Remote Procedure Call Facility for Interconnecting Heterogeneous Compute Systems*, Technical Report 86-09-10, Computer Science Department, University of Washington, Seattle (1986).

[50] David R. Cheriton, *The V kernel: A Software base for Distributed Systems*, IEEE Software, **1**(4), pp. 19–42 (April 1984).

[51] Carl Hewitt and Henry Baker, *Laws for Communicating Parallel Processes*, IFIP Congress proceedings, International Federation of Information Processing, pp. 987–992 (1977).

[52] S. T. Levi, A. K. Agrawala, and S. K. Tripathi, *Introducing the MARUTI Hard Real-Time Operating System*, Technical Report CS-TR-2010, Department of Computer Science, University of Maryland, College Park (April 1987).

[53] S. T. Levi and A. K. Agrawala, *Objects Architecture for Real-Time, Distributed, Fault Tolerant Operating Systems*, Proc. IEEE Workshop on Real-Time Operating Systems, pp. 142–148, Cambridge, MA (July 1987).

[54] S. T. Levi, *A Methodology for Designing Distributed Fault-Tolerant Reactive Real-Time Operating Systems*, PhD thesis, Department of Computer Science, University of Maryland, College Park (1988).

[55] S. T. Levi, Satish K. Tripathi, Scott Carson, and Ashok Agrawala, *The MARUTI Hard Real-Time Operating System,* Operating Systems Review, **23**(3) (July 1989).

[56] Jurgen Nehmer, *An Object Architecture for Hard Real-time Systems,* Technical Report CS-TR-2003, Department of Computer Science, University of Maryland, College Park (March 1988).

[57] Vivek Nirkhe and Satish K. Tripathi, *Object-Oriented Programming for Real-time Systems,* Technical report, Department of Computer Science, University of Maryland, College Park (1989 In preparation).

[58] B. W. Kernighan and D. M. Ritchie, *The C Programming Language,* Prentice Hall, Englewood Cliffs, New Jersey (1978).

[59] Adele Goldberg and David Robson, *Smalltalk - 80: The Language and its Implementation,* Addison Wesley (1985).

[60] Peter Wegner, *Programming Languages - The First 25 Years,* IEEE Trans. on Computers, pp. 1207–1225 (Dec. 1976).

[61] Craig Schaffert, Topher Cooper, et.al, *An Introduction to Trellis/Owl,* Special issue of SIGPLAN Notices: OOPSLA '86, Vol. 21, pp. 9–16 (1986).

[62] Norman C. Hutchison, *Emerald: An Object-Based Language for Distributed Programming,* PhD thesis, Computer Science Department, University of Washington, Seattle (Jan. 1987).

[63] M. Accetta, R. Baron, D. Golub, R. Rashid, A. Tervanian, and M. Young, *Mach: A New Kernel Foundation for UNIX Development,* in Summer USENIX Technical Conference and Exhibition, USENIX (1986).

[64] Kenneth P. Birman, Thomas A. Joseph, and Frank Schmuck, *ISIS - A Distributed Programming Environment: User's Guide and Reference Manual* (March 1988).

[65] Vivek Nirkhe and Satish K. Tripathi, *Object Groups in Distributed Systems,* Technical report, Department of Computer Science, University of Maryland, College Park (1989, In preparation).

[66] X. Yuan, S. Tripathi, and A. Agrawala, *Scheduling In Real-Time Distributed Systems - a Review*, Technical Report CS-TR-1955, Department of Computer Science, University of Maryland, College Park (Dec. 1987).

[67] X. Yuan, P. Chintamaneni, S. Tripathi, and A. Agrawala, *Scheduling Tasks in Real-Time Systems*, Technical Report CS-TR-1991, Department of Computer Science, University of Maryland, College Park (Dec. 1988).

[68] Scott D. Carson, *Derivation of Scheduling Constraints from Real-time Proofs*, Unpublished Manuscript.

[69] W. H. Kaubisch, R. H. Perrott, and C. A. Hoare, *Quasiparallel Programming*, Software Practice and Experience, 6, pp. 341–356 (1976).

[70] N. Wirth, *Modula; a Language for Modular Multi-Programming*, Software Practise and Experience, 7, pp. 3–35 (1977).

[71] W. Zhao, K. Ramamritham, and J. Stankvic. *Scheduling Tasks with Resource Requirements in Hard Real-time Requirements*, Transactions Software Engineering, pp. 564–577 (May 1987).

CHAPTER 7

COMPUTATIONAL METRICS AND FUNDAMENTAL LIMITS FOR PARALLEL ARCHITECTURES
A SURVEY OF PERTINENT RESEARCH

A.C. Hartmann
Microelectronics and Computer Technology Corp.
12100 Technology Blvd.
Austin, Texas 78727

Abstract

Computational metrics and fundamental limits from several relevant theories are outlined as quantitative measures and target goals for parallel architectures. Theory outlines are given for Lipovsky and Malek's "physics" of parallel computation, basic graph theory, VLSI complexity theory (abstracted from Ullman's text, with extensions for interconnection networks by Snir, and for parallel architectures by the author), communication "field theory", Cohn et al.'s uniform bounds on parallel computation, Cvetanovic's analysis of application parallelism, and a composite analysis of the "inductiveness" of parallel applications executing on parallel architectures. Terminology is intentionally intermingled to facilitate comparison of concepts. Apparent joint conclusions of several of the theories supports the existence of scalable parallel architectures with $O(n)$ speedup (where n is the number of processors) and $O(n^{-1/2})$ or $O(n^{-1/3})$ efficiency for sufficiently parallel problems and using conventional technology. While better technology may offer constant factor improvements, it cannot do asymptotically better than this. Also it is shown that parallel architectures can saturate, or worse, "thrash" on certain classes of applications, and that careful mappings of applications onto parallel systems is necessary in many cases to take advantage of communications locality. This study addresses

Frontiers in Computing Systems Research, Vol. 1
Edited by S.K. Tewksbury
Plenum Press, New York, 1990

only theoretical aspects of parallel architecture, and practical issues of programmability or suitability for particular purposes are not considered.

7.1 Introduction

This investigation into computational metrics and fundamental limits
is intended to identify quantitative measures for parallel computation. It
gathers and organizes relevant metrics and fundamental limits from information theory, the "physics" of parallel computation, graph theory, VLSI
complexity theory, communication "field theory", Cohn's uniform bounds
on parallel computation, Cvetanovic's analysis of application parallelism,
and a composite view of the "inductiveness" of parallel applications running
on parallel architectures. Each section is devoted to a single theory, and
expresses its elementary definitions and metrics, and any significant fundamental limits upon the metrics. This work is simply a selective summary
of several relevant theories with but little originality intended or included.

Each section is divided into two parts: definitions and metrics, and
limits on the metrics. The sections are in outline form. Wherever possible
there are corresponding limits in the limits part for each metric in the
metrics part.

The reader is warned that there is some intertwining of the theories,
and especially that the terminology developed in the "Physics of Parallel
Computation" is used throughout much of this report, as it provides some
basic value measures (notably computational *power*, *energy*, and *efficiency*).
Thus it is best to read the sections from first to last. Note that the use
of the term "physics" here is only suggestive (i.e. not referring to classical
physics), and that the notion of computational power and energy output
are based on information theoretic rather than electrical notions.

The reader should keep in mind that this survey is entirely motivated by
a hope that some one or more of these theories might cast a beacon towards
a new paradigm of parallel computation, or at least be the light by which
we evaluate new proposals. To that end the survey is not comprehensive,
but selective.

The reader should be able to note some convergence of the various
theories, especially at the final three sections. While the intermingling of
terminology among the theories was intentionally done to help uncover any
latent similarities, still the existence of an apparent common conclusion was
a surprise to the author. That this apparent conclusion pointed at least
partially in a positive direction (viz. towards the existence of arbitrar-

ily scalable general-purpose parallel processing architectures) was a further surprise, since one can easily imagine larger and larger parallel systems eventually collapsing from the weight of their increasing communications burden. Declining efficiency of larger systems remains a problem as does the apparent lack of inductive procedures 7.2 for some important classes of applications, and the apparent need for explicit mapping of some applications onto architectures with a corresponding communications topology. Also no consideration is given to practical aspects such as programmability, suitability for particular purposes, or even the desirability of scalable parallel architectures. The concluding section draws "The Bottom Line" to this theoretical review.

7.2 "Physics" of Parallel Computation

The material in this section was developed by Jack Lipovski and Miroslaw Malek [11] (with some elaborations by the author). Lipovski and Malek do not use the term "physics" in describing their theory, but it seems appropriate, at least as a unique identifier for the theory. The reader will forgive us for any lack of isomorphism with classical physics. Much of the terminology introduced here is used in subsequent sections.

7.2.1 Definitions and Metrics

Power and energy: Computational *power* is both consumed and produced by system units and processes. The power *production* of a system unit is its rate of information production (generally taken relative to a fixed process or workload). The power *consumption* of a system unit is the total power production capacity of its components and of other units blocked by it. The power consumption of a process is the total system power utilized or blocked by the execution of the process. The power production of a process is the rate of work output of the process (where "work output" is whatever the application deems it to be). Power is measured in units of computational power (UCPS) which are arbitrarily related to information production (e.g. MIPS, MOPS, MFLOPS, Mbytes/sec, or whatever is appropriate):

$$\text{power} = \frac{\text{information}}{\text{time}}$$

Switch power consumption is defined as the number of arcs in the interconnection network. This is a simple but crude metric that gives equal weight to all arcs, regardless of length or wireability. Switch power production can be defined as the average network bandwidth under a set of random requests. The bandwidth of a single arc relates power consumption to power production for efficiency calculations. In subsequent sections we will also use switch space, S_k, as a measure of switch power consumption. Especially when implemented in VLSI, this provides a more realistic measure [1].

Computational energy is the definite time integral of computational power:

$$\text{energy} = \int_0^T \text{power}\, dt$$

Efficiency: The *efficiency* of a computing system measures how effectively it utilizes its components. We define the computational efficiency of a computing system (in executing a process) as the ratio of the system computational energy production (actual work done) to the aggregate energy consumption of the system's components (defined as the total component energy consumed by the system in the execution of the process). This requires relating UCPs at the system level to UCPs at the component level:

$$\text{efficiency} = \frac{\text{system energy production}}{\sum \text{component energy consumption}}$$

The efficiency of system A relative to the efficiency of system B for a fixed process can be simplified (since the system energy production is identical) to the inverse of their component energy consumptions:

$$\text{relative efficiency (of } A \text{ to } B) = \frac{\sum_B \text{component energy consumption}}{\sum_A \text{component energy consumption}}$$

Induction: An architecture is *inductive* if:

i) there is a basis architecture and all systems use only components that are units of the basis;

ii) there is an induction mechanism that can expand a system in units of the basis;

iii) the efficiency of a system of n basis units, where efficiency is expressed as a function of n, declines strictly less rapidly than $O(1/n)$.

This last condition insures that larger systems produce more computational power than smaller systems (at least asymptotically). Inductive architectures that allow systems to be expanded without replacement of pre-existing

---

[1] S_k is a volume in k-dimensional space; S_2 is often represented as A and S_3 as V.

units are termed *strongly inductive*, while if replacement is required they are termed *weakly inductive*[2].

Any basis system unit or collection of system units (needed by processes) with a constant bound on power production (see below) but with linear (in the size of the total system) or worse power consumption is a *bottleneck*. It follows directly that any system with a bottleneck is not inductive [3]. Any basis system unit whose efficiency declines at least as fast as the reciprocal of system size is a *damper*. A bottleneck is a damper. It follows directly that any system with a damper is not inductive [4]. Any resource allocation policy that creates a damper out of a system unit or units is called a *damping policy*. [Example: circuit switching with $O(\sqrt{n})$ circuit delay is a damping policy, since $O(1)$ energy is produced from the circuit, while $O(\sqrt{n})$ resources are consumed for $O(\sqrt{n})$ time.]

A computational procedure is inductive (an *inductive procedure*) if:

i) there is a basis procedure that uses k UCPs (the "size" of the basis procedure) and contains all components needed by larger procedures;

ii) there is an induction mechanism that can expand the procedure in units of the basis;

iii) the relative efficiency (see above) of larger procedures declines strictly less rapidly than the reciprocal of the procedure size.

A procedure P is inductive *in* an architecture A if the compound efficiency of P executing on instances of A falls off less than linearly. [Example: An inductive procedure with relative efficiency $O(1/\sqrt{n})$ executing on an inductive architecture with relative efficiency $O(1/\sqrt{n})$ would have a composite relative efficiency of $O(1/n)$ and be non-inductive.] Inductive procedures are the natural algorithms to use in exploiting the power of inductive architectures since they can effectively utilize unlimited parallelism.

7.3 Graph Theory

This section reviews some elementary definitions and results of graph theory. Any reasonable text [8] may be consulted for further details, and

---

[2]Example: Depending on the particular realization chosen, a mesh network could be strongly inductive, since mesh nodes are fixed degree, independent of n, the number of nodes. On the other hand, a binary hypercube network network, where nodes are degree $\log_2 n$, would be weakly inductive since the node structure depends on n.

[3]Example: a shared bus, for which power production is the bus bandwidth (a constant) and power consumption is $O(n)$ (for n devices waiting on the bus).

[4]Example: a crossbar switch, for which efficiency is $O(n)/O(n^2) = O(1/n)$.

Fiol et al. have written on the (d, k) digraph problem [4].

7.3.1 Definitions and Metrics

A *graph* G is a two-tuple $\langle V, E \rangle$, where V is a set of *vertices* and E is a set of *edges*. If the elements of E are unordered pairs of vertices, then G is an *undirected graph*, while if the elements of E are ordered pairs of vertices, then G is a *directed graph*, or *digraph*. If the elements of E are arbitrary subsets of V, then G is a *hypergraph*.

The *distance* between two vertices is the minimum number of edges that must be traversed on any path between the two vertices, or ∞ if no path exists. The distance between two points in a digraph is not necessarily symmetric. A graph is *connected* if every pair of vertices is joined by a path, and *complete* if every pair of vertices is joined by a path of length one.

A *Moore graph* is any graph that achieves the Moore bound (see below), and a *Moore-type graph* is a graph that comes closer to achieving the Moore bound than any other known graph. In some cases the Moore bound has been proven to be unattainable.

The *diameter* of a graph, k, is the maximum distance between any two vertices. The *average distance*, $\bar{k}$, is

$$\bar{k} = \frac{1}{|V|^2} \sum_{u,v \in V} \text{dist}(u, v)$$

The *degree*, d, of a vertex is the number of edges incident to that vertex. For a digraph, it is usual to distinguish the *indegree* (edges entering a vertex) from the *outdegree* (edges leaving a vertex) and to let d be the maximum of the two. The degree of a graph is the maximum degree of any of its vertices.

The *girth* of a graph G is the length of the shortest cycle (if any) in G, and the *circumference* is the length of any longest cycle in G.

7.3.2 Limits

A moment's thought should convince one that

$$|V| \leq 1 + d + d(d-1) + \dots + d(d-1)^k - 1 = \frac{d(d-1)^k - 2}{d - 2}.$$

To see this just take a single node as a starting point. It can reach d other nodes at distance 1, each of these d nodes can reach $d - 1$ new nodes (plus the original node) at distance 1, and so on.

It is similarly obvious that, for directed graphs, we have

$$|V| \le 1 + d + d^2 + ... + d^k = \frac{d^{k+1} - 1}{d - 1}.$$

The only difference from the undirected case is that d is now the indegree or outdegree of the nodes, and so we use powers of d rather than $d - 1$ since we don't have to subtract the original connecting link to each node.

Note on the physics of Moore graphs It is interesting to apply the prior theory of the physics of parallel computation to the Moore graphs (observation attributed to Leonard Cohn), for which we note $\bar{k}$ is expressible as

$$\bar{k} = \frac{\sum_{i=0}^{k} id^i}{\sum_{i=0}^{k} d^i}.$$

For large k and $d \ll k$, $\bar{k}$ is very nearly equal to k. If each of the n nodes then produces messages at a constant rate, they will each consume $O(k)$ energy, so the Moore graph must then be capable of producing:

$$\text{power} \approx kd^k \approx n \log n.$$

Therefore, since there are approximately n edges, each edge must produce $\log n$ power, i.e. must have bandwidth proportional to $\log n$. In this respect the Moore-type graphs then resemble the less dense $n \log n$ networks (e.g. banyan, omega, delta, etc.) which have about $n \log n$ edges (whereas the Moore graphs have about n edges, since each edge is used to attach a new node).

7.4 VLSI Complexity Theory – General

J.D. Ullman has written an excellent text on general VLSI complexity theory [13], from which we borrow most of the following results, except as otherwise referenced. VLSI complexity theory is essentially information theory applied to communication over a geometric grid. It thus has applications to system structuring at all levels, not just to chip design.

7.4.1 Definitions and Metrics

The *size of a problem* is usually defined by a single parameter n (e.g. an n-point FFT) or a parameter pair k, n (e.g. sorting n k-bit numbers).

Complexity: Complexity is usually given by *asymptotic limits*. Asymptotic limits are expressed as mathematical orders of magnitude, using one of the following forms:

$f(n) = O(g(n))$, an *upper bound* within a constant factor, i.e. there exists a positive constant c for which $f(n) \leq cg(n)$ for all sufficiently large n;

$f(n) = \Omega(g(n))$, a *lower bound* within a constant factor, i.e. there exists a positive constant c for which $f(n) \geq cg(n)$ for an infinite number of values of n (and *not* necessarily for all sufficiently large n, since a function may take on high values only occasionally, e.g. a prime number tester);

$f(n) = \Theta(g(n))$, an *exact bound* within a constant factor, i.e. there exist positive constants c_1 and c_2 for which $c_1 g(n) \leq f(n) \leq c_2 g(n)$ for all sufficiently large n;

Mathematical orders of magnitude ignore constant factors, and they can be made still more approximate by ignoring powers of $\log n$, since any power of $\log n$ is asymptotically less than n^ϵ, for any $\epsilon > 0$; such a bound is indicated by a superscript asterisk (e.g. $O^*()$). In the following, binary based logarithms are usually expressed as 'lg', rather than as '$\log_2$'.

The VLSI *grid model* is a simple model of VLSI circuitry, where "wires" run along grid lines, logic elements and contacts are placed on grid line intersections, there are a fixed finite number of superimposed grid planes (layers), and there is a fixed separation distance (unit distance) between grid lines in each dimension. *Circuit normal form* is a grid model representation of a circuit in which there are only two layers, and wires in one layer run only horizontally (x-direction) and in the other layer only vertically (y-direction); it is easily shown that any k-layer circuit can be converted to normal form with a k^2 expansion in area (i.e. no order of magnitude change in area). A chip's *aspect ratio* is the ratio of the longer chip side to the shorter chip side.

Time complexity is defined as the time needed for an algorithm to execute, as a function of problem size, $T(n)$. *Area complexity* is the VLSI area consumed by a circuit, as a function of problem size, $A(n)$; this can be considered power consumption (in the sense of computational physics), since cost is largely determined by area. *Area-time complexity* is the product of area and time needed to perform a computation, as a function of problem size, $AT(n)$; note that this can be considered energy consumption, in the sense of computational physics. *Area-time-squared complexity* is the product of area and the square of the time needed to perform a computation, as a function of problem size, $AT^2(n)$. This figure is related to switch energy production, since it is based on information flow across a minimum bisection width (which is at most $\sqrt{A}T$ energy).

Information: We define problem *information content* as follows. For problem P and size parameter n, define the information content,

$$I(P,n) = \lg\left|\max_{Z \subseteq X}\left(\min_{\pi \sim P}(\max_{A \sim P}|A|)\right)\right|$$

where:

X is the set of inputs, Y is the set of outputs. Here π is a simple partition of the circuit that divides inputs and outputs into left(L) and right (R) portions, $\pi = (X_L, X_R, Y_L, Y_R)$;

A is a "fooling set" of input assignments that requires information to "cross" the partition from left to right or right to left to designate a unique member of the fooling set for each different input (viz. the chip could be fooled if the left and right chip partitions did not uniquely identify the input to each other);

Z is a subset of the inputs, X;

$A \sim P$ means that A is a fooling set for the particular P, n, and π chosen;

$\pi \sim P$ means that for particular P, n, and $Z \subseteq X$, that π divides Z roughly in half between left and right partitions;

$Z \subseteq X$ means Z is any subset of X (and in particular we seek the one giving the largest fooling set.

In other words, $I(P,n)$ is the amount of information that must cross the chip in order for the chip to always yield the correct answer (i.e. not be fooled). We minimize over all possible partitions to allow the chip designer to be arbitrarily clever in laying out the chip, so that information flow needs are minimized.

[Example: Consider any chip for performing permutations. If a partition of the chip divides the n input pads roughly in half, then roughly $n/4$ bits in each half must cross to the opposite partition to appear at the proper output pads for an arbitrary permutation. The proof is more elaborate, but it should be clear we can show $I = \Omega(n)$ for solution of the permutation problem. Since I bits must cross the chip during the time of the permutation operation, we have $\sqrt{A}T = \Omega(I)$, or $AT^2 = \Omega(I^2)$ as I/O bounds. If not, then the chip can be "fooled" into producing incorrect responses at some of its output pads (because the information they need to produce correct results couldn't get across the chip). In fact, even simple classes of permutations such as circular, left, or right shifts have $I = \Omega(n)$.]

Separators: A graph G has an $S(n)$ *separator*, or is $S(n)$-*separable*, if it can be recursively divided into two rougly equal size graphs by removal of $S(n)$ edges. If it can be exactly divided in half (to within one node for a graph with an odd number of nodes), then it is *strongly $S(n)$-separable*. The minimum separator is sometimes called the minimum bisection width. [Example: The family of binary trees is 1-separable and strongly $\log n$-separable.]

7.4.2   Limits

The following input/output bounds can readily be given. If there are *ioc* i/o connections, then $A = \Omega(ioc)$. If there are *iob* bits of input/output during a computation, then $AT = \Omega(iob)$. This implies $T = \Omega(iob/ioc)$.

Let P be a problem with information content I, and let C be a circuit of area A and time T that solves P. Then $AT^2 = \Omega(I^2)$. This is a direct result of the I/O bounds, since I bits of information must cross the chip (partition width at most $\sqrt{A}$) in time T, thus $\sqrt{A}T = \Omega(I)$, or $AT^2 = \Omega(I^2)$. Note that if C is an interconnection network, then $\sqrt{A}T$ is a limit on switch energy production in time T and $\sqrt{A}$ is a limit on switch power production (bandwidth). For sorting, it is known that $AT^2 = \Theta^*(n^2)$. If the aspect ratio is constrained to be at least a, then it can be shown that $AT^2 = \Omega(aI^2)$. If all pads must lie on the border of the chip, then it can further be shown that $AT^2 = \Omega(I \cdot iob)$.

The H-tree layout for a complete binary tree of n leaves has area $\Theta(n)$. With leaves only allowed on the border of the chip $A = \Theta(n \log n)$. For a tree of height h and nodes n, there exists a wire of length $\Theta(2^{h/2}/h) = \Theta(\sqrt{n}/\log n)$.

A linear layout ($A = O(n)$) exists for any graph whose strong separator is strictly less than $O(\sqrt{n})$. For a graph with strong separator $S(n) = \sqrt{n}$ a layout with $A = O(n \log^2 n)$ exists, and for strong separator $S(n) = n^\alpha$, $\alpha > 1/2$, an $O(n^{2\alpha})$ layout exists. *Thus wiring area dominates for graphs with separators beyond $\sqrt{n}$.* The Lipton-Tarjan planar separator theorem shows that any planar graphs of degree 4 or less have $O(\sqrt{n})$ separators, and their layout is known to lie somewhere between $\Omega(n \log n)$ and $O(n \log^2 n)$ area.

Moore-type (and other low diameter) networks are in general not planar. When non-planar graphs are drawn in the plane, they have a *crossing number*, which is the minimum number of pairs of edges that must cross. If non-planar graph G of degree 4 has crossing number c, then it it is easy to see we could model the edge crossings as dummy nodes and (by the Lipton-Tarjan Thm.) lay it out in area $O((n+c)\log^2(n+c))$.

A mesh of trees of n nodes (arranged in a square pattern with a complete binary tree connecting each row and each column) has area $\Theta(n\log^2 n)$. Very often the ith row and column tree roots are identified with each other, and termed the ith *controller*. Controllers communicate with each other by sending messages down the row trees and by receiving messages up the column trees (in $O(\log n)$ time).

The shuffle-exchange graph and the cube-connected cycles graph lay out in $\Theta(n^2/\log^2 n)$ area.

The butterfly network (and most similar networks, e.g. omega, delta, rectangular banyan, etc.) with $n\log n$ nodes lays out in $\Theta(n^2)$ area. At least the upper bound $(O(n^2))$ should be obvious, since it is not hard to see that such graphs have $O(n)$ separators. The typical three-dimensional layout result is $V = \Theta(n^{3/2})$, which again we can easily visualize if we imagine the $O(n)$ separated edges having to pass through a bisecting plane that is at most $V^{1/3}$ on a side, giving $(V^{1/3})^2 = O(n)$, or $V = O(n^{3/2})$.

Any normal algorithm that runs in $T(n)$ time on a butterfly network can be made to run in time $T(n)$ on a hypercube, and in time $O(T(n))$ on a shuffle-exchange network.

7.5 Categories of Models

The following summarizes the results of a paper by Hartmann and Ullman [10].

7.5.1 Definitions and Metrics

We shall informally define a *model category* to be a gross grouping of parallel system models according to some criteria. The criteria we shall use indicate the category's degree of physical verisimilitude, i.e. how closely it corresponds to physical reality. Many different categories are possible, depending on which physical effects one chooses to recognize and which one chooses to ignore. The principal physical effects of parallel system scaling we consider are those of layout space (typically a three-dimensional volume) and of signal propagation time in that space.

We shall refer to the physical effect of (super-linear) polynomial layout space growth to accommodate a linear increase in number of nodes or edges as *space dilation*. As discussed in the prior section on general VLSI complexity, space dilation is an information flow effect caused when nodes in k-dimensional space have to communicate across k-1-dimensional boundaries. A subsequent section on "communication field theory" discusses what limits are necessary on internodal communication to avoid space dilation. [Space dilation can be avoided when the information flow of each node possesses better than "reciprocal locality", i.e. the total communication flux associated with each node falls off strictly more rapidly than the reciprocal of the distance from the node.] Non-VLSI (discrete) parallel systems models typically ignore space dilation, while VLSI systems models incorporate space dilation effects as a rule. When used as a metric, space dilation refers to the average space per node (S_k/n for k-dimensional space and n nodes). Undilated space has $\Theta(1)$ average space per node, while dilated space has average space per node as an increasing function of n.

We shall refer to the physical effect of sub-linear average communication latency growth (typically the kth root, for a k-dimensional space) with a linear increase in layout space as *time dilation*. This is the obvious physical limitation of the speed of light. Both discrete and VLSI parallel systems models ignore time dilation effects almost universally. [The same reference locality limits (discussed in the "communication field theory" section) that avoid space dilation also avoid time dilation (since there is a uniform bound (independent of layout space size) on the average communication distance).] When used as a metric, time dilation refers to the average communication latency per edge. Undilated time has $\Theta(1)$ average latency per edge, while dilated time has average latency per edge as an increasing function of n. In cases where the communication pattern is known, a weighted average latency per edge may be computed by using the proportion of communication traversing each edge.

Based on the above concepts we propose the following categories of parallel systems models:

Category	MEANING
RSRT	Real space and real time effects considered
RSIT	Real space effects considered; idealized time
ISRT	Idealized space; real time effects considered
ISIT	Idealized notions of space and time

Real space effects are considered by the model if it provides adequate space for the necessary internodal communications bandwidth (so that communications densities are uniformly bounded independent of system size). Real time effects are considered by the model if it assumes increasing communication latencies with increasing communications distance (typically either a linear or a quadratic dependency—see the subsequent section on VLSI complexity and parallel architectures). Naive models ignore both effects.

Traditional discrete models of parallel systems are ISIT models, counting cost as a linear function of the number of nodes or edges in the system interconnection graph, and assuming unit delay along all edges. The newer VLSI models of parallel systems are RSIT models, computing space costs based on achievable layouts, but idealizing time so that all edges (regardless of length in the layout) have unit delay. The ISRT models at first seem nonsensical, computing real time delays over idealized distances, but may be useful engineering approximations to optical interconnection networks devised in an as yet unspecified optical layout complexity theory (*not* grid model based). To our knowledge the first RSRT model of a parallel system (which will subsequently be termed the *state multiplexed model*) and the first ISRT model of a parallel system (which will subsequently be termed the *linear time dilated model*) are contained in the following section on the VLSI complexity of parallel architectures.

7.5.2 Limits

Space dilation limits: Undilated space has $\Theta(1)$ average space per node. [We may consider undilated space either in an idealized model or where communications obey a sufficient locality constraint.] If the communication pattern has the number of communications sent by each node and received by each node independently identically distributed (i.i.d.), then the space, S_k, need not be dilated beyond $O(n^{\frac{1}{k-1}})$ average space per node (i.e. $O(n)$ average space per node in two-space and $O(n^{1/2})$ average space per node in three-space). This is so because under the i.i.d. assumption the minimum bisection "width" need not exceed $O(n)$. Note that the $O(n^{\frac{1}{k-1}})$ space dilation limit need not be reached in the i.i.d. case if the communication is sufficiently localized that $\Omega(n)$ minimum bisection widths are not required.

If the i.i.d. assumption is not met, then the communication pattern may be arbitrarily bad, and in general a completely connected graph may be necessary to guarantee bounded communication latencies. [For example consider a system where at each time unit all nodes send a message to a single distinguished node, and the identity of the distinguished node occasionally changes.] A completely connected graph has a minimum bisection width of $O(n^2)$, giving a space dilation limit in this worst case of $O(n^{\frac{k+1}{k-1}})$ (or, $O(n^3)$ in two-space and $O(n^2)$ in three-space).

Time dilation limits: In an undilated timeframe, communication across an edge occurs with average latency $\Theta(1)$. This may be either because we are idealizing time or because we meet the necessary locality constraints in our communications. In general we need never dilate a time-frame beyond the order of time it takes to communicate across the system physical diameter, or $O(S_k^{1/k})$, divided by the average graph theoretic distance, $\bar{g}$. (Here we use g for the graph diameter, since k is being used for the space dimensionality.) For non-trivial graphs ($\bar{g} \geq 1$) this of course means a limit of $O(S_k^{1/k})$.

7.6 VLSI Complexity Theory – Networks

These results are taken from a paper by Marc Snir [12].

7.6.1 Definitions and Metrics

These definitions address the power of various network topologies. The definitions in order of decreasing strength are:

- An *n-permutation network* has n inputs and n outputs and contains n edge-disjoint paths connecting inputs $I_1, ..., I_n$ to outputs $O_{\pi(1)}, ...,$ $O_{\pi(n)}$ respectively for any permutation π.

- An *n-superconcentrator* has n inputs and n outputs and contains for any $k \leq n$ and any subsets of k inputs and k outputs k edge-disjoint paths connecting the k inputs to the k outputs, in some order.

- An *n-hyperconcentrator* has n inputs and n outputs and contains for any $k \leq n$ and any subset of k inputs k edge-disjoint paths connecting these inputs to the fixed set of outputs $O_1, ..., O_k$ in some order.

- An *(n,m,c)-concentrator* has n inputs and m outputs, where $n \geq m \geq c$, and for any set of c inputs there are c edge-disjoint paths connecting these inputs to c distinct outputs.

This definition of *packet switching networks* is complementary to the preceding one, in that it disregards all issues of topology. It is necessary to make a watertight case for our lower bounds (viz. there is no escaping them in either circuit or packet switched networks, although we have already seen that circuit switching is a damping policy). The following model of packet switching networks is used:

(i) Each node has an infinite buffer to store messages in transit, and each message carries its destination (output) address, and possibly information about its history through the network. Since we ignore nodal area, this is the conservative assumption to make in proving lower bounds. We shall subsequently define *bandwidth* to require a uniform upper bound on the expected amount of queued messages at each node.

(ii) Messages are generated at the inputs, retransmitted at the switches, and deleted at the outputs (double-ended) *or* they are generated, retransmitted, and deleted at each node in the communications graph (un-ended).

(iii) At the beginning of each cycle each node can transmit one message through each of its output lines. The message is received at the other end of the line at the end of the cycle.

(iv) The decision on which messages to forward at each node is either global for a centrally controlled network or local for a decentralized network. Current state and history may be utilized.

In a packet switched network, *transit time* is the number of cycles it takes for a message to travel from an input to its destination. This definition makes no distinction between log n-stage networks and 1-stage recirculating networks (e.g. shuffle-exchange).

In a packet switched network, *network bandwidth* is the average number of messages the network may accept per cycle (i.e. average arrival rate, r) such that the expected transit time and the expected number of messages stored at each node is uniformly bounded. The network has *bandwidth b* if it supports all average arrival rates $r < b$. A network has *strong bandwidth b* if it supports any flow of messages with a distribution that fulfills the following two conditions:

(i) the average arrival rate, r, is less than b;

(ii) the number of messages generated at each cycle at each input, and the number of messages generated at each cycle for each output are identically, independently distributed.

[Example: An Omega network with n inputs and n outputs has bandwidth $O(n)$ but strong bandwidth $O(\sqrt{n})$.] Note that an un-ended network (e.g. hypercube) with bandwidth b has strong bandwidth at least $b/2$, since (as discovered by Valiant [14]) messages can always first be routed to a random intermediary and then on to the final destination. The equivalent result for a symmetric double-ended network (where outputs could retransmit messages to inputs) would give a strong bandwidth of at least $b/3$.

7.6.2 Limits

An n-permutation network constructed from switches of outdegree d has at least $\Omega(n \log_d n)$ switches, else every input could not even connect to every output.

It is possible to build n-superconcentrators, n-hyperconcentrators, and (n, m, c)-concentrators with $O(n)$ switches and lines.

Any of the previously defined permutation or concentrator networks lays out in area $A = \Theta(n^2)$ or volume $V = \Omega(n^{3/2})$ (where we take (n, m, c) to be $(2n, n, n)$ in the case of the (n, m, c)-concentrator). It follows that any weakening of the communication graph below the strength of an n-permutation network achieves only a constant factor improvement.

A VLSI implementation of a packet switching network with n inputs, n outputs, and bandwidth b requires area $\Theta(n + b^2)$, since obviously linear area is required for the inputs and outputs, and the network itself has minimum bisection width $\Omega(b)$. [Example: The crossbar and the butterfly networks both achieve this limit.] This limit also holds for networks with strong bandwidth b. [Example: The Benes network achieves this strong bandwidth limit.]

A recirculating shuffle-exchange network with n nodes provides a bandwidth of $P_o \equiv b = O(n/\log n)$ and consumes an area $P_i \equiv A = \Theta(n^2/\log^2 n)$ giving it an efficiency of Eff$= O(\log n/n) < O(1/n^{1-\epsilon})$ for $\epsilon > 0$, giving it the asymptotic properties of a damper (in two dimensions).

As mentioned in a previous section, an $n \times n$ crossbar has area $A = \Theta(n^2)$ and bandwidth $b = O(n)$, giving it efficiency Eff$= O(1/n)$, making it a damper in two dimensions. One can stack k copies of an $n \times n$ crossbar in the third dimension, obtaining bandwidth $b = O(kn)$ and volume $V = O(kn^2)$, for no improvement in efficiency (beyond a constant factor). Similarly one could connect n inputs and n outputs to an $n/k \times n/k$ crossbar (using time multiplexing), for $b = O(n/k)$ and $A = O(n^2/k^2)$, again for no order of magnitude gain in efficiency (i.e. it's still a damper).

An ideal interconnection network allows any two nodes to communicate in $O(1)$ time. This would require a complete graph (with $O(n)$ fanin/fanout). For a fixed nodal degree, d, the best simulation of an ideal network can achieve $O(\log_d n)$ transit time (in an idealized time model category), and hence $O(\log n)$ time dilation (assuming constant signal propagation time per edge) for the simulation. This bound can be achieved if the following two conditions are met:

(i) the network has strong bandwidth $\Theta(n/\log n)$;

(ii) in a distribution of messages that is supported by the network the expected transit time of each message is $O(\log n)$.

Thus in $O(\log n)$ time units it has sent $O(\log n) \cdot \Theta(n/\log n) = O(n)$ messages. From the previous limits, it follows that such a simulation can be realized in area $A = \Theta(n^2/\log^2 n)$.

7.7 VLSI Complexity Theory – Architectures

The following section was developed by A. Hartmann [9], with the propagation time model of Bilardi et al. [1].

7.7.1 Definitions and Metrics

We define a *parallel architecture* as an architecture for a parallel processing system, containing interconnected processing units and memory units. No assumptions are made as to whether processing units and memory units are separate or combined, or how they are assigned to nodes in the interconnection network. We only make the assumption that the average physical distance between all pairs of processing units and memory units is the same order as the system diameter. In this section we assume processing units of equal power, but the generalization to different power processing units is straightforward.

Time dilation is a slowing of the clock frequency of physically larger systems to compensate for increasing access delay, to retain a synchronous computational model wherein all accesses have unit delay.

State multiplexing is an increase in the number of locally saved process states and a multiplexing of processing unit attention among them to overlap the increased access delays in physically larger systems.

A *linear layout* is a graph layout with $A = O(n)$ and $V = O(n)$, achievable for binary trees, meshes, linear arrays, rings, and little else.

A *non-linear layout*, as used in this section, is a graph layout with $A = O^*(n^\alpha)$, $\alpha > 1 + \epsilon$ for small epsilon. Especially, for most $n \log n$ networks which layout as $O^*(n^2)$ in two dimensions and as $O^*(n^{3/2})$ in three dimensions. Recall O^* is an approximate bound, ignoring powers of $\log n$.

We here define the *system diameter* as the physical diameter of the entire parallel processing system as a function of the number of processing nodes, n. To avoid confusion with the graph theoretic diameter, k, we will call the physical diameter by the equivalent Greek letter κ. If the system is laid out in two dimensions, we sometimes write κ_2, and if laid out in three dimensions, then κ_3. [Example: For a linear layout, $\kappa_2 = O(n^{1/2})$ and $\kappa_3 = O(n^{1/3})$.]

We define *locality* as a measure of the degree to which processing units favor accesses to proximate memory units (as opposed to random accesses to any system memory units). It can be defined as:

$$\text{locality}(L) = \frac{\text{avg. access delay (uniform model)}}{\text{avg. access delay (localized model)}}$$

wherein we note that constant factor improvements in locality (e.g. by caching) will not affect our complexity results (which ignore constant factors). [Example: For perfect locality we have $L = O(\kappa)/O(1) = O(\kappa)$.] Note that this definition of locality is implementation dependent, and may or may not reflect the inherent locality of a given problem.

If we have a situation where, as we go further out from a node, the probability of access in each successively more distant region declines geometrically, then we have only a constant factor degradation over perfect locality, and hence we actually have perfect locality in order of magnitude terms. For instance, if p is my "hit ratio", then with probability p a node will access its local store, and with probability $1 - p$ it will make a remote access. If this continues in geometric fashion, so that with probability $p(1-p)$ a remote access is to the band of nodes at distance no greater than 1 away, and with probability $(1 - p)^2$ the access is beyond distance 1, then the average access distance is bounded by the series

$$\sum_{i=0}^{\infty} ip(1-p)^i = \frac{1-p}{p}.$$

In continuous form, where the probability density function is $\lambda e^{-\lambda}x$, $x > 0$, and the probability of accessing data at distance x is falling exponentially with x, we have for average access distance

$$E[x] = \int_0^\infty x\lambda e^{-\lambda}x\,dx = \frac{1}{\lambda}.$$

Thus either geometric or exponential locality converges to a constant and is, for mathematical order of magnitude purposes, as good as perfect locality.

Of course, the design of scalable parallel architectures under the assumption of perfect locality is a trivial problem.

System power and efficiency: For n processing units inside a parallel system with diameter κ and locality L, the order of magnitude of system power production, P, is bounded on the low side by the number of processors adjusted for (divided by) the average access delay:

$$P_o = \Omega(n\frac{L}{\kappa})$$

and on the high side the output power is bounded by the number of processors:

$$P_o = O(n).$$

The lower bound is $\Omega(n/\kappa)$ under uniform access assumptions (or any constant factor improvement of uniform access), or $\Omega(n)$ under the assumption of perfect locality.

We will make the assumption that system cost is proportional to physical system size (all other factors being equal), and state system power consumption (i.e., input power) as:

$$P_i = O(S_k)$$

where S_k is the size of the k-dimensional space occupied by the system. System efficiency is defined by the usual formula of

$$\text{Eff} = \frac{P_o}{P_i}.$$

7.7.2   Limits

Natural speed limit: The *speed of light* in a vacuum is 3.00×10^8 m/sec, or in more appropriate units, 30.0 cm/ns. This value is also accurate for light velocity in air (which has an index of refraction of 1.000), and for electromagnetic wave propagation (ref. Maxwell's equations) in vacuum or air.

Propagation time limits: Assume transistor Q_1 connected to transistor Q_2, with the output of Q_1 driving the gate of Q_2. We wish to know the limit on the propagation time between switching of Q_1 and the resultant switching of Q_2.

Let the signal distance between Q_1 and Q_2 be l. Let the channel of Q_1 be modeled by a lumped channel resistance R. Let the gate of Q_2 be modeled by a lumped gate capacitance C. Let the signal pathway between

Q_1 and Q_2 be modeled by an RC transmission line with resistance per unit length r and capacitance per unit length c. Then the total resistance is $R + rl$, the total capacitance is $C + cl$, and the signal propagation time, T, is expressible as:

$$T = O(RC) + O((rC + Rc)l) + O(rcl^2).$$

The $O()$ form is used to account for process parameters, which we ignore. The result is left in this form (rather than as $T = O(l^2)$) since we are not interested in asymptotic behavior for large l (where repeaters would be used), but in current and projected technological limits. If the constant term dominates, we may assume constant signal propagation time, also called the *synchronous* model. If the linear term dominates, we may assume linear signal propagation time, also called the *capacitive* model. If the quadratic term dominates, we may assume quadratic signal propagation time, also called the *transmission line* or diffusion model. Bilardi et al. [1] estimate that we are currently in the linear propagation time region, and that future technology would need to have $\lambda \approx 0.5\ \mu$ and $l \approx 50$ mm to even approach the quadratic region. We are on the verge of these dimensions today. [Installation of repeaters is normally done to remedy transmission line effects. The optimum is insertion of repeaters at separation distances so that the propagation delay between repeaters equals the repeater delay (in restoring the signal). This then achieves linear operation of the line, albeit at twice the delay and for additional cost.] Thus the VLSI signal propagation limit can reasonably be treated as $O(l)$, with the constant of proportionality being some fraction of the speed of light. An approximate table would be:

Source	Medium	Propagation speed
Light or EM wave	free space	c
Light	glass fiber	$2c/3$
Electrical signal	copper wire or trace	$c/2$
Electrical signal	chip metal layer	$c/100$?
Electrical signal	chip poly layer	$c/10\,000$??
Electrical signal	chip diffusion layer	$c/100\,000$??

We can factor *communications overhead* per message into that due to signal propagation time and that due to buffering, routing, and switching time. The first part is obviously $O(\kappa)$ (i.e. proportional to the physical system diameter) under the linear time signal propagation model, while the last part is $O(k)$ (i.e. proportional to the graph theoretic diameter) since those operations are performed only at nodes (and not along edges). Since the $O(\kappa)$ term generally dominates (at least asymptotically), we shall treat communications overhead as being an $O(\kappa)$ slowdown in average message transit time.

Power of time dilated parallel architectures: In this model the number of processes is $O(n)$, the system power is $P_o = O(n/\kappa)$ (assuming $L = O(1)$) and each process's share of this power is $O(1/\kappa)$. In time dilated parallel architectures, we effectively slow the processing unit clock to adjust to increases in average access delay so that we can still maintain processing unit utilization with $O(1)$ processes per processing unit. Whether or not the processing units are slowed down because the clock period is lengthened, or because their utilization drops with increasing access delays, the effect is the same—processing unit power output declines. This can be tabulated as follows:

Dilated model: $O(n)$ processes			
space	*diameter*	*power*	*efficiency*
$A = O^*(n^2)$	$\kappa_2 = O^*(n)$	$P = O^*(1)$	Eff$=O^*(1/n^2)$
$V = O^*(n^{3/2})$	$\kappa_3 = O^*(n^{1/2})$	$P = O^*(n^{1/2})$	Eff$=O^*(1/n)$
$A = O(n)$	$\kappa = O(n^{1/2})$	$P = O(n^{1/2})$	Eff$=O(1/n^{1/2})$
$V = O(n)$	$\kappa = O(n^{1/3})$	$P = O(n^{2/3})$	Eff$=O(1/n^{1/3})$

Thus the power obtainable from this time dilated, or synchronous, model is sublinear in the number of processing units under our locality assumptions. *The non-linear layouts under time dilation yield non-inductive (damped) systems.* The linear layouts yield inductive architectures, thus restricting time dilation to the simple types of interconnection networks, such as trees, rings, linear lists, and meshes, for which linear layouts are available. Networks with nearly linear or asymptotically linear layouts may also be acceptable (e.g. mesh of trees or non-rectangular banyans).

Note that time dilation (or else non-constant locality) is essential for a linear layout, and that (given $O(1)$ bandwidth per wire) linear layouts cannot be realized unless nodal communication rates drop as the system diameter grows. This is the same type of argument used in Sections 7.4 and 7.5, for otherwise wires must have $O(\kappa)$ bandwidth each (a physical impossibility). Consider for example a 2D square mesh, which when bisected has $O(n^{1/2})$ interconnecting wires between the halves. But for constant locality and a constant rate of message production per node there will be $O(n)$

messages crossing on these $O(n^{1/2})$ wires at each instant in time, requiring each wire to have $O(n^{1/2})$ bandwidth. Thus the layout must in fact have minimum bisection width $O(n)$ for an $A = O(n^2)$ layout. An analogous argument holds in three dimensions. Thus linear layouts are only achievable in the presence of either locality or time dilation.

Power of state multiplexed parallel architectures: In this model the number of processes is $O(n\kappa)$, the system power is $P_o = O(n)$ (assuming $L = O(1)$), and each process's share of this power is $O(1/\kappa)$. In the state multiplexed model, we save the state of $O(\kappa)$ processes locally in each processing unit and interleave instruction execution to overlap access delays (assuming $L = O(1)$). Thus processing power output is constant at $P = O(n)$, but the physical size of a processing unit grows as $O(\kappa)$. The space, diameter, number of processes, and system efficiency varies as shown below. Note that there is now no distinction between linear and non-linear layout, since the non-linear growth in aggregate processing unit space (now $O(n\kappa)$) is the same order as the non-linear layout space!

Multiplexed model: $O(n)$ power			
space	diameter	power	efficiency
$A = O^*(n^2)$	$\kappa_2 = O^*(n)$	$\# = O^*(n^2)$	Eff=$O^*(1/n)$
$V = O^*(n^{3/2})$	$\kappa_3 = O^*(n^{1/2})$	$\# = O^*(n^{3/2})$	Eff=$O^*(1/n^{1/2})$

From this we see that *two-dimensional multiplexed models yield non-inductive (damped) architectures.* The three-dimensional layout of the multiplexed model yields inductive architectures, but because of the state space expansion required in each processing node as system size increases, they are only weakly inductive.

It is not known if there are other models for parallel architectures that perhaps are more clever in compensating for the assumed linear access delays of large parallel systems. Basically these two models (time dilation and state multiplexing) offer the alternative of either ignoring the increasing delays, or of overlapping them with increasing pipelining. It is not immediately apparent that any other alternatives exist.

We note that the time dilated linear layout architectures are strongly inductive (in either two or three dimensions) and that the three-dimensional state multiplexed architectures are weakly inductive. However it is interesting to note that there exist homomorphisms [10] that reduce the linear time dilated architectures to state multiplexed architectures, and that hence they have some physical realizations in common.

The foregoing limits assume the basic grid model of VLSI complexity theory. This grid model is not valid for interconnection networks constructed from light waves propagating in free space. In this case there is no minimum separation distance similar to the λ-parameter of VLSI, but there is instead a minimum angular separation of intersecting light trajectories (of about $10°$). Two photon streams carrying separate channels of information can occupy the same space at the same time, provided their angle of incidence is at least the minimum. No complexity theory based on this (space collapsing) constraint has yet been put forward, and it is not known if nearly linear layouts could be obtained even for proportionate communications capacity networks.

7.8 Communication "Field Theory"

This section is based on a paper by Glasser and Zukowski [5], although terminology, derivations, analysis, and conclusions are principally those of the author. In particular, the following constitutes a continuous model formulation showing the physical necessity for dilation as a scaling effect under a uniform access distribution.

7.8.1 Definitions and Metrics

Model: We assume homogeneous processing nodes in an inductive parallel system with physical radius R and spherical symmetry about the origin. Isotropic communications (axis independent) among system nodes is assumed. For simplicity (and for conservatism in our estimates) we assume all communication between pairs of nodes is "straight line" along the imaginary vector between the nodes. In sympathy with our view of fine-grained, massively parallel architectures, we assume a continuous (rather than discrete) model of processors, wherein each point in the system volume is assumed to be a point processing node.

For an inductive architecture, communication density at any point in the system volume must be finite and independent of R, the system radius. As described in the prior section, this can be obtained (in the absence of significant locality of reference) through either time dilation (slow communication rates with system growth) or space dilation (grow system volume non-linearly). In this section we explore communication density and the effects of locality on it.

Communication field: At any point p in the system volume we define the *communication field* value $C(p)$ to be the amount of communication (in bits/sec) sourced, sunk, or transmitted through the point p. The scalar field C is what we had informally termed the "communication density" above. Note that C is a scalar and *not* a vector field, since two equal and opposite streams of communication of course do not cancel each other out!

We shall confine ourselves to computing $C(0)$, since our assumption of spherical symmetry about the origin makes this mathematically tractable, and the point for which C has its maximum value should lie at the origin.

Node flux: We will compute the communication field in terms of the flux contribution of a single node, which we term the *node flux*. While we need a vector field to speak of *flux*, we note that for a single node in the system, all communication with it is along radii emanating from the node, according to our model assumption. These radii are normal vectors to the surface of any sphere centered on the node. So, restricting ourselves to a single node's communication, we can speak of the communication flux (in bits/sec) passing through the surface of a sphere of radius r centered on the node. We use the term *node flux* to indicate it is relative to a single node and not to the entire system.

We use the notation $\phi(r)$ to stand for the node flux through the surface of a sphere of radius r centered on the node. As r increases, less and less of the flux extends to larger radii because some of the communication is to nodes at smaller r values. Thus $\phi(r)$ is a monotonically decreasing function of r. Strictly speaking we should write $\phi_a(r)$ for a given node a, but we have assumed a homogeneous system, and, further, we shall ignore "edge effects", where some of the radii may be truncated by the physical edge of the system (in the case a is not the origin). Thus we treat the node flux as equivalent regardless of which node we choose.

Locality: We will not define a unique metric for locality, but clearly we are interested in the relation between the node flux rate of fall-off with r, and the communication field (which we wish to be everywhere finite and independent of R). The faster the fall-off, the more the locality (nodes are communicating over shorter radii), and the lower the communication field values. If the node flux is of the form

$$\phi(r) = \frac{b}{(r_0 + r)^\alpha}$$

(for some constants b and r_0) then we shall say it *falls off with order α*. The greater the value of α, the greater the locality.

7.8.2 Limits

Communication field limits for various forms of node flux: In the following we assume that the system is laid out in k-dimensional space with volume $S_k = O(R^k)$. We wish to compute $C(0)$, the communication field at the origin, for various forms of node flux. Let $c(r)$ be the contribution to $C(0)$ resulting from a node at distance r from the origin. By symmetry we know that

$$c(r) = \frac{\phi(r)}{Kr^{k-1}}$$

since the point contribution is just the flux at that radius divided by the surface area of the corresponding sphere. The constant K is 2 for $k = 1$, 2π for $k = 2$, and 4π for $k = 3$.

Now we have

$$C(0) = \int_{S_k} c(r) = \int_0^R Kr^{k-1}c(r)\,dr = \int_0^R \phi(r)\,dr.$$

Thus the communication field is solely determined by the integral of the node flux! And thus we see the direct relationship between locality (as expressed in the form of the node flux formula) and the communication field (or communication density).

Uniform access: For uniform access we have

$$\phi(r) = \phi_0\left(\frac{R^k - r^k}{R^k}\right)$$

and

$$C(0) = \int_0^R \phi(r)\,dr = \phi_0 \frac{k}{k+1}R = O(R).$$

That is, for uniform access there is *linear* dependence on R. Clearly it is non-inductive and physically self-limiting to have the communication field intensity rising proportional to R.

Reciprocal access: We have a special case if we let the node flux fall off with order one. Then

$$\phi(r) = \frac{b}{r_0 + r}$$

and

$$C(0) = \int_0^R \phi(r)\,dr = b\left(\log(R + r_0) - \log(r_0)\right) = O(\log R).$$

Since $\log R$ is asymptotically less than R^ϵ for any $\epsilon > 0$, this is as slight a dependence as we could hope for on R, and we should suspect that this represents the dividing line between inductive and non-inductive communication. That is, for a node flux that falls off less rapidly than order one we should suspect non-inductive communication densities, while for a fall-off greater than order one we should suspect inductive communication densities (i.e. finite, independent of R). This is now shown.

Order α access: For the general case of fall-off order α, $\alpha \neq 1$, we have

$$\phi(r) = \frac{b}{(r_0 + r)^\alpha}$$

and

$$C(0) = \int_0^R \phi(r)\, dr = \frac{b}{\alpha - 1}\left(\frac{1}{r_0^{\alpha-1}} - \frac{1}{(r_0 + R)^{\alpha-1}}\right).$$

Our suspicions are realized, since for $0 < \alpha < 1$ the result is $O(R^{1-\alpha})$, or non-inductive dependence on R. However for $\alpha > 1$ we obtain $C(0) = O(1)$ and in fact the communication field is bounded by the constant

$$\frac{b}{(\alpha - 1)r_0^{\alpha-1}}.$$

Thus we see that node flux must fall off strictly more rapidly than the reciprocal of the distance from the node in order for the communication density to be finite and independent of R. This is true regardless of what dimensional space the system occupies.

Other implied limits: We can derive some corollary limits to the faster than reciprocal falloff of $\phi(r)$ derived above (in the absence of time or space dilation). The negation of the derivative

$$-\frac{d}{dr}\phi(r) = -\phi'(r)$$

will be the amount of communication between nodes at distance exactly r and the given node. If $\phi(r)$ must fall off faster than order one, then $-\phi'(r)$ must fall off faster than order two, and communication between a given node and *all* nodes at distance exactly r must fall off faster than the inverse square of the distance, $1/r^2$. Now there will be $O(r^k - 1)$ nodes at distance r, so, given symmetry, communication between any two given nodes at distance r must fall off faster than order $2 + k - 1 = k + 1$, or faster than order four in three dimensions (this last result was reported in the MIT work [5] using a more involved derivation). We thus have the table

Communication Metric	Fall-off Order
Node to beyond r, $\phi(r)$	> 1
Node to exactly r, $-\phi'(r)$	> 2
Node to node, $-\phi'(r)/O(r^k - 1)$	$> k + 1$

7.9 Uniform Bounds on Parallel Computation

The following is summarized from a paper by L. Cohn et al. [2], which borrows on the earlier work of R.L. Graham [6]. Similar results appear in a paper by Eager et al [7].

7.9.1 Definitions and Metrics

We define a *parallel computer* as a computer with n processing units, that performs an execution consisting of T unit-time tasks (i.e. $T = T_1$, the sequential runtime). Each task can run on any processor and does so without interruption. Reassignment to a new task takes place in time τ, the task switching time. Possibly τ is a function of n or some other quantity.

A precedence relation is assumed on the tasks, constraining their execution by some partial ordering. The depth of the precedence relation, D (also, the length of the longest chain in the partial ordering), gives the minimum runtime (i.e. T_∞) if an unlimited number of processors were available and $\tau = 0$.

The *runtime* is termed R for a fixed number of processors, assuming $\tau = 0$, and is $R(1 + \tau)$ if τ is positive.

The *parallel speedup*, Z, is defined as

$$Z = \frac{T}{R(1 + \tau)}.$$

That is, the sequential runtime divided by the actual runtime for the given number of processors.

The *average available parallelism*, ω, is

$$\omega = \frac{T}{D}$$

i.e., the sequential runtime divided by the minimum runtime for an unlimited number of processors.

7.9.2 Limits

Runtime limits: Certainly R is bounded below by T/n (all processors busy all the time) and by D (depth of the precedence graph, for unlimited number of processors). On the high side, R is bounded above by the worst case precedence graph, which has a sequential chain $D - 1$ in length, followed by a parallel step of $T - (D - 1)$ tasks (this is essentially Amdahl's observation that if p proportion of the program is sequential, then speedup is limited to $1/p$). Thus in the worst case R is equal to $(D-1) + \lceil (T - (D-1))/n \rceil$. Combining and simplifying the bounds yields:

$$\lceil \max(\frac{T}{n}, D) \rceil \leq R \leq \lfloor \frac{T}{n} + D\frac{(n-1)}{n} \rfloor.$$

Note that this assumes no overhead ($\tau = 0$) and should be multiplied by a factor $(1 + \tau)$.

The *speedup limits* are obtained by substituting the above limits for R into the formula for Z (i.e. $T/R(1 + \tau)$) and using the identity $\omega = T/D$. After rearranging terms we have:

$$\frac{1}{1 + \tau} \frac{n\omega}{n + \omega - 1} \leq Z \leq \frac{1}{1 + \tau} \min(n, \omega).$$

Scheduling limit: The limits for Z imply a limit on the speedup reduction for random scheduling of processors versus optimal scheduling of processors of:

$$\frac{Z_{\max}}{Z_{\min}} \leq \frac{\min(n, \omega)}{n\omega/(n + \omega - 1)} = \frac{n + \omega - 1}{\max(n, \omega)} \leq 2 - \frac{1}{\max(n, \omega)}$$

with the last inequality holding with equality when $n = \omega$. In other words, random scheduling performs within a factor of two of optimal scheduling.

The *task switching time* has an effect on the speedup limits, which is shown below for $\tau = 0, \tau = c, \tau = c \log x$, and $\tau = cx^\alpha$ for x either n (total number of processors) or ω (average available parallelism), c any constant, and $\alpha > 0$. The general case for $\tau = f(x)$ is the last table entry, and would have been sufficient in itself.

It should be apparent from the above discussions that the number of processors that can be utilized is determined by the interaction of the precedence graph for the computation and the processor scheduling algorithm. We can utilize at least ω processors, and, for a worst case precedence graph (as discussed above) at most $T - D + 1$ processors. The optimum number to utilize depends on the precedence graph, the scheduling algorithm, and the overhead factor $1 + \tau$. It is clear though that for any problem instance, there is a maximum number of processors that could be utilized, and that overhead in communication, synchronization, and result combining conspire to reduce this number. The speedup limits for various τ functions are:

Speedup limits for various τ functions			
τ	$n << \omega$	$n = \omega$	$n >> \omega$
0	$Z \approx n$	$\frac{x}{2} < Z \leq x$	$Z \approx \omega$
c	$Z \approx \frac{n}{1+c}$	$\frac{x}{2(1+c)} < Z \leq \frac{x}{1+c}$	$Z \approx \frac{\omega}{1+c}$
$c \log x$	$Z \approx \frac{n}{1+c \log x}$	$\frac{x}{2(1+c \log x)} < Z \leq \frac{x}{1+c \log x}$	$Z \approx \frac{\omega}{1+c \log x}$
cx^α	$Z \approx \frac{n}{1+cx^\alpha}$	$\frac{x}{2(1+cx^\alpha)} < Z \leq \frac{x}{1+cx^\alpha}$	$Z \approx \frac{\omega}{1+cx^\alpha}$
$f(x)$	$Z \approx \frac{n}{1+f(x)}$	$\frac{x}{2(1+f(x))} < Z \leq \frac{x}{1+f(x)}$	$Z \approx \frac{\omega}{1+f(x)}$

Note that this model can be viewed as using a communications overhead slowdown factor of $1/(1+\tau)$, whereas the model of the previous section used $1/\kappa$. Thus $\tau = f(x) = cx^\alpha - 1$ with α equal to 1/3 or to 1/2 corresponds to the physically realizeable parallel architectures described in the prior section. If we use $x = n = \omega$, for example, we obtain for the prior section's linear three-dimensional time dilated model $Z = O(n^{2/3})$. For the three-dimensional state multiplexed model we have $\tau = 0$ because of the state multiplexing trick, and $Z = O(n)$. Alternatively we could imagine each of the $N = O(n^{3/2})$ processes as being a virtual processor and use the same (last) row of the table as for the time dilated model (noting that the system volume is actually linear in N) and obtain by this alternate route $Z = O(N^{2/3}) = O(n)$.

7.10 Applications Parallelism

This section is based on a paper by Z. Cvetanovic [3], which also borrows from the earlier paper of D. Vrsalovic et al. [15].

7.10.1 Definitions and Metrics

Model assumptions: A shared memory architecture is assumed, with n processors, an interconnection network, and n memories. The problem size parameter is m and is assumed to be larger than n, so that there is sufficient work for all processors. Here we assume that communication and processing are overlapped, to the extent possible. We also assume that the algorithm used to perform the application parallelizes without additional processing cost.

The *processing decomposition function*, $D_p(n)$, is defined as the ratio of the processing time for a uniprocessor to the processing time for each processor in a multiple processor system. We shall assume the application algorithm is perfectly inductive to within a constant factor (in the sense of Section 7.2) for processing time, and that $D_p(n) = \Theta(n)$. This holds for any algorithm in which no extra local computation has to performed when the algorithm execution is distributed over multiple processes.

Communication decomposition function: The communication decomposition function, $D_c(n)$, is defined as the ratio of the data access time for a uniprocessor to the data access time for each processor in a multiple processor system. We shall assume that $D_c(n) = \Theta(n^\alpha)$, where $0 \leq \alpha \leq 1$. The case $\alpha = 0$ corresponds to constant communications overhead per processor, and system communications overhead is $\Theta(n)$, completely non-inductive communications overhead. The case $\alpha = 1$ corresponds to constant system communications overhead, i.e. the perfectly inductive case for communications overhead, where adding processors adds no additional communications overhead. *Decomposition group:* The two-tuple $(D_p(n), D_c(n))$ is defined as an application's decomposition group, for a particular algorithm. The fully inductive decomposition group would be (n, n), indicating that both the processing and the communication workload distribute linearly over all processors in the system. Some examples of decomposition groups, taken from the first cited reference are:

(i) matrix multiplication using the straightforward algorithm, group $(n, \Theta(n))$;

(ii) two-dimensional grid computations where only nearest neighbor communication is required, group $(n, \Theta(n^{1/2}))$, and three-dimensional grid computations, group $(n, \Theta(n^{2/3}))$; and

(iii) molecular motion computations, where each molecule's motion is affected by every other molecule, group $(n, \Theta(\frac{n}{n-1})) = (n, \Theta(1))$.

The *communication network bandwidth*, $BW(n)$, is the expected number of memory requests per unit time that the interconnection network completes. We shall consider the case

$$BW(n) = \Theta(n^\beta)$$

where $0 \leq \beta \leq 1$. In particular, $\beta = 0$ corresponds to a bus-based system, $\beta = 1/2$ or $\beta = 2/3$ correspond to two- or three-dimensional mesh networks with random communications traffic, and $\beta = 1$ corresponds to proportionate capacity networks such as typical crossbar or MIN networks, again with random communications traffic.

The *network depth*, Depth(n), is the number of network stages, and presumably is proportional to the network latency. For a crossbar network, Depth(n) = 1, and for a MIN, Depth(n) = $\Theta(\log n)$.

Application processing and communication: The number of processing steps required by an application execution is an integer $S_p(m)$, and the number of data access steps required by an application execution is an integer $S_c(m)$. Using our previous three examples:

(i) matrix multiplication of $m \times m$ matrices with the straightforward algorithm has $S_p(m) = m^3$ and $S_c(m) = 2m^3$;

(ii) two-dimensional grid computations on an $m \times m$ grid have $S_p(m) = \Theta(m^2)$ and $S_c(m) = \Theta(m)$, and on a three-dimensional $m \times m \times m$ grid $S_p(m) = \Theta(m^3)$ and $S_c(m) = \Theta(m^2)$; and

(iii) molecular motion computations for m molecules have $S_p(m) = \Theta(m^2)$ and $S_c(m) = \Theta(m^2)$.

Processing and communication step times: The real time required for the unit processing step is t_p, and the real time latency of a single interconnection network stage is t_c. Thus a communication that suffered no contention in its passage through the network would experience a latency of $\mathrm{Depth}(n)t_c$. Each processor executes $S_p(m)/D_p(n)$ processing steps and $S_c(m)/D_c(n)$ communication steps during an application run.

The *processing time* for the application, $T_p(m, n)$, is computed as

$$T_p(m, n) = \frac{S_p(m)}{D_p(n)} t_p$$

which we can rewrite as

$$T_p(m, n) = \frac{S_p(m)}{\Theta(n)} t_p$$

since we here restrict ourselves to a linear processing decomposition function.

The *communication time* for the application, $T_c(m, n)$, is computed as

$$T_c(m, n) = \left[\frac{S_c(m)}{D_c(n)} \frac{n}{BW(n)} + (\mathrm{Depth}(n) - 1) \right] t_c$$

which we can rewrite as

$$T_c(m, n) = \left[\frac{S_c(m)}{\Theta(n^{\alpha+\beta-1})} + (\mathrm{Depth}(n) - 1) \right] t_c$$

based on our communication decomposition and bandwidth assumptions above. The first term in the brackets is the number of time steps required to enter the communication requests into the pipelined interconnection network, while the second term is the number of time steps for the network pipeline to empty out after the last requests have been entered into its first stage. For $m \gg n$ this second term in the brackets can be ignored as negligible and we obtain

$$T_c(m, n) = \frac{S_c(m)}{\Theta(n^{\alpha+\beta-1})} t_c.$$

The *total time* for application execution is

$$T(m, n) = \max(T_p(m, n), T_c(m, n)).$$

Speedup, $Z(m, n)$, is the uniprocessor application execution time divided by the multiprocessor application execution time:

$$Z(m, n) = \frac{T(m, 1)}{T(m, n)}$$

or

$$Z(m, n) = \frac{S_p(m) t_p}{T(m, n)}$$

since $T(m, 1) = T_p(m, 1)$ as t_c is zero in the degenerate case of a single processor.

7.10.2   Limits

Speedup limits: We have from the above:

$$
\begin{aligned}
Z(m, n) &= \frac{S_p(m) t_p}{T(m, n)} \\
&= \frac{S_p(m) t_p}{\max\left(\frac{S_p(m)}{\Theta(n)} t_p, \frac{S_c(m)}{\Theta(n^{\alpha+\beta-1})} t_c\right)} \\
&= \min\left(\Theta(n), \frac{S_p(m) t_p}{S_c(m) t_c} \Theta(n^{\alpha+\beta-1})\right)
\end{aligned}
$$

If we treat m as a constant and fix it at some huge value, then asymptotically

$$Z(n) = \Theta(n^{\alpha+\beta-1})$$

which has limits of

$$\Theta(\frac{1}{n}) \le Z(n) \le \Theta(n).$$

Now for an application system to be inductive in the sense of Section 7.2 requires $Z(n)$ increase monotonically with n, i.e. we are not "standing in place" or worse, losing ground, as we add additional processes. This means we must have $\alpha + \beta > 1$. Looking at the application algorithm itself, apart from any considerations of the underlying system and its interconnection network, this means that an application algorithm is necessarily non-inductive if $\alpha = 0$.

7.11 Systems Parallelism

In this section we combine the results of the previous section on applications parallelism, with the earlier section on the complexity of parallel architectures to obtain results on the induction of entire parallel systems (consisting of parallel applications running on parallel architectures).

7.11.1 Definitions and Metrics

This section uses the definitions, metrics, and limits established in Sections 7.2, 7.7, and 7.10 to present and evaluate the combined efficiency of parallel architectures and algorithms. Our goal is as always, the "inductive system", i.e. that system which combines an application with an architecture, the composition of which continues to satisfy the induction criterion. This criterion requires that the relative efficiency of larger systems falls off strictly less rapidly than the reciprocal of the system size. If the efficiency fell at the same rate as the system grew, than performance would saturate at some fixed asymptote. If the efficiency fell faster than the system grew, then performance would decline as larger systems were used, and there would be an optimum system size beyond which additional system resources became counterproductive.

System size: There are two system size parameters, one for the application procedure and one for the underlying architecture. The application procedure size parameter is N, the number of processes. We can use the results of Section 7.10 if we treat a process as a "virtual processor" and use N, the number of processes, in place of n, the number of processors, in the results of Section 7.10. The architecture size parameter is n, the number of processors (or nodes, if you prefer). In a linear layout, as discussed in Section 7.7, both n and N are the same mathematical order of magnitude and so are interchangeable in our asymptotic formulae. In a state multiplexed architecture, n and N are not the same order of magnitude, again as discussed in Section 7.7.

Application power and efficiency: Using the results of the previous section, we will arbitrarily define the power of the application procedure (i.e. its "output" power) to be the minimum of its decomposition functions, $\min(D_p(N), D_c(N))$, since this is intuitively the speedup of the abstract procedure, ignoring the architecture. Since we are only interested in orders of magnitude, this reduces to $D_c(N)$, since $D_c(N) = O(N)$ and $D_p(N) = \Omega(N)$. The application procedure efficiency is then the quotient of power divided by size, or efficiency $= \Theta(N^\alpha)/\Theta(N) = \Theta(N^{\alpha-1})$.

Architecture power and efficiency: Using the results of Sections 7.7 and 7.10, we will take the architecture power to be the effective bandwidth of the architecture, BW, and thus have architecture power equal to $\Theta(n^\beta)$. Architecture size or cost will be dependent on both the value of n and the value of BW, according to results in Sections 7.6 and 7.7. We give the table below for both 2D and 3D linear time dilated (LTD) and state multiplexed (SM) architectures, in terms of both n and N:

Architecture	BW	Size
2D LTD	$\Theta(n^{1/2}) = \Theta(N^{1/2})$	$\Theta(n) = \Theta(N)$
3D LTD	$\Theta(n^{2/3}) = \Theta(N^{2/3})$	$\Theta(n) = \Theta(N)$
2D SM	$\Theta(n) = \Theta(N^{1/2})$	$\Theta(n^2) = \Theta(N)$
3D SM	$\Theta(n) = \Theta(N^{2/3})$	$\Theta(n^{3/2}) = \Theta(N)$

Architecture	Efficiency
2D LTD	$\Theta(n^{-1/2}) = \Theta(N^{-1/2})$
3D LTD	$\Theta(n^{-1/3}) = \Theta(N^{-1/3})$
2D SM	$\Theta(n^{-1}) = \Theta(N^{-1/2})$
3D SM	$\Theta(n^{-1/2}) = \Theta(N^{-1/3})$

The distinctions between linear time dilated architectures and state multiplexed architectures vanish when we use N instead of n as the size parameter. Thus we will say that these two classes of inductive architectures laid out in k dimensions ($k = 2, 3$) have power $\Theta(N^{(k-1)/k})$ and efficiency $\Theta(N^{-1/k})$.

[Note that in the process frame of reference (N) that two-dimensional state multiplexed architectures are inductive (Eff $= \Theta(N^{-1/2})$, while they are non-inductive in the processor (n) frame of reference (Eff $= \Theta(n^{-1})$. The former frame of reference would seem the more natural one since the units are fixed (undilated) whereas the processor units dilate depending on the value of n.]

7.11.2 Limits

System efficiency and power limits: Using the above results we obtain the system efficiency as the composition (product) of the application procedure efficiency and the architecture efficiency:

$$\text{System efficiency} = \Theta(N^{\alpha-1}) \cdot \Theta(N^{-1/k}) = \Theta\left(N^{\alpha-\frac{k+1}{k}}\right).$$

The system power would be the product of the system efficiency and the system size, or:

$$\text{System power} = \Theta\left(N^{\alpha-\frac{k+1}{k}}\right) \cdot \Theta(N) = \Theta\left(N^{\alpha-\frac{1}{k}}\right).$$

Thus the order of both system power and efficiency depend only on the order of communications decomposition, α, and the number of physical dimensions, k, used to lay out the inductive architecture. The examples given in Section 7.10 had values for α of 1 (matrix multiplication), 2/3 (3D grid calculations), 1/2 (2D grid calculations), and 0 (molecular motion simulation). For these examples we would have:

α	k	*Power*	*Efficiency*
0	2	$\Theta(N^{-1/2})$	$\Theta(N^{-3/2})$
0	3	$\Theta(N^{-1/3})$	$\Theta(N^{-4/3})$
1/2	2	$\Theta(1)$	$\Theta(N^{-1})$
1/2	3	$\Theta(N^{1/6})$	$\Theta(N^{-5/6})$
2/3	2	$\Theta(N^{1/6})$	$\Theta(N^{-5/6})$
2/3	3	$\Theta(N^{1/3})$	$\Theta(N^{-2/3})$
1	2	$\Theta(N^{1/2})$	$\Theta(N^{-1/2})$
1	3	$\Theta(N^{2/3})$	$\Theta(N^{-1/3})$

In order for the entire system (application + architecture) to be inductive, $\alpha > (k+1)/k$ must hold. However this is based on the Section 7.7 assumptions of uniformly random message traffic. It is possible to do worse than this and experience efficiency-robbing congestion and hot spots within the interconnection network. It is also possible to improve on this by explicitly mapping the application communications graph onto the interconnection network topology so that message traffic is localized and minimized. For example if a 2D grid problem is naturally mapped onto a 2D mesh network, the network bandwidth for this communications pattern becomes $\Theta(n)$ instead of $\Theta(n^{1/2})$ (which it would be for a purely random communications pattern) and the efficiency is $\Theta(1)$. Similar results occur for directly mapping a 3D grid problem onto a 3D mesh network.

In the above table we see that the last five lines represent examples of inductive systems, the third line represents a saturated system, and the first two lines represent systems that "thrash" in the sense that more resources only slow down system performance. The fourth, fifth, and sixth lines in the table represent systems that are only marginally inductive, i.e. they are well into the region of diminishing returns as the system size is increased. However if these applications are directly mapped onto a corresponding grid network architecture, as mentioned above, then architecture efficiency can be taken as $\Theta(1)$, i.e. it does not decline with system size. This would increase system efficiency for these applications from $\Theta(N^{\alpha-(k+1)/k})$ to $\Theta(N^{\alpha-1})$, and system power from $\Theta(N^{\alpha-1/k})$ to $\Theta(N^{\alpha})$. Thus the grid problem examples would change from less favorable random mapping (of processes to processors) values to more favorable direct mapping values as shown:

		Power		Efficiency	
α	k	random	direct	random	direct
1/2	2	$\Theta(1)$	$\Theta(N^{1/2})$	$\Theta(N^{-1})$	$\Theta(N^{-1/2})$
2/3	3	$\Theta(N^{1/3})$	$\Theta(N^{2/3})$	$\Theta(N^{-2/3})$	$\Theta(N^{-1/3})$

7.12   The Bottom Line

The theories outlined in the previous sections, when combined, indicate the truth of the following assertions:

- Weakly inductive parallel architectures can be shown that are examples of the state multiplexed model in three dimensions with a speedup of $O(n)$ and an efficiency of $O(n^{-1/2})$.

- Strongly inductive parallel architectures can be shown that are examples of the time dilated model in two or three dimensions with a speedup of $O(n^{1/2})$ or $O(n^{2/3})$ respectively and an efficiency of $O(n^{-1/2})$ and $O(n^{-1/3})$ respectively.

The caveat to all this is that it requires massive parallelism within the application to obtain the speedups indicated. While massively parallel *algorithms* do exist, similar *applications* (consisting of multiple algorithms of various sorts) generally do not exist, there being little incentive to create them. Since N, the number of processes, may be the more strongly limiting factor (than n, the number of processors) we give the final results for both limiters below:

3D state multiplexed model:

metric	process-bound limit	processor-bound limit
power, speedup	$P, Z = O(N^{2/3})$	$P, Z = O(n)$
efficiency	Eff$=O(1/N^{1/3})$	Eff$=O(1/n^{1/2})$
bandwidth needed	BW$=\Omega(N^{2/3})$	BW$=\Omega(n)$

3D linear time dilated model:

metric	process-bound limit	processor-bound limit
power, speedup	$P, Z = O(N^{2/3})$	$P, Z = O(n^{2/3})$
efficiency	Eff$=O(1/N^{1/3})$	Eff$=O(1/n^{1/3})$
bandwidth needed	BW$=\Omega(N^{2/3})$	BW$=\Omega(n^{2/3})$

Frames of Reference: From the forgoing we can see that a comparative evaluation of the two candidate models, three-dimensional linear time dilated model and state multiplexed model, depends on one's frame of reference. From the processors' frame of reference the time dilated model is a linear layout with sublinear performance, while the state multiplexed model is a polynomial layout with linear performance. On the other hand, from the processes' frame of reference, the two models are indistinguishable—both are linear layouts with sublinear performance ($P = O(N^{2/3})$). If cost is strictly a function of volume (i.e. interconnect volume costs as much as nodal volume, per unit) then the two models are also indistinguishable from a cost frame of reference (cost $\equiv V = \Omega(P^{3/2})$). [Asymptotically polynomial cost seems to be a fact of life for highly parallel systems.]

Architectural Interpretations: Since these candidate models are only very general paradigms for parallel computation (comparable in broadness to the von Neumann paradigm for sequential computation), they admit of unlimited architectural interpretations. There are even interpretations, such as mesh-connected networks, where the two models are physically indistinguishable. This is covered in more detail in [10].

Architecture Limits: From a processor perspective the time dilated model stretches time while the state multiplexed model stretches space and time (should we call it the *fully dilated* model?). Perhaps both dimensions should be stretched a little, but from a process perspective the effects of either transformation appear entirely relativistic. Is this all the parallel computational power obtainable in the four-dimensional space-time continuum? Can free space transmission provide a sort of space warp to free us from material interconnect limits? Even if such a solution existed (i.e. we could drive linear bandwidth through linear—not polynomial—space), without a commensurate time warp the message latencies still force a polynomial growth in the state space that annihilates the advantages of a linear interconnect space. And thus the limits.

Application Limits: In order to have an inductive system, both the application procedure and the underlying architecture must be inductive, *and* their composition must remain inductive. The examples in the final section of this collection of theories argue for acceptance of the following assertions:

- *Applications exist for which one cannot obtain an inductive procedure, and thus for these applications one cannot provide an inductive system.* Molecular motion calculations were given as an example of such applications, but they include all application procedures of zero'th order ($\alpha = 0$) communications decomposition. These are applications where local state information from each process must be known by all other processes, and would include any type of particle motion computations where each particle affected every other particle, as well as such things as neural network simulation by naive methods.

- *Applications exist which are only marginally inductive under a random mapping of processes to processors, and for which significant improvements in communication efficiency can be made by careful mappings.* Grid computations on two or three dimensional grids were seen to fall into this category, but one can easily imagine that efficiency could be substantially improved for any application that exhibited significant communications locality.

- *Applications exist for which inductive architectures provide good performance without carefully contrived mappings or locality optimizations.* Matrix multiplication was given as an example of such an application, although marginal performance improvements may still be obtained by attempts to optimize process placement. No doubt there are many application classes for which the communication pattern is dynamic and random or for which little can be gained from intricate mapping efforts. For example circuit simulation has a static communications pattern but for "rats nest" random wiring there may be little benefit to an optimal mapping of processes to processors. And even the effort to compute an optimal mapping may be computationally more difficult than the simulation itself.

Further Reading

The reader is encouraged to consult his or her own basic references in each of the broad theoretical areas discussed in this paper (e.g. graph theory, VLSI complexity theory) as any sound text should contain the elementary results we only outlined. Several of the sections however refer to more limited theoretical domains or to unpublished material. In most cases a detailed understanding of the underlying theoretical domains is unnecessary to comprehend or apply the principal results.

References

[1] G. Bilardi, M. Pracchi, and F.P. Preparata, *A critique and an appraisal of* VLSI *models of computation,* in Kung, Sproull, and Steele (eds.), VLSI *Systems and Computations,* Computer Science Press, 1981, pp. 81–8.

[2] L. Cohn, H. Sullivan, T. Bashkow, and T. Mankovich, *Uniform bounds on efficient parallel execution time and speedup,* MCC-PP Tech. Rpt., Dec. 11, 1984.

[3] Z. Cvetanovic, *The effects of problem partitioning, allocation, and granularity on the performance of multiple-processor systems,* IEEE Trans. Comput., vol. C-36, no. 4, pp. 421–32 (April 1987).

[4] M.A. Fiol, J.L.A. Yerba, and I.A. de Miquel, *Line digraph iterations and the (d, k) digraph problem,* IEEE Trans. Comput., vol. C-33, no. 5, pp. 400–3 (May 1984).

[5] L.A. Glasser and C.A. Zukowski, *Continuous models for communication density constraints on multiprocessor performance,* IEEE Trans. Comput., vol. 37, no. 6, pp. 652–6 (June 1988).

[6] R.L. Graham, *Bounds on multiprocessing timing anomalies,* SIAM J. App. Math., vol. 17, no. 2, pp. 416–29.

[7] D. L. Eager, J. Zahorjan and E. D. Lazowska, *Speedup vs efficiency in parallel systems,* IEEE Trans. Computers, vol. 38 (3), March 1989, pp. 408-423.

[8] F. Harary, *Graph Theory*, Addison-Wesley Publ. Co., 1969.

[9] A.C. Hartmann, *Computational metrics and fundamental limits for parallel architectures*, MCC Tech. Rpt. No. PP-095-85, Rev. 2, Microelectronics and Computer Technology Corp., Austin, Texas (Oct. 1987).

[10] A.C. Hartmann and J.D. Ullman, *Model categories for theories of parallel systems*, in *Parallel Computing—Theory and Comparisons*, by G.J. Lipovski and M. Malek, John Wiley & Sons, 1987.

[11] G.J. Lipovski and M. Malek, *Parallel Computing—Theory and Comparisons*, John Wiley & Sons, 1987.

[12] M. Snir, *Lower bounds on* VLSI *implementations of communication networks*, Ultracomputer Note No. 29, Courant Inst., N.Y.U., May, 1981.

[13] J.D. Ullman, *Computational Aspects of VLSI*, Computer Science Press, 1984.

[14] L.G. Valiant, *A scheme for fast parallel communication*, SIAM J. Computing, vol. 11, no. 2, pp. 350–61.

[15] D. Vrsalovic, E.F. Gehringer, Z.Z. Segall, and D.P. Siewiorek, *The influence of parallel decomposition strategies on the performance of multiprocessor systems*, in *Proc. 12th Ann. Int. Symp. Comput. Architect.*, Boston, MA, IEEE Computer Society and ACM, June, 1985, pp. 396–405.

CHAPTER 8

TEMPORAL, PROCESSOR AND SPATIAL LOCALITY IN MULTIPROCESSOR MEMORY REFERENCES [1][2]

Anant Agarwal
Laboratory for Computer Science
Massachusetts Institute of Technology
Cambridge, MA 02139

Anoop Gupta
Computer Systems Laboratory
Stanford University
Stanford, CA 94305

Abstract

The performance of cache-coherent multiprocessors is strongly influenced by locality in the memory reference behavior of parallel applications. While the notions of temporal and spatial locality in uniprocessor memory references are well understood, the corresponding notions of locality in multiprocessors and their impact on multiprocessor cache behavior are not clear. A locality model suitable for multiprocessor cache evaluation is derived by viewing memory references as streams of processor identifiers directed at specific cache/memory blocks. This viewpoint differs from the traditional uniprocessor approach that uses streams of addresses to different blocks emanating from specific processors. Our view is based on the intuition that cache coherence traffic in multiprocessors is largely determined by the number of processors accessing a location, the frequency with which they access the location, and the sequence in which their accesses occur. The specific locations accessed by each processor, the time order of access to different locations, and the size of the working set play a smaller role in determining the cache coherence traffic, although they still influence intrinsic cache performance. Looking at traces from the viewpoint of a memory block leads to a new notion of reference locality for multiprocessors, called processor locality. In this paper, we study the temporal,

[1] Preliminary results of this study were reported in Sigmetrics 1988.

[2] This work was supported in part by DARPA contracts MDA-903-83-C-0335 and N00014-87-K-0825.

spatial, and processor locality in the memory reference patterns of three parallel applications. Based on the observed locality, we then reflect on the expected cache behavior of the three applications.

8.1   Introduction

Multiprocessors use caches to reduce latency of memory accesses and network bandwidth requirements. Caches retain recently accessed data so that repeat references to this data in the near future will not require network traversals. Repeated access to the same data in a given interval of time is the property of temporal locality of memory references and has been well studied in single processor systems [1,2]. Spatial locality of memory references is another related property of memory references that places a high probability of access to data close to previously accessed data. Again, this property of single processor programs has been widely observed. The viability of cache-coherent multiprocessors is strongly predicated on whether the multiprocessor caches can exploit locality of memory referencing.

Clearly, a thorough understanding of the memory access patterns of parallel processing applications is necessary to determine a suitable organization of the memory hierarchy in multiprocessors. For example, several cache consistency algorithms proposed in the literature are based on subtle differences in the expected memory reference patterns; lacking a characterization of multiprocessor memory referencing locality, it is hard to obtain insight into the benefits of one scheme over another. While some previous studies have looked at shared-memory reference patterns (e.g., [3]), they did not analyze the temporal, spatial, and processor locality of shared data.

Unfortunately, multiprocessor locality models that we can use to aid in our understanding of the reference patterns of parallel systems do not exist. The well known notions of locality in single processor systems do not carry over straightforwardly. Consider, for example, the sequence of memory references $r_1 r_2 r_3 r_4 r_5 r_6$ to the same memory block. While such temporal locality can be usefully exploited by a uniprocessor cache, the degree to which a multiprocessor uses such locality depends on which processor made the individual references and whether the references were reads or writes. The negative extreme case would correspond to each reference being a write and emanating from a different processor.

Similarly, block size effects are hard to estimate. Increasing the block size could improve useful locality by capturing additional data words in the block that will be referenced by the processor in the near future. However, two data words being written by different processors could fall into the same block owing to a block size increase, proving harmful to cache performance.

We present a simple characterization of multiprocessor memory references and derive a locality model that is useful in a multiprocessor context. The key to the model is our focus on the set of references by one or more processors to a *given* memory block. We introduce the notion of *processor locality* as the average number of repeat references to a memory block by a processor before a reference to another processor. Specific variations of processor locality can be defined for use in different applications. For example, one interesting form of processor locality that provides insight into ownership-based cache coherence schemes is the sequences of repeat references to a given memory block by the same processor, given that at least one of the references is a write [4]. A slightly different form might count just the number of writes to a block by the same processor before a reference by another processor. Eggers and Katz [5] proposed using such a metric in characterizing multiprocessor memory references.

Besides its obvious use in gaining insight into the performance of cache coherence schemes, processor locality metrics can also be used to evaluate the efficacy of block structuring algorithms proposed to enhance locality in memory referencing of shared memory multiprocessors.

We use our locality characterization to analyze the locality patterns in three parallel applications with address trace data. Multiprocessor address traces are derived from these parallel applications running under the MACH operating system on a shared-memory multiprocessor. An extended ATUM address tracing scheme implemented on a 4-CPU DEC VAX 8350 [6] provides the trace data used in this study. The applications include ParaOPS5—a parallel implementation of the OPS5 rule-based language, P-Thor—a parallel logic simulator, and LocusRoute—a global router for VLSI standard cells.[3]

Our results suggest that shared references display a significant amount of temporal locality and only a moderate amount of processor locality. The average numbers of read and write references to a write-shared block before a remote reference are 4 and 2 respectively. This locality is exploited by the write-back class of cache coherence schemes to reduce the cost of references to shared data.

---

[3] Note that these programs were called POPS, THOR, and PEROUTE in our original Sigmetrics 1988 paper [4]. We have renamed them here to be consistent with other recent papers [7] that deal with the same applications as desired by the authors of the applications.

This paper is organized as follows. Section 8.2 defines our multiprocessor model and the terminology used throughout the paper. Section 8.3 presents background information about the ATUM address tracing technique and the applications measured. Section 8.4 constitutes the bulk of the paper and is devoted to analyzing locality in the parallel traces, and studying the impact of the reference characteristics on cache consistency algorithms. Specifically, Section 8.4.1 assesses the temporal locality in shared references, Section 8.4.2 the processor locality, and Section 8.4.3 analyzes spatial locality in the traces. Section 8.4.4 focuses on how the memory reference characteristics affect the performance of various cache consistency algorithms. Section 8.5 concludes the paper.

8.2   Characterization of Memory References

This section presents the multiprocessor model and introduces some nomenclature to help explain memory access patterns in multiprocessors. The notion of processor locality is also introduced.

8.2.1   Multiprocessor Model and Definitions

The multiprocessor model we assume for our analyses is straightforward. We assume that the system consists of several processors, each with its own cache memory. Memory is accessed through an interconnection network. We make the simplifying assumption that caches are infinite in size to concentrate on traffic caused by cache coherence related actions. The specific organization of the network and memory system is, however, unimportant to our characterization of locality.

We first introduce some nomenclature to help explain memory access patterns. A *block* is the unit of data transfer between the cache and main memory. The block size is assumed to be 1 word (4 bytes) unless otherwise stated. The small block size is chosen so that the reference behavior for each data object can be derived. However, characterization using larger block sizes is also important to study the spatial locality of shared objects, and is dealt with in Sections 8.4.3 and 8.4.4. A *read-shared* block is one that is shared (accessed by multiple processors), but never written into for the duration of the trace. A *write-shared* block is one that is shared, and written at least once. A *cpu-shared* block is one that is either read shared or write shared.

It is useful to have a notion of time in the context of multiprocessor execution. Our traces contain interleaved memory accesses by the various processors in approximately the same order they occurred. However, the exact time at which the reference was made is not clear. For example, if the processors i, j, and k each made references at real time instants t, $t+1$, and so on, the trace might have the references $i_t, j_t, k_t, j_{t+1}, i_{t+1}, k_{t+1}$, where the order of the tth references of the 3 processors might be random with respect to each other. The traces also show clusters of memory references by the same processor; the time interval between references by the same processor also varies.

Owing to such statistical variations in the reference pattern, we will use an approximation to real time. The order of occurrence of a reference in the trace is our index of time. So the rth reference in the trace is considered to have occurred at time r.[4] Because the paper considers several cases where the traces are filtered to extract specific references (e.g., shared user data), to enable comparisons, the time index used for a reference depends on its index in the original trace. For example, when we filter out operating system references while studying sharing in the user address space, the time index of a user reference corresponds to its position in the unfiltered trace.

The ensuing definitions for displaying multiprocessor locality focus on the *sequence of processors* referencing a *given memory block*. Contrast this viewpoint with uniprocessor locality that typically focuses on the *sequence of memory addresses* referenced by a *given processor*. A reference to a block B by processor i is said to *ping* if the previous reference to that block was by processor j, where $j \neq i$. We call such a reference a *pinging reference*. Conversely, a reference to a block B by processor i is said to *cling* if the previous reference to that block was also by processor i. Such a reference is called a *clinging reference*. By these definitions, a ping can occur only on a reference to a shared block. Pings and clings to a block are determined simply by keeping track of which processor last referenced a block. Similarly, the state of a block, clean or dirty, is determined solely by the references of the processor accessing it currently. A block is said to be dirty if it has been written into since the previous pinging reference to it. Therefore, a block always starts out clean following a pinging reference to it.

Figure 8.1 depicts read/write references to a given memory block, where the number in the second row corresponds to the processor accessing the

---

[4] We believe that fine time distinctions are not significant in our study. To approximate real time, one can keep a virtual system time incremented by one unit for every n references in the trace, where n is the number of processors. In other words, the times specified in our paper can be divided by 4 to get a rough idea of the real time.

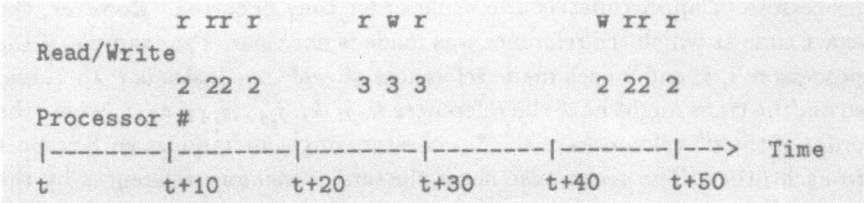

```
             r rr r          r w r            w rr r
   Read/Write
             2 22 2          3 3 3            2 22 2
   Processor #
   |--------|--------|--------|--------|--------|---> Time
   t        t+10     t+20     t+30     t+40    t+50
```

Figure 8.1: Characterizing locality in multiprocessor memory references. Various processor accesses (represented by the numbers in the second row) of a given block B are shown. r/w stand for reads or writes. The time instants with no corresponding references imply accesses of blocks other than B.

block. The reference by processor 3 at time $t+23$ is a pinging read reference, the reference at time $t+25$ is a clinging write reference.

8.2.2   Characterizing Locality

The notion of clings and pings allows the derivation of simple criteria for multiprocessor memory reference locality. The appealing feature of clings and pings is that they do not depend on implementation details such as cache sizes. In addition, they provide useful information about cache performance. For example, assuming a local cache, clinging read references do not cause a network transaction; on the other hand, pinging write references always cause a network transaction. The ensuing discussion uses statistics derived from pings and clings to study locality.

Temporal locality is displayed by references to a given block of data that are clustered in time. Small time intervals between clinging references denote a useful form of temporal locality in multiprocessors; conversely, small time intervals between pinging references is potentially harmful. In the reference sequence depicted in Figure 8.1 temporal locality of clinging references is more evident.

Time intervals between pinging and clinging references are a useful method of depicting the temporal locality of shared-memory references and can yield useful insights into the behavior of small caches in multiprocessor environments. However, a block might reside in a large cache for long periods of time without being displaced, making the relative sequence of references to a given block by various processors a more important determinant of cache performance. The form of locality that becomes more important, then, is called processor locality.

Processor locality is the tendency of a processor to access a block repeatedly before an access from another processor, and is measured by the average length of the sequences of clinging references. In Figure 8.1, the average number of clinging references before a pinging reference is $(4+3+4)/3$.

We can derive a class of processor locality metrics for use in different applications. For example, a characterization that does not distinguish between read and write references is enough to analyze cache coherence schemes such as the Dir_1NB directory scheme studied in [8]. However, this definition is unsuited for a cache coherence scheme that allows multiple cached copies of clean blocks. Therefore, a more practical definition of processor locality measures *the average length of those sequences of clinging references, where at least one reference is a write.* This definition yields $(3+4)/2$ as the measure of processor locality for our example.

In general, we can use the following notation to describe a processor locality metric: $r_c^{+/*} w_c^{+/*} t_p$. Here, r and w denote reads and writes to a block by a given processor, $+$ denotes one or more, and $*$ denotes zero or more. Sequences by the same processor are terminated by a pinging reference of type t. The type of the pinging reference can be a *read*, *write*, or *either* (denoted r, w, r/w). The length of the $r_c^{+/*} w_c^{+/*}$ sequence determines the processor locality. In this notation, the two definitions of processor locality in the previous paragraph are $r_c^* w_c^* r/w_p$ and $r_c^* w_c^+ r/w_p$ respectively.

Processor locality measures locality in shared references alone. It is meant as an aid to gain insight into the shared reference patterns of parallel programs and usually cannot be used to obtain performance data directly. For instance, an application that has very few shared references will have a low rate of cache coherency related transactions even with abysmal processor locality. Consequently, a performance model might consider using the fraction of shared references in addition to the processor locality parameter.

A direct impact of processor locality is noticed in the performance of various cache consistency schemes, which exploit different locality patterns in references to read-shared or write-shared blocks. Notice that a high temporal locality of pinging references yields a low processor locality, and negatively impacts the performance of multiprocessor caches.

Spatial locality is the tendency of processors to access data in the vicinity of a recently accessed memory word in a given interval of time. Clearly, a useful form of spatial locality increases the probability that a given processor accesses words in the neighborhood of words it accessed recently, while the opposite form of spatial locality increases the rate at which *other* processors access these words. Put another way, spatial locality can be useful in multiprocessors if a larger block size increases the processor locality of shared references. As we will show in Section 8.4.3, increasing the block size does not always increase the processor locality.

8.3   Applications and Data Collection

Our study is based on trace analysis. The traces are obtained using a multiprocessor extension of the ATUM tracing scheme [9]. ATUM stands for Address Tracing Using Microcode and works as follows: During the execution of each instruction, the microcode writes out the memory references made by the processor to a portion of memory reserved for tracing. In the multiprocessor extension of ATUM, each access to trace memory is interlocked to enable the microcode in several processors to write their references to this memory. Thus a trace contains interleaved address streams of several processors. The traces used for this study were gathered on a 4-CPU VAX 8350 machine running the MACH operating system. Each trace is roughly 3.5 million references long. In addition to addresses, ATUM records the opcodes, and the virtual-to-physical translations that occur during translation-lookaside-buffer misses. A location is considered shared when it is referenced by more than one CPU. Because different processes could access a given shared location with different virtual addresses, sharing is detected by translating the various virtual addresses of a shared location to its common physical address.

The traces used in this paper are obtained from three programs: P-Thor, ParaOPS5, and LocusRoute. ParaOPS5 [10] is a parallel implementation of a rule-based programming language called OPS5, which is a widely used language for building expert systems. It exploits parallelism at a fine granularity and makes extensive use of the shared memory provided by the architecture. P-Thor [11] is a parallel implementation of a logic simulator at Stanford University. The simulator transforms the task of circuit simulation into a series of node evaluations, where each node corresponds to a device in the circuit. The parallel implementation evaluates these nodes in parallel, while handling the dependencies between them. LocusRoute is a parallel VLSI router written by Jonathan Rose at Stanford [12].

8.3.1   General Statistics

Tables 8.1 and 8.2 present some trace statistics relevant to this study. Because the instruction space is usually read-only, it can be treated specially in memory management, and so the statistics presented in this paper

Table 8.1: Summary of dynamic trace characteristics.

Trace	User References (thousands)	Data References (thousands)	Shared References (thousands)	Shared Writes (thousands)
ParaOPS5	2817	1346	576	77
P-Thor	2727	1527	326	24
LocusRoute	3242	1528	119	6

correspond to data references alone. The columns in Table 8.1 denote the total number of user references, user data references, user data shared, and shared write references. Instruction and data references are about equal as expected. In ParaOPS5, P-Thor, and LocusRoute, shared data references comprise roughly 20%, 10%, and 3% of all user references. The corresponding fractions of shared write references are about 3%, 1%, and 0.2%.

The statistics in Table 8.2 display the number of unique user blocks, unique shared blocks, and the unique shared written blocks in the traces.

Our analyses in this paper focuses on user references alone. Except P-Thor, our applications did not have a significant amount of process migration related sharing; the few blocks that are shared by multiple processors solely due to process migration are not counted in with shared blocks. Results on sharing in the operating system, and sharing owing to process migration can be found in [4].

Table 8.2: Summary of static trace characteristics. Only user data blocks are considered.

Trace	Data Blocks (thousands)	Shared Data Blocks (thousands)	Write-Shared Blocks (thousands)
ParaOPS5	29.3	19.8	4.0
P-Thor	71.9	4.8	1.3
LocusRoute	11.6	3.3	0.7

Table 8.3: Temporal locality characteristics. Only user data blocks are considered. Block size is 1 word (4 bytes). Numbers denote the median of the frequency distribution of time intervals between three events: clinging references, pinging references, and pinging references to a dirty block.

Trace	Cling Refs	Ping Refs	Pings to Dirty Blocks
ParaOPS5	23	10	363
P-Thor	25	7	1779
LocusRoute	28188	13869	19711

8.4 Results and Analyses

This section first analyzes temporal locality in the traces. We then evaluate the processor locality in the traces and the impact of block size on this parameter. We evaluated three different cache coherence schemes by the amount of traffic they generate for various block sizes. This paper summarizes our findings and uses processor locality as a means of gaining insight into their behavior. Unless stated otherwise, we assume infinite caches and 4-byte blocks.

8.4.1 Temporal Locality

This section deals with dynamic memory access patterns and characterizes the temporal locality of cpu-shared user data references. We present the median of the distribution of time intervals between clinging and pinging references in Table 8.3 to demonstrate the temporal locality of data references.[5] The average interval of time between accesses to the same shared block tends to be large because even one reference with a very large interval (or an *outlier*) can skew the average towards large values. Such outliers are not important for two reasons. First, in practical finite sized caches the much shorter cache lifetime of blocks would preclude such large values. Second, the large values in our applications are due chiefly to clinging references that occur when the process resumes execution on the same processor after being switched out. Therefore, in the context of time intervals, a more interesting number is the median, or the time interval over which half the clinging or pinging references occur.

In ParaOPS5 and P-Thor over 50% of the intervals between clinging references are 25 time units or less. Not surprisingly, these numbers show

---

[5] For detailed frequency distribution graphs, see [4].

that blocks are re-referenced at small intervals of time, which is simply a reconfirmation of the belief that memory references display a high temporal locality, and is the precise reason why caching is successful.

LocusRoute has a much larger interval. In LocusRoute, wires are selected at random and a route is chosen using cost values from a shared matrix. Because a wire might be selected by a processor at random, there is no significant temporal locality in referencing the elements in the cost matrix. An algorithm with better temporal locality might favor routing wires in a given neighborhood rather than choosing a wire at random to increase the probability a given word is rereferenced soon. Such a choice will benefit spatial locality also.

These temporal locality results are compared with those for pinging references, or for a reference to a block by a processor followed by a reference from another processor. The time intervals here are interestingly lower than for clinging references, which says that references to shared blocks by different processors are usually at least as finely interleaved as references by the same processor. Doubtlessly, the cause of the high temporal locality of pinging references is that our applications exploit parallelism at a fine granularity, and the use of spin locks for synchronization.

As an interesting aside, in addition to a first peak at a low time interval, our frequency distribution for pings showed a small second peak at 256 time units in P-Thor owing to the process migrating to another processor following a context switch. If the level of process migration is high, this peak at a large time interval can become much taller, which falsely suggests that process migration lowers the temporal locality of shared references. In reality, process migration simply makes a large fraction of the logically private blocks appear shared, and it is references to these shared blocks alone that causes the tall second peak.

The previous results did not distinguish between read and write references. Making this distinction is necessary because in many high-performance multiprocessor architectures, writes and pinging references to dirty blocks cause bus traffic because the new value of the dirty block must somehow be transmitted to the requesting processor. The time interval between pinging references to a dirty block for the three applications is far greater than the corresponding time between *all* pinging references. The high frequency of pinging references at low time intervals is therefore attributable to read references. A possible case is the test-and-test&set synchronization sequence, where one might expect multiple reads from several processors, but less frequent writes. The low temporal locality in pinging references to dirty blocks encourages us to believe that for large time periods, blocks can be considered as private, and no traffic need be generated in maintaining consistent caches. One conclusion of this observation is that cache management schemes must support efficient read sharing of blocks.

8.4.2   Processor Locality

As caches grow bigger, blocks are expected to stay in the cache for long periods of time. Then, a better characterization uses the notion of processor locality. Our discussion here addresses processor locality in two ways. The first uses the number of clinging references to a block ($r_c^*\ w_c^*\ r/w_p$), and the second the number of clinging references to a block, given that at least one of the references was a write $r_c^*\ w_c^+\ r/w_p$.

Figure 8.2 shows the frequency histogram of the number of clinging references to a block, given at least one reference is a write. Due to the wide range of the number of references, the bins on the X-axis increase in powers of two; a bar at x with height y in the frequency histogram plot implies y sequences of clinging references of length t, such that $x \leq t < 2x$. Here, we will use averages because the average is more indicative of processor locality than the median; outliers represent a large number of references, and must be weighted accordingly.

Several observations can be made from Figure 8.2. First, the average number of clinging references to written blocks is 5.6 for ParaOPS5, 3.6 for P-Thor, and 7.5 for LocusRoute. Write references are much fewer than reads and contribute 1.6, 1.7, and 1.2 respectively to these averages. The write reference sequences correspond to the form of processor locality denoted $w_c^+\ r/w_p$.

We found a significantly lower processor locality in the distributions for clinging references when we relaxed the requirement that each sequence have at least one write [4]. For example, for P-Thor, there are about 200,000 pinging references to a block referenced only once by the previous processor. The correspondingly low average of 1.3 for P-Thor indicates that interleaved references by different processors are as frequent as clinging references, implying low processor locality. (The averages for ParaOPS5 and LocusRoute were 1.8, and 2.5 respectively.) A cache consistency scheme that allowed only one cached copy of any block [8] performed abysmally for this very reason. Another important observation is that the total number of pinging references to dirty blocks is approximately an order of magnitude lower than all pinging references, which lowers the overall rate of cache consistency related transactions.

One of the chief differences between some of the cache consistency schemes is the way they treat write references. One set of schemes, e.g., DRAGON [13] or FIREFLY [14], allows caches to hold valid copies of blocks that are being written into by others, and receive updates of the values on writes. Another set of schemes allows only one copy of a written block (e.g., Berkeley Ownership [15], or various flavors of directory schemes [8]). The performance of update versus invalidate is predicated on the locality of references to write-shared blocks. As noted earlier, the average number of writes to a block before a pinging reference is small although not unity (1.7 for P-Thor), implying that either method will not overwhelmingly outperform the other. Our results in the next section show that the invalidate and update schemes perform similarly for 1 word block sizes and bear out this intuition.

There are several possible reasons for the low value of clinging write references. We expect a low value for write references to spinlocks. We also expect this value to be low for migratory shared objects [7] which move from one processor to another, with each processor making some modifications to the object. Also mostly-read-only objects are written once, and then numerous pinging read references are made by other processors.

We also studied the distribution of the number of clinging write references. A surprising observation was that a significant fraction of clinging sequences had exactly one write. The larger average is due to a small number of clinging write sequences with several tens of writes. This dichotomous nature of clinging sequences suggests that competitive cache coherence schemes [16] that can resort to invalidations when the number of write updates crosses a threshold might be the right scheme to use. We also noticed that it was usually the synchronization objects that resulted in a clinging sequence with exactly one write. So another possibility would be to use an update-based protocol for synchronization objects, while using an invalidation-based coherence protocol for all other data objects. In an environment where processes can migrate, yet another scheme might use invalidations for private data objects spuriously shared due to process migration and use updates for other blocks.

In summary, we saw that the processor locality of shared-references is moderate, with roughly 2 writes and 4 reads on the average to write-shared objects before a pinging reference. Given the moderate processor locality of shared-data, invalidating schemes such as the Berkeley Ownership protocol or directory schemes, and the updating protocols such as the Dragon and

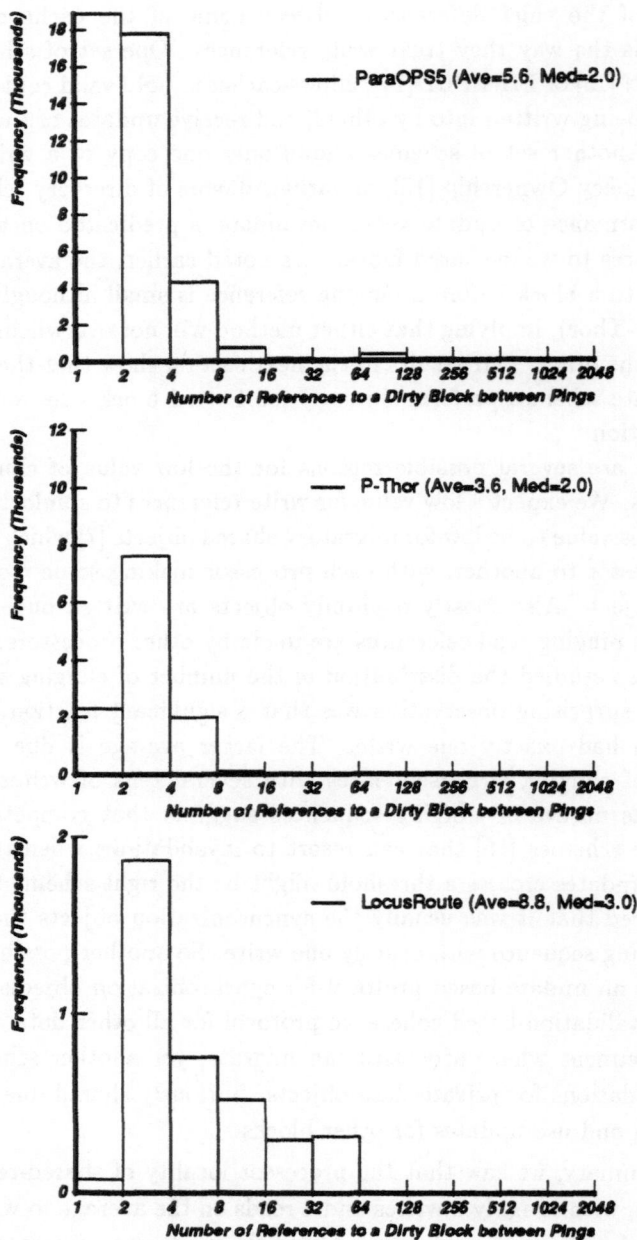

Figure 8.2: Distribution of the number of references to a block before a pinging reference to the same block, given that at least one reference was a write. Only *shared data* references of *user* are included.

Table 8.4: Spatial locality and the impact of block size. Only user data blocks are considered. Numbers denote the average of the number of clinging references to a block, at least one of which was a write.

	Block Size		
Trace	4 bytes	16 bytes	64 bytes
ParaOPS5	5.6	7.8	7.6
P-Thor	3.6	5.1	6.2
LocusRoute	8.8	29.2	117.2

Firefly schemes, are expected to have similar performance. We verified this using simulation in Section 8.4.4.

8.4.3 Spatial Locality

We now examine the effects of spatial locality on the performance of cache coherence schemes. Figures 8.3 and 8.4 plot processor locality histograms for the three applications for block sizes of 16 and 64 bytes. The averages for the three block sizes are shown in Table 8.4.

Increasing the block size impacts the various applications differently. LocusRoute shows a substantial improvement in processor locality (8.8 to 117.2) as block size is increased from 4 to 64 bytes. The reason for the substantial improvement for LocusRoute is that it has a central data structure, called the *cost array*, accessed very frequently and in a regular fashion, thus resulting in high spatial locality of references.[6] In comparison to LocusRoute, both P-Thor and ParaOPS5 show improvements of a much smaller magnitude, and in fact, the processor locality measure decreases slightly for ParaOPS5 as we go from 16 to 64 byte blocks.

Why does block size impact processor locality so differently for various shared applications? As the block size is increased, the potential for references to adjacent words increases, and two opposing forces come into play. If the probability a given processor accesses a word in the vicinity of a word it accessed before increases, then the processor locality is likely to improve. Contrarily, a larger block size increases the probability of unrelated shared

---

[6]Note that the height of the distribution becomes smaller as block sizes are increased because even small values at the tail end of the distribution correspond to a large number of references. For example, in LocusRoute, there are 18 sequences of length between 256 and 512, which account for several thousand references.

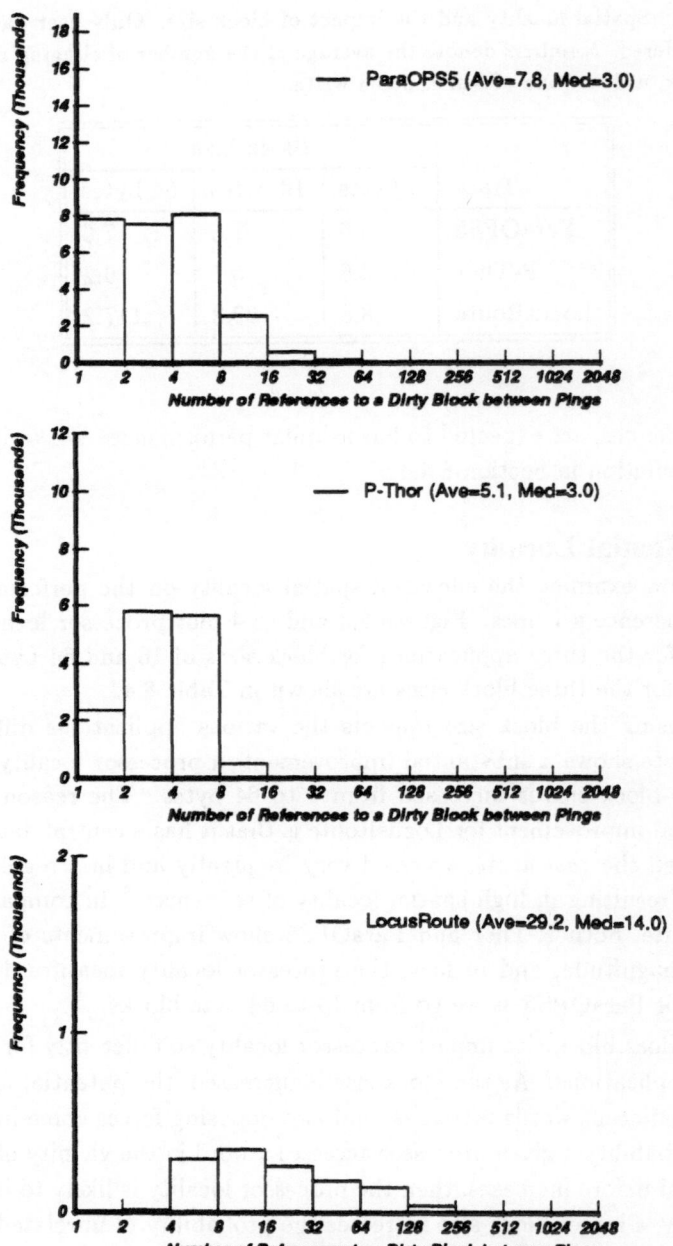

Figure 8.3: Distribution of the number of references to a block before a pinging reference to the same block, given that at least one reference was a write. Only *shared data* references of *user* are included. Block size is 16 bytes.

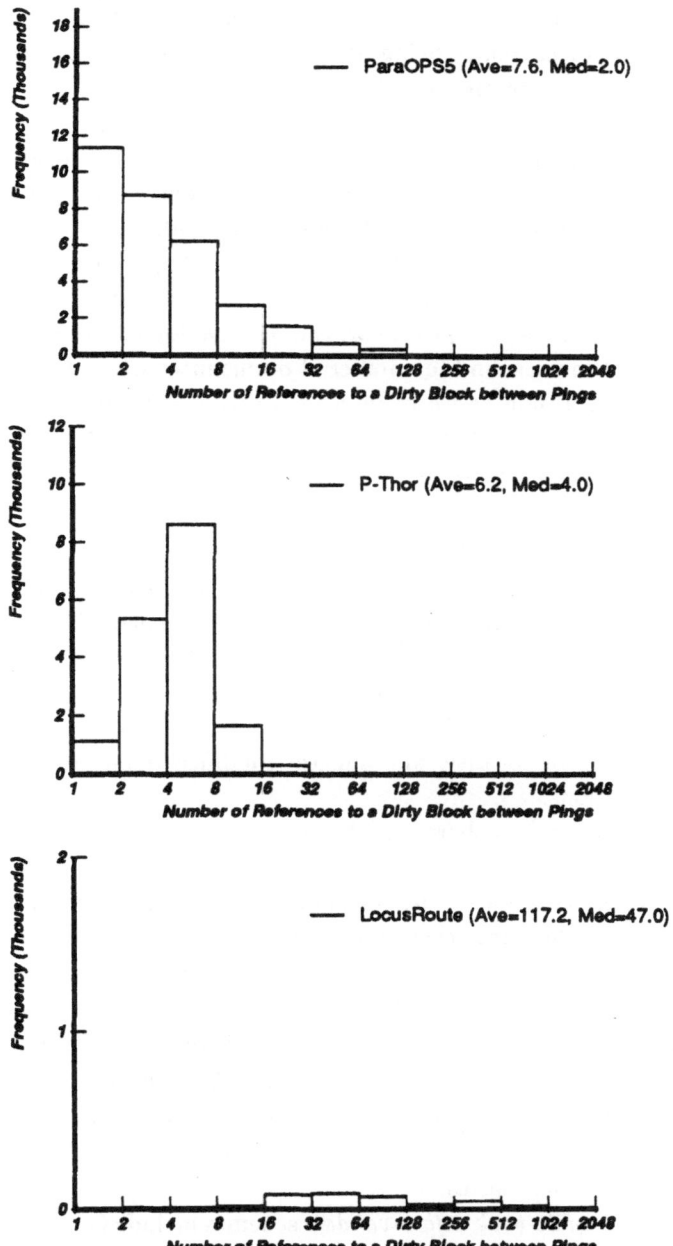

Figure 8.4: Distribution of the number of references to a block before a pinging reference to the same block, given that at least one reference was a write. Only *shared data* references of *user* are included. Block size is 64 bytes.

words residing in the same block, and a write to one word can cause a ping to the entire block currently being accessed by another processor. Clearly, the applications display differing degrees of both effects.

Let us look at the issue of same processor versus different processor accesses of a block more concretely. Examine the processor locality distributions for ParaOPS5 when the block size is 16 bytes and when it is 64 bytes (see top of Figures 8.3 and 8.4). We see a significantly larger number of occurrences with 8-16, 16-32, 32-64, and 64-128 clings before a ping as we move from 16 to 64 byte blocks. This increase is due to the spatial locality in the references of a single processor, the positive force. However, we also see a significant increase in the number of occurrences where there are only 1-2 clings before a ping as we move from 16 to 64 byte blocks. This is a result of the interference effect discussed above, and, overall, it nullifies the advantage of the large block size.

8.4.4   Cache Consistency Implications

Processor locality impacts the performance of cache coherence schemes. We examined the performance of several cache coherence schemes through simulation with the ATUM traces for various block sizes and used our notions of processor locality to gain insight into their behavior. Our findings are summarized here. We also discuss some of the limitations of our definitions of processor locality, and suggest modified definitions for use in specific applications.

Of the several cache coherence schemes proposed in the literature (e.g., [17,15,13,18,14]), we consider a representative each from the write-through with invalidate, write-back with invalidate, and write-back with update classes of cache coherence schemes assuming a shared bus as the communications medium.[7] To help explain the various phenomena we observed, we use the data presented in earlier sections. As before we assume infinite caches, and unless otherwise stated, block size is one word (or four bytes).

The *write-through with invalidate* scheme (WTI) is commonly used in low-end commercial multiprocessors. In this scheme, every write from a processor accesses the bus both to update main memory and to invalidate that location in other caches.

Examples of *write-back with invalidate* schemes include Goodman's write-

---

[7]While a detailed analysis of the numerous cache consistency schemes proposed in the literature would be interesting, it is beyond the scope of this paper. Instead, see the simulation study of several cache coherence schemes by Archibald and Baer [19], and more recently, the simulation study using real address traces by Eggers and Katz [20].

once [17], Rudolph and Segall's scheme [18], Berkeley Ownership [15], and the directory scheme [21]. We consider write-once (denoted WBI) as the second scheme in this paper. In this scheme, the first write to a location uses the bus to update main memory and to invalidate that location in other caches. Subsequent writes to that location by the same processor do not result in any bus traffic, as that location is now owned locally.

Write-back with update schemes include Dragon [13] and Firefly [14]. We use Dragon as the third scheme, and denote it WBU. In the Dragon scheme, all writes to a shared location (a location present in multiple caches) result in a bus access to update the value of that location in other caches. For non-shared locations, the cache acts like a regular uniprocessor write-back cache.

We evaluated the performance of the above three cache coherence schemes in terms of the *bus transactions* generated. A bus transaction is generated on block transfers due to misses, invalidations, or updates. Because of our interest in characteristics of shared references, we only include cpu-shared user data references for ParaOPS5, P-Thor, and LocusRoute. Because caches are infinite, a data item brought into the cache remains there until invalidated.

Before we discuss our results, we examine how we might choose an appropriate definition of processor locality for a given application. Recall the three variations of processor locality in Section 8.4.2. The first form simply counts the number of clinging references to a block (r_c^* w_c^* r/w_p). In other words, we use the average number of repeat references by a processor to a given block of data. The second form counts the number of clinging references to a block for those runs that included at least one write reference (r_c^* w_c^+ r/w_p). Figures 8.2 through 8.4 plotted distributions using this second form. The third form counts just the number of writes in sequences of the second form (w_c^+ r/w_p). Eggers and Katz define and use the same notion in their evaluation of cache coherence schemes in [5].

The first form is useful in analyzing cache coherence schemes that allow only one cached copy of a block (e.g., the Dir_1NB scheme [8]). The second form is useful in examining ownership based protocols, where a writer must first become the sole owner of a block before proceeding with the write. The third form is necessary to distinguish between invalidating and updating (or write-through) protocols.

We first compared the performance of WTI, WBI, and WBU for 4-byte blocks using the third form of processor locality. Comparing the number of transactions, we saw that the WTI scheme was worse than both WBI and

WBU. WTI loses to WBI because of the processor locality displayed by write references. While every write generates bus traffic in WTI, clinging write references do not cause bus traffic in WBI. In fact, recall from Section 8.4.2, that on the average there were 1.6, 1.7, and 1.2 writes in a sequence of clings before a ping for ParaOPS5, P-Thor, and LocusRoute respectively. Based on these numbers we verified that the greatest savings between WTI and WBI to be for P-Thor, the next greatest for ParaOPS5, and the least for LocusRoute. For example, WBI in P-Thor saves 49% bus transactions over WTI, ParaOPS5 saves 31%, and LocusRoute saves 11%.

Comparing WTI and WBU, both schemes generate an update transaction for every write to a shared location. However, WBU saves about 25% updates because before the point that a location becomes shared (a second processor requests it), only the first read or write produces a bus transaction. WBU also has fewer block transfers because, unlike WTI, it never invalidates a location from a cache.

Let us now compare WBI and WBU. WBI, in general, will be superior to WBU if there were a large number of clinging writes to an object before a ping. This is because WBI does not produce bus traffic after the first write in a sequence of clinging writes. Again, recall from Section 8.4.2 that on the average there are 1.6, 1.7, and 1.2 clinging writes for ParaOPS5, P-Thor, and LocusRoute respectively. Thus WBI has the greatest chance to win over WBU for P-Thor, next for ParaOPS5, and least for LocusRoute, which is borne out by simulations. WBI wins over WBU by 28% for P-Thor, by 3% for ParaOPS5, and loses by 21% for LocusRoute.

Dividing the total number of bus transactions generated by all three programs for the WBI scheme (161.6K) by the total number of references that resulted in these transactions (1168.7K), we see that there are approximately 0.138 bus transactions generated per reference. This number appears quite large given infinite caches, and there are two reasons for this. First, this data represents only cpu-shared user data references, which show poor processor locality as in Figure 8.2, or equivalently, which display a high temporal locality of pinging references. Consequently they do not benefit much from the read-sharing allowed by the WBI scheme. If one includes both user and OS references, and both data and instructions, then the number of transactions per reference falls to 0.031, which is much better. This reduction is primarily due to the large number of read-shared references generated by instruction fetches. When the block size is increased from 4 to 16 bytes, the number of transactions per reference further drops down to 0.016, primarily due to the high spatial locality of instruction fetch references.

We then examined the bus transactions generated by WBI, as the block size is increased, to study the spatial locality characteristics of cpu-shared user data references. For this analysis the second form of processor locality is relevant because once a block is read, a transaction takes place only on a pinging reference – on a pinging read the block must be written back to memory, while on a write the block must be invalidated.

We observed that the measure of processor locality using the second form correctly predicts the trends in ParaOPS5 and LocusRoute. For example, the transaction rate in ParaOPS5 decreases when the block size is changed from 4 to 16 bytes, and the number of transactions increases when the block size is further changed to 64 bytes. A corresponding increasing trend is observed in the second form of the processor locality parameter (see Figures 8.2 through 8.4).

A different trend is observed in LocusRoute as the block size is increased. The transaction rate decreases as we go from 4 to 16 to 64 bytes, a corresponding improving trend is displayed by the processor locality parameter for LocusRoute as the block size is increased.

The trends in P-Thor, however, did not match completely. A possible reason for the disagreement we observed is that the second form of processor locality as defined by us corresponds most closely to a protocol that invalidates a currently dirty copy of a block in a cache on a pinging read rather than just performing the writeback and making it clean. If a more accurate processor locality metric for analyzing performance of ownership protocols that clean rather than invalidate is desired, one can measure the average length of sequences of references to a block of data by a given processor, terminating the sequences only on pinging writes. This form of processor locality is denoted $r_c^* \ w_c^+ \ w_p$. The important observation is that the notion of pings and clings make it possible to customize the processor locality definition to suit a particular application.

8.5 Summary and Conclusions

We have characterized locality in memory reference patterns of shared-memory multiprocessors. Our data is based on traces obtained for three applications from a 4-processor VAX 8350 using the ATUM address tracing technique. About one-fifth of the references in the traces are to shared objects.

Shared references display a significant amount of temporal locality, but only a moderate amount of processor locality for both read and write references. For example, the average number of reads and writes to a write-shared block before a remote reference (a ping, which may possibly invalidate the data) are 4 and 2 respectively. Nevertheless, caching shared data is still highly useful because of the significant amount of read sharing. Although the average number of writes to a block before a remote reference is just 2, we observed a high variance in the length of write sequences. We believe that the use of hybrid updating and invalidating schemes, such as updating for synchronization objects and invalidating for others, may prove useful in such environments.

The locality characterization of the shared-memory reference patterns also yields insight on how various cache consistency schemes will perform. We analyzed three classes of cache consistency schemes—write-through with invalidate (WTI), write-back with invalidate (WBI), and write-back with update (WBU). For shared data references, WTI performs worse than both WBI and WBU as it uses the bus on every write. Comparing WBI and WBU, the former seems to have an edge for 4-byte blocks, while WBU does better for 16-byte and 64-byte blocks. The processor locality parameter shows that blocks larger than 16 bytes in P-Thor and ParaOPS5 cause a degradation in processor locality, and thus the total bus traffic increases rapidly with increasing block size. The WBU scheme is less influenced by the block size than WBI and WTI because it always uses single word updates. Consequently, for large block sizes, WBU performs better than WBI and WTI for all three programs.

8.6 Acknowledgments

We thank Roberto Bisiani and the Speech Group at CMU for letting us use their VAX 8350 for collecting the traces used in this study. Dick Sites at Digital Equipment Corporation, Hudson, made the ATUM microcode available for our use. Larry Soule and Helen Davis at Stanford helped with the P-Thor program and Jonathan Rose with LocusRoute. Discussions with Susan Owicki, Susan Eggers, Mark Horowitz, John Hennessy, and Rich Simoni are also gratefully acknowledged. The research reported in this paper was funded by DARPA contracts # MDA903-83-C-0335 and # N00014-87-K-0825. Anoop Gupta is also supported by a faculty development award from DEC.

References

[1] P. J. Denning, *The Working Set Model for Program Behavior*, Communications of the ACM, Vol. 11(5), pp. 323–333 (May 1968).

[2] J. R. Spirn, *Program Behavior: Models and Measurements*, Operating and Programming Systems Series, Elsevier, New York (1977).

[3] F. Darema-Rogers, G. F. Pfister, and K. So, *Memory Access Patterns of Parallel Scientific Programs*, Proceedings of ACM SIGMETRICS 1987, pp. 46–58 (May 1987).

[4] Anant Agarwal and Anoop Gupta, *Memory-Reference Characteristics of Multiprocessor Applications under MACH*, Proceedings of ACM SIGMETRICS 1988 (May 1988).

[5] S. J. Eggers and R. H. Katz, *A Characterization of Sharing in Parallel Programs and Its Application to Coherency Protocol Evaluation*, Proceedings of the 15th International Symposium on Computer Architecture, IEEE, New York (June 1988).

[6] Richard L. Sites and Anant Agarwal, *Multiprocessor Cache Analysis using ATUM*, Proceedings of the 15th International Symposium on Computer Architecture, pages 186–195, IEEE, New York (June 1988).

[7] Wolf-Dietrich Weber and Anoop Gupta, *Analysis of Cache Invalidation Patterns in Multiprocessors*, Third International Conference on Architectural Support for Programming Languages and Operating Systems (ASPLOS III) (April 1989).

[8] Anant Agarwal, Richard Simoni, John Hennessy, and Mark Horowitz, *An Evaluation of Directory Schemes for Cache Coherence*, Proceedings of the 15th International Symposium on Computer Architecture, IEEE, New York (June 1988).

[9] Anant Agarwal, Richard L. Sites, and Mark Horowitz, *ATUM: A New Technique for Capturing Address Traces Using Microcode*, Proceedings of the 13th Annual Symposium on Computer Architecture, pp. 119–127, IEEE, New York (June 1986).

[10] Anoop Gupta, Charles Forgy, and Robert Wedig, *Parallel Architectures and Algorithms for Rule-Based Systems*, Proceedings of the 13th

Annual Symposium on Computer Architecture, IEEE, New York (June 1986).

[11] Larry Soule and Annop Gupta, *Parallel Distributed-Time Logic Simulation*, IEEE Design & Test, Vol. 6 (6) (Dec. 1989).

[12] Jonathan Rose, *LocusRoute: A Parallel Global Router for Standard Cells*, Design Automation Conference, pp. 189–195 (June 1988).

[13] E. McCreight, *The Dragon Computer System: An Early Overview*, Technical Report, Xerox Corp. (September 1984).

[14] Charles P. Thacker and Lawrence C. Stewart, *Firefly: a Multiprocessor Workstation*, Proceedings of ASPLOS II, pp. 164–172 (October 1987).

[15] R. H. Katz, S. J. Eggers, D. A. Wood, C. L. Perkins, and R. G. Sheldon, *Implementing a Cache Consistency Protocol*, Proceedings of the 12th International Symposium on Computer Architecture, pp. 276–283, IEEE, New York (June 1985).

[16] Anna Karlin, Mark Manasse, Larry Rudolph, and Daniel Sleator, *Competitive Snoopy Caching*, Technical Report CMU-CS-86-164, Computer Science Dept., Carnegie Mellon University, Pittsburgh, PA (1986). {Preliminary version appeared in 27th FOCS, 1986.}

[17] James R. Goodman, *Using Cache Memory to Reduce Processor-Memory Traffic*, Proceedings of the 10th Annual Symposium on Computer Architecture, pp. 124–131, IEEE, New York (June 1983).

[18] L. Rudolph and Z. Segall, *Dynamic Decentralized Cache Consistency Schemes for MIMD Parallel Processors*, Proceedings of the 12th International Symposium on Computer Architecture, pp. 340–347, IEEE, New York (June 1985).

[19] James Archibald and Jean-Loup Baer, *Cache Coherence Protocols: Evaluation Using a Multiprocessor Simulation Model*, ACM Transactions on Computer Systems, Vol. 4(4), pp. 273–298 (November 1986).

[20] S. J. Eggers and R. H. Katz, *Evaluating the Performance of Four Snooping Cache Coherency Protocols*, Proceedings of the 16th International Symposium on Computer Architecture, IEEE, New York (June 1989).

[21] Lucien M. Censier and Paul Feautrier, *A New Solution to Coherence Problems in Multicache Systems,* IEEE Transactions on Computers, Vol. C-27(12), pp. 1112–1118 (December 1978).

CHAPTER 9

AN EXTENDIBLE
CONNECTIONIST SIMULATOR

Mark Fanty [1]
Oregon Graduate Institute
Dept. of Computer Science and Engineering
Beaverton, Oregon 97006

9.1   Introduction

Connectionist (or neural) networks consist of large numbers of relatively simple computational units. The units communicate nonsymbolically over links. The computation performed is embodied in the pattern of connectivity. Connectionist researchers hope to explain or reproduce human performance on pattern matching and other tasks which have proved resistant to traditional programming techniques. Roughly, they work on designing artificial brains. Because of the large numbers of units needed – the human brain has more than 10**10 neurons – networks useful for large, complex tasks will require hardware realizations. Work on VLSI networks is ongoing [1].

For now, most networks are simulated with software. This has the obvious advantages: low cost, easy availability, easy modification. The latter is especially important for researchers as there is no generally agreed upon definition of connectionist networks. It must be possible to add a parameter or change the behavior of the units. There are a great many software packages in use, including several which are commercially available. Many have graphical interfaces which display the units as small icons varying in size or color depending on level of activity. Some are user-programmable: the behavior of the units is determined by code provided by the user. Others simply let the user choose among several common unit types.

---

[1] This work was done while the author was at Ricoh Corporation, San Jose, California.

Frontiers in Computing Systems Research, Vol. 1
Edited by S.K. Tewksbury
Plenum Press, New York, 1990

My experience has been with the Rochester Connectionist Simulator [2] which I helped write and ported to a 100-node Butterfly Multiprocessor [3]. The Rochester simulator is highly customizable, using a separate function call for each unit and link. The simulator works best for "structured" networks which typically have more than one kind of unit and link, use complex interconnection patterns, and run for a relatively small number of iterations. It works less well for back propagation [4,5] experiments, which use networks with only one type of unit and could well use tightly coded loops rather than individual unit and link function calls when running thousands or hundreds of thousands of iterations. The Rochester simulator has been a pleasure to work with, but several years experience has led to a wish list for a redesign.

My goal in this chapter is to specify the design of a software simulator from the next generation in the family of customizable, graphics-oriented simulators like the Rochester Connectionist Simulator. The quality of the software tools is vitally important to the success of connectionist research Such software, especially graphical user interfaces, is time consuming to produce. Researchers can easily sink huge amounts of time into the software surrounding their work. My design goal is a simulation environment which is very powerful and flexible, while sacrificing as little efficiency as possible. My goal is not to realize the ideal connectionist model, but to provide the tools necessary to explore the space of possible models. The simulator is extendible because it is designed to be enhanced.

If speed of simulation is the only consideration, the only choice is custom software for each network type, or even for each individual network. This approach may make sense if experiments using the network will be running for many days or weeks and a sophisticated interface is unnecessary. If speed of simulation is ignored, the result can be almost unusable. The first simulation tool I used was written in LISP in such a way that a network with 1000 links took several minutes on our hardware to execute one simulation step. Intense frustration with this program led to a C language version which had almost the same functionality, but which took a lot less memory and was orders of magnitude faster. Ignoring size and speed, C was a much poorer language than LISP for the implementation, but a few days with the old program were enough to convince anyone that size and speed cannot be ignored. As researchers become more ambitious in the problems they tackle, size and speed will be a central issue.

Third priority, behind power and speed, is given to user-friendliness. The key here is having multiple levels of use. Predefined libraries of units and links can be used to construct networks without writing a single line of code. On-line help and good manuals make the task easier. More ambitious users can redefine the most basic simulation routines and provide arbitrarily complex interfaces. The options available are complex because the task is.

Only very preliminary implementations exist, but I will write in the present tense. The target simulator uses an object oriented language such as C++. This encourages a functional view of units and other objects, hiding the implementation details. This is important for networks with many different kinds of units and links, which don't necessarily "know" about each other but still must work together. It also allows new classes (types) to inherit the behavior of a parent class with modifications and additions. This is the key to providing common tools for a wide variety of specialized networks. Simulations have long been recognized as an ideal domain for object oriented implementations. The objects being simulated map naturally into language objects.

Some other highlights include:

- The units are statically grouped into blocks so as to make easier the modular construction of large networks from smaller, possibly quite different components. The blocks are two-dimensional and organize the default graphical display. Units can also be grouped dynamically into sets, which can be specified interactively or algorithmically.

- There is a powerful default graphical interface which displays units and links as icons or in customized windows. Large networks are most easily built algorithmically, but mouse-based interactive construction and editing is also possible. Users can easily customize the displays of network objects. Adjacent unit icons in a block may popup entirely different custom windows when selected. This customization task is eased by the inheritance of parent displays and by using a high-level toolkit. Displays are scalable so that thousands of units can be viewed simultaneously at low resolution.

- An interactive debugging environment allows specified units to run while the rest of the network is frozen, or while the inputs are temporarily fixed in some way. Breakpoints can be set to rearrange the display or stop the simulation depending on conditions. Also, it is possible to monitor and display arbitrary parameters of the network. For example, it is possible to display a plot of average activity of a block or other set of units over time, and to save the state of that block whenever it exceeds some value.

- User friendliness is a goal and tools are provided to encourage it, including standard display, keyboard and mouse conventions. Each display should have a help button explaining the available functions. A mouse window showing the bindings of the mouse keys should be available at all times. In a large network with many different kinds of units, links and displays, there could easily be dozens of mouse bindings.

In the rest of this chapter I will briefly introduce connectionist networks and object oriented programming and then describe some particulars of the proposed implementation using a few lines of C++ to illustrate.

9.2   Connectionist Networks

Connectionist networks consist of a relatively large number of computing elements which I will call "units." The units communicate via links. Each unit has a single output. A link from unit i to unit j requires that the output of i be made available as an input to j. Typically, input values are multiplied by the weight associated with the link and summed with all the other inputs. This sum is then squashed, or restricted to some range like 0 to 1 and becomes the output of the receiving unit. However, connectionist researchers have used a wide variety of other unit types, some considerably more complex, and the learning (weight change) rules which apply even to networks of weighted-sum units differ widely as well. The major purpose of the simulator is to facilitate further experimentation in unit and link behavior, and to allow maximum flexibility in combining different unit data structures and functions. Scientists have uncovered a wide variety of behaviors and interactions in the brain. It is reasonable to expect artificial networks to be heterogeneous and complex as well.

The simulator does discrete simulations. This seems a good match for the spiking behavior of neurons in the brain. However, there are also analog or continuously varying computations which may be less well approximated. This depends to a large degree on the granularity of the simulation. [6] suggest limiting output values to integers between 0 and 9, corresponding to the firing rate of biological neurons. Other researchers use output values ranging from binary to floating precision. Output representation is one of the trickier issues in a general purpose simulator since outputs are inherently public. Their value is not a question of unit-internal implementation. Floating point values could be used in all cases, but this may significantly

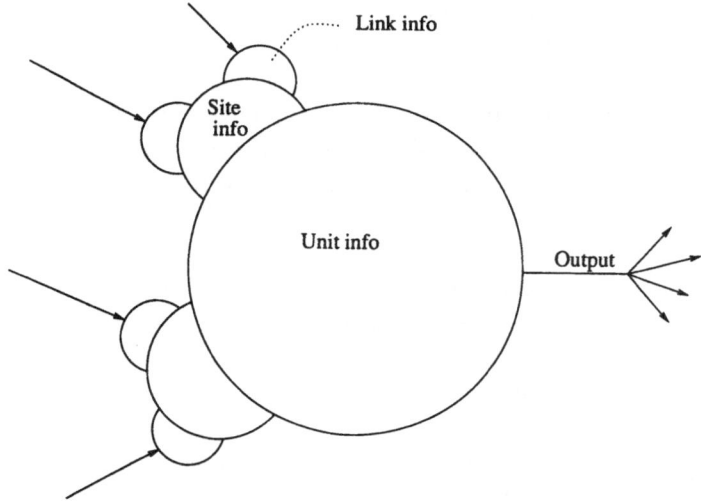

Figure 9.1: The computational entities of a connectionist network.

slow the simulation when integers could have been used. The only practical solution is to make the simulator user-configurable.

The major computational entity is the unit (Figure 9.1. Links provide communication between units, but can also perform computations; most learning algorithms modify link weights. Units are sometimes given auxiliary structures called sites. Sites are where incoming links are actually received. Sites can compute values used by the unit and perhaps by the links. Units, links and sites exist as functional objects in the simulator, though sites are optional. Units and links need not be full-fledged objects either, as will be explained below.

Several kinds of communication are possible. The most important are the output values of units, which are sent one-way down links to receiving units. This has an easy implementation. Each unit writes its output value in a public place where other units (links) can read it. There is exactly one public value for each unit. Link objects can attach to receiving units and read their inputs. In terms of implementation data structures, a unit need not have outgoing links. On multiprocessor implementations where the amount of shared memory is limited, only the output values need be shared. All the internal data structures for units and links can be kept in local memory.

The very popular back propagation algorithm also communicates backwards over links with values unique to each link. Since there are a lot more links than there are units, this greatly increases the number of distinct values to be communicated. However, unlike unit outputs, backwards link values have only a single destination. If a link object is accessed by both sending and receiving units, it is possible to back propagate error, or any other, values. Link to link communication must also be accounted for. If links are independent objects with a well-defined interface, there is no reason why other links could not access them. It is up to the user to make sure the correct values are used at the correct time. Multiprocessor implementations with limited shared memory will pose a problem for link-specific communication. Specific solutions will probably be required using general message passing primitives.

Global or broadcast communication must also be provided. This means making some information available to all units, or all units in some region, independent of any input links. Global values are used by connectionist modelers to indicate error and control simulations (sometimes implicitly). This could correspond to chemical diffusion in the brain. Accordingly, it may be desirable to have gradients or otherwise control the scope of the value.

9.3 The Object Oriented Approach

An object oriented simulation offers many advantages. Some of the key concepts will be reviewed here, using C++ [7] for illustration. A central idea in the proposed simulator is the use of classes and inheritance. Classes are data types which consist of public and private data fields as well as member functions for operating on those fields. It is best to provide a high-level functional interface leaving the details of implementation hidden as much as possible (e.g. using *get_next*() instead of direct array or linked list access.) The details of the structures can be radically altered without fear of breaking any user code, as long as the high-level interface is left alone. This is especially important for programs which are used by many people. For example, links in the Rochester simulator have a "value" field:

```
struct Link {
Output *value;
};
```

The value field is a pointer to an *Output* (which is a short integer by default). If the input value cannot be pointed to directly, say because it is in the memory of another processor on a multiprocessor machine, or because it is computed, then all the user and library code which dereferences the value field must be changed. In the new simulator, the links represent the input as

```
class Link {
    /* this part is invisible from outside the object */
    Output *inval;
    ...
  public:
    /* these functions are public */
    Output get_input() { return *inval;}
    virtual Output get_value() { return *inval}
    ...
};
```

This is a declaration of a *Link* class. It has a private *Output* pointer field, *inval*. This cannot be accessed directly. Instead, the function *get_input*() is used. (The function *get_value*() is explained below.) The definition of *get_input* can be changed without changing the behavior of the *Link* class at all. The danger here is that the added abstraction might slow down the access significantly. Sometimes this is of little importance, but millions of *Link* values may be looked up in a single simulation. C++ addresses this by providing inline functions. When these are compiled, the body of the function is inserted instead of a function call. The function *get_input*() defined above is inline by default since it is defined inside the class declaration. Code which accesses the *Link* value might look like the following:

```
Link *lp;
  sum += lp->get_input();  // x += y is equivalent
                           //  to x = x + y
  ...
```

Subclasses provide an inheritance mechanism which is central to the flexibility of the simulator. A class can be defined as a subclass of another class, in which case it inherits all the super class's fields and functions. These can be added to or redefined. The simulator provides a core of functionality in base types, with all the implementation details hidden for portability.

The built-in tools rely on this basic structure. User-defined classes inherit all this, adding any additional fields and functions they need. This allows the data structures to be very complex, with many different variables, or extremely simple, having only the needed fields.

The following declares *WeightedLink* to be a subclass of *Link*. It has an additional weight field, and it has redefined the *get_value*() function. Notice that the definition uses the parent (*Link*) *get_input*() function. Using the parent's public function is necessary, as children do not (by default) have access to the parent's private fields. (If this were not the case, many of the virtues of data hiding would be lost.)

```
class WeightedLink : public Link {
  int weight;
 public:
  virtual int get_value(){ return weight * get_input();}
  ...
}
```

A variable declared as a *Link* pointer can point to a subclass of *Link*, but only functions and fields declared in the *Link* class can be accessed. Since the compiler does not know what the actual class will be at run time, it cannot decide whether the referenced function will have been redefined in a subclass. Run-time lookup can be forced by declaring the function to be virtual. Because the *Link get_value*() function is declared virtual, then any call

```
Link *lp;
  sum += lp->get_value();
```

will be resolved to the correct *get_value*() function, so if *lp* points to a *WeightedLink*, the input will be multiplied by the weight. Unfortunately, since the correct function must be determined dynamically, this prevents simple inline expansion by the compiler. Without the virtual declaration, the declared *Link* class *get_value*() will be used whether or not *lp* points to a subclass.

Virtual functions are fundamentally important to the flexibility of the simulator. The simulator code cannot know what customizations will be made by users, and can only refer to the basic class functions. If these references can be dynamically resolved, users have much more freedom to redefine. The goal is to design the simulator so that the correct base fields, functions, and virtual functions are defined for each data type, allowing the construction of powerful tools, while making it as flexible and efficient as possible. It is important to provide a library of useful types, so that users will not, as a rule, need to define a whole host of functions. For example, the data types of the Rochester simulator could be provided, along with all the necessary support functions. It is important, though, that novel applications can customize with as little work as possible.

9.4 Units and Blocks

The unit class is the foundation of the simulator. Units are organized into blocks or two-dimensional planes. To specify a unit, it is necessary to provide a block handle and the (X, Y) coordinates of the unit. There are several reasons for using blocks. The first is to organize the display. Graphical examination and manipulation of units is fundamental to the simulator. Since computer displays are two-dimensional, it makes sense to organize the units that way. One of the goals for the user-interface is to be able to deal with a large number of units – many more than can fit on a display iconically. By using several unit blocks, a user can choose which are to be viewed (at what magnification). Also, blocks as data structures circumvent some limitations of statically typed object-oriented languages such as C++. If there were only a single block of units, then any unit retrieved from that block must have the most generic type. Functions specific to particular unit classes would not be available unless coerced to the type desired, which is very unsafe. Using multiple blocks, a user can declare an entire block to contain some specialized unit and avoid this problem. This is discussed in relation to *Link* construction below.

By putting functional groups of units in their own block, it is easier to build and test components of a complex network in a modular fashion. The addresses and display of the components are the same after they are integrated into the larger network. Blocks are also convenient for the control of simulations. Blocks can be frozen, or simulated in isolation (other blocks frozen). They also provide a level at which multi-unit functionality can be provided. This could include global parameters available to the units, such as error signals, as well display parameters such as average activity. Using block statistics and displays is a small step towards understanding and debugging massive networks too large to deal with at the unit level. As for the two-dimensional layout, it is somewhat encouraging to note that the human cortex can be viewed as a two-dimensional sheet with several layers, though no direct correspondence is intended.

9.4.1 The Basic Unit

Most of the simulator's functionality is found at the unit level. Ideally, units can be customized internally while maintaining a uniform external interface. All units need to generate an output. Also, each unit must provide several support functions such as writing its state to a file and reading that state back, resetting, and displaying itself. The following C++ declaration illustrates the idea:

```
/******** unit class **************/
class Unit {
  /* private data fields */
  short x,y;              // location indices
  Output output;         // local output value
  UnitBlock *ub;         // ub is a pointer to a UnitBlock
 public:
  Unit(UnitBlock *,short,short);     // constructor; needs
                                     //     location
  Unit(UnitBlock *);                 // default location
  int loc_x() { return x; }
  int loc_y() { return y; }
  int get_output() {return output;}
  UnitBlock *get_block() { return ub;}
  void set_output(Output ot) {output = ot;}
  void sync() {ub->set_output(x,y,output);} // make output
                                            //    public
  virtual void simulate();
  virtual void reset();
  virtual void printme(stream& ,int = 1);
  virtual void receivelink(Link *);
  virtual void sendlink(Link *);
  /* a couple of graphics functions -- more will
     be needed */
  virtual void disp_icon();       // color icon according to
                                  // activity level
  virtual void disp_window();     // pop up a window with a
                                  // detailed display
}; // end unit class declaration
```

The final definition could be much longer. The space required for the individual unit objects is not so large. Only the data must be allocated. The fixed functions (not labeled "virtual") can be resolved by the compiler. The virtual functions require run-time indirection, but there need only be one pointer per object to the list of class functions. This indirection incurs some overhead, but superefficiency at the unit level is not really necessary. In large networks, the link to unit ratio could easily be hundreds or thousands to one. Links take most of the time and space.

Output values used for communication between units are stored in the unit block of the sending unit. A new output value is not seen by other units until it is copied to the unit block by the *sync()* function. (Multiprocessor simulation may not have shared memory, in which case the unit block *set_output*() function may be more complex than an assignment. The exact nature of the communication is transparent to the user since it is provided in the base class definitions.)

The functions named "Unit" are constructors, one of which is called every time a Unit instance is made. Two are declared above. Which will be called is resolved at compile time, depending on the number and type of the arguments. The first constructor expects a unit block pointer and a location (two short indices) within the block. (When the function is defined elsewhere, the declarations lists the parameter types, but not the parameter names.) The second constructor does not expect a location; it uses a default. Using function overloading like this increases flexibility and ease of use and can speed up run time by reducing the number of parameters which must be passed. Users who find the use of (x,y) coordinates for each unit unhelpful and tedious can avoid them entirely by allowing the units to be placed be default and referring to them by pointer or with some other naming mechanism. Except for very simple functions, the definitions occur elsewhere and are not shown.

The *simulate()* function is responsible for updating the entire unit. The Rochester simulator has a loop over the units which loops over the sites calling all the link functions, then the site function, then the unit function is called last. This will not work with the new simulator as there is no guarantee of the expected site and link structure. The alternative is to loop over the units calling the *simulate()* function for each of them. This virtual function can be defined separately for each class and is responsible for the simulation of sites and links as well, which may require a loop to call the *simulate()* function of each, or which may be more involved.

This organization forces any change in unit behavior to be realized as a new unit class. Defining a new unit behavior is somewhat more involved than it currently is for the Rochester simulator. For one thing, unit functions are not as interchangeable as they are now, since they can, in general, expect different unit data structures and perhaps even different representations of inputs. This extra work is not so harmful. More parsimonious models are better, so perhaps each different unit type should be a full-fledged, clearly declared class. In any case, new classes which use old data structures can inherit almost everything.

The *reset()* function is responsible for putting the unit in an initial state. What this means depends on the application. The inflexibility of this command in the Rochester simulator has often proved frustrating: Should the data value be reset? What about the link weights and data? In the new simulator the user can easily specify what is meant by a reset, and vary it among unit classes. Parameterized resets might be useful as well. A weak reset could just affect the output, while a strong reset could affect internal parameters as well. The *receivelink()* and *sendlink()* functions allow greater flexibility in how links are managed. Link construction will be discussed below. Other functions are necessary, including those which display the unit and interpret input events as will be discussed later.

Also not shown are the data fields and functions to control set membership. Blocks organize units into manageable and functionally coherent groups, but are static. Sets are dynamic. Units can be added to sets by hand using a mouse. More important, they can be added algorithmically, either by the unit's own simulate function, or with monitoring code at the unit block level. It is easy to isolate and view or gather statistics for all units which changed during the last simulation step, or have not been active since the last reset of a global variable. Set membership is indicated by setting the corresponding bit in a unit object field. This puts a hard limit on the number of possible sets, but is much more efficient than keeping central rosters for each set, especially for parallel implementations.

9.4.2   The Basic Unit Block

A bare-bones unit block class looks something like:

```
struct UnitDesc {
    Output output;              // the output seen by other
                                //    units
```

```
    Unit *body;                 // the unit instance
    /* more stuff */
};

class UnitBlock {
    short width, height;        // size of block
    UnitDesc *entry;            // holds units and outputs
  public:
    UnitBlock(int, int);        // constructor
    Output get_output(int,int); // return global output for
                                //     unit
    void set_output(int,int,Output);  // set output at the
                                       // location
    virtual Unit *get_unit(int,int);   // return unit at
                                       //    location
    short get_width(){return width;}
    short get_height(){return height;}
    virtual int *enter(Unit *);   // enter a unit (location
                                  // in unit)
    virtual int *outref(int,int); // return a pointer to
                                  //    global output
    /* more stuff */
};
```

A unit block is rectangular grid. Initially, it contains no units, but does allocate an empty slot for each location. Some functions may operate on the locations before they contain a unit. For example, locations could be marked using a mouse, then a "build units" command given, specifying the type of unit to be built in each marked location. It is not possible in the new simulator to simply allocate "empty" unit structures ahead of time as is now done with the Rochester simulator, because the size of the unit structure can vary with class. Even if they could be pre-allocated, filling each location with a unit would waste more space than using the *UnitDesc* structure above, and if the block is very sparse, even the *UnitDesc* structures could be allocated as needed. Because the block layout determines the default display, it should be expected that many locations will remain unfilled in order to make the display more appealing. For example, a simple network consisting of eight input units, three hidden units, and eight output units might put in an eight by five block, with every other row empty and only the three hidden units in the middle row. The empty locations should use little memory. The details of the allocation are hidden in the implementation of *enter, get_output*, etc.

There are various subclasses of *UnitBlock* which can be defined. One interesting possibility is a *UnitBlock* object which contains no *unit* objects. The *UnitBlock* can simulate the presence of many unit objects by maintaining the outputs. This would allow space- and time-efficient simulation of large numbers of simple units. For example, an input block simulating a simple retina could read its output values from an image file. During a simulation these values would not change; no unit simulate() functions would be called. The unit block could also change the outputs according to some simple algorithm. Much of the functionality of the simulator might be lost on this block, but the block's output values could still be displayed graphically. More important, the outputs of such a block would look normal to units in other blocks. It would even be possible to take outside simulation code written in C or C++, copy its outputs into a *UnitBlock* at each simulation step and thereby integrate it into the simulator. Of course, links into arbitrary outside code would not be so simple.

It is sometimes desirable to have a *UnitBlock* which is defined to hold a particular subclass of *Unit*. If a specialized *Unit* has functions which were not declared (virtual) in the base *Unit* class, then they are hard to get at externally. Jumping ahead a bit, suppose we define a *Link* class which expects a *get_error*() function in its destination unit. In particular, it expects a unit which is in the class *ErrorUnit*. If we specify the destination in the *Link* constructor as a generic *Unit* block and location, there is no guarantee that the specified unit is of the correct type. In fact, the result of the *get_unit*() function must be cast (forced type change, in C++) to be of type *(ErrorUnit *)* before the *get_error*() function can even be called. Such casts are unsafe – the unit may not have been an *ErrorUnit*. We could include a type identifier in the unit class which should be checked by all careful programmers, but this defeats much of the elegance of the object oriented approach. The other solution is to declare subclasses of *UnitBlock* which only hold *ErrorUnits* (and their subclasses, of course). The *get_unit*() function of such a block would be defined to return *ErrorUnits*. No cast is necessary. No non-*ErrorUnits* can exist in that block. If the unit classes are given a flexible set of virtual functions, it should not often be necessary to define special *UnitBlock* subclasses. Some Languages, such as *Eiffel* [8], allow parameterized classes. This means that a single *UnitBlock* declaration could be used to create *UnitBlock* objects which only hold particular *Unit* subclasses. To the type specifier "UnitBlock" must be added a parameter: the *Unit* subclass that block holds.

Specialized unit blocks can also contain specific display and simulation parameters. They can be used to define global (in the sense of being shared by many units) parameters, such as error and alertness signals. Since it is impossible to anticipate such parameters, the user must be able to add them arbitrarily. Units expecting such parameters would need to declare the correct unit block subclass in their constructors so the correct parameter access functions would be available.

9.5 Links and Sites

There are various possible approaches to links. They can be full-fledged computational objects or simple data structures. In the latter view, links merely describe the pattern of communication between units. They may be stored as an explicit list of weights and pointers to remote output values, or they may be implicit. For example, a single stored location may be enough to represent a large number of links emanating from surrounding locations. Addresses for the surrounding units could be computed as needed. In this view, the only simulated objects are the units which look at the outputs of other units in order to compute their value. Because link computations are the inner loop of simulations, this approach leaves open the possibility of very efficient implementations but places more work on the unit functions. For example, the unit function responsible for full-sized displays must also display the links in some form. It cannot pass this task on to the link objects.

Links as objects are also natural and especially well suited to networks where the link computations (e.g. weight change rules) are complicated and varied. If such computations are to be monitored or debugged, it is very helpful to be able to manipulate them as separate entities. This leads to a clean design and a great deal of flexibility, but may exact a fairly large performance penalty. The simulator provides link classes, but units are not required to use them. This means that unit and link objects do not fit together arbitrarily. This would be a highly desirable situation but is unobtainable in an experimental setting. Researchers must be able to invent new link and unit values and design units to expect particular kinds of links and vice versa. A statically typed language such as C++ or Eiffel helps control the improper mix of types.

For now, let's consider the base link class definition. The link data structure usually attaches to the receiving unit because that is where its value is used. We could get by with just a pointer to the source unit, but the output of the source unit must be taken from the unit block for synchronization. We could go indirect through the unit to the block and back to the public unit output, but this would be slow, so we should probably have a direct pointer to the public output value. Links often have a weight, but by not including the weight in the base class the space need not be allocated if it is not used. It would be wise to include virtual functions for weights anyway. This link class definition ends up something like:

```
/********** link class *****************/

class Link {
  Output *inval;        // incoming value
  Unit *source;         // source unit
  Unit *sink;           // destination unit
 public:
  Link(UnitBlock *,int,int,UnitBlock *,int,int);
  Link(Unit *, Unit *);
  Output get_input() { return *inval;}
  virtual Output get_value() { return *inval;}
  int from_x() {return source->loc_x();}
  int from_y() {return source->loc_y();}
  int to_x() {return sink->loc_x();}
  int to_y() {return sink->loc_y();}
  Unit *source() {return source;}
  Unit *sink() {return sink;}
  UnitBlock * from_block() {return source->get_block();}
  UnitBlock * to_block() {return sink->get_block();}
  virtual int val(){return *inval;}
  virtual void update(){};
  virtual void printme(int);
  virtual void reset(){};
  virtual int get_weight() { return UNIT_WEIGHT;}
                                          // implicit weight
  virtual int set_weight() { sim_error("link has no weight");]
  /* some graphics interface functions */
};
```

Link objects are created one at a time with calls like:

```
new mylink(front,x1,y1,back,x1,y1);
```

This will allocate space for the link and call the constructor:

```
Link::Link(UnitBlock *ubf, int xfrom, int yfrom,
           UnitBlock *ubt, int xto, int yto)
{
    inval = ubf->outref(xfrom,yfrom);
    source = ubf->get_unit(xfrom,yfrom);
    sink = ubt->get_unit(xto,yto);
    source->receivelink(this);
    sink->sendlink(this);
}
```

The first three lines of the constructor assign the proper values to the *Link* data fields. The last two provide the hooks for attaching the link to the receiving and sending units. (The variable "this" is a pointer to the *Link* object being constructed.) How the units record the link is of no concern to it. Most likely, the receiving unit will keep a linked list or array of pointers to link objects. The sending unit need not keep pointers to outgoing links except for display purposes and in those cases where links must communicate in two directions, such as with the back propagation algorithm.

Links can be treated as more passive objects holding inputs and other values such as weights and pointers to sending and receiving units. In this case, during a simulation, the unit's simulate function will loop over all the links getting their values and, perhaps, changing their weights. Except for the indirection involved, this will be time efficient. Even if links are computationally passive, they can inherit display and debugging functions. They also insulate the unit function from the exact method of communication. There is still reason to keep them independent objects.

More generally, each link's update function could be called for each simulation step. The unit's view of the link is simplified: it provides a value and, perhaps, changes state using rules of its own. A wide variety of links can be made to a single, simple unit which need know nothing about them. The price to be paid is the function call at the innermost loop of the link simulation. Of course, if a link which is designed to have its update function called is made to a unit which does not call its link's update functions, unexpected behavior could result. All links have a default, null update function, so there will never be any harm in calling it. It cannot be expected that every class of unit and link which can be used with the simulator will work together. The object-oriented approach furthers that goal but does not work magic.

9.6   Graphical Interface

A powerful graphical interface is very important to the simulator. In this section I will discuss desirable interface behavior and how it might be realized. Since no prototype implementation has yet been done, the implementation account will be somewhat general. In the proposed simulator, interface tools are provided at several levels. The most generic interface relies on the base definitions only. Common unit and link classes in the library come with their own displays when appropriate. For making custom displays, the user can work with a library which not only provides high-level primitives, but which eases integration with the rest of the display. For example, in a Postscript display, the user might be given a unit square in which to display information. Errant drawing outside the boundaries would be clipped, and the display scaled and placed correctly.

The default display is organized by unit block. Each block appears as a rectangular window. Units in the block appear as icons in the correct (x, y) position. Thus, if the units are placed in visually meaningful locations at creation, a good display follows automatically. The icon color and (relative) size are selected by a unit function and so are completely customizable. The block display is scalable in two ways: icon size and overall window size. In the limit, each unit is represented by a single pixel in the display. This is useful for viewing images and image transforms. In case not all units will fit in the display window, there are scroll bars to adjust the view.

Block displays can be iconified. The icons fit into a main grid. There is a main control panel for global commands and parameters, notably the "go" command which does some number of simulation steps. Of course, the iconic representation of unit blocks is controlled by a function. In so far as it is possible to summarize the activity of a large number of units with a single icon, it is possible to monitor a large number of large blocks simultaneously. Even a simple representation such as average activity might be useful. The blocks with the most activity could be opened and examined more carefully. Another possible representation is to use an $N \times N$ portion of the block's units at one pixel representation – a sort of peep hole. Or an individual unit could be singled out to represent the whole block. This process could be applied indefinitely so that a block of unit blocks can be iconified. While it is not at all clear that such high-level icons can meaningfully represent the activity of the contained units, such a hierarchical organization would serve to organize very large networks.

Going the other way, unit icons in a block can be opened to reveal a detailed display of the unit. What is displayed is controlled by a unit function, so side-by-side units could pop up completely different displays. The default shows all the units parameters and puts up displays for subordinate objects such as links and sites. The unit's (site's, link's) parameters can be edited from the display. The link's display can include a display of the source unit, so that source, link and sink can be simultaneously displayed in great detail. The displays can remain open during simulation to monitor the behavior of selected components.

The display also works as a command and network construction interface. The master window, which holds the unit block icons, is also the central control area. Builtin and user-defined command buttons can be used to run the simulation. Typed commands are available as well. All display windows have a control panel with command buttons and editable parameter fields. This should actually be a separate popup window so it is not forced to scale with the display. As usual, there are default commands and parameters which appear on all block displays as well as any customization added to *UnitBlock* subclasses. For example, simulated annealing networks might have a temperature display which is set by the annealing algorithm or with the mouse.

Many commands apply to sets of objects. In each icon grid (whether for unit blocks or units), a small border around the icons is reserved for use as a set marker. At least two sets are bound to particular displays, say gray and black on monochrome displays. Objects in the black set have a black border. Objects in the gray set have a gray border. Objects can be assigned to these sets in many ways, including assignment of set expressions and by using the mouse to select individuals or regions. For example, some unit blocks could be selected and put in set black followed by the command "freeze black," meaning do not change the state of any units in that set. Units can place themselves in sets dynamically based on whatever criteria the experimenter finds useful. Visually displaying these sets provides quick feedback on, say, the number of units with saturated weights and allows the experimenter to investigate further by opening the marked units.

In the unit block display, empty regions of the grid can be selected and a large number of units created with one command. The name of the unit class can either be typed or selected from a menu. The unit block and location arguments to the constructor are provided automatically. Any extra parameters must be entered in a template. Links between two sets of units can be made using various protocols such as total connectivity, ordered one-to-one, random with some probability, etc. Manual construction is no substitute for algorithmic construction, but it is sometimes a useful option. Unit and link objects can also be destroyed individually or by sets.

Being able to quickly display a unit's fan in (set of units send links to the target unit) or fan out (set of units to which the target unit sends links) is very useful. To this end, the Rochester simulator has a link mode which changes the interpretation of unit icons to be the weight on the link from that unit to some selected unit (or vice versa). By selecting unit icons in turn, it is possible to see the connectivity of several units in just a few seconds. A similar mechanism exists in the new simulator, with some modifications. Rather than change all displayed icons into link weight indicators, only those icons in selected blocks will be changed. Optionally, a separate window will appear for the link weight icons which is isomorphic to the main unit block window. This means that the weights and other unit parameters can be viewed simultaneously. It also permits several windows to simultaneously display the weights to different units. In order to implement this feature, each unit has a function which returns a list of indices and weights for all links from a given block. If a unit is unable to comply with the request, it can return an empty list, but should also pop up an error window stating this fact.

The unit block display described is fixed and somewhat limited. Each unit has a fixed (x, y) position and must use a simple rectangular icon to display a single value. This provides a uniform interface for all units. More flexibility is provided by using additional windows. Sets of units can be "copied" into new general purpose windows (canvases) and the resulting icons placed arbitrarily. The units in a canvas can come from different blocks and can display whatever they wish. For example, in a network where units can be meaningfully labeled, the display can be the text label with boldness representing output value. Links and sites can also be displayed in canvases. Another useful display tool plots values over time. A general-purpose plot tool need only be given a function call or other hook to return a value and it could plot it at a chosen scale with a chosen line type, etc.

The ideal is to design display tools with a "universal" interface that works with any computational object in the network. A user may add a "delta error" field to his units. If he then wants to watch a plot of this value over time for some unit, he can call up a plot tool and "plug it into" this field. The simulator should provide a rich set of tools and the mechanism by which new tools and displays can be created. Object-oriented design is appropriate here as well [9,10]. Because of the complexity of the interface, ample help facilities are necessary. Each display should have a help button explaining the use of that display. Subclass displays can of course call the parent help and follow it with their specializations. The interpretation of mouse events varies from window to window, so these bindings will be especially difficult to remember. Design consistency helps, e.g., always left click on icons to open them. A mouse map showing the current bindings is always available on the screen. This makes it practical to have various command modes, each with its own mouse bindings.

9.7 Other Issues

The simulations are discrete. The order of simulation is flexible. The main control loop simply calls the *simulate()* functions of the units in an arbitrary sequence. The newly calculated output is not visible to the other units until the *sync()* function is called. An asynchronous simulation control function might call the *simulate()* functions in an random order, each followed immediately by a *sync()*. A synchronous control function would call all the unit *simulate()* functions and when finished call all the *sync()* functions. Though not commonly used with connectionist networks, event-driven simulations may in some cases be appropriate, say with networks where unit outputs only change when their inputs change and not many inputs are changing at any time. A mechanism for placing units in the run queue is necessary. One possibility: each unit could keep a list of other units to which it has a connection, and add them to the run queue if its output changes. The point is that, because of the extensibility of the simulator, event-driven control could be added with orders of magnitude less effort than doing a new simulator from scratch.

It is tempting to organize the simulation control by block, but this would be a problem with asynchronous simulations. If each block finished a time step of simulation before the next block started, the simulations would only be locally asynchronous. In general, asynchronous simulation presents a problem. A global function must be able to efficiently choose a random unit from any block and be assured that it is ready to run. If various specialized control mechanisms are used in the different blocks, e.g. temperature for simulated annealing and control of forward and backward passes for back propagation, this may be no easy task. Specialized unit blocks which don't actually have unit objects cannot be handled in the same way of course. Here the unit block must be responsible for the simulation and, unless the programmer wants to go to considerable difficulty, the simulation must be externally synchronous. The simulation of any objects subordinate to a unit is controlled by the unit. In particular, the *simulate()* function of a unit might call the *simulate()* functions of several sites, which call the *simulate()* functions of all the links. Or the unit's *simulate()* function could directly and more efficiently manipulate link data structures.

Because a network simulation is just a lot of unit simulations, it is very easy to parallelize. Multiprocessors with shared memory are especially well suited. Each processor can run its own mini-simulator, which could have either a fixed set of units or take waiting units from a ready queue. On multiprocessors with limited shared memory, unit and link objects can reside in local memory. A message-based machine would be easier to work with if outputs were the only values to be communicated. However, the simulator allows link-specific values to be sent to units and other links using pointers to the objects in question. This could be difficult to port. A compromise might be possible organized around unit blocks. If the objects within a block were guaranteed to reside on the same processor they could easily access one-another. Inter-block communication would be restricted to unit outputs. How outputs would be communicated would be an implementation question. They could be written into remote caches from the source, or read, as needed, by the sink.

By and large, users must be able to program in the language of the simulator. They may want to define new classes, for example. A general purpose language is also useful for building networks algorithmically and keeping statistics on performance. Forcing users to program does have some disadvantages. It may intimidate some researchers with little experience. Also, because no object oriented language is in widespread use, the resulting simulator would only be portable to sites which also acquired the language. Avoiding source language altogether cannot be done. Too much customizability would have to be sacrificed. However, it may be possible for many users to avoid programming if they use standard library functions (these can be enhanced at the research sites with local favorites, of course) as long as they can specify the structure of the network algorithmically (building by hand with the mouse quickly becomes tedious). To this end, it would be worthwhile to add simple construction languages to the library.

Only a very preliminary version of the simulator has been implemented using C++. C++ has many advantages. It compiles into fast, small executables. Efficiency (both time and speed) is too important to tolerate large, slow object oriented environments. C++ is widely available at no cost and runs on a wide variety of machines. It is compatible with plain C, so existing and/or low-level code and libraries can be used. Eiffel is another promising language. It compiles into C so it is portable and it has multiple inheritance. A class can have several parents and inherits attributes from each. It also has parameterized classes. A class definition can have a type argument. This would be useful for *UnitBlock* classes, among others. A unit block containing units from the class *SumUnit* would be declared as "*block_name : UnitBlock[SumUnit]*."

There are two major candidates for implementing the graphical interface: the X window system and NeWS. Both are network-based which is important. It is reasonable to anticipate running large simulations on large, shared machines. The simulation can still be run from a desktop workstation running X or NeWS. X is much more widely available and can be freely distributed with source. It is also faster. NeWS is proprietary and much less widely used. However, it uses Postscript, augmented to be made object oriented and interactive. This is a very good match to the simulator's needs, assuming users who want custom displays are willing to use a new language. With NeWS, scaling of displays comes for free. The use of clipping and user-coordinates also makes it easy to integrate user-provided displays into a global context. Unfortunately, the implementation of NeWS which I have used was too slow. Combined with its greater availability, X is the obvious choice at this time.

References

[1] Carver Mead, *Analog VLSI and Neural Systems*, Addison-Wesley Publishing Company, Reading, Massachusetts (1989).

[2] Nigel Goddard, Kenton Lynne, and Toby Mintz, *The Rochester Connectionist Simulator*, Technical Report 233, Computer Science Department, University of Rochester 1987.

[3] Mark Fanty, *A Connectionist Simulator for the BBN Butterfly Multiprocessor*, Technical Report 164, Computer Science Department, University of Rochester (1986).

[4] David B. Parker, *Learning Logic*, Technical Report, Center for Com-

putational Research in Economics and Management Science, MIT (1985).

[5] David E. Rumelhart, Goeffrey E. Hinton and Ronald J. Williams, *Learning Internal Representations by Error Propagation*, in Rumelhart and McClelland (editors), *Parallel Distributed Processing: Exploring the Microstructure of Cognition, Volume 1: Foundations*, Bradford Books/MIT Press, Cambridge, Massachusetts (1986).

[6] James Feldman and Dana Ballard, *Connectionist Models and their Properties*, Cognitive Science, 6, pp. 205-254 (1983).

[7] Bjarne Stroustrup, *The C++ Programming Language*, Addison-Wesley Publishing Company, Reading, Massachusetts (1986).

[8] Bertrand Meyer, *Object-oriented Software Construction*, Prentice Hall, New York (1988).

[9] Paul S. Barth, *An Object-Oriented Approach to Graphical Interfaces*, ACM Transactions on Graphics, 5(2), pp. 142-172 (April 1986).

[10] Mark A. Linton, John M Vlissides, and Paul R. Calder, *Composing User Interfaces with InterViews*, Technical Report CSL-TR-88-369, Computer Systems Laboratory, Stanford University (1988).

CHAPTER 10

PARADIGMS FOR OPTICAL COMPUTING

Neil Collins
STL Ltd.
London Road
Harlow, Essex CM17 9NA
UNITED KINGDOM

10.1 Introduction

The subject matter of this chapter is the design of parallel computers using optoelectronic device hardware. The hardware does not exist except in developmental form; however, there is a reasonably general awareness of what can and cannot be achieved in terms of performance. The subsystem development is also in a rudimentary state, with a large gap between the predicted performance of devices and their actual performance in the system. In spite of this, it is timely to examine the optical alternatives to electronic hardware, particularly with respect to what are generally known as AI applications. In the AI field there is a requirement for new functionality in terms of the computational primitives [1]. Although this new functionality is still within the capabilities of electronics, a number of overheads such as microcode, compilers, intermediate languages, interpreters, software tools, etc., have to be introduced. This added complexity is to the detriment of both the programmer and the hardware designer. It complicates the thinking of the former and adds to the reliability design problems of the latter. The present proposition is for a modest excursion into the realm of alternative technologies, in order to find a match with what is really required.

The top-down approach to the design of parallel computers starts with the computational paradigm, proceeds through the computational model to the abstract machine, and ends with a particular implementation. The paradigm is a format for expressing the problem. It may be a particular language (e.g. procedural, functional, object-oriented, event-sequencing), or a form of knowledge representation (eg. semantic network, neural network). An algorithm is developed as a solution to the problem, and the computational model forms a basis for implementation. Examples of models include control flow; data flow; reduction; actor; and Hopfield. There is frequently an association between the paradigm and the model, such as procedural-control flow; functional-reduction; and neural network-Hopfield. The abstract machine is the familiar diagram of labelled boxes joined by lines, and the implementation is the particular architectural model of parallel computing, such as tightly coupled multiprocessor, shared memory, or SIMD machine. The implementation also constrains the abstract machine with regard to hardware limitations, such as number of nodes, communication, and memory distribution.

The bottom-up design approach starts with the capabilities of optical devices and aims towards the implementation of a useful computational primitive. A useful technique for formulating the capabilities is by writing down the functional specification of the devices.

This chapter presents examples of both approaches. On the one hand, we describe an extrapolation of work carried out with Graham Pratten and Alastair Tocher on the novel implementation of a reduction model of computation. On the other hand, we briefly summarise work carried out with Jeremy Jacob and Ali Abdallah of the Programming Research Group at Oxford University, on the functional specification of spatial light modulators. Although neither aspect will be pursued commercially, the specification study is perceived as being worthy of more consolidated effort. The reason for this is that it seems to provide a well defined path to novel functionality. However, the study of paradigms would be an important accompanying activity. This work is expected to become relevant when optical interconnects at the board-to-board and interchip level have given the performance improvement required to maintain conventional electronic processor architectures. In order for optics to improve the intra-chip communications in a meaningful way it will be necessary to revolutionise the processor architecture, and new functionality can be incorporated.

10.2　The Functional and Logic Paradigms

As an example of the level at which paradigms might be analysed, the functional and logic styles have been selected since they are of most relevance to my general work. The relevant question is which primitive operations would we wish to support in each case. For example, each functional language has a set of primitive functions together with a set of combining forms which are the rules for combining the primitive functions. When we come to consider the functionality of optical devices, then it will be easier to support some of these primitives and combining forms than others. The question eventually arises whether a novel functional language which is tuned to the strengths of optical hardware can be formulated, and the means of answering this question lies with the synergy between top-down and bottom-up approaches. In the case of logic languages, the situation is less diverse. Prolog is the main language, and there is a desire to support the operations of resolution and unification more efficiently in hardware. We are dealing with list and graphical (tree-structured) data representations, and operations on these such as restructuring, sorting, pattern matching, etc. There are attempts to merge the best features of the two approaches, functional and logic, in a single language [2]. Such studies are interesting for the hardware designer, because they give a clue to what constitutes a coherent blend of useful functionality. However, there appears to be some diversity of opinion on what the correct blend should be. The present time seems to be an appropriate point at which some hardware considerations might crystallize one or a small number of useful systems. The importance of optics stems from the facility for parallel processing. There is a belief that both the functional and logic languages (or even a combined approach) would run more efficiently on parallel hardware, in view of the modular construction of the former and the large element of searching involved in the latter.

In this chapter we concentrate on the functional approach. In contrast to the need for a store to implement backtracking in the logic languages, there is no need for permanent storage in the functional style, which should allow efficient implementation using the pipeline optical computing architecture.

10.3   Pipeline Optical Computing Architecture

This architecture was suggested by Alan Huang [3], and forms the underlying basis for the support of functional styles considered here. Communication between the stages in the pipeline is a regular interconnect, and the propagation delay between stages provides the temporary storage for the data stream. The unique feature of an optical data stream is that it can be two-dimensional. The data written across a cross-section of the beam is a pattern of binary digits. The zeroes and ones can be distinguished according to intensity, polarisation, or phase. Most designs for digital optical computing architectures employ intensity coding, because that is the most readily explained. However, where polarisation coding can be used, the overall computation dissipates less light power. Intensity coding has been chosen to exemplify the system below, but polarisation coding is also possible.

The limitation on the number of digits contained in the pattern is set by the number of pixels in the input device, which is called the spatial light modulator, or SLM. A large number of groups around the world are working on SLM technology, although only a few types of device are commercially available at the present time. A good review is presented by Fisher [4]. Electrically addressed devices with a pixel complexity of 128 by 128, and a frame rate of 160 Hz, are currently available, with a near-term future goal of 512 by 512 and 1kHz frame rate [5]. The frame rate of the SLM sets an upper limit to the throughput of the pipeline.

Where the present study differs from the Huang approach is the relatively smaller importance of combinatorial logic elements. The pipeline optics to be presented contains a 2-D packet routing backbone, with specialist modules for copying and splitting the data tree. When the tree has been simplified it is passed on to electronic logic for further computation. As a prelude to the description of the optical machine design, a brief survey of the two computational models which have been applied to functional program execution is given in the next section.

10.4 Dataflow and Reduction Models

Perhaps the best known example of the dataflow model is the systolic array processor. The computation proceeds by the synchronous pumping of data through the pipeline, rather than by the flow of control from one line of the program to the next (control flow). The general dataflow architecture is more complex than the systolic array and requires, inter alia, buffers for the instruction packets which are waiting for data, and a fine-grained communications network. Unless the computation is harnessed in some way, all possible instructions are elaborated (eager evaluation), rather than just those which are important for reaching the answer (lazy evaluation). For example, all three calculations in an *IFTHENELSE* line would be evaluated. This consumes processing resources, and lazy evaluation, which is supported by reduction machines, is preferred. An example of a working machine is the Manchester Data-flow machine [6]. An efficient aspect of this machine is the ability to handle recursion.

Reduction models are classified as either string or graph reduction. In a graph the data is represented more compactly than in a string, because common parts of the data structure are represented just once and referenced from the overall structure by means of pointers. When such a part of the structure is reduced, it is reduced simultaneously for all occurrences within the structure. Conversely, where the reduction must take place separately for each occurrence of a common part, it is known as string reduction. The graph reduction model is considered superior because the problem domain is much larger. The use of pointers prevents the size of the data tree expanding beyond the capacity of the memory in the course of program execution. Machines have been implemented for both types of reduction using conventional memory/processor hardware: the GMD machine for string reduction [7], and the ALICE machine for graph reduction [8]. However, it is interesting to see that when novel hardware is contemplated, then cellular logic implementations have been posited. The Mago design performs string reduction [9]; and the Cobweb architecture graph reduction [10]. Neither has, to my knowledge, been implemented, but they do provide a good analogy with the optical solution in that the computation is fine grained and highly parallel. The spirit of graph reduction can be captured in optics by coding up the common areas of the data structure with a code that is not recognised by the processing part of the system. The code will be carried through intact, and can be replaced when the structure is no more reducible by table look-up (which can be implemented efficiently using, for example, holograms). In the worked example in the next section, the reduction of factorial, the code for factorial has to be called up recursively, so that some form of table look-up is implied.

10.5 Optical Graph Reduction

As a first attempt to assess how optical hardware might be used, we tackled combinator reduction. Combinators are a reduced instruction set for functional programs [11]. We avoided the issue of implementing the compiler, which uses variable abstraction to generate the combinators from the source text. One complexity with combinators is that they are higher order functions, i.e. they can take other combinators as arguments. Typically, a function such as factorial is represented by a sequence of combinators, each

def fac = S(S(S(K cond) (S(S(K eq) (K 0))I)) (K 1))
                    (S(S(K times)I) (S(K fac) (S(S(K minus)I) (K 1))))

**In order to simplify the text below the function names – cond eq time fac minus –
have been replaced with – Y V X W T – in the expression above, giving:**

def W = S(S(S(K Y) (S(S(K V) (K 0))I)) (K 1))
                    (S(S(k X)I) (S(K W) (S(S(K T)I) (K 1))))

The capitals stand for the following transformations:

```
S f g x  ♦ f x (g x)
K x y    ♦ x
I x      ♦ x
X x y    ♦ x X y
T x y    ♦ x – y
Y x y z  ♦ y if  x=1
         ♦ z if  x=0
V x y    ♦ 1 if  x=y
         ♦ 0 if  x=y
W        ♦ recursive call of fac
```

In addition the identities

```
(f  x) y = f x y
(f  x)  = f x
```

are used.

Figure 10.1: Combinator reduction: function represented as sequence of combinators.

of which acts on the bracketed term immediately to the right, as shown in Figure 10.1. In addition to the difficulty of processing a string where the control functions (combinators) are mixed with the data variables, there is the added difficulty of control acting on control. An alternative (perhaps easier) option, which we are currently progressing, is to move over to first order languages where functions only operate on variables, and not on themselves.

The order in which the expressions are reduced has important consequences for the efficiency of the overall reduction. For example, the Mago design performs applicative order reduction where the innermost expression is reduced at each step. This technique controls the expansion of the data structure, but does not always guarantee a result [12]. The alternative, normal order reduction, proceeds through the bracketed representation of the data structure from left to right. Normal order reduction guarantees termination but the data tree can grow unmanageably, which is why graph reduction with its compact data representation is preferred. In our work we applied optics to normal order reduction because it is easier to identify control information which is on the left of the data structure rather than embedded control. Spatial intensity coding was used for control, data, and pointers. The pointers remain in small irreducible packages at the end of

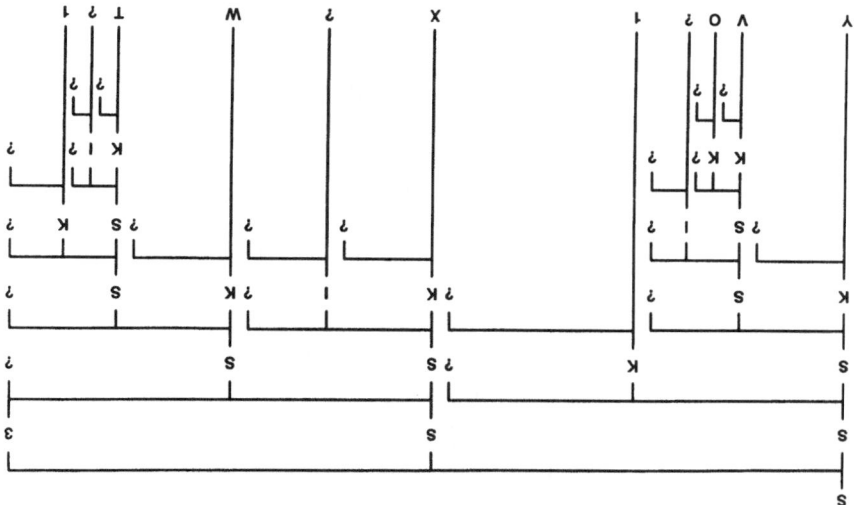

Figure 10.2: Fractal coding.

the first stage of reduction. They can be sent to look-up tables which either generate new combinator code (e.g. in the case of recursive call of factorial), or perform the combinatorial logic (e.g. in the case of multiply). The new combinator code is further reduced by the same optical hardware. The reduction is complete when no new code can be generated, and the original data tree has been simplified to a line of compact code which can be manipulated electronically.

We chose the basic set of S,K,I combinators [11] for simplicity of explanation, although some of the extensions result in more compact code [13]. The entire tree of factorial can be coded on a 300-by-300 pixel array, even using the basic set, as shown in Figure 10.2. An alternative format is to arrange the tree in depth along the direction of propagation of the beam, such that successive cross-sections represent deeper layers of the tree (Figure 10.3). The latter approach does not fully exploit the parallelism available in the light beam, and the data density is significantly lower due to the low frame rate of the SLM. However, extension of these implementation ideas to trees larger than factorial N must involve splitting the tree up in some manner between successive frames.

The reduction of the tree in Figure 10.2 can be viewed as a mechanism for percolating the integer 3 down through the tree to the bottom line, which can then be read from left to right to give $X2W3$. The main concern here is the optical system which performs the reduction, rather than the treatment

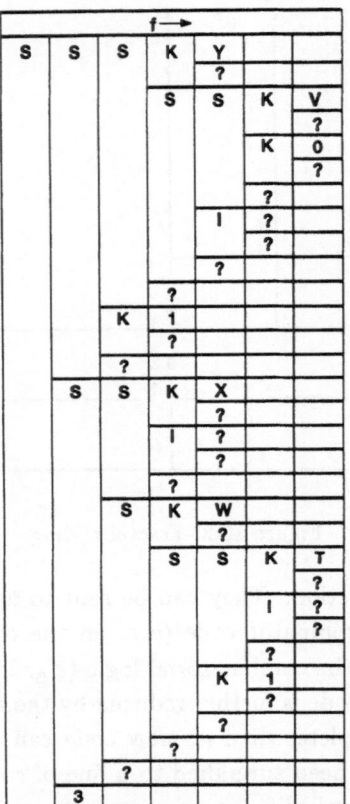

Figure 10.3: Tree arranged in depth along beam propagation direction.

of the bottom line. The S, K, I combinators control the movement of the 3 as follows:

- An S in the line above the line with the 3, causes the 3 to be copied into the succeeding line in two positions, one immediately below the S, and the second midway between the S and the 3.

- A K results in the loss of the 3 because it retains only the variable/integer directly below it.

- An I moves the 3 into the bottom line directly below the I.

Clearly, the most complex restructuring is the S rule. In order that this rule is obeyed down through the tree, a fractal tree structure is adopted. Unfortunately, this is wasteful of coding space.

In implementing these rules using optical techniques some general comments are in order. It is important that the tree is efficiently registered on the light beam so that single lines can be abstracted from the top of the array. The first line contains a single combinator, but thereafter the lines contain more than one, and the question arises whether to implement parallel reductions. Up to this point the advantage of using optics lay in the parallel program representation, which facilitated the structural transformations of the tree. If parallel combinator reduction is employed, then a further advantage would be that when the reduction is complete the leaf line at the bottom of the tree would contain the result. The alternative would be to break up the tree into subtrees which could be reduced in a pipeline fashion. Then there is the additional problem of collecting up the partial results at the end of the reduction. Because the control mechanism for single combinators is easier to illustrate, the second alternative has been chosen.

In order to decide whether an S,K, or I combinator is present on the first line, the beam enters a packet switch where the first line is stripped off and identified (Figure 10.4). The intensity coding in the first line is relayed to the write side of an optically addressed beam deflector such as the VGMLCD [14]. In this device, the resolution of a diffraction grating formed

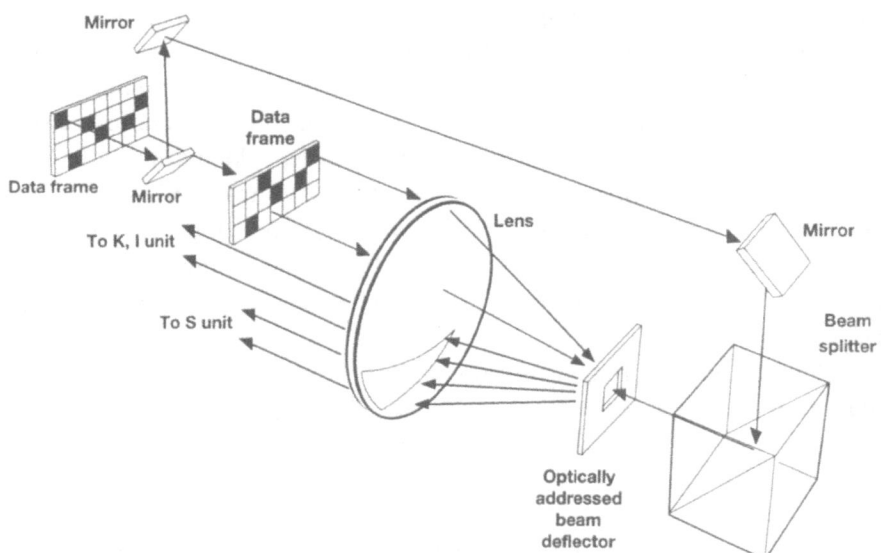

Figure 10.4: Packet switch.

in the device is a function of the write light intensity. The result of this is that the program frame is diffracted to either an S unit or a K, I unit. A lens affords data compression on the deflector for cases where real estate should be minimised. The VGMLCD is an analogue deflector which can access about 32 different spot positions, given that there is sufficient dynamic range on the write light intensity. This capability could be useful if we were to choose an expanded combinator set, where the number of destinations extends beyond two. Although the VGMLCD represents the idea quite well, it is too slow for practical application, and a better alternative for fast, binary routing would be to use polarisation-based ferroelectric liquid crystal gates [15]. The switching of the liquid crystal can be optically controlled by means of a photosensitive amorphous silicon layer [16]. This device would also be used as a temporary store for the program frame before it impinged on the deflector, because there will be some delay in switching the deflector on. This buffering is not shown on the figure for simplicity.

The S reduction unit consists of a copy and a splitting unit (Figure 10.5. In order to copy the digital coding for 3 into the correct locations in the succeeding line, a similar methodology to that of the control unit is employed. Again, exact registration of the array is required. Since the copying of the 3 will involve a halving of the light intensity associated with each coding, the copy unit is an appropriate stage at which to double the lateral dimension of the array prior to splitting and recirculating through the packet switch. Two important consequences follow from this. The light intensity in each pixel is halved uniformly across the array, and the coding is extended laterally. The coding expansion can be accommodated at compile time when the array is formulated. The level restoration of the light intensity is performed by amplification in the splitting unit. This is most conveniently performed by using an optically addressed SLM [16]. The clocking of this SLM via the electrical drive waveform can be used in order to temporally order the data frames. As far as the S unit is concerned, therefore, there is no requirement to tag the frames other than by retaining their temporal order.

The K, I unit is brought into the picture when direct insertion of variables into the leaves of the tree is required. This may be physically realised by extracting the data block below the combinator, to test whether it is a K or I subtree.

- If there is a data block, then it is a K subtree and the block is transferred directly to the leaf line.

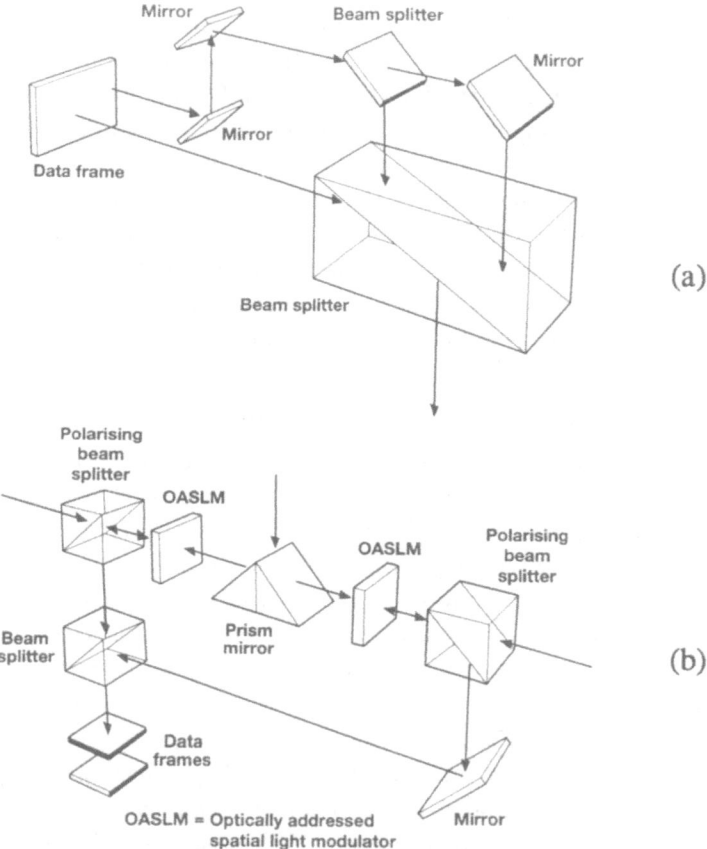

Figure 10.5: Reduction unit: (a) Copy unit. (b) Splitting units.

- If there is no data block, then it is an I subtree and the block adjacent to the I combinator is transferred to the leaf line.

A similar methodology for the optical system could be followed. The tagging of these data blocks is important in this case, because these K, I reductions can occur at any level of the tree, and the correct ordering of the leaves depends on it. If we assume that these data blocks are contained within the original page size, then there is ample room on the page for associating some tag with the block. The reconstruction of the leaf line is more complex now than if combinator reduction was performed in parallel. The latter option should be the aim for a serious implementation.

Similar issues arise in the processing of the data format of Figure 10.3. In this case the control frame precedes the data frame on which it is to act, so that the correct path for the following frames can be set up without requiring the temporary storage which was referred to in the previous approach. The 3 is extracted from the second frame and copied into the third frame. At this point arises the choice of whether to reduce the two S combinators in the third frame in parallel, or split the data stream into two, then four, etc. As before, the former is preferable because it maintains the coherency of the data stream. Clearly, the implementation issues are more complex in this case and will not be pursued here.

10.6 Functional Specification of Optical Devices

The bottom-up approach to optical system design proceeds from a functional specification of the relevant devices. There is good evidence to show that this works in the case of electronic VLSI design [17]. For example we take the case of an SLM. The SLM is divided into pixels which modulate either the intensity, the phase, or the polarisation. For binary modulation, the pixel can be transmitting or opaque; or it can invert the phase or maintain it; or it can rotate the polarisation to an orthogonal state or leave it. We may ultimately wish to know how these different modes can be combined in system usage. To this end, each type of modulation is described in a common specification language. The effect of a single pixel is straightforward to express in this manner. This can be extended to a block of pixels using the map function. When rays of light are expressed as infinite lists, the temporal sequence of pixel states is the zip function of the sequence with the ray list. A one-bit store was specified by this means, using a source, an amplitude modulating pixel, a phase modulating pixel, and a switch. The extension to beams was not quite so clear, because there are two routes to the functional composition of beams and it is not clear whether the specifications are equivalent. However, this extension allows one to specify a store processing unit, using the specification for the one-bit store.

10.7 Conclusion

Two approaches to machine design have been presented. Both are in early stages, but they are important for building bridges between the optical system designer and the software engineer. We hope to pursue the second approach more exhaustively over the coming years.

Acknowledgements

I wish to thank Alastair Tocher, Graham Pratten, Jeremy Jacob, Ali Abdallah, and Prof. John Hughes for their technical input on the computing side, without which none of this could have been realised.

References

[1] S.E.Fahlman and G.E.Hinton, *Massively parallel architectures for AI: NETL,THISTLE, and BOLTZMANN machines*, Proc. Nat'l Conf. Artificial Intelligence, AAAI, pp.109-113 (1983).

[2] D.DeGroot and G.Lindstrom, *Logic programming – functions, relations, and equations*, Prentice-Hall (1986)

[3] A.Huang, *Architectural considerations involved in the design of an optical digital computer*, Proc. IEEE, Vol. 72(7), pp.780-786 (1984).

[4] A.D.Fisher and J.N.Lee, *Current status of two-dimensional spatial light modulator technology*, Proc. SPIE, Vol. 634, pp.352-371 (1986).

[5] N.Collings et al., *Evolutionary development of advanced liquid crystal spatial light modulators*, Appl. Opt. (August, 1989).

[6] J.R.Gurd et al., *The Manchester prototype dataflow computer*, Communications of the ACM, Vol. 28(1), pp.34-52 (1985).

[7] R.Treleaven and M.Vanneschi (Eds),*Future parallel computers*, Springer-Verlag Lecture notes in Computer Science, Vol. 272 (1986).

[8] M.D.Cripps et al., *The design and implementation of ALICE: A parallel graph reduction machine*, in *Functional programming: Languages, tools and architectures*, S.Eisenbach and C.Sadler (Eds), Ellis Horwood Ltd. (1986).

[9] G.A.Mago, *A cellular computer architecture for functional programming*, COMPCON 1980, pp.179-187 (March 1980).

[10] M.J.Shute and P.E.Osman, *Cobweb – a reduction architecture* in *Wafer Scale integration*, C.Jesshope and W.Moore (Eds), Adam Hilger (1986).

[11] D.A.Turner, *A new implementation technique for applicative languages*, Software-Practice and Experience, Vol. 9, 31 (198?).

[12] S.L.Peyton Jones, *The implementation of functional programming languages*, Prentice-Hall (1987).

[13] D.A.Turner, *Another algorithm for bracket abstraction*, The Journal of Symbolic Logic, Vol. 44(2), pp.267-270 (1979).

[14] B.H.Soffer et al., *Optical computing with variable grating mode liquid crystal devices*, Proc. SPIE, Vol. 232, pp.128-136 (1980).

[15] K.M.Johnson et al., *Optical interconnection network using polarisation based ferroelectric liquid crystal gates*, Appl.Opt., Vol. 27(9), pp.1727-1733 (1988).

[16] D.Williams et al., *An amorphous silicon/chiral smectic spatial light modulator*, J.Phys.D: Appl.Phys. Vol. 21, pp. S156-S159 (1988).

[17] M.Sheeran, *μFP, a language for VLSI design*, ACM Symp. on Lisp and Functional Programming, Austin,Texas (August 1984).

CHAPTER 11

TECHNICAL REPORTS LIST

Stuart K. Tewksbury
Room 4B505
AT&T Bell Laboratories
Crawfords Corner Road
Holmdel, NJ 07733 USA

The listings provided in this chapter were compiled by the editor from lists submitted by various individuals and institutions from whom the unpublished, internal reports are available (possibly with a modest charge). In some cases, full listings of technical reports from institutions were provided, in which case the editor has selected a few typical reports. The address information for requesting either individual reports or lists of technical reports is provided, along with brief descriptions of the reports. Neither Plenum Press nor the editor take responsibility for the accuracy of the information listed below. However, advertising such reports is felt to be important, mainly since such unpublished reports often convey the personalized view of research topics which we seek to highlight in these volumes.

Those wishing to include listings of technical reports should submit information such as that included in the following listings to the editor at the address above.

University of Arizona, Dept. of Computer Science, Tucson, AZ 85721: *Attn: Technical Reports.*

Selected from Technical Reports list, available above.

TR 89-3 *Implementing fault-tolerant replicated objects using Psync,* S. Mishra, L. L. Peterson and R. D. Schlichting.

Psync is an IPC protocol that explicitly preserves the partial order of messages exchanged among a set of processes. Report describes use of Psync to implement replicated objects in the presence of network and host failures.

TR 89-7 *On total delay in virtual circuits with parallel links,* S. Chowdhury.

Computer networks with multiple links may deliver packets to the destination out of sequence. With numerical examples, report studies the dependence of the mean resequencing delay and mean queuing delay on the mean service time, the squared coefficient of variation of service time and the number of links.

TR 89-8 *Parallel LISP on the BBN Butterfly,* C. J. Turner and J. C. Peterson.

Report discusses research in the area of parallel LISP compilation and execution, including work in automatic parallelization of sequential user programs (obtained by a static analysis phase within the compiler itself).

Boston College, Computer Science Department, Fulton Hall 423, Chestnut Hill, MA 02167: *Attn: Technical Reports Coordinator.*

Selected from Technical Reports list, available above.

BCCS-89-03 *On generalizing the concept of hypertext,* M. Bieber.

Paper discusses author's generalization of the basic hypertext concept, including generalizations of the node, link and link traversal concepts.

BCCS-89-04 *A structured, holistic framework for the creation of information systems,* G. Schiavone.

Paper proposes a unified and structured approach to thinking about information systems, on both a conceptual and operational level.

BCCS-88-01 *Myhill's thesis: There's more to musical cognition than computing,* P. Kugel.

Considers some arguments favoring suggestion that some features of musical cognition might require more than computing and asks what precise accounts of the uncomputable aspects of musical cognition might look like.

Brown University, Dept. of Computer Science, Box 1910, Providence, RI 02912: *Attn: Technical Reports.*

Selected from Technical Reports list, available above.

CS-89-32 *The B-SYS programmable systolic array,* D. P. Lopresti and R. Hughey.
Report introduces a general architecture for programmable systolic arrays, incorporating regular topology with nearest neighbor connections, synchronous SIMD control, interprocessor communication using shared registers and stream-based I/O. The Brown Systolic Array (B-SYS), using above philosophy, is a highly parallel array of simple processing elements, tuned for combinatorial problems, being implemented in 2 micron CMOS.

CS-89-30 *TANGO: A framework and system for algorithm animation,* J. T. Stasko.
Algorithm animation abstracts the data, operations and semantics of computer programs and then creates animated graphical views of those abstractions. TANGO (Transition-based ANimation GeneratiOn) supports two-dimensional color animations in a window-based workstation environment, allowing programmers to produce sophisticated, real-time views of their programs with a minimum of graphics coding.

CS-89-23 *A logic for emotions: A basis for reasoning about common-sense psychological knowledge,* K. E. Sanders.

CS-89-18 *I/O overhead and parallel VLSI architectures for lattice computations,* M. H. Nodine, D. P. Lopresti and J. S. Vitter.

CS-89-09 *Algorithms for drawing graphs: An annotated bibliography,* P. Eades and R. Tamassia.
Report presents a bibliographic survey of algorithms whose goal is to produce aesthetically pleasing drawings of graphs

CS-88-19 *A Threads tutorial — Fortran version,* T. W. Doeppner, Jr.
Threads is a system for efficient support of concurrency, running on either single processor or multiprocessor computers (presenting the programmer with the same "view of the world" no matter how many processors are available). This view is that a number of concurrent threads

of control are executing in a single shared address space and share a common view of which files are open.

CS-88-09 *Elements of relational database theory,* P. C. Kanellakis.

The goal of this paper is to provide a systematic and unifying introduction to relational database theory, including some of the recent developments in database logic programming. The exposition closes with a discussion of how relational database theory deals with problems of complex objects, incomplete information and database updates.

California Institute of Technology, Computer Science Dept., 256-80, Pasadena, CA 91125: *Attn: Technical Reports.*

Selected from Technical Reports list, available above.

CS-TR-89-06 *The first asynchronous microprocessor: The test results,* A. J. Martin, et al.

CS-TR-89-02 *Design of an asynchronous multiprocessor,* A. J. Martin.

CS-TR-88-20 *Neural network design and the complexity of learning,* J. S. Judd.

CS-TR-88-16 *Programming parallel computers,* K. M. Chandy.

CS-TR-88-04 *Cochlear hydrodynamics demystified,* R. F. Lyon and C. A. Mead.

CS-TR-88-01 *C Programmer's abbreviated guide to multicomputer programming,* C. Seitz, J. Seizovic and W-K. Su.

Univeristy of California - Los Angeles, Computer Science Department, 3413 Boelter Hall, Los Angeles, CA 90024: *Attn: Ms. Brenda Ramsey or Ms June Myers.*

Selected from Technical Reports list, available above.

CSD-890003 *The Tangram Project: Publications 1987-88,* R. R. Muntz, D. S. Parker and G. J. Popek.

The Tangram Project at UCLA is aimed at the development of an environment for modeling of dynamic systems. It is an integration of DBMS and KBMS technology with distributed processing techniques. This report summarizes technical reports over first year of project.

CSD-890009 *Support for fault tolerance in VLSI processors,* M. Tremblay and Y. Tamir.

Hardware supported concurrent error-detection and limited fault tolerance in system components, implemented by coding or replication, are often required. This report describes alternative implementations of such circuits and ways they can be connected to VLSI modules. As a concrete example, authors present area and performance measurements of alternative microarchitectures and circuits for a VLSI RISC processor.

CSD-890050 *A taxonomy of parallel simulated annealing techniques,* D. R. Greening.

This paper provides a comprehensive, taxonomic survey of parallel simulated annealing techniques, highlighting their performance and applicability.

CSD-890052 *Queuing networks: Solutions and applications,* E. De Souza de Silva and R. R. Muntz.

During the past decade, queuing network models have proven to be a versatile tool for computer system and computer communication system performance evaluation. The report provides a survey of the field with a particular emphasis on applications.

Carleton University, Computer Related Technical Reports, Dept. of Systems and Computer Engineering, Ottawa, Ontario, CANADA K1S 5B6: *Attn: Department Librarian.*

Selected from list provided by Prof. Karam.

SCE-88-3 *MLog: A language for prototyping concurrent system designs,* G. M. Karam (Jan. 1988).

SCE-88-16 *Survey in machine learning: Techniques and programs,* B. Pelletier (Aug. 1988).

SCE-89-19 *TimeBench: A next generation CASE tool,* G. M. Karam, R. J. A. Buhr, C. M. Woodside and R. Casselman.

SCE-89-20 *Visibility analysis: A formulation aid for all classes of network models,* J. W. Chinneck.

Carnegie Mellon University, CMU Research Center for Dependable Systems, Dept. of ECE, Pittsburgh, PA 15213: *Attn: Roxann Martin.*

Selected from Research Report list, available above.

CMUCDS-89-2 *Interprocessor traffic scheduling and multicommodity network flows,* R. P. Bianchini, Jr.

CMUCDS-89-3 *Automatic synthesis of reliable systems,* P. Edmond.
ASSURE (Automatic Synthesis of Reliable Systems) Version 2 is a general purpose expert advisor to automate the process of design for dependability in the domain of single board computers. The tool has been implemented as part of the MICON system.

University of Colorado at Boulder, Dept. of Computer Science, Campus Box 430, Boulder, Colorado 80309: *Attn: Technical Reports.*

Selected from Technical Reports list, available above.

CU-CS-404-88 *Research trends in formal semantics: Report of a discussion,* M. Main and M. Mislove.

CU-CS-420-89 *Benchmarking Fortran and Ada programs on parallel machines,* L. D. Fosdick, C. J. C Schauble and K. M. Olender.

CU-CS-422-89 *Characterizing distributed computer paradigms,* M. F. Schwartz and I. M. Demeure.

CU-CS-429-89 *New approaches to programming,* C. Lewis.

CU-CS-433-89 *Current developments in parallel computation,* O. McBryan.

CU-CS-438-89 *Simulation of parallel computations,* L. D. Fosdick and C. J. C. Schauble.

CU-CS-440-89 *Performance characteristics of scientific computation on the connection machine,* R. Pozo and A. E. MacDonald.

University of Colorado at Boulder, Dept. of Computer Science, Boulder, Colorado 80301: *Attn: A. G. Graefe.*

Oregon Grad Center Reports: submitted by Graefe.

89-013 *Set processing and complex object assembly in Volcano and the REVELATION project,* A. G. Graefe.

89-009 *The one-to-one match operator of the Volcano query processing system,* A. T. Keller and A. G. Graefe.

89-008 *Parallel external sorting in Volcano,* A. G. Graefe.

89-007 *Encapsulation of parallelism in the Volcano query processing system,* A. G. Graefe.

89-006 *Volcano: extensible and parallel dataflow query processing system,* A. G. Graefe.

Columbia University, Dept. of Computer Science, 450 Computer Science Building, New York, NY 10027: *Attn: Tech Report Librarian.*

Selected from Technical Report list, available above.

CUCS-415-89 *Parallel vision algorithms: Final technical report,* J. R. Kender, H. A. H. Ibrahim and L. G. Brown.

CUCS-421-89 *A visual language for browsing, undoing and redoing graphical interface commands,* D. Kurlander and S. Feiner.

CUCS-425-89 *Concurrency control in advanced database applications,* N. S. Barghouti.

CUCS-436-89 *Exploring "multiple worlds" in parallel* and **CUCS-437-89** *System support for "multiple worlds",* J. M. Smith and G. Q. Maguire, Jr.

CUCS-467-89 *A survey of machine learning systems integrating explanation-based and similarity-based methods,* A. Danyluk.

CUCS-493-89 *Image understanding and robotics research at Columbia University,* J. R. Kender, P. K. Allen and T. E. Boult.

Cornell University, Dept. of Computer Science, 4130 Upson Hall, Ithaca, NY 14853: *Attn: Technical Reports Librarian.*

Selected from Technical Reports list, available above.

TR 87-849 *ISIS — A distributed programming environment, Version 1.3 — User's guide and reference manual,* Birman, Joseph and Schmuck (July 1987).

TR 89-997 *Implementing fault-tolerant sensors,* Marzullo (May 1989).

TR 89-1014 *How robust are distributed systems,* Birman (June 1989).

TR 88-904 *Computational foundations of basic recursive function theory,* R. L. Constable and S. F. Smith (March 1988).

TR 88-908 *New developments in structural complexity theory,* J. Hartmanis (April 1988).

TR 88-914 *Critical (of) issues in real-time systems: A position paper,* F. B. Schneider (May 1988).

TR 89-1001 *The role of order in distributed programs,* K. Marzullo and K. Birman (May 1989).

TR 89-1002 *Space bounded computations: Review and new separation results,* J. Hartmanis and D. Ranjan (May 1989).

TR 89-1021 *Nupri as a general logic,* R. L.Constable and D. J. Howe (June 1989).

TR 89-1032 *Fault-tolerant computing based on Mach,* O. Babaoglu (Aug. 1989).

TR 89-1053 *What should a roboticist do next? A progress report from the Cornell Computer Science Robotics Dept.,* B. Donald, D. Pai and P. Xavier.

University of Delaware, Dept. of Computer and Information Science, 103 Smith Hall, Newark, DE 19716: *Attn: Prof. Paul Amer.*

Submitted by Amer.

89-14 *Adding graphics and animation to Estelle,* D. New and P. D. Amer.

GROPE (Graphical Representation Of Protocols in Estelle) is a window-based tool which pictorially represents and animates the dynamic evaluation of a protocol. This report describes the design, implementation and use of GROPE.

Ecole Polytechnique, Laboratoire d'Informatique, 91128 Palaiseau Cedex, FRANCE: *Attn: Michel Weinfeld.*

Selected from list provided by Weinfeld, above.

Implementation of a fully connected digital CMOS integrated Hopfield neural network with included learning and annealing, M. Weinfeld, J-D. Gascuel, P-Y. Alla and J. Roman.

Describes circuitry and design of an integrated CMOS digital Hopfield neural network with 64 binary neurons, semi-parallel update, Widrow-

Hoff internal learning capability and internal noise generator for improved convergence.

George Mason University, Machine Learning and Inference Laboratory, Center for Artificial Intelligence, 4400 University Drive, Fairfax, Virginia 22030: *Attn: Technical Reports.*

Selected from Publications list, available above.

MLI 89-1 *Hierarchical model-based diagnosis,* I. Mozetic.

MLI 89-12 *EMERALD 1: An integrated system of machine learning and discovery programs for education and research, Users guide,* K. Kaufman, R. S. Michalski and A. Schultz.

MLI 89-15 *Characterizing machine learning programs, a European compilation,* Y. Kodratoff.

The George Washington University, Inst. for Information Science and Technology, Dept. of Electrical Engineering and Computer Science, Washington, DC 20052: *Attn: Technical Reports.*

Selected from Index of Reports, available above.

89-01 *Probabilistic image models and their information-theoretic properties,* Y. Zhang, M. Loew and R. Pickholtz.
Authors propose a new method to construct the joint probability model from a specified first-order distribution and correlation structure. Approach is intended to remove limitations imposed by earlier methods and make for more realistic modeling of medical images.

89-08 *The Banyan-Hypercube network: A synthesis of Banyans and Hypercubes,* A. Youssef and B. Narahari.
Authors introduce a new family of networks that are a synthesis of banyans and hypercubes, seeking to combine best features of each for better communications capabilities. An optimal routing algorithm for Banyan-Hypercubes and an efficient partitioning strategy are also given.

89-09 *Fuzzy command grammars for user modeling in intelligent interfaces,* H. Senay.
Report considers design of interfaces exhibiting intelligent behavior in

user-computer interactions. A fuzzy set theoretic view of user-computer interactions incorporating knowledge acquired using a simple learning mechanism is presented.

89-18 *Neural network: Theory and VLSI implementation,* F. I. Hamama and M. E. Zaghloul.

Report reviews the biological functions of neural networks and briefly summarizes learning algorithms. Grossberg, Hopfield and Kohonen models are discussed. A summary of recent VLSI circuit implementations is provided, along with a summary of GWU research activities in VLSI implementation.

89-24 *Multidimensional control system research at the George Washington University,* R. Carroll.

An overview of current research in control systems and applications at GWU is provided. Emphasis is on theory and applications of two-dimensional (and higher dimensional) discrete dynamical systems. Current research includes modeling and zero-input stability of systems; modeling, simulation and control of flexible systems; multidimensional identification; model order-reduction; adaptive and learning control of multidimensional systems. Recent research has considered optimal control of chaotic systems and the adaptive control of robots.

88-20 *Simulation of parallel computer architectures,* S. Ziavras and N. Alexandridis.

Report describes simulation tools allowing parallel programs to be developed, debugged and executed on various parallel computer architectures, including variable dimensions hypercubes, pyramids, meshes and rings.

88-27 *Towards a formalization of communication complexity,* B. Narahari and Y. H. Ma.

The communication overhead in parallel processing systems depends on both the algorithms and the interconnection network. Authors propose a classification of tasks based on the communication complexity, which is identified using the dependency graph. They propose an additional metric of relative dilation cost to evaluate the relative efficiency of networks in supporting an algorithm.

Georgia Institute of Technology, School of Information and Computer Science, Atlanta, GA 30332: *Attn: Liya Pan, Technical Report Librarian.*

Selected from Technical Reports list, available above.

GIT-ICS-89/22 *The Grid protocol: A high performance scheme for maintaining replicated data,* S. Y. Cheung, M. H. Ammar and M. Ahamed (June 1989).

Authors present a new protocol for maintaining replicated data that can provide both high data availability and low response time. Includes an analysis of the availability of the new protocol, using simulation to study the effect of load sharing on the response time of transactions.

GIT-ICS-89/28 *Gateway performance analysis in interconnection networks,* I. F. Akyildiz and J. Liebeherr (August 1989).

The performance of interconnection networks is highly dependent on the performance of the gateways. Storage capability of gateways and effect on performance are studied for different configurations of networks. Approximation methods for computing throughput performance of networks are given and results are validated with simulation.

GIT-ICS-89/13 *A reconfigurable supercomputer architecture,* W. B. Ligon and U. Ramachandran (Feb. 1989).

GIT-ICS-88/04 *Program development for processor arrays,* W. F. Appelbe, J. D. Anderson and P. Darvas (June 1988).

Report introduces a general model for SIMD processor arrays (PAs) together with a simple language, PAPL, for expressing parallel algorithms. A portable compiler for PAPL, and simulator for PAs, have been developed.

GIT-ICS-88/15 *Improved algorithms for distributed resource allocation: Extended abstract,* E. F. Styer and G. L. Peterson (May 1988).

GIT-ICS-88/45 *The Clouds distributed operating system,* P. Dasgupta, R. L. LeBlanc Jr., and W. F. Appelbe (Nov. 1988).

Clouds is a distributed operating system targeted at providing the integration, reliability and structure necessary to make a distributed system usable. Clouds is designed to run on a set of general purpose computers connected via medium-to-high speed LAN. Report overviews paradigm, operating system and 1st & 2nd implementations of Clouds.

The Hebrew University of Jerusalem, The Leibniz Center for Research in Computer Science, Institute of Mathematics and Computer Science, Givat Ram, 91904, Jerusalem, ISRAEL: *Attn: Secretary, Computer Science Dept.*

Selected from Technical Reports list, available above.

89-2 *Multiresolution shape from shading*, G. Ron and S. Peleg (Jan. 1989).

Multiresolution approaches are often used in computer vision to speed
up computationally extensive tasks. A solution is computed for a smaller
image, and that solution helps to guide towards the complete solution
on a larger image. Trying to adopt this multiresolution approach for
the computationally extensive shape from shading problem proved to be
harder than expected. The correspondence between grey level and shape
resolutions is discussed and a method is proposed to use multiresolution
in the case of shape from shading.

89-5 *Adaptive algorithms*, Y. Ossia and L. Rudolph (March 1989).

Given a dynamically changing environment, a method is presented that
automatically adapts to the best strategy based on a game of market interactions between autonomous agents. The system was implemented on
top of a parallel environment to avoid the artificial introduction of time-
sharing. Authors develop a theory for pricing, show how the number
of actors remains bounded and force the system to adapt to the correct
strategy. Authors present results of several experiments, one yielding a
surprising resemblance to the behavior of simulated annealing.

89-12 *Motion based segmentation of 2D scenes*, H. Rom and S. Peleg
(June 1989).

Automatic segmentation of independently moving objects in image sequences is performed. Both the camera and the object may be moving; at
present the motion is limited to rigid motion of 2D scenes. The segmentation is performed by clustering pixels based on their agreement with
their motion estimates. The process is iterated and the motion estimates
become more accurate every iteration until an accurate segmentation is
obtained, with accurate motion parameters for each segment. A method
is also suggested to accurately detect occluded regions that are visible
in one image and occluded in another.

University of Illinois at Urbana-Champaign, Dept. of Computer
Science, 1304 West Springfield Ave., Urbana, IL 61801: *Attn: Technical Reports.*

Selected from Quarterly Publications lists, available above.

1506 *Fast algorithms for scheduling imprecise computations with timing constraints,* W-K. Shih, J. W. S. Liu and J-Y. Chung (May 1989).
Report considers problem of scheduling tasks each of which is logically decomposed into a mandatory subtask and an optional subtask. Authors describe (1) a preemptive algorithm for scheduling n independent tasks on a uniprocessor system and (2) two algorithms for optimum schedules of dependent tasks when all optional tasks have identical processing times.

1510 *Principles of object-oriented operating system design,* R. H. Campbell, G. M. Johnson, P. W. Madany and V. F. Russo (April 1989).
For design and construction of object-oriented operating systems, authors present three principles: (1) model hardware/system software by a framework of interacting components, (2) provide a uniform mechanism for application-to-system and application-to-application communication and (3) organize object-oriented operating system as a member of a family of operating systems. Implemented on Encore Multimax and written in C++.

1525 *Asynchronous integration of ordinary differential equations on multiprocessors,* S. Aslam and C. W. Gear (July 1989).
Report describes an asynchronous iterative algorithm for Picard method of solving the initial value problem for ordinary differential equations. Algorithm is implemented on Encore Multimax.

1528 *Dynamic scheduling of medium-grain processes on multicomputers,* W. Shiu and L. V. Kale (July 1989).
Report considers allocating work to processors (distributed memory parallel machines) for computations with unpredictable dynamic behavior or irregular structure. Authors present Adaptive Contracting Within Neighborhood (ACWN), a dynamic, distributed, load dependent and scalable scheme. It is contrasted with two previously proposed schemes, using results from a 64 processor iPSC/2 hypercube.

1498 *Kyma: An interactive graphic environment of object-oriented music composition and real-time software sound synthesis written in Smalltalk-80,* C. Scaletti (Feb. 1988).
Kyma uses a co-processor to perform software sound synthesis in real time. Compositions are specified by manipulating graphic representations of 'sound' objects on the display.

1504 *An integrated performance data collection, analysis and visualization system,* A. D. Malony, et al (March 1989).
Report describes an integrated performance environment being devel-

oped for the Intel iPSC/2 hypercube. The visualization environment is
based on the X windows system.

Universität Kaiserslautern, Department of Computer Science, Post-fach 3049, D-6750 Kaiserslautern, WEST GERMANY: *Attn: Rolf Socher-Ambrosius.*

Selected from SEKI: List of Abstracts, available above.

SR-88-11 *Opening the AC unification race,* H.-J. Bürckert et al.
This report discusses the implementation of AC (associative-commuta-
tive)-unification algorithms, based on the variable-abstraction method
of Stickel and on the constant-abstraction method of Livesey, Siekmann
and Herold. Authors give 105 benchmark examples and compare execution times for implementations of the two approaches. This documents
for other researchers what authors consider to be the state-of-the-art
performance for elementary AC-unification problems.

SR-88-19 *Structuring computer generated proofs,* C. Lingenfelder.
A main disadvantage of computer generated proofs of mathematical the-
orems is their complexity and incomprehensibility. Author describes a
procedure to transform proofs represented as abstract refutation graphs
into natural deduction proofs. During this process, topological properties of the refutation graphs can be successfully exploited to obtain
structured proofs and to remove trivial steps from the proof formulation.

Universität Kiel, Institut für Informatik und Praktische Mathematik, Olshausenstrasse 40, D-2300 Kiel 1, West Germany: *Attn: Techni-cal Reports.*

Selected from Technical Reports list, available above.

Report 8902 *MIMOLA reference manual, Version 3.45,* R. Jöhnk and
P. Marwedel (1989).
MIMOLA (machine independent microprogramming language) is a computer language supporting design, test, simulation and programming
of digital computing. MIMOLA is a high-level programming language

(HLL), a register transfer language (RTL) and a computer hardware description language (CHDL).

Report 8718 *Transitive closure on an instruction systolic array,* H-W. Lang (1988).

The instruction systolic array (ISA) is a parallel processor architecture, which is characterized by a systolic flow of instructions (instead of data as in standard systolic arrays).

Report 8715 *Time-distorted cellular algorithms,* B. Bleck and H. Kröger (1987).

Paper investigates transformation of a given cellular algorithm, with simultaneous activation of the cells, into a modified "time-distorted" cellular algorithm. Problem arises in composing a cellular algorithm out of smaller ones.

Katholieke Universiteit Leuven, ESAT Laboratory, Dept. of Electrical Engineering, Kardinaal Mercierlaan 94, 3030 Heverlee, BELGIUM: *Attn: Dr. Sabine Van Huffel.*

Submitted by Van Huffel.

ESAT-KUL-88/1 *Documented Fortran 77 programs of the extended classical total least squares algorithm, the partial singular value decomposition algorithm and the partial total least squares algorithm,* S. Van Huffel.

The extended classical total least squares algorithm is an extension of the classical total least squares method, described by Gulob and Van Loan. Partial singular value decomposition and partial total least squares algorithms are also described.

TIM3/IMAG/INPG, 46 avenue F. Viallet, 38031 Grenoble Cedex, FRANCE: *Attn: Bernard Courtois.*

Selected from list provided by Courtois, above.

Computer architecture group activity report – 1988, B. Courtois.

Research in group includes architecture of IC's, silicon compilation, architecture of AI oriented machines, testing (including e-beam) and self-checking circuits.

NAUTILE: A physical design environment based on an object oriented data manager, A. A. Jerraya, P. Bondono, J. P. Geronimi, A. Hornik and B. Courtois.

Discusses a physical environment system, built around an object oriented data manager that handles hierarchical design. Proposes multiple views of different elements composing the whole circuit.

Fault simulation and test pattern generation at the multiple-valued switch level, J. P. Caisso and B. Courois.

Concerns simulation and test of almost all possible faults which may occur in a CMOS switch-level circuit.

New testing equipment for SMT boards, L. Balme, A. Mignotte, J. Y. Monari, P. Pondaven and C. Vaucher.

Describes project aimed at testing printed circuit board, including interface using anisotropic elastomer conductors, PC test interface and software.

SYCO: A silicon compiler for VLSI ASIC's specified by algorithms, A. A. Jerraya, N. Mhaya, J. P. Geronimi and B. Courtois.

SYCO system starts with an algorithmic description (high level hardware description language) and produces circuit that realizes algorithm.

University of Massachusetts, Dept. of Electrical and Computer Engineering, Amherst, MA 01003: *Attn: Prof. Imrich Chlamtac.*

Submitted by I. Chlamtac.

A software emulator for computer communication networks, I. Chlamtac and M. Chlamtac.

Report presents CONSIP II, a software tool for the design and evaluation of computer communication networks based on the introduced "software emulation" approach. The software, in the case of networks, can execute processes virtually in parallel while mimicking interprocess communications procedures found in actual computer networks.

University of Michigan, Dept. of Electrical Engineering and Computer Science, 3402 EECS Bldg, 1301 Beal, Ann Arbor, MI 48109: *Attn: CSE Technical Report Series.*

Selected from Technical Reports list, available above.

CSE-TR-04-88 *Structure from motion – a critical analysis of methods,* C. P. Jerian and R. Jain.

Report classifies and analyzes many existing methods to solve the SFM problem, which has yielded few practical solutions.

CSE-TR-10-88 *A formal metalanguage for Nupri,* T. B. Knoblock.

An automated theorem prover is said to be metamathematically extensible if a metalanguage can be employed by the user to soundly extend the reasoning capabilities of the system. A formal metalanguage called Metapri is defined that represents the proof theory of Nupri in a natural and computationally-oriented fashion.

CSE-TR-24-89 *The complex behavior of simple machines,* R. Machlin and Q. F. Stout.

This paper interprets work on understanding the actions of Turing machines operating on an initially blank tape. Normalization and computer techniques drastically reduced the number of arbitrary Turing machines considered, isolating exotic machines which would be exceedingly difficult to develop directly. These exotic machines show that it is difficult to estimate the number of states needed to produce given behavior, and hence subjective estimates of complexity may be poor approximations of the true complexity.

CSE-TR-31-89 *Analysis and design of latch-controlled synchronous digital circuits,* K. A. Sakallah, T. N. Mudge and O. A. Olukotun.

Authors present a succinct yet complete formulation of the timing constraints for latch-controlled synchronous circuits. They show the constraints are mildly nonlinear and prove the equivalence of the nonlinear optimal cycle time calculation problem to an associated and simpler linear programming problem.

University of Newcastle Upon Tyne, Computing Laboratory, Claremont Tower, Claremont Road, Newcastle upon Tyne, NE1 7RU, UNITED KINGDOM: *Attn: M. J. Elphick, Editor of Technical Report Series.*

Selected from List of Technical Reports, available above.

TR254 *An introduction to integrated project support environments,* A. W. Brown (Feb. 1988).

It is widely accepted that current software development techniques are unacceptable to produce high quality software at the rate required by the rapidly expanding applications of computer technology. This report analyzes the motivation for providing integrated support for production of software, follows the history of environments for software development and provides the context for describing current and future research trends in this area.

TR262 *A technical overview of Arjuna: A system for reliable distributed computing,* S. K. Shrivastava, G. N. Dixon, F. Hedayati, G. D. Parrington and S. M. Wheater (July 1988) and **TR298** *An overview of Arjuna: A programming system for reliable distributed computing,* S. K. Shrivastava, G. N. Dixon and G. D. Parrington (Nov. 1989).

Arjuna is an object-oriented fault-tolerant distributed programming system being designed and implemented in C++ on a set of UNIX workstations connected by an Ethernet. The report describes how several mechanisms are integrated into Arjuna's object model.

TR264 *Security and databases: A methodological approach,* J. E. Dobson (Sept. 1988).

There is a sharp distinction between a software-oriented view of information and a social view. A case study is examined to support argument that reconciliation of security and privacy issues with data modeling issues through gross over-simplifying assumptions is not only a retreat from the problems identified but can be positively damaging and counter-productive. Relevant ideas from philosophy are raided to show how a methodological approach may be structured, and the details of a design scheme are outlined.

TR273 *Expressibility, complexity and comparative schematology,* I. A. - Stewart (Nov. 1988).

Report considers connection between expressibility of a given problem and its computational complexity using new results concerning classes of program schemes. Many of the proofs of old results (employing non-trivial mathematics) can be couched in a style familiar to programmers, through a link between complexity theory and programming formalisms. Author provides new setting in which to attack previously unsolved problems in logic and complexity theory.

New York University, Courant Institute of Mathematical Sciences, Dept.

of Computer Science, 251 Mercer St., New York, NY 10012: *Attn: Victoria Macaulay.*

<u>Following items were selected by NYU.</u>

435 *Compilation techniques for VLIW architectures,* F. Gasperoni (Mar. 1989).

Experiments have shown that reasonable amounts of fine grain parallelism are available globally in serial programs. New compaction algorithms, as well as a new architecture, have been put forward to exploit such parallelism.

443 *Polymorphic type inference and semi-unification,* F. Henglein (April 1989).

Author investigates several polymorphic type systems, the most powerful of which, termed Milner-Mycroft Calculus, extends the so-called let-polymorphism. Shows that semi-unification (problem of solving inequalities over first-order terms) characterizes type checking in Milner-Mycroft Calculus to polynomial time. This permits extension of some infeasibility results for related combinatorial problems to type inference and to correct several claims and statements in the literature.

453 *Random B-Trees with inserts and deletes,* T. Johnson and D. Shasha (June 1989).

Authors first present two models for computing B-tree utilization, the more accurate of which remembers items inserted and then deleted in a node. After analyzing the leaf level of a random B-tree, they analyze the upper levels, and show that they have the structure of the leaf level of a pure-insert tree, independent of the percentage of operations that are deletes (if that percentage is less than 50%).

465 *Automated inversion of a unification parser into a unification generator,* T. Strzalkowski (Sept. 1989).

Report describes an algorithm for an automated conversion of a unification parser for natural language into an efficient unification generator for the same language. The scope of applicability of the algorithm is discussed and possible avenues of extension are suggested. The algorithm is tested on an actual grammar derived from a larger string grammar for English.

467-R213 *On the error analysis of 'Geometric Hashing',* Y. Lamdan and H. J. Wolfson (Oct. 1989).

Report presents an experimental and theoretical analysis of the noise model in the *Geometric Hashing* technique. In particular, the accuracy of the technique is discussed in the cases of affine transformations, similarities and rigid motions. The efficacy of the voting procedure in *Geometric Hashing* is discussed and it is shown that its introduction significantly reduces the expected burden of the verification stage. The discussion is illustrated by results of numerous simulations which have been performed to test the expected performance of the algorithm.

University of North Carolina, Dept. of Computer Science, Campus Box 3175, Sitterson Hall, Chapel Hill, NC 27599: *Attn: Mrs. Sandra Rudd.*

Selected from Textlab Technical Reports list, available above.

TR87-033 *A Hypertext writing environment and its cognitive basis,* J. Smith, S. Weiss and G. Ferguson.
WE is a hypertext writing environment to create both electronic and printed documents. Paper includes discussion of underlying cognitive model, a description of WE and a brief outline of evaluation experiments.

TR88-031 *An overview of the architecture for WE 1.0,* P. E. Bush, G. J. Ferguson, J. B. Smith, S. F. Weiss, J. D. Bolter and M. Lansman.

TR88-036 *WE 1.0 user's information,* Y-P. Shan, J. Thorn and M. C. Rooks.

TR88-042 *An overview of the architecture for MicroArras 1.0,* S. Southard, J. B. Smith and S. F. Weiss.
Report describes MicroArras, a full-text retrieval system being developed at the University of North Carolina.

TR86-017 *Microarras: An overview,* J. B. Smith, S. F. Weiss, G. J. Ferguson.

Northeastern University, College of Computer Science, 161 Cullinane Hall, Boston, MA 02115: *Attn: Beth Nicholson.*

Selected from Technical Reports list, available above.

NU-CCS-89-1 *Oracles for structural properties: The isomorphism problem and public key cryptography,* S. Homer and A. Selman.

NU-CCS-89-10 *Class modules: An integration of classes, modules and macro grammars for object-oriented design,* K. J. Lieberherr.

NU-CCS-89-13 *A connectionist learning algorithm with provable generalization and scaling bounds,* S. I. Gallant.

NU-CCS-89-15 *An introduction to the Biological Knowledge Laboratory,* R. Futrelle.

Ohio State University, Dept. of Computer and Information Science,
2036 Neil Avenue, Columbus, OH 43210-1277: *Attn: Ginny Strawser.*

Selected from Technical Reports Series List, available above.

OSU-CISRC-10/89-TR 44 *Recent developments in load sharing in locally distributed systems,* N. G. Shivaratri and M. Singhal.

OSU-CISRC-7/89-TR 36 *Animation of gaseous phenomena using turbulent flow based solid texturing,* D. Ebert and R. Parent.

OSU-CISRC-6/89-TR 23 *An overview of the MANDEN project: A computerized system to support scholarly writing,* S. A. Mamrak.

OSU-CISRC-6/89-TR 19 *A paradigm for developing portable and efficient parallel programs for MIMD architectures,* P. R. Vishnubhotla.

OSU-CISRC-3/89-TR 11 *Efficient initialization and finalization of data structures: why and how,* D. E. Harms and B. Weide.

OSU-CISRC-1/89-TR 2 *A system for simulating human facial expression,* B. Guenter.

OSU-CISRC-11/88-TR 37 *Computerized systems to support scholarly writing: A survey and assessment,* S. A. Mamrak.

OSU-CISRC-3/88-TR 10 *Music formatting guidelines,* D. Roush.

Old Dominion University, Dept. of Computer Science, Norfolk, VA
23529: *Attn: Technical Reports.*

Selected from Technical Reports list, available above.

TR-89-05 *Systolic implementation of neural networks,* M. Zubair and B. B. Madan (Feb. 1989).

TR-89-27 *Reasoning about software specifications: A case study,* C. Wild, J. Chen and D. Eckhardt (June 1989).

Oregon State University, Dept. of Computer Science, Computer Science Building 100, Corvallis, OR 97331: *Attn: Technical Reports.*

Selected from Publication Announcement list, available above.

CSTR-88-60-12 *Internal hashing for dynamic and static tables,* T. G. Lewis and C. R. Cook.

Tutorial discusses one of the oldest problems in computing: how to search and retrieve keyed information from a list in the least amount of time. Surveys techniques which have evolved over the past 25 years and introduces more recent research results.

CSTR-88-70-2 *A new strategy for processor allocation in an n-cube multiprocessor,* A. Al-Dhelaan and B. Bose.

Report describes two known strategies (buddy system and gray code) for allocation in an n-cube multiprocessor and proposes a new strategy, suitable for static and dynamic allocation. Implementation details of new strategies are given.

CSTR-88-60-17 *Software development in Parallax: The ELGDF language,* H. El-Rewini and T. Lewis.

ELGDF (Extended Large Grain Data Flow) is a robust syntax (graphical and heirarchical) to allow construction and viewing of a wide variety of parallel programs. ELGDF serves as the foundation of a parallel programming environment called Parallax under development at Oregon State University.

CSTR-88-50-3 *Genetic algorithms as function optimizers,* W. Langford.

Report surveys the use of genetic algorithms in function optimization. Two distinct camps are Holland's camp and Rechenberg's camp. Annotated bibliography included.

CSTR-89-70-3 *A benchmark suite for parallel processors: Part 1,* T-J. Sun and T. G. Lewis.

Seven benchmark programs (parallel matrix multiplication, disk file I/O, saturating, parallel enumeration sort, memory transfer, system math functions, Linpack routines) — implemented using "C" and Dynix parallel programming library on Sequent Balance 21000 shared memory multiprocessor and "Linda" parallel programming primitives on the Cogent XTM distributed system — are discussed and results presented.

Universitá di Pisa, Dipartimento di Informatica,Corso Italia, 40, 56100 Pisa, ITALY: *Attn: Francesca Bernardini.*

Selected from Technical Report List, available above.

9/89 *Prolog as a database language,* M. E. Occhiuto and R. Orsini.

Paper surveys approaches to integrate Prolog and databases both at a linguistic and pragmatic level. All the proposals of integrations turn out to be unsatisfactory either because they result in a juxtaposition of two very different languages or because they do not offer adequate mechanisms to deal with persistent data. The aim of the paper is to point out the critical issues of such integration, in order to overcome some limitations of the proposed systems and to support the design of future integrated systems.

12/89 *Communication cost and process mapping in massively parallel systems: A static approach,* S. Antonelli, F. Baiardi, S. Pelagatti and M. Vanneschi.

An integrated approach to the mapping of processes of a concurrent program onto processing nodes of a massively parallel system is presented. Only general purpose systems in the Microcomputer Array class (Seitz 84), and hence with a regular communication structure, are taken into account. No constraints are imposed on the communication structure of the program to be mapped but, since process mapping is solved during compilation, the proposed solution may be applied only to programs whose structure is statically derivable. Since the problem is NP-hard, a heuristic algorithm has been developed to approximate the optimal mapping.

30/89 *System programming with logic languages,* P. Ciancarini.

Logic programming languages are well known as very high level specification and prototyping languages. Their use as system programming languages has been advocated but not deeply investigated. In this paper, authors survey and examine the family of logic languages, both sequential, with respect to their features for system programming. The logic languages Prolog, Aurora Prolog, Concurrent Prolog, Parlog, Guarded Horn Clauses, DeltaProlog and Shared Prolog will be surveyed.

41/89 *Coordination languages for open system design,* P. Cianacarini.

The concept of "coordination language" has been recently introduced by Carriero and Gelernter to designate a class of parallel programming languages suitable for describing the behavior of "open" systems composed of a dynamic collection of asynchronous communicating agents.

In this paper, three parallel languages, Linda, Flat Concurrent Prolog and DeltaProlog, are discussed with respect to their features for open system design. Although they seem to be equivalent with respect to their expressive power, current implementations of both Flat Concurrent Prolog and DeltaProlog miss the efficiency of Linda, for reasons discussed in this paper. Author has introduced Shared Prolog, a new logic language that is closer to the Linda coordination model.

The Queen's University at Belfast, Dept. of Computer Science, Belfast

BT7 1NN, NORTHERN IRELAND: *Attn: R. H. Perrott – Tel: (0232)245133 ext. 3246.*

Submitted by R. H. Perrott.

Autoparallelisation, R. H. Perrott, R. W. Lyttle and T. F. Lunney.
Authors provide a survey of the language approaches being used to program MIMD computers, with particular emphasis on systems which are available to automatically translate sequential Fortran programs into code which will execute on multiple processor machines.

University of Rochester, VLSI Group, Dept. of Electrical Engineering,

Rochester, NY 14627: *Attn: Technical Reports.*

Selected from Publications List, available above.

EL-89-01 *Displaying a system of interconnected modules,* R. Molyneaux and A. Albicki.
Paper addresses topological issues associated with the display of a system of interconnected modules. The need to display and manipulate the elements of a VLSI design described at the register transfer level provided the motivation for this work.

EL-88-05 *Prospects on cellular automata application to test pattern generation,* A. Albicki, S-K. Yap, M. Khare and S. Pamper.
The consensus is that the simplest approach to test generation in Built-In Self Test structures is the use of linear feedback shift registers. Authors show that cellular automata based techniques can serve as an alternative when test application time is a concern.

University of Rochester, Dept of Computer Science, Rochester, NY 14627: *Attn: Technical Reports.*

Selected from Technical Reports list, available above.

TR 244 *Time, space, and form in vision,* J. A. Feldman (Nov. 1988). Paper presents a fairly detailed connectionist computational model of how the perception and recognition of objects is carried out by primate brains. Central construct in intermediate-level vision is taken to be the *trajectory,* used in recognition of dynamic situations called *scenarios.* Work is an extension of the author's 1985 Four Frames model.

TR 257 *The Rochester robot,* D. H. Ballard, et al (Aug. 1988). The Rochester robot was built to study use of real-time vision in cognition and movement. Major feature is the robot head, with binocular cameras movable at over 400°/sec. Body is Puma 761 six degree-of-freedom arm. Visual information is analyzed with a pipeline processor and used to control motion of body.

TR 273 *Machine-independent complexity theory,* J. I. Seiferas (Jan. 1989). Report provides an accessible and straightforward tour through some of the most basic notions and remarkable phenomena in machine-independent computational complexity.

TR 224 *Why we can't program multiprocessors the way we're trying to do it now,* D. Baldwin (Aug. 1987). Author argues that a key cause of problem is that models of computation on which current programming languages are based are inadequate for describing parallelism. Paper closes with comments on recent work on constraint languages, which may reduce problem of programming multiprocessors.

State University of New York — Binghamton, Dept. of Electrical Engineering, Binghamton, NY 13901: *Attn: Prof. J. G. Delgado-Frias.*

Provided by Delgado-Frias.

A fault tolerant WSI semantic network architecture, J. G. Delgado-Frias and W. R. Moore (Tech. report QUEL-1767/88, University of Oxford). A multiprocessor architecture for AI semantic networks is studied. This architecture is designed for knowledge manipulation and representation processing.

Simon Fraser University, Center for System Science, Laboratory for Computer and Communications Research, Burnaby, BC, CANADA V5A 1S6: *Attn: Dorothy Wong.*

Selected from Technical Reports list, available above.

CSS/LCCR TR 88-26 *Discontinuous grammars,* V. Dahl.

Article ties together several years of research on discontinuous grammars – logic grammars in which non-explicit sequences of symbols can be alluded to in the rules, and sometimes repositioned by them. Author also discusses implementation issues, related work and extensions.

CSS/LCCR TR 88-27 *Distributed C: An environment for designing and testing algorithms for distributed systems – Preliminary system specifications,* J. G. Peters.

Distributed C is a software package for the design and testing of algorithms for distributed systems. It provides a powerful and flexible environment in which both synchronous and asynchronous distributed algorithms can be developed for many different types of network environment. It has been designed to be both a research tool and a teaching tool. The system features a graphical interface for drawing and labelling networks, a template-driven editor for the specification of processes, a symbolic debugging package and an interactive simulator which includes a statistical package and (maybe) graphical output.

CSS/LCCR TR 89-07 *Simulation of a polling system for token passing networks using GPSS,* E. Lo and R. H. S. Hardy.

A token passing computer network uses a token to control access to the network and can be modeled as a polling systems. The ANSI standard X3T9.5 and the IEEE Standards 802.4 and 802.5 all use token passing as their medium access method. This paper presents a simulation model written in GPSS block statements that can simulate the performance of token passing networks.

University of Texas at Austin, Dept. of Computer Sciences, Taylor

Hall, Austin, Texas 78712: *Attn: Technical Report Center.*

Selected from Technical Reports list, available above.

TR-88-23 *A new explanation of the glitch phenomenon,* J. H. Anderson and M. G. Gouda.

Report considers a discrete model for asynchronous circuits and shows that under very mild restrictions this model excludes the existence of glitch-free arbiters, contradicting a long standing conjecture that the nonexistence of glitch-free arbiters is due to the continuous nature of such circuits.

TR-89-04 *Distributed file systems,* E. Levy and A. Silberschatz.

Report provides a survey of current systems (Unix United, Locus, Sprite, Sun's Network File System and ITC's Andrew), illustrating a variety of concepts and demonstrating various implementations and design alternatives.

TR-89-22 *A collection of 120 computer solved geometry problems in mechanical formula derivation,* S-C. Chou and X-S. Gao.

This is a collection of 120 geometric problems mechanically solved by a program based on methods introduces by the authors. Researchers can use this collection to experiment with their methods/programs similar to authors' experiments. A typical example consists of an informal description of the geometric problem, the input to the program, the result of the program and a diagram.

TR-88-29 *Adaptive programming,* M. G. Gouda and T. Herman.

An adaptive program is one that changes its behavior based on the current state of its environment. In this paper, the notion of adaptivity is formalized and a logic for reasoning about adaptive programs is presented.

University of Twente, Dept. of Computer Science, PO. Box 217, 7500 AE Enschede, THE NETHERLANDS. *Attn: Secr. SPA.*

Selected from Technical Reports list, available above.

INF-88-5 *PROPER, A performability modelling and analysis tool,* B. R. Haverkort and I. G. Niemegeers.

Performance modelling is a technique which incorporates aspects of both performance and reliability modelling. It therefore provides means of trade-off between the two. In this paper, we briefly discuss the mathematical background of performability modelling as a start-up for the main discussion topic: the PROPER system. The PROPER system allows users to specify at a high level, via the language PDL, performability models which are automatically translated into low level Markov-Reward processes. Invisible for the end user, this translation incorporates multiple performance analyses for obtaining the rewards. The PROPER system combines a high level specification technique with a number of state-of-the-art calculation methods and forms in that sense a new approach in quantitative systems modeling.

INF-88-6 *Exploring AI in VLSI-CAD systems*, G. R. Tjon Joek Tjien.

In order to reduce the development time for VLSI, artificial intelligence is one of the new methods and approaches being studied. This report gives a structured overview of some VLSI design systems based on AI and will investigate if this is indeed a step in the right direction or merely an optimistic approach.

INF-88-12 *On identifying resources in multiprocessor systems*, E. G. Zondag.

In any data processing environment, all kinds of resources must be identified in order to be able to manage and manipulate them, both by human beings and by machine processes. Uniform approaches to identification seem an important – and often underestimated– topic in resource management. This paper surveys issues and gives some suggestions on identification concerns. Also an experiment toward a general resource identification scheme for the TUMULT multiprocessor system is discussed.

INF-88-18 *TUMULT-64: A real-time multi-processor system*, P. G. Jansen and G. J. M. Smit.

TUMULT is a modular extendible multi-processor system (MIMD) with distributed memory. The processors communicate via a high performance switching network. A distributed real-time operating system has been designed and implemented, which offers high performance communications at the application level. Processors can connect dynamically to links after which they may pass messages or call remote procedures. This article gives a brief description of the system and emphasizes architectural and communications aspects. Also, **INF-88-28**, *The Twente University Multiprocessor* by J. Scholten and P. G. Jansen, describing the implementation of TUMULT.

INF-88-22 *An exercise in tranformational programming – backtracking* *and branch-and-bound,* M. M. Fokkinga.

Author presents a competely formal development of program schemes that are usually called Backtracking programs and Branch-and-Bound programs. Development consists of a series of transformational steps, or better, algebraic manipulations, on the initial specification until the desired programs are obtained. The notation and algebraic transformation laws are those of Meertens' paper, "Algorithmics – towards programming as a mathematical activity."

INF-88-42 *Integrated Services Digital Network overview and architectural concepts,* E. G. Zondag.

In any data processing environment, all kinds of resources must be identified in order to be able to manage and manipulate them, both by human beings and by machine processes. Uniform approaches to identification seem an important – and often underestimated– topic in resource management. This paper surveys issues and gives some suggestions on identification concerns. Also an experiment toward a general resource identification scheme for the TUMULT multiprocessor system is discussed.

INF-88-46 *Processor controlpath synthesis: Literature survey and preliminary analysis,* A. J. W. M. ten Berg.

Synthesis at the implementation level in the design of today's processors in VLSI technology is gaining attention due to the large complexities of the circuits and the shorter development periods. The processor's controlpath however stays out of focus compared to the other processor module, the data path. In this paper, the literature on and related to controlpath synthesis is surveyed in order to get an idea about the state of the art and also of the unaddressed problems at this moment.

INF-88-50 *An overview of some methods for the high-level specification of synchronization,* J. J. Luursema.

A large number of experimental languages and notations for parallelism and synchronization have been developed. There are however fundamentally different points of view for high-level synchronization, resulting in different groups of languages like the regular expression based methods and temporal logic based methods. This paper gives a short description of the different approaches. Per approach, a number of different languages are discussed.

INF-88-61 *Review of the Graham-Glanville code-generation scheme,* A. Nijmeyer.

A code generator is a part of a compiler that translates an intermediate representation into target-machine code. Historically, code generators have been written in an informal and ad hoc manner. Over the last decade, however, research into code-generation methodology has been steadily gaining momentum. The most popular method to have been developed to date is the Graham-Glanville schem. The author reviews the main implementations of the Graham-Glanville scheme, in particular considering the syntactic and semantic approaches to parsing the target-machine description, and the various techniques used to overcome the deficiencies of the scheme.

Villanova University, Dept. of Electrical Engineering, Villanova, PA 19085: *Attn: Prof. Julia V. Bukowski.*

Selected from list submitted by Bukowski.

Preliminary evaluation of software reliability models, J. V. Bukowski and *An investigation of issues impacting software reliability,* J. V. Bukowski, J. H. Goodman and M. Baykal-Gursoy.
Reviews of software reliability models (first paper through 1983, second paper through 1985).

Washington University, Dept. of Computer Science, Campus Box 1045, One Brookings Drive, St. Louis, Missouri 63130: *Attn: Technical Reports.*

Selected from Technical Reports list, available above.

WUCS-89-10 *Asynchronous algorithms for optimal flow control of BCMP networks,* A. D. Bovopoulos and A. A. Lazaar.
The decentralized flow control problem in BCMP networks is studied, with power based optimization criterion used to obtain optimal flow for each user. It is shown that optimal arrival rates correspond to the unique Nash equilibrium point of a noncooperative game problem. Asynchronous algorithms (particularly the nonlinear Gauss-Seidel algorithm) are presented to compute the network's Nash equilibrium point.

WUCS-89-19 *The next generation of internetworking,* G. M. Parulkar.
Report describes a research effort concerned with the next generation of

internet architecture, motivated by the orders of magnitude increase in data rates of communications networks over the next few years and the use of communication infrastructures by researchers from several disciplines to solve bigger and more complex problems.

WUCS-89-36 *Axon: A high speed communication architecture for distributed applications,* J. P. G. Sterbenz and G. M. Parulkar.
Report describes Axon, a new host communications architecture including an integrated design of hardware, operating systems and communications protocols. Architecture is motivated by bottleneck imposed by host-network interface as higher performance communication networks evolve.

University of Washington, Dept. of Electrical Engineering, FT-10, Seattle, Washington 98195: *Attn: Dr. Arun Somani.*

Selected from list provided by Somani.

Hypercube-based compact neural networks and their comparison with other artificial neural networks, A. K. Somani and P. Rostykus.
Report presents mapping of neural networks on hypercube architectures and presents their performance results.

Meshkin: A fault tolerant architecture with distributed fault detection, diagnosis and reconfiguration A. K. Somani, M. Bagha and B. Sullam.
A new fault tolerant architecture for managing redundancy efficiently is presented. The performance loss due to the fault tolerant mechanism is minimal.

Wayne State University, Dept. of Computer Science, Detroit, Michigan 48202: *Attn: Technical Report Committee.*

Selected from Technical Reports list, available above.

CSC-88-001 *Intraneural computation and evolutionary learning,* K. G. Kirby.
CSC-88-005 *Constraint satisfaction algorithms,* B. A. Nadel.
Constraint satisfaction problems are ubiquitous in artificial intelligence

and many algorithms have been developed for their solution. This paper provides a unified survey of some of these, in terms of three classes – tree search, arc consistency and hybrid tree search/arc consistency algorithms. This unified view suggest several new algorithms.

University of Wisconsin — Madison, Computer Sciences Dept., 1200 W. Dayton St., Madison, WI 53706: *Attn: Computer Related Technical Reports.*

Selected from Technical Report list, available above.

TR-843 *Brain-structured connectionist networks that perceive and learn,* V. Honavar and L. Uhr (April 1989).
Specifies main features of Brain-like, Neuronal and Connectionist models; argues for need for, and usefulness of, structuring networks of neuron-like units into successively larger brain-like modules; examines Recognition Cone models of perception from this perspective.

TR-844 *Number-theoretic algorithms,* E. Bach (April 1989).
Report on algorithms to solve problems in number theory, concentrating on methods to test primality, to find the prime factor of numbers and to solve equations in various finite groups, rings and fields. Describes both algorithms and underlying mathematics.

TR-856 *On the algebraic properties of program integration,* T. Reps (June 1989).
The need to integrate several versions of a program into a common one arises frequently but it is a tedious and time consuming task to merge programs by hand. The program-integration algorithm recently proposed by Horwitz, Prins and Reps provides a way to create a *semantics-based* tool for integrating a base program with two or more variants. This paper studies the algebraic properties of the program-integration process.

TR-860 *Cache memory design considerations to support languages with dynamic heap allocation,* C-J. Peng and G. S. Sohi (July 1989).
Paper considers the design of cache memories to support the execution of languages that make extensive use of a dynamic heap. Defines several characteristics of dynamic heap references and measures them for several benchmarking programs using Lisp.

ETH Zurich, Department of Computer Science, Department Informatik, Stabsstelle Administration, ETH-Zentrum, CH-8092 Zurich, SWITZERLAND: *Attn: Technical Reports.*

Selected from Recent Technical Reports list, available above.

Report 111 *From Modula to Oberon: The programming language Oberon,* N. Wirth.

Oberon is the result of a concentrated effort to increase the power of Modula-2 while simultaneously reducing its complexity. This report describes and motivates the changes.

Report 115 *Solving linear equation by extrapolation,* W. Gander, G. H. Golub and D. Gruntz.

This is a survey paper on extrapolation methods for vector sequences.

CHAPTER 12

UNIVERSITY SOFTWARE LIST

Stuart K. Tewksbury
Room 4B505
AT&T Bell Laboratories
Crawfords Corner Road
Holmdel, NJ 07733 USA

The listings provided in this chapter were compiled by the editor from lists submitted by various individuals and institutions from whom research-oriented software is available (possibly with a modest charge) to friendly users. In some cases, full listings of software from institutions were provided, in which case the editor has selected a few typical examples. The address information for requesting either individual reports or lists of software is provided, along with brief descriptions of the software. Neither Plenum Press nor the editor take responsibility for the accuracy of the information listed below.

Those wishing to include listings of software, developed during research programs and available for a modest charge, should submit information such as that included in the following listings to the editor at the address above.

The University of Arizona
Beth Stair, Dept. of Computer Science, Tucson, Arizona 85721
Tel: (602)621-2018.

Software below are in public domain and are available by anonymous ftp over Internet from host "cs.Arizona.edu." They can also be acquired on tape for a nominal charge from Beth Stair, address above.

SNOBOL4
The SNOBOL4 distribution is fairly old now but still receives requests and is listed here.
Project head: R. Griswold.

Icon
Icon is a more recent, and much more powerful, language for the same application domain as SNOBOL4, i.e. non-numeric programming, especially string and list processing.
Project head: R. Griswold.

SR
The SR programming language is a recent concurrent programming language, one especially suited for distributed programming. A synopsis of SR is given in the Dept. of Computer Science's technical report TR 89-6, which is the reference manual for the most recent release.
Project head: Prof. G. R. Andrews.

SB-Prolog
SB-Prolog is a recent implementation of Prolog.
Project head: Prof. S. Debray.

Brown University
Kathleen P. Krause, Software Librarian
Computer Science Dept. Box 1910
Providence, RI 02912

BAGS (Brown Animation Generation System)
BAGS is a suite of software tools directed towards the non-technical user for creating high-quality 3D animation sequences.
Developer: Brown University Computer Group

BWE (Brown Workstation Environment)
BWE is an integrated toolkit for 2D graphics programming. BWE runs on top of X11 (R3 or earlier).
Developer: S. Reiss.

FIELD (Friendly Integrated Environment for Learning and Development)
The Field environment is an integrated collection of programming tools and interfaces to existing UNIX tools. It utilizes a simple message-based integration mechanism to provide a powerful environment for full-scale UNIX programming.
Developer: S. Reiss.

GARDEN (A graphical programming environment)
The GARDEN system is an environment for programming in two dimensions. Its goal is to allow programmers to write programs with the diagrams they use to design a system.
Developer: S. Reiss.

OBSERVER (ObServer II database)
ObServer is a general purpose object server. Its purpose is to provide secondary storage of arbitrarily sized objects for database transactions and to facilitate cooperation between these transactions.
Developer: S. B. Zdonik.

TANGO
TANGO is an algorithm animation design and execution system designed to allow the user to easily create animations of their programs. TANGO provides sophisticated, 2-D color animations in workstation-based windows.
Developer: J. T. Stasko.

THREADS (Brown Workstation Environment)
THREADS provides lightweight processes for concurrent programming, whether on a uniprocessor (e.g. workstation) or on a shared-memory multiprocessor (e.g. parallel machine).
Developer: T. W. Doeppner.

California Institute of Technology
Computational Neural Systems Program, Division of Biology, 216-76
Pasadena, California.

GENESIS (a GEneral NEural SImulation System)
Increased interest in the use of computer simulations in the study of the structure and function of biological and computational neural networks has led to the development of GENESIS, a general purpose neural network modeling platform. GENESIS was created to provide neural network researchers with an interactive object-oriented tool for the rapid development of new neural network simulations with graphical interfaces.
Developers: M. A. Wilson, U. S. Bhalla, J. D. Uhley, D. H. Bilitch, M. E. Nelson and J. M. Bower.
Request forms available via: (1) by calling (818)356-6818 or (2) anonymous ftp from genesis.cns.caltech.edu.

University of Colorado at Boulder
Software Engineering Group
Dept. of Electrical and Computer Engineering
Boulder, Colorado 80309-0425 Tel: (303)492-7204

Eli
Eli is an integrated system for generating complete compilers from specifications. It allows end users who are not compiler experts to rapidly and reliably implement special purpose languages.
Developers: V. P. Heuring, U. Kastens and W. M. Waite.

The University of Connecticut
Systems Optimization Laboratory
Dept. of Electrical and Systems Eng.
260 Glenbrook Road, Storrs, Connecticut 06269

START (System Testability Analysis and Research Tool)
START is a comprehensive, interactive, window-based software that allows the users to graphically enter functional models of large-scale, hierarchical and modular systems; obtain optimal/near-optimal testing strategies; and obtain testability analysis reports and figures of merit. The software runs on a SUN workstation.
Developers: K. R. Pattipati, S. Deb and M. Dontamsetty.

MAPPER
MAPPER is an interactive, window-based software hosted on a SUN workstation. MAPPER allows users to graphically enter the computation flow graphs and computation resource graphs, and obtain optimal/ near-optimal allocation of tasks on processors, subject to constraints on local memory, redundancy, precedence relations, and security of individual processors.
Developers: K. R. Pattipati and R. T. Lee.

HQN (Hierarchical Queuing Network analyzer)
HQN is a software package written in FORTRAN 77 for analyzing large-scale systems modeled as hierarchical queuing networks. The queuing networks may be closed, open or mixed.
Developers: K. R. Pattipati and J. L. Teele.

Cornell University

DPE: Datapath Editor
DPE is a simulated annealing based high level synthesis system. Starting with a behavioral specification, an optimized RTL output is produced. DPE is described in *Progress in Computer-Aided Design*, G.

Zobrist (Ed), Vol. 4 (Feb. 1990).
Requests: Prof. Lov K. Grover, Cornell University, School of Electrical Engineering, 445 Phillips Hall, Ithaca, NY 14853.

Synthesizer Generator

The Synthesizer Generator is a general tool for creating language-based environments for formal specifications. Using a declarative language, an editor designer prepares a specification that includes rules defining a language's context-free abstract syntax, context-sensitive attributions, concrete input syntax, concrete display format, and transformations. From this specification, the Generator creates a full-screen editor for manipulating the objects according to these rules. The Synthesizer Generator uses attribute grammars to compute derived information about the object being edited. The fundamental algorithmic importance of the Synthesizer Generator are its algorithms that incrementally recompute attribute values after an editing change. These incremental algorithms permit immediate response when objects are being manipulated through a generated editor. The Generator is currently licensed to 235 research sites worldwide. A wide variety of editors have been written using the Generator including ones for high-level languages like Pascal, C, and Fortran 77; an editor for partial-correctness programs in Hoare-style logic; and proof editors based on the Theory of Constructions and the Logical Framework.

Project Manager/Requests: Prof. Tim Teitelbaum, Cornell University, School of Electrical Engineering, 4147 Upson Hall, Ithaca, NY 14853.

Nuprl (Version 3.0)

Nuprl is a formal proof development system. The Nuprl package includes a tape and the book *Implementing Mathematics with the Nuprl Proof Development System*. The tape includes the source code for Nuprl, the Symbolics binaries for the system, some of the Nuprl libraries constructed at Cornell University, and some documentation files that supplement the book. Version 3.0 should allow Nuprl to run on any machine that supports a Common Lisp and an implementation of CLX (the standard primitive interface between Common Lisp and X-windows). Nuprl 3.0 has been run with (1) Lucid 3.0 on Sun 3 and Sun 4 using Lucid's interface to Sun's SunView window system, (2) Lucid 3.0 on Sun

3 and Sun 4 running X-windows using the CLX implementation distributed with Lucid 3.0 or the May 1989 version of CLX for X11R3 from ucbarpa.berkeley.edu (the latter version supplied with Nuprl tape) and (3) Symbolic machines (36xx with Genera 7.2 and MacIvory with Genera 7.4I) using the Symbolics window system. It is reasonably likely that some implementation dependencies will appear when an attempt is made to compile and run Nuprl in a new context.

Information: Liz Maxwell, Nuprl Distribution Coordinator, Cornell University, Dept. of Computer Science, Upson Hall, Ithaca, NY 14853.

University of Illinois at Urbana-Champaign
National Center for Supercomputing Applications
605 East Springfield Ave., Champaign, IL 61820
Attn. Documentation Orders

The "Technical Resources Catalog" from the National Center for Supercomputer Applications above provides a comprehensive list of NCSA documentation, video training materials, software and newsletters. Items below are summary.

Software documentation for CRAY Computers
General areas: systems and utilities; languages, libraries and compilers; chemistry and molecular systems software; computational fluid dynamics software; electrical engineering; solid mechanics; graphics; numerical and statistical libraries.

NCSA Scientific Visualization Software Suite
Designed for color-equipped Macintoshes, these tools support both internal and external copying and pasting, and are designed to form a complete and complementary computing environment in which to analyze 2D raster datasets and images. Suite includes NCSA DataScope, NCSA Image, NCSA Layout, NCSA PalEdit, NCSA HDF and NCSA Telnet packages.

University of Illinois at Urbana-Champaign

Dept. of Computer Science, 1304 West Springfield Ave.
Urbana, Illinois 61801. Tel: (217)333-3426

CHOICES

Choices (Class Hierarchical Open Interface for Custom Embedded Systems) provides a foundation on which to construct sophisticated scientific applications. CHOICES embodies the notion of customized operating systems that are tailored for particular hardware configurations and for particular applications. Within one large computing system, many different specialized application servers can be integrated to form a computing environment. A prototype CHOICES kernel is now operational on an Encore Multimax. Unlike more conventional operating systems, CHOICES is intended to exploit large parallel processors interconnected by shared memory or high-speed networks. It provides a set of software classes that can be used to build specialized software components for particular applications. CHOICES uses a class hierarchy and inheritance to represent the notion of a family of operating systems and to allow the proper abstraction for deriving and building new instances of a CHOICES system. At the basis of the class hierarchy are multiprocessing and communication objects that unite diverse specialized instances of the operating system in particular computing environments. In the attempt to build a high-performance operating system, many of the traditional implementation schemes used in the kernel of operating systems like UNIX were modified or abandoned.

Principal Investigator: Prof. Roy Campbell.

LEIF

Leif is a language oriented editor that supports a full set of text editing commands as well as commands based on the program's syntax. The editor uses an incremental parser to update syntactic information about the program. Leif can be used with several different context free languages simultaneously. Leif is implemented as a minor-mode within GNU Emacs. Leif can be used for writing programs in the following: C, ada, elisp, (GNU emacs lisp), pascal, yacc.

Developers: William Smith, Dan LaLiberte and Roy Campbell.

SAFloorplan

SAFloorplan is a new algorithm for floorplan design in VLSI circuit layout using the method of simulated annealing. The major contributions are (1) a new representation of floorplans (normalized Polish expressions) which enables us to carry out the neighborhood search effectively and (2) a simultaneous minimization of area and total interconnection length in the final solution.
Developers: D. F. Wong and C. L. Liu

UNIX Notesfile

The UNIX notesfile system was developed at the University of Illinois. The Notesfile concept was taken from PLATO (trademark CDC), a University of Illinois project, which is a nationwide network for computer-assisted instruction based here at the university. The Notesfile software is used nationwide by many sites on the Arpanet and Internet, as well as sites served by UUNET.
Contact: Raymond B. Essick.

XGKS (Version 1.01)

XGKS is a X11 window system based version of the ANSI Graphical Kernel System. XGKS is a full GKS system (level 2C). The project was headed by Prof. Bill Kiubitz and Prof Roy Campbell. Development of XGKS was done by Greg Rogers, Sung Hsien Ching and Yu Pan.
Contact: Prof. Roy Campbell.

Fred

Fred is a screen-based structured editor. It can be used to construct and modify any text file but it is especially useful for editing computer programs. The editor acts as the programmer's companion: it points out syntax errors in the file being edited and does automatic pretty printing to provide readable programs. The user can explicitly provide fred with syntactic rules for various languages of interest or the user can allow fred to choose a default language description. Ones available are basic, C, cobol, fortran, list and pascal. Documented in *Fred User's Manual*, Report 84-1151 (1984) from the Dept. of Computer Science.

Katholieke Universiteit Leuven

ESAT Laboratory, Dept. of Electrical Engineering
Kardinaal Mercierlaan 94, 3030 Heverlee, BELGIUM
Tel: 32/16/22 09 31

See listing of technical report ESAT-KUL-88/1 for documentation on Fortran 77 programs for (1) the extended classical total least squares algorithm, (2) the partial singular value decomposition algorithm, and (3) the partial total least squares algorithm.

Michigan State University

<u>GMP</u> (Graph Manipulation Package)
GMP is an interactive tool for manipulation of graphs, for SUN workstations. Users construct graphs using a mouse. Graph properties may be examined by invoking algorithms from within the package.
Developers: A.-H. Esfahanian and G. W. Zimmerman.
Contact: Dr. A.-H. Esfahanian, Computer Science Dept, A714 Wells Hall, Michigan State University, East Lansing, MI 48824-1027. Tel: (517)353-4389. email: esfahani@cps.msu.edu.

Microelectronics Center of North Carolina (MCNC)

PO Box 12889, Research Triangle Park, North Carolina 27709
Tel: (919)248-1800

For a full catalog of CAD software tools available from MCNC (and prices), contact Jeri C. Williams at address above.

<u>CAzM</u> (Circuit Analyzer with Macromodeling)
CAzM is a circuit simulator developed jointly by Duke University and MCNC. CAzM uses modern numerical techniques including look-up tables and an automatic time step adjustment scheme to ensure an accurate and fast simulation. CAzM contains standard MOS levels I, II,

III, and BSIM models, JFET models and bipolar models. Circuits containing as many as 80,000 transistors have been successfully simulated. CAzM is netlist compatible with SPICE.

PREDICT (PRocess Estimator for Design of IC Technologies)
The PREDICT program is an accurate multilayer process simulator for advanced silicon technologies. The goal in developing the program was to couple physical models together, verify the models and the coupling with a large measured data base, and embed the calculations in a fast numerical integration scheme. The program is intended for use by silicon process engineers as well as researchers needing to simulate experimental data. The 1,500 models in the PREDICT program include RTA, RTO and silicidation and are based on extensive, detailed data generated as part of the Center's submicron program.

SIGVIEW
SIGVIEW is a tool for viewing digital and analog waveforms. SIGVIEW presents one unified interface for viewing results from CAzM, SPICE, ESIM, RNL, and HILO. A powerful and consistent command set allows the designer to superimpose waveforms (even when produced by different simulators), display digital output as a bus, scroll through and zoom in on segments of the simulation data (input and output), and search patterns in digital data. SIGVIEW can also produce hardcopy for Postscript printers, Textronix 4510 and HP 7580A plotters.

VPNR (Vanilla Placement aNd Route)
The VPNR tool, developed jointly by the MCNC and Duke University, is useful for automatically placing and routing standard cell circuits. A standard cell library (MOSIS Scalable CMOS) is included as part of the VPNR program. The VPNR tools have been benchmarked against other placement and routing tools and VPNR gives competitive results in much less computing time. VPNR accepts several netlist inputs including HILO and RNO and outputs a Magic command file. Through use of a unifying language to describe placement and routing of standard cells (the VPNR language), users can mix and match various placement and routing approaches to meet their specific needs.

VIVID

The VIVID System is a set of tools for symbolic, virtual grid layout of custom digital VLSI circuits. These tools facilitate topological circuit design, allowing the designer to concentrate on circuit function rather than on device composition and adherence to design rules. The designer places circuit icons, such as transistors and wires, in various layouts on the graphics display's virtual grid. To generate the mask layout, the VIVID System then compacts (or translates) the symbolic icons into a corresponding physical design mask representation and spaces them according to user-specified design rules. Simulation is done with FACTS, a fast timing simulator.

University of Rochester

Peg Meeker, Computer Science Dept., Rochester, NY 14627

The Rochester Connectionist Simulator

The Rochester Connectionist Simulator is a tool that allows you to build and experiment with connectionists networks. It provides the basic mechanism for running a simulation (iterate through all units, call functions, update values). It also provides a graphic interface that lets you examine the state of a network. It provides convenient facilities for defining and manipulating your network: names for units, set manipulation, etc. It also has a dynamic loading facility, so you can compile and load new functions on the fly, and to customize the simulator by adding your own commands. There is also a library to help you implement back-propagation networks. The Simulator runs at Rochester on VAX, SUN-3 and SUN-4 systems. The latest version (4.2) has also run on the Digital DECstation 3100 and the MIPS RS2030. The simulator comes with a choice of two graphics interfaces: an X11 interface (using the Athena toolkit) which should be relatively portable, and a SunView interface, which only runs on Sun workstations at present. The simulator can also be run without a graphics interface. Code is generally pretty generic C.

The TimeLogic System

The TimeLogic system is an interval-based, forward-chaining inference engine and database manager of temporal constraints. Relational constraints, indicating relative order between intervals, are based on James Allen's interval logic. The TimeLogic system also supports durational constraints, used for the explicit or automatic construction of interval hierarchies. Constraints are posted and propagated in user-defined contexts with inheritance. Source in Common Lisp.

Rhet Software

This is a knowledge representation system based on concepts proved with HORNE. It includes 2 major modes for representing knowledge (as Horne clauses or as frames) which are interchangeable; a type subsystem for typed and type restricted objects (including variables). Features include: E-unification; negation; forward and backward chaining; complete proofs (prove, disprove, find the KB inconsistent or claim a goal is neither provable nor disprovable); incremental compilation (next version); contextual reasoning; default reasoning (soon); truth maintenance; intelligent backtracking; full LISP compatibility (can call or be called by LISP); upward compatible with HORNE; user-declarable reasoning subsystems (soon); Allen & Koomen's TimeLogic time interval reasoning subsystem; frames have KL-1 type features, plus arbitrary predicate restrictions on slots within a frame as well as default values for slots; separate subsystem providing advanced user-interface facilities, graphics, and ZMACS interface on the lispms.

University of Southern California

ADAM (Advanced Design AutoMation system) is a system for register-transfer level design of VLSI chips. Software release includes items below.

ADAM VLSI Synthesis Program

- SLIMOS selects the module style for each function.

- Sehwa and MAHA schedule operations into time steps and determine how many modules are required for pipelined and non-pipelined operations respectively.

- MABAL decides which module will perform each function and how the modules are to be interconnected.

ADAM VLSI Area Estimation Program

- PLEST estimates standard cell area.

- PASTA calculates the PLA controller area on the chip.

- PSAD-P and PSAD-NP provide lower bounds on cost and performance for pipelined and non-pipelined designs.

Contact: Dr. Alice C. Parker, SAL 300, MC-0781, University of Southern California, Los Angeles, CA 90089-0781. Tel: (213)743-5560. email: PARKER%EVE.USC.EDU@USC.USC.EDU.

University of Wisconsin – Madison
Computer Science Dept., 1210 West Dayton Street
Madison, Wisconsin 53706. Tel: (608)262-1204

Generalized Timed Petri Net Analyzer (GTPNA)
A Generalized Timed Petri Net Analyzer for Sun workstations or DEC VAX machines that run Berkeley Unix. The code is written in Pascal and can be ported to other machines.
Developer/Requests: Prof. Mary Vernon, Computer Science Dept. Tel: (608)262-7893. email: vernon@cs.wisc.edu.

DineroIII Cache Simulator, Version III
DineroIII reads user-provided traces to simulate a cache specified by a dozen parameters. See Mark D. Hill, *Test Driving Your Next Cache*, Magazine of Intelligent Personal Systems (MIPS), pp. 84-92 (Aug. 1989).
Developer/Requests: Prof. Mark D. Hill, Computer Science Dept. email: markhill@cs.wisc.edu.

Tycho Cache Simulator
Tycho reads user-provided traces to simulate numerous alternative caches

having the same block size but different capacities and associativities. See M. D. Hill and A. J. Smith, *Evaluating associativity in CPU caches,* IEEE Trans. Computers, Vol. C-38(12) (Dec. 1989).
Developer/Requests: Prof. Mark D. Hill, Computer Science Dept. email: markhill@cs.wisc.edu.

The EXODUS Extensible Database System Toolkit
The EXODUS software is intended for use in developing data/object managers for applications that require database support for which a relational DBMS is insufficient. The software includes a flexible storage manager for objects, a persistent programming language (E) based on extending C ++, and a tool for generating a database query optimizer from a rule-based specification.
Developers: M. Carey, D. DeWitt, D. Haight, D. Schuh, et al.
Requests: Sheryl Pomraning, Computer Science Dept. Tel: (608)262-5776.

DeNet (Discrete Event Networks)
Modula-2 based discrete event simulation environment. Has been used to simulate distributed systems, databases, communication networks and multiprocessors.
Developer/Requests: Miron Livny, Computer Science Dept. Tel: (608)262-0856. email: miron@cs.wisc.edu.

BERMUDA
Loose coupling of C+Prolog to the IDM-500 database machine. It offers full transparency of the database under Prolog, and employs various optimizations for efficiency. It works over the network and supports multiple Prolog processes requesting data from the same database.
Developers: M. Tsangaris (mostly), J. Chen, M. Friedman, D. Nara, M. Sturdevant.
Requests: Miron Livny, Computer Science Dept. Tel: (608)262-0856. email: miron@cs.wisc.edu.

Xproof
A previewer for device independent troff on X windows.
Developer/Requests: Prof. Marvin Solomon, Computer Science Dept.

Tel: (608)262-2844. email: solomon@cs.wisc.edu.

CONDOR
System for utilizing idle workstations.
Developers: A. Bricker and M. Litzkow.
Requests: Mike Litzkow, Computer Science Dept. Tel: (608)262-6122.
email: mike@cs.wisc.edu.

Index